GEOFFREY CHAUCER

The Wife of Bath

Case Studies in Contemporary Criticism

SERIES EDITOR: Ross C Murfin

Case Studies in Contemporary Criticism

SERIES EDITOR: Ross C Murfin, *University of Miami*

GEOFFREY CHAUCER
The Wife of Bath

Complete, Authoritative Text with
Biographical and Historical Contexts,
Critical History, and Essays from
Five Contemporary Critical Perspectives

EDITED BY

Peter G. Beidler
Lehigh University

Bedford Books
BOSTON NEW YORK

Dedicated to J. Burke Severs

For Bedford Books
President and Publisher: Charles H. Christensen
General Manager and Associate Publisher: Joan E. Feinberg
Managing Editor: Elizabeth M. Schaaf
Developmental Editor: Stephen A. Scipione
Editorial Assistant: Alanya Harter
Production Editor: Michelle McSweeney
Production Assistant: Maureen Murray
Copyeditor: Nancy Bell Scott
Text Design: Sandra Rigney, The Book Department
Cover Design: Richard Emery Design, Inc.
Cover Art: Composite image from the miniature and some of the elements of the decorative borders in the Ellesmere Chaucer. Reproduced by permission of the Huntington Library, San Marino, California.

Library of Congress Catalog Card Number 95–80788

Manufactured in the United States of America.

0   9   8

f   e   d   c

For information, write: Bedford Books, 75 Arlington Street, Boston, MA 02116
(617-426-7440)

ISBN: 0-312-11128-2 (paperback)
ISBN: 0-312-15859-9 (hardcover)

Published and distributed outside North America by:

MACMILLAN PRESS LTD.
Houndmills, Basingstoke, Hampshire RG21 2XS and London
Companies and representatives throughout the world.

ISBN: 0-333-65706-3

About the Series

Volumes in the Case Studies in Contemporary Criticism series provide college students with an entrée into the current critical and theoretical ferment in literary studies. Each volume reprints the complete text of a classic literary work and presents critical essays that approach the work from different theoretical perspectives, together with the editors' introductions to both the literary work and the critics' theoretical perspectives.

The volume editor of each Case Study has selected and prepared an authoritative text of the classic work, written an introduction to the work's biographical and historical contexts, and surveyed the critical responses to the work since its initial publication. Thus situated biographically, historically, and critically, the work is examined in five critical essays, each representing a theoretical perspective of importance to contemporary literary studies. These essays, prepared especially for undergraduates, show theory in praxis; whether written by established scholars or exceptional young critics, they demonstrate how current theoretical approaches can generate compelling readings of great literature.

As series editor, I have prepared instructions, with bibliographies, to the theoretical perspectives represented in the five critical essays. Each introduction presents the principal concepts of a particular theory in their historical context and discusses the major figures and key works that have influenced their formulation. It is my hope that these introductions will reveal to students that effective criticism is informed by a set of coherent assumptions, and will encourage them to recognize and examine their own assumptions about literature. After each introduction, a selective bibliography presents a partially annotated list of important works from the literature of the particular theoretical perspective, including the most recent and readily available editions and translations of the works cited in the introduction. Finally, I have compiled a glossary of key terms that recur in these volumes and in the discourse of contemporary theory and criticism. We hope that the Case Studies in Contemporary Criticism series will reaffirm the richness of its literary works, even as it introduces invigorating new ways to mine their apparently inexhaustible wealth.

Ross C Murfin
Series Editor
University of Miami

About This Volume

This edition is intended to help instructors in a variety of courses introduce their students to contemporary critical approaches to reading literature. Perhaps most usefully, it can serve as a supplement in the Chaucer course, alongside complete editions of Chaucer's works such as the *Riverside Chaucer,* or in more general introductory courses in medieval literature. It may also help instructors teaching the general survey course in English literature who wish to introduce critical perspectives right away, when students are reading medieval literature.

In Part One of this volume I present a biographical sketch of Chaucer, some of the historical highlights of the fourteenth century, and a brief guide to reading and pronouncing Chaucer's verse. In Part One I also present newly edited and glossed versions of the description of the Wife of Bath from the General Prologue to the *Canterbury Tales,* the complete text of the Wife of Bath's Prologue, and the complete text of the Wife of Bath's Tale. I briefly considered using one of the many translations of Chaucer or even writing my own, but quickly decided that a translation of Chaucer would provide the wrong foundation for the five critical studies that make up Part Two. In the end I prepared a totally new edition, designed for students with no previous knowledge of either Chaucer or Middle English. It is based on the best of the Chaucerian manuscripts, the Hengwrt manuscript, and provides full glosses of difficult words, phrases, and concepts. For more on the edition, see my "Introduction to the Text."

In Part Two I present my own history of the criticism on the Wife of Bath, her prologue, and her tale, followed by five contemporary critical views, each introduced by a general discussion by Ross Murfin giving background on the critical approach being exemplified: new historicist, Marxist, psychoanalytic, deconstructionist, and feminist. The five critical essays that appear in this volume were written especially for this volume. I chose not to reprint five of the many, many essays already in print because almost all of them are too specialized and footnote-laden for a volume like this. Rather, I sought out five distinguished scholars and invited each of them to write an original essay. My requirements for those essays were few and simple: they should touch on both the Wife of Bath's Prologue and Tale; they should exemplify the designated critical approach so that readers could learn not only about the Wife of Bath's performance, but also about a particular contemporary critical approach to literature; they should be jargon-free, or at least include simple and clear definitions of any terms that the approach requires; and they should be accessible to a non-specialist audience.

All five of the approaches argue for a more complex reading than the older approaches gave us. Things are not so simple as many of the earlier scholars assumed they were. Lee Patterson's new historicist essay on the Wife of Bath reminds us that women, wives, and widows were all historical as well as literary personages, and that the Wife of Bath had a more optimistic view of marriage than most readers have acknowledged. Laurie Finke's Marxist essay shows us how to examine the text in the light of Chaucer's, and the Wife of Bath's, positions in an emerging middle class that was working in a money-based rather than a land-based economy. Louise O. Fradenburg's psychoanalytic essay takes us into the fantasy world of the Wife of Bath, a world in which her prologue is a confession of the appetites, pleasures, and pains that have driven her, and in which her tale is an escape into a place where lovelessness and old age are but temporary afflictions. H. Marshall Leicester's deconstructionist essay warns us against trying to resolve contradictions or give "determinate" answers when dealing with the Wife of Bath or with the performance of this deliciously undecidable teller. And Elaine Tuttle Hansen's feminist essay invites us to consider the ways Chaucer does — or does not — give adequate expression to a woman's point of view in his creation of a prologue and tale for his most famous woman character.

The five essayists sometimes break away from the narrow labels of "new historicist," "Marxist," "psychoanalytic," "deconstructionist," and "feminist," and, indeed, sometimes make use of the methods of an older or a rival approach. The five often do not agree with one another on the issues they write about — but, of course, that is the whole point of a volume like this, designed in part to show that different approaches lead to different conclusions. Because the five contributors have not seen each others' essays, they have had no opportunity to respond to each other or to resolve the areas where they differ. All five of the essayists would insist that they are speaking for themselves more than for a whole approach. Lee Patterson would be the first to admit, for example, that other new historicists would focus on different aspects of the Wife of Bath's Prologue and Tale, and that they might well reach quite different conclusions. He is giving *his* new historicist approach, not *the* new historicist approach.

Acknowledgments

Like every new editor of Chaucer, I must acknowledge my debt to the many editions that have preceded mine. I have found the glosses and notes of Walter W. Skeat, E. Talbot Donaldson, Albert C. Baugh, John Hurt Fisher, and Larry D. Benson to be invaluable, though it is both impossible and unnecessary to acknowledge every individual debt. In addition, virtually every page profits from the work of modern Chaucerians, whose published opinions about hundreds of words, lines, and concepts have helped lend to this text whatever authority it has.

The five who contributed new essays to this volume deserve my warm thanks. Without their cheerful striving to meet deadlines, and without their gracious refusal to be visibly annoyed when I asked for revisions, there could have been no such volume as this.

I am grateful to publisher Charles Christensen, to associate publisher Joan Feinberg, to series editor Ross Murfin, and to editor Steve Scipione for their willingness to consider a Bedford volume on Chaucer. We had considered trying to do a complete *Canterbury Tales,* but we all felt a sense of relief when we decided that a volume focusing on the character and performance of Chaucer's most stimulating Canterbury pilgrim was more in keeping with the aim of this series.

I am grateful to a dutiful group of graduate students from Lehigh University and Baylor University who read through an early draft of my edition of the Wife of Bath materials and made many suggestions. Each of them is directly responsible for at least one addition or correction that none of the rest saw: Jennifer McNamara Bailey, Sheila Bauer, Elizabeth M. Biebel, Christine Lynch Berg, Tracey Cummings, Anne Dickson, Sister Elaine M. Glanz, Sandra Guy Salla, Nicole Matson, Nancy Rodgers, Julienne Roe, Jian "Stan" Shi, and Martha Kalnin. Mark Allen, of the University of Texas at San Antonio, one of the editors of the forthcoming *Variorum Chaucer* edition of the Wife of Bath materials, was particularly helpful in making many and sensitive suggestions for improving my introductory materials, my text, my glossarial materials and notes, and my critical history of the Wife of Bath. Beverly Kennedy, of Marianopolis College, was generous enough to make suggestions about my glosses and shared with me a prepublication copy of her article on the five disputed passages in the Wife of Bath's prologue.

Many of the members of the staff at Bedford Books, particularly Elizabeth Schaaf, Michelle McSweeney, Maureen Murray, and Mark Reimold, proved to be congenial but tough companions in the work of bringing the manuscript into print.

I close with gratitude to three important inspirations in my life. The first is Geoffrey Chaucer himself, without whom there could be no such book as this. No doubt Chaucer would be puzzled and amused by much of what contemporary scholars say about his work, but surely he would be thrilled to know that, after six hundred years, people still read it with such vigor. The second is my mentor in medieval studies, J. Burke Severs, who first brought the dead words of a dead poet to life for me. My appreciation to him is expressed in the dedication to this volume. The third is my wife Anne, for her generous understanding of my need to spend many hours in the library and office working devotedly and lovingly with another Wife.

Peter G. Beidler
Lehigh University

Contents

PART ONE

The Wife of Bath:
The Complete Text

Biographical and Historical Contexts

Geoffrey Chaucer is usually considered to be second only to Shakespeare among British writers. Chaucer preceded Shakespeare by some two centuries and unquestionably influenced him. Although the sexist terms "seminal" and "the father of English literature" are now fortunately out of favor, there is no question that Chaucer introduced into English many of the genres, verse forms, and fictional techniques that were to help make English one of the most important literary languages the world has ever known. Who is this Geoffrey Chaucer?

CHAUCER'S LIFE

In fact, we know not nearly as much about Chaucer as we would like to know. Personal records were few in the fourteenth century, and of those that might once have existed most have disappeared or disintegrated in the six hundred years since his death. Not born to a noble family, Chaucer was not an important enough man in his youth that the world took note of his birth. We think that he was born in the early 1340s, son of John Chaucer, a reasonably wealthy London wine merchant, and Agnes de Copton.

To judge from his later writing of poetry, Geoffrey apparently received a decent enough education, probably at one of the schools near his home on Thames Street, London. John Chaucer apparently had enough money that, although he was not noble, he was able to purchase for young Geoffrey a position as a page in the household of the Earl of Ulster. As a page he would have performed certain domestic tasks — serving, kitchen work, whatever — in exchange for small amounts of money and for training in the skills necessary to court attendance. The earliest life record that we have for Chaucer was preserved, quite by accident, in the binding of a book that had nothing to do with him. This 1357 record, made when Chaucer would have been perhaps fifteen or so, indicates that young Geoffrey was given a sum of money by the Countess of Ulster for some clothes and other items at Christmas. As a member of the Ulster household, Chaucer would have observed proper manners and begun to learn French. Ever since France's conquest of England in 1066, French had been very much the language of high society in London.

A few years later, in 1360, Chaucer accompanied Ulster on a military campaign to France, where he was taken captive. His growing value to the British royalty is suggested by the fact that his ransom was paid by England's King Edward III. Somewhere around this time Chaucer might have attended the Inns of Court or, more likely, the Inns of Chancery, a kind of London school of law for chancery clerks. Around age twenty-five Chaucer became a squire in the king's court. He would have had a few duties in connection with that post, but it would have given him ample opportunity to observe at close hand the manners of court and to make contacts with the royal family. One member of that royal family was John of Gaunt, son of Edward III, brother to Edward the Black Prince, and uncle to the Black Prince's young son who would take over the throne of England as Richard II. John of Gaunt was to become Chaucer's chief patron over the years. As patron he encouraged and supported the young poet, who was already beginning to imitate the French love poems that were in vogue in the English court.

Despite the so-called Hundred Years' War that flared up intermittently between England and France during most of Chaucer's lifetime, the two countries were culturally close, and it seems that Chaucer served his poetic apprenticeship by imitating French models. His first long poem was a translation into English of the French allegorical poem the *Roman de la Rose,* although only a portion of Chaucer's translation survives. In the French poem the role of a love-experienced old woman may have planted the early seeds in Chaucer's fertile imagination for the five-times-married Wife of Bath, the subject of this volume.

Chaucer spent much of his life acting as a public servant. Indeed, though his current fame rests almost exclusively on his poetry, during his own lifetime poetry seems to have been little more than a diverting sideline. In the 1370s he was sent by King Edward III on two diplomatic journeys to Italy to negotiate commercial and religious matters. He was selected to go in part, we assume, because he would have had some fluency in Italian, a language he probably learned by his early association with the Italian wine merchants who dealt with his father. On those trips to Italy Chaucer apparently became acquainted with the Italian literature that was then being written by Italy's own triumvirate of poets — Dante, Petrarch, and Boccaccio.

On one of those trips to Italy Chaucer may well have become acquainted with Boccaccio's *Decameron*. Originally written around 1350, shortly after the bubonic plague ravaged Italy, the *Decameron* is a collection of one hundred tales told by ten noble young travelers who agree to entertain each other with tales on ten days of their escape from Florence during the worst ravages of the plague. It may well have given Chaucer the initial inspiration for his own masterpiece, the *Canterbury Tales,* in which a group of pilgrims agree to tell stories to entertain one another on a journey. Not until some years later, however, did Chaucer have the time to work seriously on the *Canterbury Tales,* and there is in the *Decameron* no one like the Wife of Bath.

Chaucer's various civil duties took most of his time. He was alternately a diplomat, a justice of the peace, a customs officer, and a forester. He was also for a time a member of Parliament from Kent, the county the Canterbury pilgrims would have had to travel through to get to Canterbury. He became clerk of the king's works — an important job that involved him in various administrative, construction, and maintenance duties in connection with various royal properties.

Creative, resilient, and versatile, Chaucer seems to have prospered well enough during most of his life. Some records indicate, however, that at times he must have been short of money because he was sued for nonpayment of his debts. He was robbed a time or two, and he was fined two shillings for beating a friar. We know almost nothing about any of these matters except the bare-bones factual record of them, usually with no explanation whatever.

About Chaucer's love life we are also mostly in the dark. He married a woman named Philippa, with whom he had two sons and possibly two daughters. Judging from the sardonic attitude toward marriage that we see reflected in some of Chaucer's works — including the Wife of Bath's Prologue and Tale — we might be tempted to assume that Chaucer's marriage was not entirely satisfying to him, but that is mere speculation. Chaucer also at times portrays successful marriages, and in fact we just don't know about his domestic strife or tranquillity. There is an ambiguous legal record in which a woman named Cecilia Chaumpaigne, in consideration of a payment of ten pounds, releases Geoffrey Chaucer from the charge of *raptus*. The import of the charge and the circumstances surrounding it are sufficiently vague that various scholars have attempted to clear Chaucer of the charge of sexual rape by pointing out that *raptus* might have meant something more like our modern "abduction." In fact, we know neither that he was guilty of raping, or attempting to rape, Cecilia, nor that he was not guilty. Chaucer would have been around forty at the time of the charge in 1380. We have no idea what Cecilia's age would have been. Indeed, we know almost nothing about Cecilia except that she was the daughter of a London baker. In the absence of conclusive evidence, it is perhaps best to speak only of probabilities: Chaucer probably was accused of sexual rape by a woman named Cecilia Chaumpaigne, and his paying her ten pounds — roughly equivalent to Chaucer's annual salary as a customs official — to settle the matter suggests that he was probably guilty, either of the attempt or of the act. More than that we cannot say.

Philippa apparently died in 1387 after a twenty-year marriage to Chaucer. Chaucer lived for thirteen more years before dying in 1400, at about age sixty. By fourteenth-century standards, he would have exceeded the average life expectancy by a considerable number of years.

CHAUCER'S APPEARANCE

We know almost nothing of Chaucer's appearance. We do have the miniature portrait of him in the Ellesmere manuscript, perhaps made ten years after his death by someone who remembered what he looked like, but no one can claim accuracy. The proportions of the portrait, perhaps the result of the need to provide an equestrian likeness in the narrow margin of a manuscript, make the man appear to dwarf the horse he rides on, and make his torso large in comparison with his short legs. Another early portrait of Chaucer in a Hoccleve manuscript in the British Library in London, made about the same time, shows a face with somewhat similar features.

Portrait of Chaucer from the Ellesmere manuscript. Used by permission of the Huntington Library in San Marino, California.

Perhaps the most interesting "portrait" of Chaucer comes from Chaucer himself, when he has Harry Bailly, the Host of the pilgrimage to Canterbury, ask the pilgrim Chaucer for a tale:

And thanne at erst he looked upon me
And seyde thus, "What man artow?" Quod he,
"Thou lookest as thou woldest fynd an hare,
For evere upon the ground I see thee stare.
Approche neer, and looke up myrily.
Now war you, sires, and lat this man have place,
He in the wast is shape as well an I.
This were a popet in an arm t'enbrace
For any womman, small and fair of face.
He semeth elvish, by his contenance." (B² 1884–93)

In reading these lines we must recall that when they were first put before an audience, Chaucer was himself probably standing before a live audience reading or reciting the lines so that auditors would have been able to see for themselves whether the Host was being accurate. The Host describes Chaucer as shy and reticent, looking down as if for rabbits rather than boldly up at his fellow pilgrims. The Host also describes Chaucer as having a large enough waistline that he could be compared to himself — a tavern keeper whose life kept him in the vicinity of rich food all the time. Chaucer's girth was such, it seems, that the Host had to ask others to step aside to make room for him to come forward. It is entirely possible, at any rate, that the sedentary life of a middle-aged poet and civil servant might well have contributed to a certain portliness of appearance. That Chaucer was short is suggested by the Host's saying that he was "small," "elvish," and a little doll or "puppet." Perhaps more important than Chaucer's possibly retiring and unprepossessing appearance is his ability to poke fun at that appearance in the portrait he has the Host give of him. Chaucer's own self-portrait is briefer and less developed than the self-portrait we find coming from the mouth of the Wife of Bath, but Chaucer's has some of that same self-critical humor and shows a similar willingness to let us see aspects of himself that he might have had reason not to be proud of.

HISTORICAL EVENTS

If we are to understand most fully Chaucer's life and his poetry, we need to know something of the times Chaucer lived in. Five of the major historical events that influenced Chaucer's life and literary output are the murder of Thomas à Becket, the Black Death, the troubled reign of Richard II, the English Rising of 1381, and the Great Schism.

Thomas à Becket

From the point of view of Chaucerians, one of the most important historical events in England took place three centuries before Chaucer's time: the death of Thomas à Becket, archbishop of Canterbury, in the cathedral itself. Thomas, a capable ecclesiastical administrator, became the friend and counselor of the young King Henry II. When the old archbishop of Canterbury died in 1161, Henry decided to name his trusted friend as the new archbishop, thus bringing firmly under his own control both the church and the state. Canterbury was, after all, the seat of the Christian church in England, and to control the archbishop was to control much of the wealth and power in England. Once he became archbishop, however, Thomas refused to act like a royal appointee. Increasingly he saw himself as serving God rather than the king.

After Henry made moves indicating that he was considering elevating the archbishop at York to be the real head of the church in England, Thomas secured from the pope a bull excommunicating the rival archbishop. When Henry heard that news, he muttered in the presence of four of his trusted knights, "Will no one free me of this wretched priest?" The knights took Henry at his word and rushed to Canterbury, entered the cathedral there, and murdered Thomas. King Henry was later to do public penance at Canterbury for his former friend's death. When Thomas was named a saint, his tomb at Canterbury became one of the most popular shrines in all of England, the destination of thousands upon thousands of pilgrims. Among those pilgrims some three centuries later were thirty fictional men and women whose gathering at the Tabard Inn in London and whose tales told along the Pilgrim's Way were to be immortalized by Geoffrey Chaucer.

The Black Death

At the middle of the fourteenth century, when Chaucer would have been a boy of around ten, the bubonic plague, sometimes known as the Black Death, hit Europe. It struck first in the south and east, then made its way inexorably north and west.

We now know that the plague is carried by a species of black rat and that it is conveyed to humans by fleas leaving their dead hosts seeking new ones. In Chaucer's time, however, most people assumed that the plague was the result of strange movements of the heavenly bodies or, more likely, was God's way of punishing evil people for their sins. Only one thing was absolutely clear: that people were dying in agony and in unprecedented numbers. In its pneumonic form the disease killed swiftly and with little warning. The more widespread bubonic form of the disease was not quite as swift, but swift enough. Starting with the appearance of buboes or lumps in the armpits and groin, it proceeded to spread widely over the rest of the body. The buboes were followed by black splotches over the body, and finally by death. The plague was especially widespread in cities, but it seemed to travel along the various trade routes with infected cloth and people. It was a democratic disease, affecting men, women, children, the poor, the rich, the laity, the clergy — many of them buried hastily in mass graves. To come up with accurate figures is impossible, but reasoned estimates claim that between 1348 and 1350 a quarter to a third of the population of Europe was carried off. We don't know whether anyone in Chaucer's own family died of the plague, but we do know that in a later onslaught of the plague in 1368, Duchess Blanche, the wife of John of Gaunt, contracted the disease and died. Chaucer commemorated her death in one of his early poems, *The Book of the Duchess.*

Far greater than its effect on literature, however, was the plague's effect on the European economy. With all those people dying, labor was suddenly in short supply, and workers who survived the ravages of the plague found themselves in a far stronger economic position. No longer locked into a feudal system that kept them tied to a single manor, they were mobile and able to insist on certain wages and working conditions. One of the most important effects of the plague, then, was its boost to the rise of an independent middle class — that class of merchants, weavers, millers, taverners, and cooks that joined Chaucer on the road to Canterbury.

Richard II

Richard succeeded his grandfather Edward III in 1377 and reigned as King Richard II until his deposition in 1399, just before Chaucer's death. In part because he was sandwiched between two far stronger and more prominent kings (Edward III and Henry IV), in part because he began his twenty-two-year reign as a boy of eleven, and in part because the times seemed not to provide much opportunity for such a man, Richard II has never figured large in the histories of English royalty or of England itself.

In the early years of his reign he was dominated by the policies of his uncles, especially the ambitious Duke of Gloucester and the kindly John of Gaunt. In the later years Richard tried to lead, but he lacked the vision and the confidence to rise very far above the petty squabbles that seemed to surround him. The so-called Hundred Years' War with France was in one of its many lulls during his reign, and at home his barons were more interested in protecting their own interests than in helping the young king gather a large national treasury or provide a strong central government or military force. When Richard was off in Ireland in 1399 trying to consolidate his power there, his cousin Henry, eldest son of the now-deceased John of Gaunt, won the support of the barons and effectively deposed the weak Richard. On his return from Ireland, Richard had no choice but to abdicate, and within a year, a prisoner in his own country, he died. Looking back on his reign, he may have been proud of at least one heroic act — his handling of the English Rising of 1381 when he was a teenaged king.

The English Rising

Sometimes referred to as the Peasants' Revolt, the English Rising of 1381 resulted from a series of causes, among them the weakness of King Richard and the new freedom that the rising middle class was beginning to feel as a result of the reduced workforce following the bubonic plague. The more immediate cause was an unpopular poll tax that some angry laborers or villeins in Essex — the area east of London — refused to pay. When the London magistrates sent out a small delegation to try them and punish them for not paying, the men of Essex angrily beheaded the members of the delegation. Word of their audacious action spread immediately, and a large group of supporters from Essex and, farther to the southeast, from Kent joined them. Soon thousands of Englishmen — not just laborers but also freemen and merchants — started off to London to talk with the king. They were less angry at this fourteen-year-old boy-king than they were at his ministers, but they rode to the Tower of London and demanded a royal audience. Most of the king's army was at that time in faraway Portugal, and no civil force was big enough to disperse so large a group of Englishmen, the likes of which had never stormed into London before with such demands.

Acting on the advice of his counselors, the young Richard bravely rode out of the Tower of London and listened to the revolutionary demands of the people: the abolition of the hated system of villeinage whereby workers were bound to the land as near-slaves of the lord of the manor; an end to feudal dues; and total amnesty for those who came into London. Richard hastily granted the demands, which he had no intention of honoring, and asked the men to go home. After an altercation that ended with the wounding of Wat Tyler, a leader of the rising, the men surrounded the king and drew their arrows on him. Richard shouted out, "Let ME be your leader." Impressed with his bravery, they lowered their arrows and followed him to the edge of the city and went home. Tyler was soon beheaded.

The English Rising was over, but Chaucer, who was probably in London at the time, must have been impressed by this unprecedented show of rebelliousness from a group of people previously considered insignificant. Chaucer makes only a brief and passing direct reference in one of his Canterbury stories to the storming of London, but it seems likely that the whole structure of the *Canterbury Tales* was influenced by the spirit that made the rising possible. One of the most amazing features of Chaucer's collection of tales is, after all, that those tales are told by a group of men and women from many strata of English society. On the pilgrimage to Canterbury a drunken miller can challenge a noble knight, and a weaving wife from beside Bath can challenge virtually any authority that tries to tell her who she is or what she can do. The fictional gathering that is the *Canterbury Tales* is usually assumed to be set in 1387 — just six years after the English Rising. Such a gathering, with such challenges, would have seemed unrealistic earlier than 1381.

The Great Schism

A year after young Richard ascended to the English throne in 1377, a severe disruption in the politics of the Christian church took place in southern Europe, known as the Great Schism. To understand this event we need to remind ourselves that in Chaucer's time there was but one Christian church, what we now call Roman Catholic. The Protestant revolution, like the printing press that helped to popularize it, was still a century away, and the Bible was a document that few, except clergymen who knew Latin, read. In 1377, then, just as to be English was by definition to recognize the authority of the king and the civil hierarchy of barons and government officials, so to be Christian was by definition to recognize the authority of the pope and the church hierarchy of bishops, priests, and other church officials. In 1378, that church hierarchy was complicated and confused because suddenly there were two popes, one in Rome, Italy, and one in Avignon, France. The French cardinals, not satisfied that Urban VI, the new pope in Rome, was adequately reflecting the interests of France, decided to elect a French pope, Clement VII, and seat him at Avignon. When Chaucer was sent to Italy on a diplomatic mission in 1378, one of his tasks may have been to assure Urban that England's sympathies were with him rather than with the French pope.

For the next four decades, including the richest period of Chaucer's own artistic development, the Christian church was divided. Two different popes insisted on being the head of the church and the one true vicar of the one true God. The situation was eventually resolved in 1417, but during those four decades, seeds of doubt must have been planted in the minds of many people. If there were two popes, could there be two Christianities? If both popes claimed to speak directly for God but spoke differently, might both be speaking only for themselves? If so, should Christians perhaps look elsewhere — to the Scriptures themselves, perhaps? — for a more reliable authority on God's own messages to the men and women on earth? If the papacy were a function more of nationalism than of God, then might not Christianity itself be more a religion of men than a religion of angels, and if it were a religion of men, might it not also be a religion of women? References to corrupt clergymen are everywhere in the *Canterbury Tales,* which is full of allusions to the dishonesty of those who should be honest, the sexuality of those who should be chaste, the greed of those who should be poor servants of the Lord. Chaucer's Wife of Bath, in an astounding display of independence, challenges the words of some of the great interpreters of religious doctrine, and even takes on Jesus himself at one point. It was not merely the papacy that was being called into question in Chaucer's time; it was the very structure, meaning, and basis of Christianity itself.

THE *CANTERBURY TALES*

Chaucer's *Troilus and Criseyde* — a wonderful poem — is sometimes called the first English novel. It is a long fictionalized account of the love of the Trojan prince, Troilus, for Criseyde, the daughter of a Trojan traitor who defects to the side of the enemy Greeks. The beauty of their love, the role played by Pandarus, Criseyde's uncle, in helping it along, the tragedy of Criseyde's final abandonment of Troilus in favor of the protection of a Greek soldier, and the death of Troilus make for a captivating and enduring story. The stunning complexity of pilgrims like the Wife of Bath, however, and the richness and variety of the individual tales cause most scholars to agree that the *Canterbury Tales* is truly Chaucer's masterpiece.

The general scheme of the *Canterbury Tales* is well known. One April, Chaucer — or a fictional persona named Chaucer — spends the night at the Tabard Inn in Southwark, on the south bank of the

Thames River in London, at the start of a trip to Canterbury to pay homage at the tomb of English martyr Thomas à Becket. At the Tabard he meets a richly varied group of twenty-nine other pilgrims, all headed in the same direction: a knight, a miller, a prioress, a ship-man, a merchant, a friar, a monk, and so on. The group seems so var-ied and lively that Harry Bailly, the innkeeper, suggests that they all set off to Canterbury together the next morning and that, to entertain and enlighten one another along the way, they tell each other tales. Whoever tells the best story — the story that best combines entertain-ment and morality — is to get a free dinner at the Tabard, to be paid for by the rest of the pilgrims when the group returns to London. They all agree, and the next morning they set off.

Although Chaucer's plan for the *Canterbury Tales* appears to have changed in the process of composition, one of his plans seems to be the one outlined in the General Prologue: to write some 120 tales — 4 for each of the Canterbury pilgrims, including 2 each for the trip to Canterbury and 2 each for the trip back. Other obligations, however, and his own death in 1400, prevented Chaucer from completing that ambitious scheme, and we are left with only twenty-odd tales, some of them incomplete. At his death Chaucer seems to have left his working copies of the Canterbury stories in some disarray. We cannot be sure even of what his working copies looked like, because we have not a single one that was written in his own hand. Rather, we have only copies made by scribes — professional copyists — in the fifteenth cen-tury, at least a decade after Chaucer's death.

Some eighty separate manuscripts contain materials related to the Canterbury collection, some fifty of them with more-or-less complete sets of the tales. No two of these manuscripts are exactly alike, though it is possible to construct family relationships among them. Identifying the half-dozen oldest and most authentic manuscripts is relatively easy. Of those, two stand out for special attention. The most authentic of them, and the one that most probably comes closest to reflecting the state of Chaucer's own manuscripts of the individual tales, is known as the Hengwrt manuscript (variously pronounced "hengert" and "hengwrit"), the MS Peniarth 392, now in the National Library of Wales at Aberystwyth. The manuscript is not elegant, its sheepskin leaves having been damaged in its nearly six-hundred-year history by the gnawings of mice and the more subtle ravages of water, mildew, binding, and rough handling. The order of the tales that the Hengwrt manuscript provides is flawed — a fact that suggests that Chaucer himself never placed them in any final order — but its text of the individual tales is generally considered the best we have.

Not long after the Hengwrt was completed, the same scribe set to work on a more elegant and polished version, now known as the Ellesmere manuscript. The Ellesmere, labeled as El.26.C.9 at the Huntington Library in San Marino, California, was much better managed than the Hengwrt. It has the tales in a more logical order, it is variously "improved" by intelligent editing, and it is beautifully illustrated with colorfully artistic renderings of some large initial letters and with miniature drawings of the Canterbury pilgrims — including both Chaucer and the Wife of Bath. Lovely though it is, and polished though its text of the Canterbury stories is, the Ellesmere manuscript introduces some corrections that are scribal or editorial rather than Chaucerian. I have chosen the Hengwrt as the base text for my edition of the General Prologue description of the Wife of Bath and the Wife of Bath's Prologue and Tale. A more extended discussion of my editing principles appears in the "Introduction to the Text" (p. 28).

It is important to remember that the *Canterbury Tales* is incomplete, unfinished, fragmentary. At his death Chaucer appears to have left ten fragments or groups of tales. Within each group are links connecting one tale to the next. In Group A, for example, we have the General Prologue, ending with the Knight's drawing of the shortest straw to indicate that he will tell the first tale; the Knight's romance about two young royal prisoners who both fall in love with the same young woman; the Miller's drunken reaction to it and his response with a delightfully realistic comedy that annoys the aging Reeve; the Reeve's revenge with a tale about a thieving Miller, which pleases the Cook; and the start of the Cook's story about the London underworld of con men and prostitution. The Cook never finishes his tale, which ends in midsentence and is linked to nothing after it. So ends Group A. There are ten such groups of tales, with links between the tales in each group, but little or no indication of where the groups would have fit into Chaucer's final ordering. Chaucer's literary executors took those groups and recopied them, sometimes apparently adding links and titles between the fragments to make the *Canterbury Tales* seem more like a completed book.

In Group D we find the Wife of Bath's performance. It is followed by and linked to the tales of the Friar and the Summoner, but the fragment breaks off after the Summoner's Tale. It is linked to nothing before the Wife of Bath's Prologue, which begins abruptly with the

Wife of Bath's insistence that experience, not authority, is her own guiding principle when it comes to sexuality and marriage. It might perhaps eventually have followed a tale in which the teller proclaimed the importance of some authority — perhaps religious or biblical — in matters of sexuality and marriage, but that is mere speculation. In fact we simply do not know what Chaucer's final detailed intentions for the *Canterbury Tales* were, and there is no evidence that he even had any intentions that could realistically be called "final." Because he wrote no more than a fifth of the 120 tales he at one point intended to write, there could be nothing final about any plan he might have dreamed up.

Equally problematic is the notion of a Marriage Group of tales. In this supposed group the Wife of Bath initiates a debate about marriage that is picked up and extended by other pilgrims — notably the Clerk, the Merchant, and the Franklin. Most arguments about the Marriage Group are based on certain assumptions about Chaucer's final order of three of the fragments, and all such assumptions are suspect. The *Canterbury Tales* was still fragmentary, still growing in Chaucer's mind, at his death. All we have are the pieces he had completed. We can safely assume almost nothing about what order he would have arranged them in, what other tales might have intervened between the fragments we now have, or even whether Chaucer would have kept the tales he did complete in the fragments or groups we now find them in.

Although he did not live to complete the *Canterbury Tales,* Chaucer wrote enough of the stories, and wrote them so well, that they provide the foundation for a towering reputation. Chaucer scholars agree on little, but most agree that he was a world-class writer, that the Wife of Bath is Chaucer's most memorable character, and that her prologue and tale are among the most remarkable of Chaucer's creations.

THE WIFE OF BATH'S PROLOGUE AND TALE

The Wife of Bath is one of the most fascinating and controversial of Chaucer's Canterbury pilgrims. When her turn comes to talk, Alisoun of Bath begins with a long prologue — variously called by modern critics an autobiography, a confession, a lecture, a sermon, a harangue — in which she talks about her ideas on virginity and multiple marriages and about her first five husbands. Then she launches into her tale about an Arthurian knight who rapes a young maiden, is sent on a quest to discover what women most desire, and pays the price for the correct answer by being forced to marry the ugly old woman who gives him that answer.

We know little about when Chaucer wrote the Wife of Bath's Prologue and Tale, though most readers assume that it was written when Chaucer was at the very height of his powers, probably in the late 1380s or early 1390s. We can only speculate about whether Chaucer wrote this prologue and tale for a specific occasion, but we assume that it was designed initially to be presented orally by Chaucer himself, either in the royal court or at some other gathering — a bachelor party, for example, or a visit by a diplomat, or a trade guild festival. In fact, however, we just don't know. The prologue itself may have been written originally as two separate pieces. The first may have been on the relative advantages of virginity, marriage, and multiple marriages; the second, on the relative advantages of young and old husbands. The tale of the various misadventures of the Arthurian knight was probably written specifically for the Wife of Bath to tell on the road to Canterbury, but there is strong evidence that Chaucer at one time envisioned another tale for her, the one now known as the Shipman's Tale. That tale is about a merchant's wife who engages in commerce and sex with both her own husband and her husband's best friend, a monk. Whatever the developmental history of the Wife of Bath and the various pieces of her Canterbury performance, at his last reworking of the Wife of Bath material Chaucer almost certainly meant to have her long prologue presented as a single piece, as it is here, to be immediately followed by the Arthurian tale.

SOURCES OF THE WIFE OF BATH'S PROLOGUE AND TALE

For almost everything he wrote Chaucer appears to have had a literary source, some earlier narrative that served as a starting point for his own work. If to us that seems like cheating or like a failure of originality, we must recall that Chaucer lived in an age when people were not impressed with the "new." Anyone could make up a new plot, but to tell an old story as well as, or better than, it had been told before — now *that* was genius. For some of Chaucer's tales we know without question what the source was. No one doubts, for example, that the Knight's story of Palamon, Arcite, and Emily is based on Boccaccio's

Teseida, a tale about Palamone, Arcita, and Emilya. But Chaucer did not simply translate the Italian. Rather, he rewrote it, focusing on the love story, tightening the plot, reducing the length to about a quarter of the original. Chaucer rarely simply retold old stories. Rather, he rewrote them and recombined them, giving them his own quite distinctive stamp in the process.

He did the same for the materials he assigned to the Wife of Bath. Some of the material in the prologue, for example, will sound vaguely familiar to anyone who has read Guillaume de Lorris and Jean de Meun's *Roman de la Rose* (originally in French) and Jerome's letter *Adversus Jovinianum* (originally in Latin). Relevant portions of these and other sources pertinent to the Wife of Bath's performance are available in the Bryan and Dempster volume cited in full in the Works Cited at the end of this chapter. Bryan and Dempster provide the original-language texts of the four works I give in my own summaries that follow as well as those of certain other materials possibly relevant to the Wife of Bath's Prologue and Tale. Because they provide only brief side summaries of the materials they quote, that volume will be of limited use to readers who are unfamiliar with medieval Latin, Old French, and Middle English.

The *Roman de la Rose* is an allegorical dream tale about a young man who falls asleep in May and dreams about his love for a Rose. As he tries to win his love he has a series of adventures with people — Envy, Avarice, Poverty, Old Age, and so on — who try to dissuade him. A friend named Fair Welcoming tries to help him, but soon Fair Welcoming is imprisoned in a tower and put under the guard of the Old Woman (called La Vieille in the French, the Duenna in some English translations). The section we are mostly concerned with — lines 12740–14546 — is the Old Woman's long speech to Fair Welcoming in which she tells him, out of motives that are not entirely clear, about her life and the wiles of women.

Summary of the Old Woman's Speech in the *Roman de la Rose*

Your time of joy is yet to come, but mine is past. Before you plunge into Venus's bath, listen to my instructions. I speak from a lifetime of experience. I used to be so young and pretty and popular with men, but now I am old and wrinkled and neglected. I will avenge the wrong done to me by teaching you my doctrine, so that you can get revenge for me. And yet, the sweet memories of my love-filled youth still give me pleasure.

I don't encourage you to engage in love, but if you do, at least do so wisely and with your eyes open. Because I know all about the games of love, you will do well to listen to me. Always get what you can from the rich, promising them everything but giving them as little as possible. Always look out for your own needs, and plan ahead for more than one lover. Never concentrate your love on just one person. The mouse who has but one hole to run to is in a bad way indeed. And be aware that you cannot trust women. They are all deceitful and eager to have sex with anyone they can. They know that they must carefully conceal their shortcomings with fine dresses, their foul breath and ugly teeth by closing their mouths. They know when to use tears to their best advantage and that they must appear generous and genteel in serving and eating food. They are careful about drinking too much, because a drunken woman has no defenses and can keep no secrets. They go about to dances, games, weddings, and festivals to meet new lovers.

A woman knows that she should take everything she can from her lovers, filling her coffers and collecting fine dresses, demanding whatever she can before she yields. In this way she can accumulate enough to live the life she wants to live, free and independent. Women, after all, naturally desire freedom. They hate being tied down, just as the birds hate being caged, no matter how sumptuous the cage. All men desire to make love to all women, and women love to receive them — whether they are secular men or men of religion, dressed in leather or fine cloth. Nature has inclined women's hearts to desire pleasure, and men give us that pleasure. It is absurd for husbands to think that they can have their wives to themselves. They might as well not even try to cage their wives, but would do better to look the other way and not enquire too much about what their wives do or with whom they do it. When they do that they just make themselves miserable. The wives will always have their way anyhow and will always have excuses and alibis.

A woman knows that it is best to make love in the dark so that if she has some blemish or ugly mark or filth about her body, her lover will not notice it and lose his desire. She knows that she must strive to reach climax at the same time the man does, or at least pretend to do so. He won't know the difference and will be pleased at her enjoyment.

I should have been far more careful to hold on to the wealth I acquired in the days when I was young and in great demand by many

men. I did acquire much, but I foolishly squandered it all, and now I
have nothing. Alas, I gave it away to a no-good man. He was the one
I loved best, but he did not care a fig for me. He was an evil man. He
called me a whore and never really loved me to begin with, but I was a
fool. The men who loved me I did not love, but this one, who did not
love me, was the one I loved the most. He beat me and cracked my
skull and dragged me about and insulted me, but he always made
peace before we went to bed and made love. Ah, what a fine lover he
was! I would have followed him anywhere. But he stayed with me
only long enough to spend all of my money. He threw it all away in
riotous living and gambling, and I let him do it. In the end we were
both left with nothing, and now I am reduced to begging.

I hope that you, fair son, will live your life more wisely than I have
lived mine, so that when your hair is white you will be able to live
more comfortably than I.

Chaucer's Wife of Bath is related to the Old Woman of the
Roman de la Rose, but of course she is far different. She is not so old,
for example, and she is far more interested in questions of virginity
and marriage than the Old Woman is. And, most important, the Wife
of Bath is a fictional woman who tells her own story, not a minor alle-
gorical abstraction in someone else's story.

The other central source for much of the material in the Wife of
Bath's Prologue is Jerome's letter *Adversus Jovinianum.* We know al-
most nothing of Jovinian except that he wrote, in Rome in the fourth
century, certain opinions about virginity and marriage, food and eat-
ing, baptism, the nature of sin, and the rewards and punishments of
the afterlife. What Jovinian actually wrote we do not know because no
copies of any document by him has survived. What has survived is
Saint Jerome's treatise of A.D. 393, in which the venerable church Fa-
ther cites Jovinian's arguments as heretical, wrongheaded, and stupid,
and then proceeds to refute them, one after the other, in his own long
treatise *Adversus Jovinianum,* or "against Jovinian." There is no
question that Chaucer was familiar with Jerome's treatise, especially
those portions having to do with Jovinian's opinion that a married
woman — even a woman married more than once — was potentially
just as good and pure of soul as a virgin, and had every right to marry
more than once, if she so desired. It is important to note that by "vir-
gin" Jerome meant either a male or a female, and that "chastity"
could be achieved by anyone who decided, even after experiencing
sex, to give up sex. The multiple-married Wife of Bath, of course, ap-

proved of Jovinian's ideas, even as they are represented — or perhaps misrepresented — in the words of the man who was out to prove him wrong. Below is a summary of some of the key arguments of Jerome about the superiority of virginity over marriage, and single marriage over multiple marriage (taken from *Adversus Jovinianum*, Book I, sections 1, 7–9, 12–16, 36, 40, 47–48).

Summary of Arguments from Jerome's *Adversus Jovinianum*

Only a few days ago I received from friends a copy of some treatises by a certain Jovinian, along with the request that I reply to his foolish ideas. His whole work, however, is so full of vile language, foolish blunders, and mad notions that I scarcely know where to begin. But to take up the matter of virginity and marriage, the Scriptures themselves, and particularly Saint Paul's letter to the Corinthians, tell us precisely what we are to believe.

Paul tells us that it is good for a man not to touch a woman, but for the man who cannot resist, let him have his own wife and render to her the marriage debt. In marriage, neither husbands nor wives have power over their own bodies, but their bodies belong to their spouses. Paul says to the unmarried and the widows that it is good for them to remain chaste, but if they cannot do so then it is better for them to marry than to burn. Paul means that wheaten bread is better than barley bread, but for those who cannot achieve the wheaten, then eating the barley is better than eating excrement. It is a question of degree, not a question of absolutes. It is clear that chastity is the highest virtue, but for people who cannot live chastely, marriage is better than undisciplined fornication. We are speaking here of better and best, not wrong and right.

Our opponent Jovinian goes wild with exultation when citing Saint Paul's statement that "concerning virgins I have no commandment of the Lord," as if that proves that the Lord does not value virginity. But it is clear what the Lord means. Of course the Lord would not command virginity, because then the end of mankind would come. It is a recommendation, not a commandment, to pursue the chaste life, but we are all free to choose for ourselves. There is no question that the Lord loves virgins more than others. They have chosen willingly in a way that was merely recommended, not commanded, and their free choice makes them superior.

Similarly, when the Apostle says of a wife that "if the husband be dead, she is free to be married to whom she will," he means that it would be *better* for a wife freed from marriage by the death of a husband to exercise that freedom and choose to be chaste from then on. As long as a person is married, he or she should stay bound and not seek divorce, but once the marriage is ended by death, the survivor is free to seek a higher life. There is no commandment that one *must* seek that life, but it is better, and more pleasing to the Lord, if one does. Surely it is better voluntarily to embrace chastity than to return to the filth of marriage. To be sure, Paul said that second and even more marriages are permitted to a widow, but that is only because it is better for a woman who cannot or will not remain chaste to prostitute herself to one man than to many. But still, commandment or not, chastity is always preferred to the marriage state. That is why we say that, while marriage fills the earth, virginity and chastity fill paradise.

Jovinian argues that if everyone were a virgin, then the human race would soon die out because there would be no wailing infants in the world. But that argument is absurd. Many are called, but few are chosen. We are all called to virginity, but few will choose it, and it is clear that there are plenty of wailing infants in the world. You ask, why were organs of generation made by the all-wise Creator, and why did He give us the natural desire for intercourse if he wanted us to refrain from that desire? My reply is, just because we have such organs below our waists and have the desire to use them in intercourse, that does not mean we are required to use them all the time, or that we cannot choose a higher way of life than engaging in the activities that join us to the animals. Besides, why would the Apostle urge us to be chaste if chastity were impossible or contrary to nature? In heaven there is no sexuality among the angels, so why should those who aspire to be angels not refrain from sexuality here on earth?

By going only once to a wedding, Jesus taught us by example that we should marry only once. It is not that the Church condemns marriage, but merely subordinates it and regulates it. The Church knows that in any great house there are vessels not only of gold and silver, but also of clay and wood.

In his wonderful book on marriage, Theophrastus advises wise men not to marry because it is almost impossible for a man to provide for the needs of a wife and also study philosophy. Wives want too many things — dresses, jewelry, servants, furniture. Then there are the never-ending curtain-lectures at night in which wives complain that they do not have as much as their neighbors, or that their husbands are looking lustfully at other women. Theophrastus says that we never learn the faults of our wives until after we marry them. We are ever so careful in purchasing horses and cattle and slaves and clothes and crockery, and do not buy them until we have thoroughly inspected them. But we do not know the women we marry until after we marry them, and then it is too late. We must always praise them and remember their birthdays. If we give them the management of the household, then we become their slaves, and still they will have the poison ready for us. If a wife is beautiful, she will soon find other lovers; if she is ugly, she will be wanton and throw herself at anyone.

Theophrastus says that some men marry to get a good household manager, but a faithful slave is a far better manager, and more submissive to the master. Some men marry to have children, to carry on their name, to support them in their old age, and to inherit their property, but those are the stupidest of reasons. It is better to choose as heirs relatives whom you love and trust. If you have children you have no choice but to give your goods to them.

Many men have suffered with bad wives. After Socrates' quarrelsome wife Xantippe cast dirty water on him, what could he say but, "After such thunder comes the rain." And a certain Roman nobleman, married to a woman whom everyone thought lovely and virtuous, said, "This shoe I have on looks elegant and lovely, but only I know where it pinches." Sometimes wives turn out to be so awful that men get divorced the day after they are married.

Although the Wife of Bath draws on many of these materials from Jerome, she does so selectively. She seems at times to be almost a caricatured composite of the heretical Jovinian and the sort of wife that Theophrastus most thoroughly condemned. Yet somehow Chaucer manages to turn the qualities that were negative in Jerome into qualities that are at least ambiguous, at best downright engaging, in the autobiographical portrait of the Wife of Bath. In any event, the Wife of Bath's Prologue is remarkable both for the variety of its sources and for its striking freshness. There was, quite simply, nothing quite like it before Chaucer wrote it, and the Wife of Bath stands out as at once the most fully developed and the most dramatically original of Chaucer's creations.

For the tale itself, the story of a knight-rapist's attempt to save his life by finding out what women most desire and of his then being tricked into marrying a "loathsome lady," we don't know precisely what Chaucer's literary source was. There are, however, several somewhat similar tales, usually called "analogues," that Chaucer could well have been familiar with. One of the unique features of the Wife of Bath's Tale is its "Englishness." Chaucer looked to the continent — particularly France and Italy — for most of his narrative materials, but for this tale he apparently looked closer to home. The narrative most likely to have been known to Chaucer was the Tale of Florent, taken from the *Confessio Amantis* — a long collection of stories by John Gower, Chaucer's friend and contemporary. The tale would probably have been available to Chaucer before its publication in the *Confessio Amantis* in 1390, although it is possible that Gower drew from Chaucer's tale the general outlines of his own, or perhaps both men drew on another version, now lost. In any case, to have a summary of Gower's tale before us for comparison with Chaucer's is useful, if only to show that the word *source* is itself a problem, so different from Chaucer's tale is Gower's.

Summary of John Gower's Tale of Florent

The worthy Florent, nephew of the emperor, is a kind, courteous, and chivalrous young knight. One day he is captured by enemies and in the struggle he kills Branchus, son of the enemy captain. Branchus's parents vow vengeance against Florent but are reluctant to punish the emperor's near relative directly. The evil grandmother of Branchus comes up with a plan to send Florent on an impossible quest — to discover what women most desire — so that when he fails, they can legitimately kill him for that failure. Florent agrees to the quest. He promises to come back on the appointed day with the answer and, if he fails, to submit to his own death.

Florent goes back to the emperor's court and takes a hasty survey of what women want, but he can find no clear or consistent answer. Discouraged, but telling the emperor not to avenge his death, he heads back to Branchus's relatives to accept his fate. On the way through the forest he comes upon a loathsome old woman. She beckons to him and says that she can give him the correct answer, but that in exchange he must agree to marry her. He offers her other payment, but she refuses. Finally Florent agrees, thinking that she will probably not live long anyhow. She then tells him the answer: women want to be sovereign over men's love.

When Florent gives that answer to Branchus's grandmother, she suspects trickery but angrily admits that it is the correct answer and releases him. On his way back through the forest he returns to the old woman. She is truly ugly: she has a low nose and high brows, small and deep eyes, cheeks wet with tears, wrinkled skin, shrunken lips, short neck, stooped shoulders, large body. Marry her he must, however, so Florent leads her back to his castle by night, hoping no one will see her. She bathes and dresses in good clothes but then looks even worse than she did before. After their night-time wedding, the old woman leads her bridegroom to bed. They lie together naked, but Florent turns away from her in disgust. She urges him to be a good husband and turn toward her. When he reluctantly does so he is delighted to see in place of the old woman a lovely young woman. She asks him whether he would rather have her lovely by day and ugly by night, or vice versa. Torn and unable to decide, he gives her the choice.

She is pleased to be thus sovereign over him, because she is thereby released from the spell her evil stepmother had cast upon her. The only way she could break this spell was to gain the love and sovereignty of the knight who surpassed all others in reputation. They laugh and play all night long and have a long and happy life together.

Another version of the loathsome lady story is an Arthurian tale called the Wedding of Sir Gawain and Dame Ragnell. Although it is taken from a manuscript that Chaucer could not have known (it is dated some fifty years after his death), it may itself be derived from an earlier version, now lost to us, that Chaucer could have known. It is also possible, of course, that its anonymous author might have been influenced by Chaucer's tale. It has a number of features that Gower's Tale of Florent does not have: the Arthurian setting, the presence of Arthur's queen, the year's respite (Florent is apparently given only a few days to seek his answer). Again, a summary may be useful for comparison.

Summary of the Wedding of Sir Gawain and Dame Ragnell

After King Arthur, hunting alone in Ingleswood, kills a deer, a strong knight named Sir Gromer Somer Joure appears and threatens to kill him. When Arthur pleads for his life the knight tells him that unless he returns after a year with the correct answer to the question of what women love best, he will behead him. Arthur agrees, then leaves to seek the comfort and help of his court.

The noble Sir Gawain offers to help Arthur by riding around to different regions seeking the correct answer. He and Arthur part, both carrying books in which to write the various answers they receive. When they later compare lists, Arthur despairs of finding any one answer to the question. With only a month remaining, Arthur goes into the forest at Ingleswood where he encounters Dame Ragnell, a profoundly ugly, barrel-shaped old woman with a snotty nose, enormous bleary eyes, huge pendulous breasts, and yellow teeth protruding tusklike out of her sagging lips. She says she will give Arthur the answer if he will promise to give her Sir Gawain as her bridegroom. Arthur seeks out Gawain and tells him the condition. "Is this all?" Gawain asks, and readily agrees to marry Dame Ragnell in order to save his king's life. Arthur returns to Dame Ragnell and receives the answer: what women love most is to have sovereignty over men.

Arthur takes the answer to Sir Gromer in Ingleswood and the knight spares him his life. When Arthur returns to Dame Ragnell she insists on marrying Gawain in a large public ceremony despite both Arthur's and the queen's requests for a small private ceremony. She dresses up in fancy wedding clothes, and afterward she and her new husband go to dinner. She uses her long fingernails to rip apart the food, then gorges herself with chickens and baked meats — so much so that all the wedding guests marvel to see her eat so voraciously.

[There is a page from the manuscript missing here, presumably containing about 70–80 lines.] Dame Ragnell, now in bed with Gawain, asks him to show her his courtesy in bed and invites him to kiss her. When he turns to kiss his bride he finds instead of the repulsive old woman a lovely young woman. She offers him a choice: Does he want her to be lovely during the days but ugly at night, or vice versa? He ponders the question, but finally asks her to decide. She is delighted and tells him that she had been enchanted by her evil stepmother. The only way she could break the enchantment, she says, was to marry the finest man in England and get him to yield sovereignty to her. They spend the night in joyful bliss and the next morning sleep late.

Around mid-day King Arthur, along with others in his court, comes up to the bedroom and, fearing that Gawain may have been killed by the loathsome lady, asks Gawain why he is sleeping so long. Gawain joyfully displays his lovely bride and tells them all the story of her disenchantment. Dame Ragnell corroborates the story and, delighted at being saved by so noble a knight as Gawain, promises to be obedient to Gawain always, and never argue with him. Gawain and Dame Ragnell have a son and live happily for five years before she dies.

Chaucer's version of the story is far different from either the Tale of Florent or the Wedding of Sir Gawain and Dame Ragnell. It opens with a recollection of the old days when fairies, not friars, bothered women, and moves on quickly to describe a most ignoble young knight's rape of a maiden. In Chaucer's tale the queen intervenes to save the knight's life, and at the edge of the forest the knight is first beckoned not by the old woman but by more than twenty-four dancing ladies. The foul old bride on her wedding night delivers a long pillow lecture on the nature of true gentility, offers him a choice of having her foul but faithful or lovely but perhaps not so faithful, and never claims to have been bewitched by an evil stepmother. There are other differences, of course, but the most striking difference of all is that the teller of this tale is the Wife of Bath. We know from her long prologue that the Wife is interested in sexuality and marriage, and we know that she has strong views, some of them expressed in the tale, about these and other subjects. All in all, the Wife of Bath's Tale is unique, and its uniqueness is due in large part to the fact that a woman narrates it.

Peter G. Beidler

WORKS CITED

Bryan, W. F., and Germaine Dempster, eds. *Sources and Analogues of Chaucer's Canterbury Tales.* Chicago: U of Chicago P, 1941. New York: Humanities, 1958. 207–68.

Guillaume de Lorris and Jean de Meun. *Le Roman de la Rose.* Ed. Ernest Langlois. 5 vols. Paris: Didots (vols. 1–2), Champion (vols. 3–4), 1914–24. Trans. Charles Dahlberg as *The Romance of the Rose.* Hanover, NH: UP of New England, 1971, 1983. Alternate trans. Frances Horgan. Oxford: Oxford UP, 1994.

Jerome, Saint. *Against Jovinianum.* In *Letters and Select Works.* Trans. W. H. Freemantle. Vol. 6 of *A Select Library of Niceen and Post-Niceen Fathers of the Christian Church.* Grand Rapids: Eerdmans, 1961. 346–416.

Introduction
to the Text

This edition contains the most important materials in the *Canterbury Tales* relating to the Wife of Bath: (1) the 32-line description of the Wife of Bath from the General Prologue to the *Canterbury Tales*; (2) the 856-line Wife of Bath's Prologue, containing the two interruptions (the first by the Pardoner, separating the 162-line expository section on marriage and virginity from the 636-line autobiographical account of the Wife of Bath's experiences with five husbands; the second by the Friar, separating the prologue from the tale proper); and (3) the 408-line Wife of Bath's Tale, the story of a young knight who rapes a maiden and is sent on a quest to discover what women most desire. The first of these is taken from the first fragment of the *Canterbury Tales* (usually referred to as Fragment I or Group A); the second two are taken from the fragment (usually referred to as Fragment III or Group D) that contains the prologue and tale of the Wife of Bath and the tales of the Friar and the Summoner. This edition of the three pieces dealing with the Wife of Bath, along with the various glosses and notes designed to help modern readers, was prepared especially for this Bedford Case Study.

THE TEXT

There is no "authorized" text of Chaucer's *Canterbury Tales*. Indeed, we have not a single word that we are sure is in Chaucer's own hand-writing. Instead, we have some eighty scribal manuscripts, each containing some or all of Chaucer's tales. It appears that copies of individual tales and of some groupings of tales were distributed during Chaucer's lifetime, but all of the existing manuscripts were made after his death. Most of the manuscripts were made not from an authorized Chaucerian original but from other scribal copies. Scholars have identified a half-dozen or so of the oldest and most authoritative manuscripts, and all modern editors look to those as they try to build a text that is most like what Chaucer probably wrote. The *Canterbury Tales* has been edited by many modern editors, most notably Walter W. Skeat (1900), John M. Manly and Edith W. Richert (1940), Fred N. Robinson (1933, 1957), A. C. Cawley (1958), E. Talbot Donaldson (1958, 1975), Albert C. Baugh (1962), Robert A. Pratt (1966), Donald R. Howard (1969), John H. Fisher (1977, 1989), N. F. Blake (1980), and Larry D. Benson (1987). Like these other editors I have examined the various early versions and have tried to make informed guesses about what Chaucer may have meant us to read.

The situation is complicated by a number of difficulties. First, there is textual evidence that Chaucer revised his work, although it is not always clear which revisions are Chaucer's own and which are the work of later copyists and editors who wanted to improve on Chaucer or smooth over what they thought of as rough spots or gaps in his text. In many of the later manuscripts of the Wife of Bath's Prologue, for example, five short passages of from 4 to 10 lines each (32 lines total) are suspect because they do not appear in some of the earliest manuscripts. They are not in the Hengwrt manuscript, the oldest and most authentic, for example, but they are in the lovely Ellesmere manuscript, made by the same scribe slightly later. Are these 32 lines Chaucerian revisions or scribal interpolations? We cannot be sure. I call attention to these passages in the text below by bracketing them and pointing out their questionable status in the notes. Second, Chaucer's spelling was erratic by modern standards. Like the copyists after him, he spelled the same word in different ways, sometimes to make it fit the metrical or rhyming needs of particular lines, sometimes merely because he forgot or did not care how he spelled it a previous time. Some of the spelling, of course, may reflect more a scribe's decision than Chaucer's. In any case, the notion of a single correct spelling of a word did not develop until centuries after Chaucer. Third, and perhaps most important, Chaucer and his copyists gave us almost no punctuation. They set off most of the text in ten-syllable iambic lines, and they put into most lines virgules or slash marks (/). The positioning of these virgules seems rather arbitrary, however, and is, in any case, not a useful guide to modern editors about where to put periods, commas, question marks, exclamation marks, colons, semicolons, and quotation marks. Paragraph indentations are for the most part the responsibility of modern editors.

In this edition I have tried to be faithful to the words and lines in the manuscripts, particularly in my base manuscript, the Hengwrt, but I have slightly modernized some of the spelling to make the text more readily understandable to modern students. I have, for example, generally regularized the spelling of *yow* to *you;* of *youre* to *your;* of *wel* to *well;* of *se* to *see;* of *thre* to *three;* of *myn* to *mine;* of *nat* to *not;* of *hir* to *her;* of *seyn* to *sayn;* and of *al* to *all.* I have made a few other small changes to avoid confusion. Where such changes would alter the actual pronunciation of a line, however, I made no change. I have not, for example, changed *hir* to *their,* even though that would have made the text easier for modern audiences to understand. I have made no effort to regularize the spelling of medieval words that have dropped out of the language. Thus, *eek* and *eke* — meaning "and" — remain unregularized. Realizing that Chaucer often used the letters *i* and *y* interchangeably, I have generally used the more modern choice. Thus, *wyves* becomes *wives* and *mayde* becomes *maide.* I have used the "Alys" of Hengwrt 548, however, rather than the "Alis" of Hengwrt 320 because "Alys" is the form usually used by modern scholars in referring to the shortened form of "Alisoun." I have not changed the past-participial prefix *y-,* so words like *ytaught* (meaning "taught") remain. This edition, then, may be considered to be minimally modernized, the modernization done with a view to making more friendly the task of reading Chaucer's language for the first time. The text still looks — and is — sufficiently medieval that modern readers will have plenty to challenge them in dealing with Chaucerian meanings and inconsistencies in spelling.

The lack of punctuation in most medieval manuscripts meant that readers were expected to resolve for themselves syntactic ambiguities that modern editors resolve. The punctuation and paragraphing in the pages that follow are my own. Readers should be aware that with this edition, as with every other modern edition, the meaning can vary somewhat depending on the positioning of the editor's placement of punctuation marks. Let me give an example. When the old woman in the Wife of Bath's Tale quotes Juvenal in lines 1192–94, in the Hengwrt manuscript we read

> Iuuenal seith / of pouerte myrily
> The poure man / whan he gooth by the weye
> Biforn the theues / he may synge and pleye

In Larry Benson's *Riverside* edition we read

> Juvenal seith of poverte myrily:
> "The povre man, whan he goth by the weye,
> Bifore the theves he may synge and pleye."

In my edition we read

> Juvenal seith of poverte, "Myrily
> The poure man, whan he goth by the weye,
> Before the theves he may singe and pleye."

The difference in punctuation at the end of the first line above may seem slight, but it is important. In Benson's edition Juvenal speaks merrily about the poor man who walks along not fearing that he will be robbed. In my version the poor man sings and plays merrily as he walks along because he need not fear that he will be robbed. My point here is not to argue for one reading over another, but to warn all readers that I have made editorial decisions like this on every page. Readers should in their own reading, therefore, consider other possible punctuation of the lines they are seeking to interpret.

To give readers of this book an opportunity to try their own hand at editing Chaucer, I reproduce here a transcription of 30 lines from the Hengwrt manuscript of the *Canterbury Tales*. The lines are numbered 163–92 in the Wife of Bath's Prologue. They appear just after the Wife has talked about her views of the relative merits of marriage and virginity and the relative merits of multiple and single marriages. The Pardoner, another of the Canterbury pilgrims, comes forward and tells her that he was thinking about getting married himself, but, having heard her, may not after all. She tells him to listen to the rest of her discourse and then decide whether to marry. The Pardoner politely invites her to carry on and teach him and other young men about her practices. She agrees, but asks her audience not to take what she says too seriously, since she just means to have fun. Perhaps you will want to try your hand at producing a modern edition of these lines, crossing out the virgules or slash marks and using modern punc-

tuation to break the lines into the kinds of sentences and speeches that
will make the lines accessible to modern readers:

Up stirte the Pardoner / and that anon

Now dame quod he / by god and by Seint Iohn

165   Ye been a noble Prechour / in this cas

I was aboute / to wedde a wyf allas

What/sholde I bye / on my flessh so deere

Yet hadde I leuere / wedde no wyf to yere

¶Abyd quod she / my tale is nat bigonne

170   Nay/thow shalt drynken / of another tonne

Er þ^t I go / shal sauoure wors than Ale

And whan that I / haue toold thee forth my tale

Of tribulacion / in maryage

Of which I am expert / in al myn age

175   This is to seye / my self hath been the whippe

Thanne maystow / chese/wheither þ^t thow wolt sippe

Of thilke tonne / that I shal abroche

Be war of it / er thow to neigh approche

For I shal telle ensamples / mo than ten

180   Who so þ^t nyle / be war by othere men

By hym / shal othere men corrected be

Thise same wordes / writeth Protholome

Rede in his Almageste / and take it there

¶Dame I wolde pray yow / if youre wyl it were

185   Seyde this Pardoner / as ye bigan

Telle forth youre tale / spareth for no man

And techeth vs yonge men of your praktyke

¶Gladly quod she / syn it may yow lyke

But that I praye / to al this compaignye

190   If that I speke / after my fantasye

As taketh nat agrief / of that I seye

For myn entente / nys but for to pleye.

My own version of these lines appears on pages 50–51. Readers will immediately see the kinds of changes I have made: modernizing the spelling (for example, by changing a *y* to an *i*), expanding the abbreviation þ^t to *that*, changing the paragraph markers ¶ to indentations, changing capitalization, adding some words (like *it* in line 167) from the Ellesmere manuscript, and, of course, supplying modern punctuation.

PRONOUNCING CHAUCER

For most of us in the twentieth century, poetry is a private and visual art: we read the words on a page silently to ourselves. In the fourteenth century, however, before the invention of printing made books inexpensively available, poetry was largely a communal and auditory art: poets read their works aloud before live audiences. Chaucer was one of the first important oral poets in English. It is beyond the scope of this volume to attempt to show modern readers in any detailed or highly systematic way how to pronounce Chaucerian poetry, but I give here twenty-five rules to help those who wish to try. For readers who are not so ambitious I give at the end of this section information about how to purchase an inexpensive tape of the Wife of Bath's Prologue and Tale.

Chaucerian English is called Middle English to distinguish it from the Old English of the *Beowulf*-poet and other early writers and the Modern English of Shakespeare and other later writers. A century ago scholars were convinced that Chaucer was a quaintly primitive poet who did not understand rhyme or meter. More recently we have discovered how to read him, and now we know that he was very much in control of both rhyme and meter. Indeed, we can learn to read his poetry with some general accuracy if we master the twenty-five rules I give below. Some are more important, more easily confused, or more frequently applied than others: 1, 3, 4, 7, 8, 10, 15, 16, 18, 21, 23, 24, and 25. (Note: In this section I generally use *italics* for Middle English words, quotation marks for Modern English ones.)

Consonants

Most of the consonants have not changed in the six hundred years since Chaucer wrote. A *g*, for example, was for Chaucer very much like the modern *g*. Sometimes it was pronounced hard (for example, before the vowel *o* as in *good*), sometimes soft (for example, before *e* as in *gentle*). Modern pronunciation is almost always a reliable guide to Middle English pronunciation of consonants. I call attention to three special features of Chaucerian consonants:

1. *k, g, l, r*   Because Chaucer wrote phonetically, most consonants were pronounced, even if they have become silent in Modern English. The *k* in *knight* would have been pronounced, for example, as would the *g* in *gnaw*, and the *l* in *folk*, even though all are silent now. The letter *r*, which is now virtually silent, would have been trilled in Chaucer's time, as it still is in Scottish pronunciation.

2. *y*   The letter *y* is usually a vowel (generally interchangeable with the letter *i*), but sometimes, as in *yellow*, it serves as a consonant. When it is a consonant it is pronounced as in Modern English. See rules 15 and 16 below for pronouncing it when it serves as a vowel.

3. *gh*   The noun cluster *gh*, now silent as in "though" or pronounced "f" as in "enough," would have been given a heavily Germanic gutteral sound, something like our modern "k" but deeper in the throat, as in the German "ich." The Middle English word *knight*, then, would have been pronounced something like "caneekt." For the sound of the vowel *i* in *knight*, see rule 16 below.

Vowels

In the fifteenth and sixteenth centuries the sounds of many English vowels gradually changed quality. That series of changes has come to be called the Great Vowel Shift. To read Chaucerian Middle English with any accuracy we need to be aware of those changes. Fortunately the changes were reasonably regular, and it is possible, knowing the pronunciation of Modern English words, to leap back through the Great Vowel Shift to a good approximation of Middle English pronunciation. Of course, if the Middle English word has dropped out of the language, then these rules will be of no help and we need to make bold guesses as we read aloud. Still, the rules cover more than 90 percent of the words we find, and if we stick with them and practice, we will soon be spouting Middle English in a downright Chaucerian way. The key is to start with the Middle English spelling of the vowel and find the letter or letters at the start of one of the rules below. Note that several vowels can have various pronunciations, and that I give at the end of each possible pronunciation examples of Middle English words in which that sound is used. Note also that some of the vowels are really diphthongs — vowel clusters that involve a glide from one vowel sound to another, as in the Modern English "ou" in "house." In Chaucer's time that word rhymed with our "goose" — a single vowel sound, "oo." In our time the vowel is a glide, from "ah" to "oo." I indicate these diphthongs with hyphenation, such as "ah-oo."

4. *a, aa* Pronounced "ah," like the *a* in Modern English "father." Middle English examples: *that, bath*.
5. *ai, ay* Pronounced "ah-ee," like the *ai* in the Modern English "aisle." Examples: *day, lai*.
6. *au, aw* Pronounced "ah-oo," like the *ou* in Modern English "house." Examples: *faught, lawe*.
7. *e, ee* Pronounced "eh," as in Modern English "men" and "bed," if the *e* in the word has the short-*e* sound today (that is, these short-*e* words have not changed in pronunciation in the six hundred years). Examples: *gentil, end*.
8. *e, ee* Pronounced "ay," as in Modern English "hay" and "play," if the word is pronounced "ee" now. Examples: *she, fredom*.
9. *e, ee* Pronounced like the *a* in Modern English "math" and "at," if the word in which it appears is spelled with the letters *ea* and is pronounced either "ee" or "ay" today. Examples: *heeth, great*.
10. *e* Pronounced "uh," like the unaccented *a* at the end of

Modern English "sofa," if the letter *e* appears at the end of a line or if Chaucer's iambic pentameter seems to require it elsewhere in the line (see rules 24 and 25). Example: *chapeleyne* (the first and final *e*'s might be pronounced "uh").

11. *e* Pronounced "ah," like the *a* in Modern English "dark" and "barn," in certain words in which it precedes the letter *r*. Example: *ferther, clerk, sterte.*

12. *ei, ey* Pronounced "ah-ee," like the *ai* in Modern English "aisle." Examples: *feith, veyne.*

13. *eau, ew* Pronounced "eh-oo" (sound not duplicated in a Modern English word) in the following Middle English words: *fewe, lewed, dew, shewe, shrewe, beaute, hewe.*

14. *eu, ew* Pronounced "ee-oo," like *ew* in Modern English "few" and "mew," in most words except the seven listed in rule 13. Examples: *new, reule.*

15. *i, y* Pronounced "ih," like the *i* in Modern English "him" and "thin," if the vowel in that word has the short-*i* sound today (that is, these short-*i* words have not changed in pronunciation since Chaucer's time). Examples: *skille, offring.*

16. *i, y* Pronounced "ee," like the *ee* in Modern English "sheet" and "free," in words where the vowel is pronounced "eye" today, as in "bright." Examples: *wif, ryde.*

17. *oi, oy* Pronounced "oh-ee," like the *oy* in Modern English "boy" and "decoy." Examples: *boidekyn, coy.*

18. *o, oo* Pronounced "aw" usually, as in Modern English "claw" and "hawk," if the word in which the Middle English *o* or *oo* appears is now pronounced like the vowel sound in "stone," "hot," "would," or "thong." Examples: *ofte, hooly.*

19. *o, oo* Pronounced like the vowel in Modern English "look" and "full," if the word in which *o, oo* appears is now pronounced like the vowel in "monk" and "shove." Examples: *love, above.*

20. *o, oo* Pronounced "oh," like the *o* in Modern English "most" and "stone," if the word is now spelled *oo* or pronounced like the *oo* in Modern English "food." Examples: *roote, good.*

21. *ou, ow* Pronounced "oo" usually, like the vowel in Modern English "ooze" and "shoe." Examples: *fowles, flour.*

22. *ou, ow* Pronounced "aw-uh," like a two-syllable *au* in Modern English "Paul" or a two-syllable *aw* in "crawl," in words in which the Modern English equivalent is pronounced "oh" as in "know." Examples: *knowen, soule.*

23. *u* Pronounced like the vowel sound in Modern English "look" and "full." Since there is only one alternative in this

list of rules for the single *u,* you can always assume that it rhymes with the vowel sound of "book." Examples: *ful, muchel.*

To determine the pronunciation of most Chaucerian words, then, we should assume that all consonants were pronounced, start with the spelling of the vowel and find the correct pronunciation in rules 4–23, and remember that *i* and *y* were usually interchangeable. We should also recall that in all of the poetry in this text, Chaucerian words are to find their proper pronunciation in a line that is in iambic pentameter.

Iambic Pentameter

In writing most of his poetry in what is now called iambic pentameter, Chaucer set the pattern for much of the poetry that followed, including Shakespeare's. It is impossible to read Chaucer's poetry well without understanding the fundamentals of iambic pentameter. An iamb is a two-syllable poetic unit in which the first syllable is unaccented, the second accented. Some examples of iambic words in Modern English are "alone," "return," and "pretend," although we must understand that while some two-syllable words can be iambic, as these are, two different words can together form an iamb as well: "the cow," "in tune," "on top." An iambic pentameter line is a joining together of five iambic units in such a way that we end up with a ten-syllable line in which the first is unaccented, the second accented, the third unaccented, and so on until the tenth syllable, which is accented. Here are examples of three Modern English iambic pentameter lines:

When Tom was young he ate a lot of corn.
The yellow dog was on the roof asleep.
My cow ate up my aphrodisiac.

Note that the first line has ten words, the second eight, and the third six, yet each has ten syllables and each is made up of five iambic units. The key to their being in iambic pentameter is not the number of words or merely the number of syllables, but that each line can be scanned without a great deal of forcing into five repeating units each of which has an unstressed syllable followed by a stressed one. To fully appreciate Chaucer's poetry in the Wife of Bath materials in this volume we need to be able to read his lines in more-or-less regular iambic pentameter lines. Two important final rules have to do with Chaucer's way of putting his English into iambic pentameter:

24. **Final** *e*   When an *e* appears at the end of a word at the end of a line, it should be read unstressed as an eleventh syllable. Although that final syllable technically renders the line not precisely an iambic pentameter line, most scholars now believe that Chaucer expected us to read that final *e* as a weak "uh"-sounding syllable.

25. **Internal** *e*   Some of the *e*'s within the line can either be pronounced or not, depending on the metrical requirements of the line. That is, Chaucer had a flexibility that modern poets do not have in that he could choose whether to pronounce certain internal *e*'s in the line. To approximate Chaucer's reading of the lines, then, we need to determine which *e*'s need to be pronounced to make the lines most iambic. It will help to consider lines A459–60 from the Wife of Bath's Prologue:

> She was a worthy womman all her live.
> Housbondes at chirche dore she hadde five.

First, we notice that when we read those Middle English lines as if they were in Modern English, the first scans pretty well ("She **was** a **wor**thy **wom**an **all** her **life**"), but the second ("**Hus**bands at **church door** she **had five**") yields us only eight syllables, and those not iambic at all. If we look more closely at the Middle English line 460, however, we notice that there are four "extra" *e*'s that do not appear in the modern rendition: one in *housbondes,* one in *chirche,* one in *dore,* and one in *hadde.* If we keep in mind our need for two additional syllables to bring the eight syllables up to ten, if we experiment with different ways of reading the line, and if we recall our rule 24 about the *e*'s at the end of the line, we can come up with a more regular scansion:

> She **was** a **wor**thy **wom**an **all** her **live**.
> Hus**bondes** at **chir**che **dore** she **had**de **five**.

Other readers might scan the lines slightly differently. They might choose, for example, to give an extra syllable to *Hus-bondes* rather than my choice of *chirche,* but the point is that Chaucer has given himself — and us — at least one way to scan his lines as iambic pentameter. Not all of his lines can be made to scan perfectly, any more than all of his lines rhyme perfectly. Indeed, there is considerable evidence that he was more interested in his meaning than his scansion or rhyming. But his verse is without question far more regular than scholars a century ago thought it was, and we now have the means, with a little time and effort, to hear him aright.

One of the best ways to start reading Chaucer correctly is to learn to pronounce his personal pronouns. For Chaucer,

he, she, me, and *we* were pronounced "hay," "shay," "may," and "way";

they was pronounced as a diphthong or vowel glide, something like "thy-ee" — almost but not quite two syllables;

I, my, and *mine* were pronounced "ee," "mee," and "meen";

our would have rhymed with Modern English "moor" and "lure," but with the *r* trilled;

you, your, his, her, and *it* were pronounced as they still are, "you," "your," "his," "her," and "it," except that the *r*'s would have been trilled.

It will be extremely helpful to read through the text while listening to a tape of the Wife of Bath's Prologue and Tale put out by the Chaucer Studio. To get a copy of the tape, write a check for $5.00 to The Chaucer Studio and send it to Paul R. Thomas, The Chaucer Studio, Department of English, Brigham Young University, Provo, UT 84602–6218. Indicate that you want the Wife of Bath tape. The different parts are read in different voices, with Mary Hamel, for example, reading the lines of the Wife of Bath and Jane Chance reading those of the old woman in the tale. This production was directed by Paul R. Thomas. Ideally, of course, you should try applying the twenty-five rules, listen to the tape, and boldly practice reading the lines out loud.

GLOSSES AND NOTES

Perhaps the most easily recognized feature of any modern edition of Chaucer is the number and placement of the glosses and explanatory notes it provides. Anticipating the needs of readers not previously familiar with Chaucerian words and phrases, I have tended to include more glosses but fewer technical explanatory notes than readers will find in editions designed for graduate courses. For the last 73 lines of the Wife of Bath's Tale, for example (from the Juvenal reference in line 1192 to the end of the tale), the *Riverside* edition devotes nearly fifty words to same-page glossing but about two hundred words to detailed explanatory notes in a separate section at the back of the volume. Some of those words at the end are in Latin, and most deal with remarks (not written by Chaucer) in the margins of the Ellesmere manuscript. For the same 73-line passage I devote nearly one hundred fifty words to glossing and nearly one hundred fifty to explanatory footnotes. These words are all in English and make no reference to the editorial glosses in the Ellesmere manuscript. All of my glosses and notes appear on the same page as the text to which they refer. I do not cite the work of other scholars in the notes. For some of the most important scholarship on the Wife of Bath, readers are referred to my Critical History following the text section of this volume.

Even though I have tried to provide full glosses and paraphrases, readers might do well to become familiar with the meanings of a number of Middle English words that appear with some frequency in the Wife of Bath materials:

al: "although"

atte: contraction of "at the"

aventure: "chance"

ay: "always"

bad: "bade," "asked"

benedicite: from the Latin meaning "(God) bless you," an interjection often used with little more meaning than "by heaven"

but: "unless," "but"

certes: "certainly"

clepe: "say," "name," "call"

daungerous: "coy," "standoff-ish"

eek, eke: "and," "also"

er: "before"

han: "have"

hem: "them"

hir: "their"

ilke: "same"

koude: "could" or "knew"

list (n): "desire"

list (v): "pleases"

make (n): "mate"

make (v): "make"

nas: contraction for "not was" ("wasn't")

nil: contraction for "not will" ("won't")

nis: contraction for "not is" ("isn't")

nolde: contraction for "not would" ("wouldn't")

noon: "none"

o, oon: "one"

pardee: from the French *par-dieux*, an interjection meaning "by God" or "indeed" but often used as a filler with little substantive meaning

parfit: "perfect"

quit, quite: "repay," "requite"

seistow or *seystow:* "you say," but note similar constructions such as *hidestow*: "you hide" and *wenestow* and *wostow*: "you know"

siker: "sure"

sikerly: "surely"

sinne: "sin"

sith, syn: "since"

thee: "you" or "thrive"

tho: "those" or "then"

unnethe: "scarcely"

verray: "true" or "veritable"	*yaf:* "gave"
(not "very")	*yif:* "give"
wight: "person"	*yifte:* "gift"
wood: "mad"	*yiven:* "given"
woot: "know"	*ywis:* "indeed," "certainly"

In addition, readers should know that poets in Chaucer's time still sometimes used the Old English inflectional marker to indicate the past participle of the verb. This marker was a *y-* preceding the verb form (pronounced as a separate syllable as if it were an *i*). Some examples:

ybroght: "brought"	*yhad:* "had"
yflatered: "flattered"	*ywroght:* "made"

Readers should also be aware of certain grammatical features of Chaucer's Middle English. For example, our modern notion that double negatives cancel one another would have seemed absurd to Chaucer. He used double, triple, and even quadruple negatives to intensify the negative. When Chaucer tells us of Alisoun — the given name for the Wife of Bath — that in all the parish such a "wif ne was there noon" (A449), he is telling us not that there were other wives like Alisoun, but that there *really* was no other wife quite like her. When Alisoun says that clerks can speak well neither of wives "Ne of noon oother womman never the mo" (691), she means not that clerks sometimes *do* speak well of women, but that they never, *ever* speak well of *any* of them. Readers should also know that the possessive case of nouns did not for Chaucer require the apostrophe. Thus "Goddes" in line 50 of the Wife of Bath's Prologue means "God's" rather than "Gods," and "Venus seel" (604) means the seal or mark of Venus.

In the pages that follow, short translations are given in the right-hand margin, adjacent to the line that contains the defined word or phrase. Longer explanations are at the bottom of the page, referenced by a superscript bubble at the end of the word or passage being glossed.

Peter G. Beidler

The Wife of Bath

DESCRIPTION OF THE WIFE OF BATH
FROM THE GENERAL PROLOGUE°
TO THE *CANTERBURY TALES*

A445 A good wif° was there of beside Bathe,	*just outside Bath*
But she was somdel deef, and that was scathe.	*somewhat deaf / regrettable*
Of clooth-making she hadde swich an haunt,	*such skill*
She passed hem of Ypres and of Gaunt.°	*surpassed them*
In all the parissh, wif ne was there noon	
A450 That to the offring before her sholde goon.°	

General Prologue: In the General Prologue, Chaucer describes the gathering of his fellow pilgrims at the Tabard Inn in London before their journey to Canterbury. He also describes most of the individual pilgrims he meets there. This is Chaucer's 32-line description of the Wife of Bath — identified later (line 320 in her prologue) by the name "Alys" and (in 804) "Alisoun." The letter at the start of the line numbers indicates that the lines are from the first fragment, known as Fragment I or Group A, of the *Canterbury Tales.*

A445. wif: The term could refer to a married woman, but also simply to a woman. In any case, the Wife of Bath is more technically a widow than a wife at this time, and the old woman in her tale, also referred to as a "wif" in line 998, is not a married woman.

A448. Ypres and Gaunt: Two towns in what is now Belgium noted for their fine cloth-making. The second is now called Ghent.

A450. before her . . . goon: Before she goes to make her offering. She apparently considers that her wealth gives her a right to make first offering — probably to be taken as a sign of her pride.

And if there did, certeyn so wrooth was she   *so angry*
That she was out of alle charitee.   *unforgiving*
   Her coverchiefs ful fine weren of ground —   *head-scarfs / finely spun*
I dorste swere they weyeden ten pound —   *weighed ten pounds*
A455 That on a Sunday weren upon her heed.   *head*
Her hosen weren of fin scarlet red,   *stockings*
Ful streite yteyd, and shoes ful moiste and newe.   *tightly laced / supple*
Boold was her face, and fair, and reed of hewe.   *red-colored*
She was a worthy womman all her live.   *life*
A460 Housbondes at chirche dore° she hadde five,
Withouten° oother compaignye in youthe.
   But therof nedeth not to speke as nowthe.   *at the present time*
   And thries had she been at Jerusalem.   *thrice*
She hadde passed many a straunge strem.°
A465 At Rome she hadde been, and at Boloigne,
In Galice at Seint-Jame, and at Coloigne.°
   She koude muchel of wandring by the weye.   *She knew much*
   Gat-tothed° was she, soothly for to seye.   *to say the truth*
Upon an amblere esily she sat,   *smooth-riding horse*
A470 Ywimpled° well, and on her heed an hat   *head*
As brood as is a bokeler or a targe,°
A foot-mantel about her hipes large,   *apron*
And on her feet a pair of spores sharpe.   *sharp spurs*
   In felaweship well koude she laugh and carpe.   *jest*
A475 Of remedies of love° she knew per chaunce,
For she koude of that art the olde daunce.   *knew / all the old tricks*

    A460. at chirche dore: Marriages were often performed publicly at the door or vestibule of the church, before the bride and groom went inside to attend a service. By stipulating the location, the Wife would have been legitimizing her marriages and her right to certain properties.
    A461. Withouten: Not to mention. The line is usually taken to mean that she had other sexual company before she was married, but Chaucer is ambiguous about the point. It could mean simply that she was "without other company before she was married."
    A464. passed many . . . strem: Crossed many foreign rivers.
    A465–66. At Rome . . . Coloigne: Sites of several of the most famous religious shrines of medieval Europe, all of which Alisoun has visited in addition to the three pilgrimages to Jerusalem mentioned in line A463.
    A468. Gat-tothed: According to some physiognomists (scientists who studied the relationship between the physical configuration of the head and face and the moral and intellectual qualities of the person), having gaps between the teeth could indicate pride and heightened sexuality. The word "gat" may be related to the word "goat" — an animal noted in Chaucer's time for its sexuality.
    A470. Ywimpled: With her head and neck covered by a "wimple" or linen cloth.
    A471. a bokeler or a targe: A "buckler" is a small shield; a targe is a larger one.
    A475. remedies of love: Solutions to love problems, or erotic stimulants, perhaps associated with Ovid's *Remedia Amoris*.

THE PROLOGUE°
TO THE WIFE OF BATH'S TALE

"Experience, though noon auctoritee
Were in this world, is right ynogh for me   *sufficient for me*
To speke of wo that is in mariage.°
For, lordinges, sith I twelve yeer was of age,   *gentlemen / since*
5 Thonked be God that is eterne on live,   *lives eternally*
Housbondes at chirche dore I have had five —
If I so ofte myghte have wedded be° —
And all were worthy men in hir degree.   *in their rank*
    "But me was toold certeyn, not longe agoon is,   *not long ago*
10 That sith that Crist ne wente nevere but ones   *only went once*
To wedding in the Cane of Galilee,
That by the same ensample taughte he me   *his example*
That I ne sholde wedded be but ones.°   *only once*

Prologue: The Wife of Bath's Prologue, as well as her tale, following, are taken
from the third fragment (Fragment III or Group D) of the *Canterbury Tales*.
    1–3. Experience, though . . . mariage: Even if there were no authorities on the
woes of marriage, I could speak from experience on the subject. The Wife of Bath
speaks as if in response to someone who had spoken about the woes of marriage, but
Fragment III is not clearly connected with any preceding tale. Some scholars believe
that Chaucer may have constructed this passage intending to link her prologue with the
epilogue to Man of Law's Tale at the end of Fragment II or Group B[1]. The blank space
is variously filled by "Squire," "Summoner," or "Shipman" in the manuscripts that con-
tain this passage:

> "Nay, by my fader soule, that schal he nat,"
> Seyde the _____. "Heer schall he nat preche.
> He schal no gospel glosen here ne teche.
> We leven alle in the grete God," quod he;
> "He wolde sewen some difficulte,
> Or springen cokkel in our clene corn.
> And therfore, Hoost, I warne thee biforn,
> My joly body schal a tale telle,
> And I schal clynken you so mery a belle,
> That I schal waken al this compaignie.
> But it schal nat ben of philosophie,
> Ne phisylas, ne termes queinte of lawe.
> Ther is but litel Latyn in my mawe."

    7. If I . . . be: If it is possible to be wedded so often.
    10–13. That sith . . . ones: Because Christ only attended one wedding in his life
(the one at Cana at Galilee, John 2:1), he taught that people should marry only once.
This interpretation is taken from Jerome's letter *Adversus Jovinianum* I, 40. Saint
Jerome (c. 340–420) is best known for his version of the Bible, known as the Vulgate.
Little is known of Jovinian except for what Jerome refers to in his letter refuting his
heretical and "stupid" ideas. The Wife of Bath, however, argues in favor of many of the
ideas of the more liberal Jovinian, particularly those having to do with virginity and
marriage. Chaucer certainly was familiar with Jerome's long epistle against Jovinian,
which provides much of the antifeminist material found in the Wife of Bath's Prologue.

Herkne eek, which a sharp word for the nones
15 Biside a welle, Jhesus, God and man,
Spak in repreeve of the Samaritan,°
'Thou hast yhad five housbondes,' quod he,
'And that ilke man that now hath thee   *same*
Is not thine housbonde.'° Thus he seyde certeyn.   *for sure*
20 What that he mente therby, I kan not sayn.   *say*
   "But that I axe why that the fifthe man   *But now I ask you*
Was noon housbonde to the Samaritan?   *not a*
How manye mighte she have in mariage?
Yet herde I nevere tellen in mine age   *As yet I have not heard*
25 Upon this nombre diffinicioun.   *this number defined*
Men may devine and glosen up and doun,   *speculate and interpret*
But well I woot, expres, withoute lye,   *I know without doubt*
God bad us for to wexe and multiplye.°
That gentil text kan I well understonde!
30 Eek well I woot he seyde mine housbonde   *And well I know*
Sholde lete fader and mooder and take to me.°   *Should leave / cleave*
But of no nombre mencioun made he,   *made no mention*
Of bigamye or of octogamye.   *marrying twice or eight times*
Why sholde men speke of it vileynye?
35   "Lo, here the wise king, daun Salomon,   *hear (of) / master Solomon*
I trowe he hadde wives many oon!°   *I believe*
As wolde God it were leveful unto me   *Would that God allowed me*
To be refresshed half so oft as he.
Which yifte of God hadde he for alle his wives!
40 No man hath swich that in this world alive is.
God woot, this noble king, as to my wit,   *in my opinion*
The firste night had many a myrie fit   *The wedding night*
With ech of hem, so well was him on live.   *so lusty was he*
Blessed be God that I have wedded five.   *Thank God*
44a [Of whiche I have picked out the beste
Bothe of hir nether purs° and of hir cheste.

All of my references to Jerome are to Book I of his two-volume *Adversus Jovinianum*.
   14–16. Herkne eek . . . Samaritan: Listen, also, to the sharp words Jesus spoke in reproof of the Samaritan. Notice that the Wife of Bath goes on to take on even Jesus.
   17–19. Thou hast . . . housbonde: See John 4:17–18.
   28. God bad . . . multiplye: God told us to procreate. See Genesis 1:28.
   31. Sholde lete . . . me: See Matthew 19:5.
   36. many oon: Many a one. In 1 Kings 11:3 Solomon is said to have had seven hundred wives and three hundred concubines.
   44b. nether purs: Presumably a reference to her husbands' genitalia. The "cheste" refers to their financial wealth.

Diverse scoles maken parfit clerkes°
And diverse practik in many sondry werkes
Maketh the werkman parfyt sikerly.°
44f Of fyve husbondes scoleiyng am I.]°
45 Welcome the sixte, whan that evere he shall!
    "For sith I wol not kepe me chaast in all   *entirely chaste*
Whan mine housbonde is fro the world agon,   *dies*
Some Cristen man shall wedde me anon,
For then th'apostle° seith that I am free
50 To wed, a Goddes half, where it liketh me.   *in God's behalf / pleases*
He seith that to be wedded is no sinne:°
'Bet is to be wedded than to brynne.'°
What rekketh me, thogh folk say vileynye   *What do I care*
Of shrewed Lameth and his bigamye?   *wicked*
55 I woot well Abraham was an hooly man,
And Jacob° eek, as fer as ever as I kan,   *so far as I know*
And ech of hem hadde wives mo than two —
And many another holy man also.   *And so did*
Wher can ye seye, in any manere age,   *in any period*
60 That heighe God defended mariage   *the high God forbade*
By expres word? I pray you, telleth me.   *In explicit words*

44c. Diverse scoles . . . clerkes: Attending diverse schools causes students to be "perfect."

44d–44e. And diverse . . . sikerly: And different practical experiences make the workman perfect, surely. In these lines and the next the Wife of Bath is bragging about how she has been well schooled in the ways of marriage by her five husbands. Chaucer may not have written the lines, however. See next note.

44a–44f. Of whiche . . . scoleiyng am I: I bracket these six lines because they are of questionable authenticity. They do not appear in some of the oldest and most reliable manuscripts, and may well have been late additions either by Chaucer or by an editor. Their authenticity is suspect in part because they interrupt the otherwise nice continuity between lines 44 and 45: "Thank the Lord that I have had five husbands. . . . Welcome the sixth!" The line numbering of 44a–f is different from the rest of these materials because the lines are in neither the Hengwrt nor the Ellesmere manuscript, and because Walter W. Skeat, whose line numbering most subsequent editors follow, did not include the six lines in his 1894 landmark edition.

49. th'apostle: Saint Paul. The reference here is to 1 Corinthians 7:39. Most of Chaucer's knowledge of Pauline materials, and, indeed, other biblical materials in the Wife of Bath's Prologue, comes by way of Jerome. For this passage, for example, see Jerome 14. In general, however, I shall give in these notes only the biblical reference. For Chaucer, "the" apostle — that is, with the definite pronoun — always refers to Paul.

51. to be . . . sinne: See 1 Corinthians 7:28.

52. Bet is . . . brynne: It is better to marry than burn (with desire). See 1 Corinthians 7:9.

54–56. Lameth . . . Abraham . . . Jacob: In Genesis 4:19 Lameth is said to have two wives. According to Jerome 5, Abraham had three wives, Jacob four.

"Or where comanded he virginitee?
I woot as well as ye, it is no drede,   *know / there is no doubt*
Th'apostel, whan he speketh of maidenhede,   *maidenhood*
65 He seyde that precept thereof hadde he noon.°   *precise ruling*
Men may conseille a womman to been oon,   *advise / one*
But conseilling nis no comandement.·
He put it in oure owene juggement.
For hadde God comanded maidenhede,
70 Thanne hadde he dampned wedding with the dede.   *at the same time*
And, certain, if there were no seed ysowe,   *sown*
Virginitee thanne wherof sholde it growe?°
Poul dorste not comanden, atte leeste,   *Saint Paul*
A thing of which his maister yaf noon heeste.   *gave no law*
75 The dart is set up for virginitee.
Cacche whoso may. Who renneth best lat see.°   *let's see*
"But this word° is not take of every wight,   *every person*
But there as God list give it of his might.   *God pleases to*
I woot well that th'apostel was a maide,   *know / Paul was a virgin*
80 But nathelees, thogh that he wroot and sayde
He wolde that every wight were swich as he,°
All nis but conseil to virginitee.   *nothing but advice (not command)*
And for to been a wif he yaf me leve   *gave*
Of indulgence.° So nis it no repreve   *it is no reproof*
85 To wedde me if that my make die,   *my mate*
Withoute excepcioun of bigamye.   *accusing me of*
Al were it good no womman for to touche,°   *Although*
He mente as in his bed or in his couche,
For peril is both fire and tow t'assemble.°
90 Ye know what this ensample may resemble!   *example, metaphor*
"This all and som: he heeld virginitee   *To summarize*
Moore parfit than wedding in freletee.   *frailty*

64–65. Th'apostel . . . noon: See 1 Corinthians 7:25.
69–72. For hadde . . . growe: From Jerome 12.
75–76. The dart . . . see: A "dart" or small spear was sometimes given as the prize to the winner of a footrace. The Wife of Bath's point is that people who want to pursue that prize may do so, but she has other "darts" in mind.
77. this word: Paul's word that people should strive for a life of abstinence.
81. He wolde . . . he: He would prefer that everyone be like him (in chastity). See 1 Corinthians 7:7.
83–84. leve Of indulgence: Special permission or dispensation to marry.
87. Al were . . . touche: See 1 Corinthians 7:1.
89. For peril . . . t'assemble: For it is dangerous to bring fire and flax close together. That the Wife of Bath has a sexual comparison in mind is clear enough from the previous and the following lines.

'Freletee,' clepe I, but if that he and she   *say I, unless*
Wolde leden all hir lif in chastitee.°

95 I graunte it well: I have noon envye   *no argument*
Thogh maidenhede preferre bigamye.°   *virginity is preferred to*
It liketh hem to be clene in body and goost.   *It pleases them / spirit*
Of mine estaat I nil not make no boost.°
For well ye know, a lord in his houshold,
100 He hath not every vessel all of gold.   *container, bowl*
Somme been of tree, and doon hir lord servise.°   *wood*
God clepeth folk to him in sondry wise,   *calls / various ways*
And everich hath of God a propre yifte:
Some this, some that, as him liketh shifte.°

105   "Virginitee is greet perfeccioun,
And continence eek, with devocioun.   *abstinence*
But Crist, that of perfeccioun is welle,   *the well of all perfection*
Bad not every wight he sholde go selle   *Bade*
All that he hadde and give it to the poore,°
110 And in swich wise folwe him and his foore.   *his path, footsteps*
He spak to hem that wol live parfitly,
And lordinges, by your leve, that am not I!
I wol bistowe the flour of all mine age   *the flower of my life*
In th'actes and in fruit of mariage.

115   "Tell me also, to what conclusioun   *for what purpose*
Were membres maad of generacioun,   *Were sexual organs made*
And of so parfit wis a wight ywroght?°
Trusteth right well, they were not maad for noght.   *nothing*
Glose whoso wole and seye both up and doun   *interpret any way you will*

93–94. 'Freletee,' clepe . . . chastitee: I call it "frailty" unless the partners desire
not to have sex. The Wife of Bath here makes reference to the idea that there are several
degrees of chastity: virginity, celibacy, and "chastity" in marriage. This last degree
could mean abstinence from sex in marriage, but could also refer merely to sexual
fidelity to one's spouse (as in line 155). The Wife has no objection to this last degree
of chastity — although there are hints (see lines 227–34 and 333–34) that she may not
always have been entirely faithful herself.

95–96. I have . . . bigamye: I have no quarrel with women who prefer to keep
chaste rather than submit to bigamy. "Bigamy" here may refer to a widow's having sex
with successive husbands.

98. Of mine . . . boost: For myself I will make no such boast — that is, no boast
that I prefer virginity.

100–01. He hath . . . servise: Not every utensil is made of gold; even wooden
utensils can be of service. See 2 Timothy 20.

103–04. And everich . . . shifte: Some are given one talent or task in life, some
another. For the notion that each of us has a certain "gift," see 1 Corinthians 7:7.

108–09. Bad not . . . poore: See Matthew 19:21.

117. And of . . . ywroght: And made by so perfect a creator.

120 That they were maked for purgacioun
    Of urine, and oure bothe thinges smale   *sexual organs*
    Were eek to knowe a femele from a male,   *tell the difference between*
    And for noon oother cause. Say ye no?
    Th'experience woot well it is noght so.   *proves conclusively*
125   "So that the clerkes be not with me wrothe   *angry*
    I sey this, that they beth maked for bothe,   *were made*
    This is to seye, for office and for ese
    Of engendrure, there we not God displese.°
    "Why sholde men elles in her bookes sette
130 That man shal yelde to his wif her dette?°
    Now wherwith sholde he make his paiement,
    If he ne used his sely instrument?   *his foolish organ*
    Thanne were they maad upon a creature   *Therefore*
    To purge urine and eek for engendrure.
135   "But I seye noght that every wight is holde
    That hath swich harneys as I to you tolde,   *sexual equipment*
    To goon and usen hem in engendrure.
    Thanne sholde men take of chastitee no cure.   *pay no heed to chastity*
    Crist was a maide and shapen as a man,   *virgin*
140 And many a seint sith that the world bigan.   *since*
    Yet lived they evere in parfit chastitee.
    I nil envye no virginitee.   *will not argue against chastity*
    Lat hem be breed of pured whete-seed,   *wheat grains*
    And lat us wives hoten barly-breed.°   *be called barley-bread*
145 And yet with barly-breed, Mark telle kan,
    Oure Lord Jhesu refresshed many a man.°
    "In swich estaat as God hath cleped us   *rank as God has called us to*
    I wol persevere° — I nam not precius.   *fastidious*
    In wifhode I wol use mine instrument
150 As frely as my makere hath it sent.
    If I be daungerous, God yeve me sorwe.   *stingy with it, God give*
    Mine housbonde shal it have both eve and morwe,
    Whan that him list com forth and paye his dette.
    An housbonde wol I have, I wol not lette,   *I'll never quit*

127–28. for office . . . displese: For function (in eliminating urine) as well as for the joy of procreation, so long as we do not displese God.
   130. dette: Debt, referring to sexual services. See 1 Corinthians 7:3.
   143–44. Lat hem . . . barly-breed: From Jerome 7.
   145–46. And yet . . . man: The biblical reference to Christ's multiplication of the loaves and fishes is probably to John 6:9–11, not to Mark 6:38–41. Note the Wife's sexual use of "refreshed" at line 38 above.
   147–48. In swich . . . persevere: See 1 Corinthians 7:20.

155 Which shall be both my dettour and my thral,   *my slave*
And have his tribulacioun withal   *troubles*
Upon his flessh° whil that I am his wif.
    "I have the power duringe all my lif
Upon his propre body, and noght he.°   *physical body*
160 Right thus th'apostel tolde it unto me
And bad oure housbondes for to love us weel.°
All this sentence me liketh every deel!"°

    Up stirte the Pardoner,° and that anon.
"Now dame," quod he, "by God and by Seint John,
165 Ye been a noble prechour in this cas.
I was aboute to wedde a wif.° Allas!   *Why*
What sholde I bye it on my flessh so deere?   *been wiser to*
Yet hadde I levere wedde no wif to-yeere."°
    "Abide," quod she, "my tale° is not bigonne.   *tale*
170 Nay, thou shalt drinken of another tonne   *cask*
Er that I go, shall savoure wors than ale.
And whan that I have toold thee forth my tale
Of tribulacioun in mariage,
Of which I am expert in all mine age —
175 This is to saye, myself have been the whippe —   *pain-giver*
Than maystow chese wheither that thou wolt sippe   *choose whether*

156–57. tribulacioun withal . . . flessh: See 1 Corinthians 7:28.
158–59. I have . . . he: See 1 Corinthians 7:4.
161. And bad . . . weel: See Ephesians 5:25.
162. All this . . . deel: This message — that our husbands should love us well —
pleases me very well indeed!
163. Pardoner: The Pardoner is another of the Canterbury pilgrims. His interruption here serves as a kind of interlude and transition in the Wife's performance. Before
this interruption Alisoun has been talking about the relative merits of multiple versus
single marriages, and of active sexuality versus abstinence. After her exchange with the
Pardoner she moves into straight autobiography, focusing first on her three old husbands and then, individually, on her fourth and fifth ones.
166. aboute to wedde a wif: This is not the place to discuss the Pardoner at
length, but it is interesting that Chaucer in the General Prologue describes him as "a
gelding" (castrated male horse) or a "mare" (female horse). If there is, indeed, something ambiguous about the Pardoner's sexuality, it is curious that he brags here of being
nearly ready to get married.
167–68. What sholde . . . to-yeere: Why should my flesh pay so heavily for marriage? I would rather not marry this year.
169. tale: The reference here is not to her fictional Arthurian tale, which starts at
line 857, but to the factual account of her own life story, which she insists she has
barely begun. Compare line 193, where the Wife uses the term *tale* to refer to the factual account of her five marriages.

Of thilke tonne that I shall abroche.°	*From that cask / open*
Be war of it, er thou to neigh approche,	*approach too near*
For I shall telle ensamples mo than ten.	*stories (of marriage)*
180 'Whoso that nil be war by othere men,	
By him shal othere men corrected be.'°	
The same wordes writeth Protholome.	
Rede in his Almageste and take it there."	
"Dame, I wolde praye you, if your will it were,"	*if it pleases you*
185 Seyde this Pardoner, "as ye bigan,	
Telle forth your tale. Spareth for no man,	
And techeth us yonge men of your praktike."	*practices*
"Gladly," quod she, "syn it may you like.	*since it pleases you*
But yet I praye to all this compaignye	
190 If that I speke after my fantasye	*according to my whim*
As taketh not agrief of that I seye,	*don't take me wrong*
For mine entente nis but for to pleye.	*intention is only*
Now, sire, now wol I tell you forth my tale.	
"As evere moote I drinken wine or ale,	
195 I shall seye sooth.° Tho housbondes that I hadde,	*Those*
As three of hem were goode and two were badde.	
The three men were goode, and riche, and olde.	
Unnethe mighte they the statut° holde	*Scarcely*
In which that they were bounden unto me.	
200 Ye woot well what I meene of this, pardee.	
"As help me God, I laughe whan I thinke	
How pitously a-night I made hem swinke!	*work*
And, by my fey, I tolde of it no stoor.	*by my faith, I was unpitying*
They had me yiven hir lond and hir tresoor.	*given*

176–77. Than maystow . . . abroche: After (you hear my account of marital tribulation) you can decide whether you will sip from the barrel I am opening. In the metaphor of marriage as a cask of wine, the Wife may be alluding to the story of one cask filled with sweet wine, one with vinegar.

180–81. Whoso that . . . be: He who will not learn from other men's mistakes will serve as an example to other men of how not to behave. As the next lines suggest, Chaucer probably read the proverb in some version of Ptolemy's *Almagest*, a treatise on astrology. The proverb (and the proverb in lines 326–27) is found in a medieval preface to a Latin translation of Ptolemy's work. Ptolemy was a second-century mathematician and geographer.

194–95. As evere . . . sooth: I will tell the truth, or may I never drink wine or ale again.

198. statut: Law. The reference is almost certainly to the Wife's "legal" right to have her husband pay the "marital debt" of sex (see lines 130–31). As the following lines show, the three old husbands had their "work" cut out for them, partly because of their age, partly because of the Wife of Bath's sexual appetite — real or feigned.

205 Me neded not do lenger diligence
    To winne hir love or doon hem reverence.°
    They loved me so well, by God above,
    That I ne tolde no deyntee of hir love.
      "A wis womman wol bisye her evere in oon
210 To gete her love, ye, there as she hath noon.
    But sith I hadde hem hoolly in mine hond,
    And sith they hadde yiven me all hir lond,
    What sholde I take kepe hem for to plese
    But it were for my profit and mine ese?
215 I sette hem so a-werke, by my fey,
    That many a night they songen 'weilawey.'
    The bacon was not fet for hem, I trowe,
    That some men han in Essex at Dunmowe.°
      "I governed hem so well, after my lawe,
220 That ech of hem ful blisful was and fawe
    To bringe me gay thinges fro the faire.
    They were ful glad whan I spak to hem faire,
    For, God it woot, I chidde hem spitously.°
      "Now herkneth hou I baar me proprely.
225 Ye wise wives,° that kan understonde,
    Thus shul ye speke and bere hem wrong on honde,
    For half so boldely kan there no man
    Swere and lyen as a womman kan.°
    I sey not this by wives that been wise,
230 But if it be whan they hem misavise.
    A wis wif, if that she kan her good,

did not value their love
busy herself continually
herself love
in my power

Why / bother to
Unless

'woe is me'

happy and willing
fair
kindly

behaved so well

accuse them falsely

Swear and lie

are misguided
knows her worth

205–06. Me neded . . . reverence: I had neither to show them respect nor to win their love (because I already had their land and money).

217–18. The bacon . . . Dunmowe: At Dunmowe, a town in Essex, a side of bacon was offered as a prize to any couple that could swear, after a year and a day of marriage, that they had neither quarreled nor regretted getting married. The Wife of Bath's husbands, of course, could not claim the bacon because she made them so miserable.

219–23. I governed . . . spitously: I managed things so well, after my custom, by chiding them so angrily that, God knows, they were glad to bring me anything just to put me in a better temper.

225. Ye wise wives: A curious statement, since there are no other wives on the pilgrimage to Canterbury. Perhaps Chaucer has in mind a wider court or reading audience for the Wife of Bath's bragging performance, or perhaps he means to have the Wife of Bath offer to the men on the pilgrimage a dramatic display of the way clever wives trick them. Compare line 524.

227–28. For half . . . kan: Compare *Roman de la Rose*, lines 18136–37. There are many echoes in the Wife of Bath's performance of this long allegorical poem by Guillaume de Lorris and Jean de Meun. I mention in these notes only a half-dozen or so of the most prominent ones.

Shall beren him on hond the cow is wood,°
And take witnesse of her owene maide
Of her assent.° But herkneth how I sayde:°   *listen*
235   "'Sire olde kaynard, is this thine array?   *grouch, dotard*
Why is my neighebores wif so gay?°
She is honoured over all there she gooth.   *wherever she goes*
I sitte at hoom. I have no thrifty clooth.   *decent clothing*
What dostow at my neighebores hous?
240 Is she so fair? Artow so amorous?
What rowne ye with oure maide, benedicite?   *whisper / by God*
  "'Sire olde lecchour, lat thy japes be.   *forget your tricks*
And if I have a gossib or a freend   *companion*
Withouten gilt, thou chidest as a feend   *complain like a devil*
245 If that I walke or pleye unto his hous.
Thou comest hoom as dronken as a mous
And prechest on thy bench. With yvel preef,   *With a rotten attitude*
Thou seist° to me it is a greet meschief
To wedde a poure womman, for costage.   *because of the cost*
250 And if that she be riche, of heigh parage,   *high birth*
Thanne seistow that it is a tormentrie   *thou sayest / torment*
To suffre her pride and her malencolie.
And if that she be fair, thou verray knave,   *true villain*
Thou seyst that every holour wol her have:°   *lecher*
255 "She may no while in chastitee abide°   *stay chaste*

232. Shall beren . . . wood: Shall browbeat them into believing that the chough, or crow, is crazy, an allusion to the traditional fable of the tattle-tale bird. The Wife of Bath is suggesting that a wise wife will convince her husband that the bird that reports her indiscretions is mad.

233–34. And take . . . assent: And shall arrange for her maid to corroborate her stories.

234. how I sayde: The following 144 lines are the Wife of Bath's self-quoting recital of the typical speeches she gave to her husbands. This long speech is all part of her advice to the would-be "wise wives" she imagines as her pupils.

235–36. is this . . . gay: Is this your clothing? Why is the wife of my neighbor so finely dressed (when I have nothing decent to wear)? Much of the material in lines 235–302 comes from Theophrastus as summarized in Jerome 47. For more on Theophrastus, see the note to line 671.

248. Thou seist: You say. Alisoun pretends to quote back at her husband things he says when he comes home drunk. What she says he says is a catalog of misogynist commonplaces that men, especially clerics, often *did* say about women. The implication is that her husbands did not really say them, but are so cowed by her that they do not defend themselves against her accusations. An alternative explanation is that, since they did not seem to defend themselves, they really were guilty of saying — or at least believing — these things.

253–54. And if . . . have: There are close parallels in these and the next 16 lines to *Roman de la Rose*, lines 8587–8600.

255. in chastitee abide: Remain chaste. Here "chastity" clearly refers not to virginity or celibacy but to faithfulness in marriage. See note to lines 93–94.

That is assailled upon ech a side."   *every side*
    "'Thou seyst some folk desiren us for richesse,
Somme for oure shap, and somme for oure fairnesse,   *figure / beauty*
And some for she kan either singe or daunce,
260 And some for gentillesse and daliaunce,   *gentility and flirtatiousness*
Some for her handes and her armes smale.
Thus goth all to the devel, by thy tale.   *according to you*
    "'Thou seyst men may not kepe a castel wall   *defend a castle wall*
It may so longe assailed been over all.
265 And if that she be foul, thou seist that she
Coveiteth every man that she may see,   *Lusts after (covets)*
For as a spaynel she wol on him lepe   *spaniel*
Til that she finde some man her to chepe.   *who will take her*
Ne noon so grey goos gooth there in the lake
270 As, seistow, wol been withoute make.   *mate, lover*
    "'And seyst it is an hard thing for to wolde   *control*
A thing that no man wole, his thankes, holde.   *wishes to keep*
Thus seistow, lorel, whan thow goost to bedde,   *rogue*
And that no wis man nedeth for to wedde,
275 Ne no man that entendeth unto hevene.   *intends to get into*
With wilde thonder-dint and firy levene   *thunder and lightening*
Moote thy welked nekke be tobroke!   *withered neck*
    "'Thou seyst that dropping houses and eek smoke   *leaking*
And chiding wives maken men to flee°   *noisy*
280 Out of hir owene hous — a, benedicitee!   *ah, good Lord!*
What eyleth swich an old man for to chide?   *ails*
    "'Thou seyst we wives wol oure vices hide
Til we be fast, and thanne we wol hem shewe.   *secure*
Well may that be a proverbe of a shrewe!
285   "'Thou seist that oxen, asses, hors, and houndes,
They been assayed at diverse stoundes.   *tested / various times*
Bacins, lavours, er that men hem bye,   *basins, washbowls*
Spoones and stooles, and all swich housbondrye,   *household utensils*
And so been pottes, clothes, and array.   *adornment*
290 But folk of wives maken noon assay   *assessment*
Til they be wedded, olde dotard shrewe!   *foolish*
And thanne, seistow, we wol oure vices shewe.
    "'Thou seist also that it displeseth me
But if that thou wolt preise my beautee,   *Unless*

278–79. dropping houses . . . flee: Chaucer probably took this antifeminist proverb, as he did so much in the Wife of Bath's Prologue, from Jerome. See section 28.

295 And but thou poure alwey upon my face   *unless you gaze always*
    And clepe me "faire dame" in every place
    And but thou make a feeste on thilke day
    That I was born, and make me fressh and gay,   *dress me fresh and new*
    And but thou do to my norice honour,   *nurse*
300 And to my chamberere withinne my bour,   *chambermaid / bedroom*
    And to my fadres folk and his allies.   *family and relatives*
        "'Thus seistow, olde barelful of lies!
    And yet of oure apprentice Janekyn,   *And again*
    For his crisp heer, shininge as gold so fin,   *lustrous*
305 And for he squiereth me bothe up and doun,   *escorts*
    Yet hastow caught a fals suspecioun.   *have you*
    I wol him noght, thogh thou were deed tomorwe.°   *I would not have him*
        "'But tel me, why hidestow, with sorwe,
    The keyes of thy cheste awey fro me?   *keys of your coffer*
310 It is my good as well as thine, pardee.   *property / by heaven*
    What wenestow make an idiot of oure dame?°
    Now by that lord that called is Seint Jame,
    Thou shalt noght bothe,° thogh that thou were wood,   *mad*
    Be maister of my body and of my good.   *goods*
315 That oon thou shalt forgo, maugree thine eyen.   *despite your watching*
    What helpeth it of me enquere and spyen?°
    I trowe thou woldest loke me in thy chiste.   *would lock me*
        "'Thou sholdest seye, "Wif, go where thee liste.   *wish*
    Taak your disport, I wol not leve no talis.°
320 I knowe you for a trewe wif, dame Alys."°
    We love no man that taketh kepe or charge   *charge of*
    Wher that we goon. We wol ben at oure large.   *at large, free*
    Of alle men yblessed moot he be,
    The wise astrologien, daun Protholome,   *astrologer / Ptolomy*

307. **I wol ... tomorwe:** I would not have him if you died tomorrow. Compare lines 593–99.

311. **What wenestow ... dame:** Why would you make a fool of the lady of the house?

313. **bothe:** Refers to the next line: You shall not be master of both my body and my goods.

316. **What helpeth ... spyen:** What good does it do you to inquire about and spy on me?

319. **Taak your ... talis:** Have your fun, and I will not believe any stories I hear about you.

320. **dame Alys:** This is the first reference to the Wife of Bath's name, later used by her husband in the form "Alisoun" (line 804) — the form used by most scholars in referring to the Wife of Bath. The Hengwrt manuscript here has the spelling "Alis," but I have adopted, for consistency, the form given in line 548.

325 That seith this proverbe in his Almageste,
     "Of alle men his wisdom is the hyeste
     That rekketh nat who hath the world in honde."°
     By this proverbe thou shalt understonde:
     Have thou ynogh, what thar thee recche or care
330 How myrily that othere folkes fare?°
     For certes, olde dotard, by your leve,
     Ye shul have queynte° right ynogh at eve.   *skinflint / refuse*
     He is to greet a nigard that wolde werne
     A man to lighte a candle at his lanterne.°
335 He shall have never the lasse light, pardee.
     Have thou ynogh, thee thar not pleyne thee.°
         "'Thou seyst also that if we make us gay
     With clothing and with precious array
     That it is peril of oure chastitee.   *a threat to*
340 And yet, with sorwe, thou most enforce thee,   *strengthen your control*
     And seye thise wordes in th'apostles name:
     "In habit maad with chastitee and shame   *clothing*
     Ye wommen shul apparaille you," quod he,
     "And noght in tressed heer and gay perree,   *jewelry*
345 As perles, ne with gold, ne clothes riche."°
     After thy text, ne after thy rubriche,
     I wol not wirche as muchel as a gnat.°
         "'Thou seydest this, that I was like a cat,
     For whoso wolde senge a cattes skin   *burn*
350 Thanne wolde the cat well dwellen in his in,   *stay in its house*
     And if the cattes skin be slik and gay
     She wol not dwelle in house half a day
     But forth she wole, er any day be dawed,   *dawned*
     To shewe her skin and goon a-caterwawed.   *caterwauling around*

326–27. Of alle . . . honde: The wisest man is the one who does not care who has
control or dominion. See note to lines 180–81.
329–30. Have thou . . . fare: If you have enough, why do you care how much
others have? Read in conjunction with the following lines, the Wife is probably talking
about sex here: If I give you all you want, why would you care if others get some too?
332. queynte: Pretty little thing. This is one of several euphemisms that the Wife
of Bath uses to refer to genitalia: "belle chose," "instrument," "small thing," "candle,"
"lantern," "tow."
333–34. He is . . . lanterne: Compare *Roman de la Rose,* lines 7410–14.
336. Have thou . . . thee: As long as you get enough, don't complain if others
get some.
342–45. In habit . . . riche: For Saint Paul's requirement that women should
dress in chaste clothing, see 1 Timothy 2:9.
346–47. After thy . . . gnat: I will pay attention neither to your text nor to your
title, any more than a gnat would.

355 This is to seye, if I be gay, sire shrewe,   *gaily dressed*
    I wol renne out my borel for to shewe.   *fine clothing to show off*
    "'Sire olde fool, what helpeth thee t'espyen?
    Thogh thou preye Argus with his hundred eyen°
    To be my warde-corps, as he kan best,   *warden*
360 In feith, he shall not kepe me but me lest.   *unless I want him to*
    Yet koude I make his berd, so moot I thee!°
    "'Thou seydest, eek, that there been thinges three
    The whiche thinges troublen all this erthe,
    And that no wight may endure the ferthe.°   *person / fourth*
365 O leeve sire shrewe, Jhesu shorte thy lif!   *dear sir shrew / shorten*
    Yet prechestow and seyst an hateful wif   *you preach*
    Yrekened is for oon of thise mischaunces.   *Reckoned*
    Been there none othere maner resemblances   *similarities*
    That ye may likne your parables to,
370 But if a sely wif be oon of tho?°
    "'Thou liknest eek wommenes love to helle,   *compare also*
    To bareyne lond there water may not dwelle.   *desert land where*
    Thou liknest it also to wilde fir,
    The moore it brenneth, the moore it hath desir
375 To consume every thing that brent wole be.
    "'Thou seyest, right as wormes shende a tree,   *destroy a piece of wood*
    Right so a wif destroyeth her housbonde.   *In the same way*
    This knowe they that been to wives bonde.'°
    "Lordinges, right thus, as ye have understonde,
380 Bar I stifly mine olde housbondes on honde   *accused*
    That thus they seyden in her dronkenesse.
    And all was fals, but that I took witnesse
    On Janekyn and on my nece also.°
    O Lord, the peyne I dide hem and the wo,   *pain*

---

358. Argus with . . . eyen: In classical literature, Argus was a monster with one hundred eyes whom Zeus sent to guard Io. Compare *Roman de la Rose,* lines 14381–84, but the ultimate source of the passage is Ovid's *Metamorphoses.*
361. Yet koude . . . thee: Still I could trick him, so may I thrive.
362–64. Thou seydest . . . ferthe: Probably an allusion to Proverbs 30:21–23, but see also Ecclesiasticus 26:5–6. Ecclesiasticus, an apocryphal biblical text, is not to be confused with Ecclesiastes.
368–70. Been there . . . tho: Can't you think of any other characters for your stories than the poor wife?
378. wives bonde: On this note of husbands being "bound" to wives, Alisoun ends the long recital about how she controlled her three old husbands by accusing them of drunkenly accusing her of transgressions. The "lordinges" of the next line are her fellow pilgrims, not her husbands.
382–83. And all . . . also: It was all lies, though I got both Jankyn and my niece to verify what I said.

385 Ful giltelees, by Goddes sweete pyne!   *though they were innocent*
    "For as an hors I koude bite and whine.   *like a horse*
    I koude pleyne — and I were in the gilt —   *complain / guilty*
    Or elles often time hadde I been spilt.   *caught, defeated*
    Whoso that first to mille comth, first grint.   *grinds*
390 I pleyned first, so was oure werre ystint.   *battle stopped*
    They were ful glad to excusen hem ful blive   *ask forgiveness quickly*
    Of thing of which they nevere agilte hir live.   *never were guilty of*
         "Of wenches wolde I beren hem on honde,
    Whan that for sik they mighte unnethes stonde.°
395 Yet tikled it his herte, for that he
    Wende that I hadde of him so greet chiertee.°
    I swoor that all my walking out by nighte
    Was for t'espye wenches that he dighte.   *to spy out / slept with*
    Under that colour hadde I many a mirthe.   *by that trick*
400 For all swich wit is yiven us in oure birthe.   *us women at birth*
    Deceite, weping, spinning God hath yeve   *spinning lies*
    To wommen kindely whil they may live.   *by nature*
    And thus of o thing I avaunte me,   *one thing I boast*
    At ende I hadde the bettre in ech degree,   *At the end / in every way*
405 By sleighte or force, or by some maner thing,   *trick*
    As by continuel murmur or grucching.   *whining or grumbling*
         "Namely abedde hadden they meschaunce.   *Especially / misfortune*
    There wolde I chide and do hem no plesaunce.   *give them no fun*
    I wolde no lenger in the bed abide
410 If that I felte his arm over my side
    Til he had maad his raunceon unto me.   *paid a ransom*
    Thanne wolde I suffre him do his nicetee.   *have sex with me*
    And therfore every man this tale I telle:
    Win whoso may, for all is for to selle.
415 With empty hand men may none haukes lure.   *lure hawks*
    For winning wolde I all his lust endure   *To achieve victory*
    And make me a feyned appetit.   *faked desire*
    And yet in bacon° hadde I nevere delit.
    That made me that evere I wolde hem chide.
420 For thogh the pope hadde seten hem biside,

393–94. Of wenches ... stonde: I accused them of whoring around when they were so sick they could scarcely stand. The Wife of Bath's accusation, of course, is meant to be a form of flattery.
   395–96. for that ... chiertee: Because he thought that I had such great affection for him.
   418. bacon: Apparently a euphemism for penis or sexual intercourse, though it may simply mean "dried up meat" or old men. Alisoun seems to be saying that, at least with her three old husbands, sex was more a bartering tool than a source of delight for her.

I wolde not spare hem at hir owene bord.°
"For, by my trouthe, I quitte hem word for word.   *repaid*
As helpe me verray God omnipotent,
Though I right now sholde make my testament,   *will*
425 I ne owe hem not a word that it nis quit.°   *every word has been paid back*
I broghte it so aboute by my wit
That they moste yeve it up as for the beste,°
Or elles hadde we nevere been in reste.   *at peace*
For thogh he looked as a wood leoun,   *like a mad lion*
430 Yet sholde he faille of his conclusioun.   *goals*
    "Thanne wolde I seye, 'Goode lief, taak keep,   *My good husband*
How mekely looketh Wilkyn, oure sheep.°
Com neer, my spouse, lat me ba thy cheke.   *kiss your cheek*
Ye sholden been all pacient and meke,
435 And han a sweete-spiced conscience.   *tender demeanor*
Sith ye so preche of Jobes pacience,°
Suffreth alwey, syn ye so well kan preche.
And but ye do, certein we shall you teche
That it is fair to have a wif in pees.   *it is best*
440 Oon of us two moste bowen, doutelees,   *yield, undoubtedly*
And sith a man is moore resonable
Than womman is, ye moste been suffrable.   *the one to suffer*
What eyleth you to grucche thus and grone?
Is it for ye wolde have my queynte allone?   *my genitalia all to yourself*
445 Why, taak it al! Lo, have it, every deel!   *every bit of it*
Peter, I shrewe you, but ye love it weel.   *By Saint Peter, I declare*
For if I wolde selle my bele chose,   *lovely thing*
I koude walke as fressh as is a rose.
But I wol kepe it for your owene tooth.   *your private use*
450 Ye be to blame, by God, I sey you sooth.'
    "Swiche manere wordes hadde we on honde.
Now wol I speken of my fourthe housbonde.
    "My fourthe housbonde was a revelour —   *riotous man*
This is to sayn, he hadde a paramour —   *a mistress*
455 And I was yong and ful of ragerye,   *passion*

420–21. **For thogh . . . bord:** Even though the pope himself sat beside them at their own dinner tables, I still would not spare them my chiding.
425. **I ne . . . quit:** Every nasty word I owed them I have paid back.
426–27. **I broghte . . . beste:** By my own cleverness, I arranged things in such a way that they had to call it quits.
432. **How mekely . . . sheep:** How crestfallen looks my little sheep Willikin. Imagine the line to be said in a kind of condescending baby talk.
436. **Jobes pacience:** Job's patience was proverbial. The reference, of course, is to the biblical Job, who was tested by God with almost every imaginable affliction.

Stibourne, and strong, and joly as a pie.   *Stubborn / chipper as a magpie*
How koude I daunce to an harpe smale,
And singe, ywis, as any nightingale,   *surely*
Whan I had dronke a draughte of sweete wine!
460 Metellius — the foule cherl, the swine,
That with a staf birafte his wif her lif
For she drank wine° — thogh I hadde been his wif,
He sholde not han daunted me fro drinke!   *dissuaded me from drinking*
    "And after wine on Venus moste I thinke,   *on sex*
465 For all so siker as cold engendreth hail,
A likerous mouth moste han a likerous tail.   *lecherous*
In wommen vinolent is no defence.°
This knowen lecchours by experience.
    "But, Lord Crist, whan that it remembreth me
470 Upon my youthe and on my jolitee,
It tikleth me about mine herte roote.   *right to the heart*
Unto this day it dooth mine herte boote   *it does my heart good*
That I have had my world as in my time.°
    "But age, allas, that all wole envenyme,   *will poison everyone*
475 Hath me birafte my beautee and my pith.   *robbed me of / vigor*
Lat go. Farewell. The devel go therwith!   *I let it go*
The flour is goon. There is namoore to telle.   *wheat flour*
The bren, as I best kan, now moste I selle.   *bran*
But yet to be right myrie wol I fonde.   *strive to be merry*
480   "Now wol I tellen of my fourthe housbonde,
I seye. I hadde in herte greet despit   *anger*
That he of any oother had delit.
But he was quit. By God and by Seint Joce,   *repaid*
I made him of the same wode a croce,°
485 Not of my body, in no foul manere,
But certeinly I made folk swich chiere

460–62. Metellius . . . wine: Based on a story in *Facta et dicta memorabilia* 6:3 written by the Roman writer Valerius Maximus in the first half of the first century A.D. Metellius clubbed his wife to death for drinking wine.

467. In wommen . . . defence: Women who are inebriated have no defenses (against sexual advances).

473. That I . . . time: That I lived life to the fullest while I could. For these and the previous four lines, compare *Roman de la Rose*, lines 12932–48.

483–84. Seint Joce . . . croce: Saint Judocus was a Breton saint of the seventh century who was perhaps associated with the staff of a pilgrim and with neglect of his wife. There may, in the second line, be a pun on "croce," for the word can mean both "staff" and "cross." Alisoun seems to be saying that she can make both a staff to beat her fourth husband with and a cross to crucify him on. Saint Judocus's bones were brought to Winchester at the start of the tenth century.

That in his owene grece I made him frye
For angre and for verray jalousye.°
By God, in erthe I was his purgatorie,
490 For which I hope his soule be in glorie.   *suppose his soul is in heaven*
For, God it woot, he sat ful ofte and song   *sang (a bitter tune)*
Whan that his shoo ful bitterly him wrong.°
There was no wight save God and he that wiste,
In many wise, how soore I him twiste.   *sorely I tortured him*
495 "He deyde whan I came fro Jerusalem,   *back from pilgrimage to*
And lith ygrave under the roode-beem,°
Al is his tombe noght so curius   *Although / elaborate*
As was the sepulcre of him, Darius,   *tomb*
Which that Appelles wroghte subtilly.°   *made so cleverly*
500 It nis but wast to burye him preciously.   *wasteful*
Lat him fare well. God yeve his soule reste.   *God let*
He is now in his grave and in his cheste.   *coffin*
  / "Now of my fifthe housbonde wol I telle.
God let his soule nevere come in helle.°
505 And yet was he to me the mooste shrewe.   *cruelest, most shrewish*
That feel I on my ribbes all by rewe,   *one after the other*
And evere shall unto mine ending-day.
But in oure bed he was so fresshe and gay,
And therwithal so well koude he me glose,   *talk to me, flatter me*
510 Whan that he wolde han my bele chose,
That thogh he hadde me bet on every bon,   *bone*
He koude winne agayn my love anon.   *afterwards*
I trowe I loved him best for that he

485–88. Not of . . . jalousye: I did not actually sleep with other men, but I was so openly friendly with them that he was jealous and angry. I made him fry in his own grease!

492. Whan that . . . wrong: When his shoe pinches (wrings) him. The metaphor of a wife as pinching shoe was common (it appears in Plutarch and Walter Map). Chaucer most likely encountered it in section 48 of Jerome's *Adversus Jovinianum,* with Jerome's anecdote about a man whose friends found fault with him for having divorced his lovely, chaste, and wealthy wife. The Roman held out his foot and said that the shoe looked new and elegant to others, but only he could say where it pinched. Chaucer refers to a wife as a pinching shoe in E1549–93 (Justinus's speech in the Merchant's Tale).

496. And lith . . . roode-beem: And lies buried under the crossbeam that often divided the chancel from the nave of the medieval church. That he is buried in the church rather than outside suggests he was a man of some importance.

497–99. Al is . . . subtilly: Darius's tomb was reputed to be unusually fine. Appelles was the craftsman supposed to have built it. As the next line shows, the Wife of Bath's point is that it would have been wasteful and ostentatious to bury her fourth husband in such a tomb.

504. God let . . . helle: Compare line 525. These lines are usually taken to mean that the fifth husband is dead, but there is some disagreement on the point.

Was of his love daungerous to me.°
515   "We wommen han, if that I shall not lye,
In this matere a queynte fantasye.   *strange way of thinking*
Wayte what thing we may not lightly have,   *Whatever / easily*
Therafter wol we crie all day and crave.
Forbede us thing, and that desiren we;
520   Preesse on us faste, and thanne wol we fle.   *Force it on us*
With daunger oute we all oure chaffare.
Greet prees at market maketh deere ware,
And to greet cheep is holde at litel pris.°
This knoweth every womman that is wis.
525   "My fifthe housbonde — God his soule blesse —
Which that I took for love and no richesse,   *for love, not money*
He somtime was a clerk of Oxenford,   *used to be*
And hadde left scole and wente at hom to bord
With my gossib, dwellinge in oure toun —
530   God have her soule. Her name was Alisoun.°
She knew mine herte and eek my privetee   *personal affairs*
Bet than oure parisshe preest, so moot I thee.°
To her biwreyed I my conseil all.   *I confided everything*
For hadde mine housbonde pissed on a wall,
535   Or doon a thing that sholde have cost his lif,
To her, and to another worthy wif,
And to my nece,° which that I loved weel,
I wolde han toold his conseil every deel.   *his secrets right away*
And so I dide ful often, God it woot,   *God knows*

514. daungerous to me: Coy, standoffish, distant. The word here is usually taken to mean that the Wife of Bath likes her fifth husband the most because he played hard to get, but the word "daungerous" could also mean dangerous. The first meaning is suggested by the following lines, especially line 519: Forbid us something, and that is what we want the most. That he puts her in danger is suggested by the previous lines, especially lines 505–07: He was the most shrewish to me, as I can tell by the pain in my ribs, row after row.

521–23. With daunger . . . pris: We are careful about how we sell our wares. At market, when everyone presses around to buy something, the price goes up, but if the price is too low, the thing is considered worthless.

530. Alisoun: Confusingly, her "gossip" or friend has the same name she does, a fact that may be explained by the fact that this gossip (literally "god-sibling") is her godmother: perhaps she was named for her godmother. Compare line 548 where this gossip is called "dame Alys," suggesting that the two forms of the name were equally honorific and were used interchangeably. It was apparently through this close friend that the Wife of Bath met Jankyn, who was to become her fifth husband.

532. so moot I thee: So may I thrive (get to heaven). This expression is common in Chaucer (compare line 361). In this context it seems to mean, "I'll wager my soul that she knew more about my private affairs than even the parish priest did."

536–37. To her . . . nece: The Wife of Bath seems to have had three close women friends — the "gossip" Alisoun, her niece, and another wife.

540 That made his face often reed and hoot
    For verray shame, and blamed himself for he   *regretted that he*
    Had toold to me so greet a privetee.
      "And so bifel that ones in a lente° —
    So often times I to my gossib wente,
545 For evere yet I loved to be gay,
    And for to walke in March, Averill, and May,
    Fro hous to hous, to heere sondry tales —   *to listen to various stories*
    That Jankyn clerk and my gossib, dame Alys,
    And I myself into the feeldes wente.
550   "Mine housbonde was at Londoun all that Lente.   *My (fourth) husband*
    I hadde the bettre leyser for to pleye,   *leisure*
    And for to see and eek for to be seye   *to see and be seen*
    Of lusty folk. What wiste I wher my grace   *By pleasure-loving people*
    Was shapen for to be, or in what place?°
555 Therfore I made my visitaciouns
    To vigilies and to processiouns,   *services before religious holidays*
    To preching eek, and to thise pilgrimages,   *To sermons also*
    To pleyes of miracles,° and to mariages,°
    And wered upon my gaye scarlet gites.   *had on my red gowns*
560 Thise wormes, ne thise motthes, ne thise mites,
    Upon my peril, frete hem never a deel.
    And wostow why? For they were used weel.°
      "Now wol I tellen forth what happed me.   *to me*
    I seye that in the feeldes walked we,
565 Til trewely we hadde swich daliance,   *such fun, such wantonness*
    This clerk and I, that of my purveiance   *because of my foresight*
    I spak to him and seyde him how that he,
    If I were widwe, sholde wedde me.
    For certeinly, I sey for no bobance,   *boast, bragging*
570 Yet was I nevere withouten purveiance   *a future plan*
    Of mariage, n'of othere thinges eek.

---

   543. And so . . . lente: And it so happened that once during the spring. The term "lente" may not yet have had its more specific meaning as the period between Ash Wednesday and Easter.
   553–54. What wiste . . . place: How was I to know where I was destined to find my good fortune (a new husband)?
   558. pleyes of miracles: Miracle plays, or plays of saints' lives. English drama was in its infancy in Chaucer's time. Indeed, references to medieval drama by Chaucer, here and in the Miller's Tale, are among the few bits of proof that there even were such plays in fourteenth-century England. The surviving plays are in fifteenth-century, or later, manuscripts.
   555–58. Therfore I . . . mariages: Compare *Roman de la Rose,* lines 13522–28.
   560–62. Thise wormes . . . weel: I did not have to fret about worms, moths, and mites destroying my gowns, because I wore them constantly.

I holde a mouses herte not worth a leek   *not worth an onion*
That hath but oon hole for to sterte to,   *jump to*
And if that faille, thanne is all ydo.°   *all is finished*
575 [I bar him on honde he hadde enchanted me —   *I persuaded*
My dame taughte me that soutiltee —   *mother / subtle trick*
And eek I seyde I mette of him all night,   *And also I said I dreamt*
He wolde han slayn me as I lay upright,   *(In the dream) he tried to*
And all my bed was ful of verray blood.
580 But yet I hope that he shall do me good,
For blood bitokeneth gold,° as me was taught.
And all was fals. I dremed of it right naught,
But as I folwed ay my dames loore,   *always my mother's advice*
As well of this as of othere thinges moore.]°
585 But now, sire, lat me see, what I shall sayn?
A ha! By God, I have my tale ageyn.
   "Whan that my fourthe housbonde was a-beere,   *(dead) on his bier*
I weep algate and made sory cheere,   *wept constantly*
As wives mooten, for it is usage,   *must / customary*
590 And with my coverchief covered my visage.   *my face*
But for that I was purveyed of a make,   *provided with (another) mate*
I wepte but small, and that I undertake.   *guarantee*
   "To chirche was mine housbonde born a-morwe   *carried the next day*
With neighebores that for him maden sorwe.   *grieved*
595 And Janekyn oure clerk was oon of tho.   *one of the mourners*
As help me God, whan that I saugh him go
After the beere, me thoughte he hadde a paire   *the coffin, it seemed to me*

572–74. I holde . . . ydo: Compare *Roman de la Rose*, lines 13150–52.

581. blood bitokeneth gold: Gold was often described as "red," so the association of the red color of blood with the color of gold may be referred to here. Keep in mind, however, that Alisoun is addressing a prospective future husband, and that the whole account of the dream of his trying to kill her is a fiction. The reference to gold may be a kind of come-on to a young man who might not otherwise be attracted to the older Alisoun. If this passage was not by Chaucer, however, then the question is moot. See next note.

575–84. I bar . . . moore: I bracket these ten lines because there is some question about their authenticity. They do not appear in some of the oldest manuscripts. We cannot be certain whether they are late additions by Chaucer himself or the work of an unusually skillful editor or scribe. Because the matter will not likely be settled for some time — if ever — it seems best to present these lines in their "proper" place, but to call attention to their problematic authorship. There are also questions about the authenticity of lines 609–12, 619–26, and 717–20. One theory is that, since many of these lines appear to be antifeminist, they may be the work not of Chaucer but of a clerk annoyed at what the Wife of Bath has to say about her clerkly fifth husband. In MS Cambridge Dd, the earliest manuscript in which they appear, there are a number of antifeminist marginal comments, possibly made by the same person who added the lines in question. Still, the dominant view is that the lines are Chaucer's own. I have glossed "dame" as "mother," but the reference is probably to "dame Alys," her godmother.

Of legges and of feet so clene and faire *clean and lovely*
That all mine herte I yaf unto his hoold. *gave over to him*
600 "He was, I trowe, a twenty winter oold, *I think*
And I was fourty, if I shall seye sooth.
But yet I hadde alwey a coltes tooth. *the spirit of a colt*
Gat-tothed° I was, and that bicam me weel.
I hadde the prente of Seinte Venus seel.°
605 As help me God, I was a lusty oon,
And faire and riche and yong and well bigon. *well dispositioned, happy*
And trewely, as mine housbondes tolde me,
I hadde the beste quoniam mighte be. *genitalia that might be*
[For certes, I am all Venerien
610 In feelinge, and mine herte is Marcien.
Venus me yaf my lust, my likerousnesse,
And Mars yaf me my sturdy hardinesse.]°
Mine ascendent was Taur, and Mars therinne.°
Allas, allas, that evere love was sinne!
615 I folwed ay mine inclinacioun *always my impulses*
By vertu of my constellacioun
That made me I koude noght withdrawe
My chambre of Venus° from a goode felawe.
[Yet have I Martes mark° upon my face,
620 And also in another privee place.
For God so wis be my savacioun, *As God is my salvation*
I ne loved nevere by no discrecioun, *according to reason*
But evere folwede mine appetit,
All were he short, or long, or blak, or whit.°
625 I took no kepe, so that he liked me, *did not care, so long as*

603. **Gat-tothed:** See line A468 in the General Prologue, and my note to it.

604. **Seinte Venus seel:** A birthmark, probably in some concealed place on her body.

609–12. **For certes ... hardinesse:** See note to lines 575–84. In these lines of questionable authorship the Wife of Bath explains that she gets her warm and loving feelings from Venus but her tough combativeness from Mars. She is portrayed in this section as the medieval equivalent to a schizophrenic, pulled in two ways at once, a woman "venerian" enough to attract husbands in the game of courtship, but "martial" enough to hold her own on the battleground of marriage.

613. **Mine ascendent ... therinne:** The Wife of Bath is explaining her character by describing the astrological situation at her birth: Mars was in Taurus, one of the "houses" of Venus. This planetary association would have made her extraordinarily amorous.

618. **chambre of Venus:** To judge from a parallel phrase in the *Roman de la Rose* (line 13336), this "chamber" is her genitalia, but it may also refer to her heart.

619. **Martes mark:** The mark of Mars, apparently another birthmark. See line 604.

622–24. **I ne ... whit:** I always followed my impulsive appetites, whether the man were short or tall, black-haired or blond.

How poore he was, ne eek of what degree.]°   *of what rank*
What sholde I seye, but at the monthes ende
This joly clerk, Jankyn, that was so hende,   *close at hand*
Hath wedded me with greet solempnitee,   *solemnness*
630 And to him yaf I all the lond and fee   *gave all the land and property*
That evere was me yiven therbifore.
"But afterward repented me ful sore.
He nolde suffre nothing of my list.°
By God, he smoot me ones on the lyst,   *struck me once / ear*
635 For that I rente out of his book a leef,   *because I tore / leaf*
That of the strook mine ere wax all deef.   *the blow my ear became*
Stibourne I was as is a leonesse,   *Stubborn*
And of my tonge a verray jangleresse,   *chatterbox*
And walke I wolde, as I had doon biforn,
640 From hous to hous, although he had it sworn.   *forbidden*
"For which he often times wolde preche,
And me of olde Romayn geestes teche.   *stories*
How he Simplicius Gallus left his wif,
And her forsook for terme of all his lif,
645 Noght but for open-heveded he her say   *bareheaded/saw*
Lokinge out at his dore upon a day.°
Another Romayn° tolde he me by name
That for his wif was at a someres game°
Withouten his witing, he forsook her eke.   *his knowledge*
650 "And thanne wolde he upon his Bible seke   *in his Bible search*
That ilke proverbe of Ecclesiaste   *very same*
Where he comandeth and forbedeth faste   *absolutely*
Man shall not suffre his wif go roule aboute.°   *roam about*
"Thanne wolde he seye right thus, withouten doute:
655 'Whoso that buildeth his hous all of salwes,   *willow twigs*
And priketh his blinde hors over the falwes,   *new-plowed field*
And suffreth his wif to go seken halwes,°

619–26. Yet have . . . degree: See note to lines 575–84. Absent from some of the most reliable manuscripts, these lines portray Alisoun as sexually promiscuous, eager to make love with virtually any man who liked her.
633. He nolde . . . list: He paid no attention to what I wanted.
643–46. How he . . . day: How Simplicius Gallus left his wife because of no other offense than that he saw her look outside with her head uncovered. This story and the next one are from Valerius Maximus, *Facta et dicta memorabilia* 6:3.
647. Another Romayn: Sempronius Sophus, referred to in Valerius Maximus, *Facta et dicta memorabilia* 6:3.
648. someres game: A midsummer rural picnic involving, by some accounts, potentially indecent sports and dancing.
650–53. And thanne . . . aboute: The reference is to Ecclesiasticus 25:34–35.
657. to go . . . halwes: To travel to seek holy shrines (to go on pilgrimages).

Is worthy to been hanged on the galwes.'°   *gallows*
But all for noght. I sette noght an hawe   *fruit of the hawthorne*
660 Of his proverbe n'of his olde sawe,   *For / saying*
Ne I wolde not of him corrected be.   *by him*
I hate him that my vices telleth me,
And so doon mo, God woot, of us than I.   *more . . . of us*
This made him with me wood all outrely.   *openly angry with me*
665 I nolde noght forbere him in no cas.   *tolerate him at all*
    "Now wol I seye you sooth, by Seint Thomas,   *honestly*
Why that I rente out of his book a leef,   *Why I tore*
For which he smoot me so that I was deef.   *struck me*
He hadde a book that gladly, night and day,
670 For his desport he wolde rede alway.   *own entertainment*
He cleped it Valerie and Theofraste,°
At which book he lough alwey ful faste.   *laughed out loud*
And eek there was somtime a clerk at Rome,
A cardinal, that highte Seint Jerome,   *was named*
675 That made a book agayn Jovinian.°
In which book eek there was Tertulan,
Crisippus, Trotula, and Helowis,°
That was abbese not fer fro Paris.
And eek the parables of Salomon,°
680 Ovides Art,° and bookes many on.   *many other books*
And alle thise were bound in o volume,   *one*
And every night and day was his custume,   *it was his habit*
Whan he hadde leyser and vacacioun   *leisure*
From oother worldly occupacioun,

655–58. Whoso that . . . galwes: This four-line proverb may predate Chaucer, but this is the first recording of it. The point is that for a man to let his wife go on a pilgrimage is as stupid as building a house out of flimsy materials or galloping a blind horse across a freshly furrowed field.

671. Valerie and Theofraste: These are two authors whose works were apparently included, along with other antifeminist works, in Jankyn's book of wicked wives, referred to in line 685. "Valerie" was *The Advice of Valerius to Rufinus the Philosopher Not to Marry*, sometimes attributed to the ancient Roman Valerius Maximus but actually written by Walter Map, archdeacon at Oxford in the twelfth century. "Theofraste" was *The Little Golden Book of Theophrastus on Marriage*, preserved only in summary in Jerome's *Adversus Jovinianum* I, 47.

674–75. Seint Jerome . . . Jovinian: Jerome's letter *Adversus Jovinianum*. See note to lines 10–13.

676–77. Tertulan . . . Helowis: Four writers known or thought to have written antifeminist or antimatrimonial letters or treatises. Tertulian and Chrissipus are identified by Jerome as having written such pieces. Trotula was a female gynecologist said to have written a treatise about the diseases of women. Eloise was a nun who wrote letters to Abelard stating why she should not marry him.

679. parables of Salomon: See, for example, Proverbs 7:5–27.

680. Ovides Art: Ovid's *Ars amatoria*.

685 To reden on this book of wikked wives.°
    "He knew of hem mo legendes and lives   *tales and life stories*
    Than been of goode wives in the Bible.   *Than there are about*
    For trusteth well, it is an impossible   *an inconceivable event*
    That any clerk wol speke good of wives,
690 But if it be of hooly seintes lives,
    Ne of noon oother womman never the mo.°
    "Who peyntede the leon, tel me who?°
    By God, if wommen hadde writen stories,
    As clerkes han withinne hir oratories,   *cells, places of prayer*
695 They wolde han writen of men moore wikkednesse
    Than all the mark of Adam° may redresse.
    "The children of Mercurie and Venus°
    Been in hir wirking ful contrarius.   *contentious*
    Mercurie loveth wisdam and science,
700 And Venus loveth riot and dispence,   *revelry and extravagance*
    And for hir diverse disposicioun   *opposed dispositions*
    Ech falleth in otheres exaltacioun.°
    And thus, God woot, Mercurie is desolat
    In Pisces wher Venus is exaltat,

685. book of wikked wives: This anthology of antifeminist and antimatrimonial anecdotes and tales was apparently designed in part to convince young men to consider the celibate priesthood rather than a secular calling. Alisoun, of course, is infuriated by having to listen to Jankyn read to her from this book, which would have denigrated women, wives, and marriage.

688–91. For trusteth . . . mo: Alisoun exaggerates, but medieval clerics were known for their antifeminist views, and books like Jankyn's exist to this day. For clerics, Eve was the archetypal human woman whose gluttony and pride caused man to be driven out of heaven. Eve is counterbalanced by Mary, of course, whom clerics would have thought of as utterly sinless, and certainly not human in the same sense that Eve was.

692. Who peyntede . . . who: The reference here is to an old fable, originally by Aesop, about the man who painted a picture of a man defeating a lion. A lion remarks that if lions did the painting, they would naturally paint scenes depicting a lion defeating a man. Alisoun's point is that if women told about men, the wickedness of men would be apparent.

696. all the mark of Adam: All who are in the image of Adam — that is, all men. The idea here is that women could tell such stories about the wickedness of men that all the men in the world could not "redress" or make amends for them or set them right.

697. Mercurie and Venus: Learned men, or clerks, were associated with Mercury, god of learning and literature, while most women in the secular world were associated with Venus, goddess of love. The following lines suggest in a complicated manner that clerks and women are by nature "contrarious." The conflict between Mars and Venus (see lines 610–18) leads to divisiveness within the Wife of Bath. This conflict between Mercury and Venus leads to dissension between the Wife of Bath and others, especially the clerk Jankyn, who was her fifth husband.

702. Ech falleth . . . exaltacioun: A complicated astrological reference that means that when one of the planets is "exalted" or increases its influence, the other "falls" or loses its influence.

705 And Venus falleth there Mercurie is reysed. *where*
Therfore no womman of no clerk is preysed.
The clerk, whan he is oold and may noght do
Of Venus werkes worth his olde sho, *love-works / worth an old shoe*
Thanne sit he doun and writ in his dotage *writes in his old age*
710 That wommen kan not kepe her mariage. *remain faithful*
   "But now to purpos, why I tolde thee
That I was beten for a book, pardee. *because of*
Upon a night Jankyn, that was oure sire, *my husband*
Redde on his book, as he sat by the fire,
715 Of Eva first, that for her wikkednesse *Eve / because of*
Was all mankinde broght to wrecchednesse.
[For which that Jhesu Crist himself was slayn
That boghte us with his herte blood agayn. *redeemed us*
Lo, heere expres of womman may ye finde *explicitly / find (it said)*
720 That womman was the los of all mankinde.]°
Tho redde he me how Sampson° loste his heres, *his hair*
Slepinge. His lemman kitte it with her sheres, *lover cut / shears*
Thurgh which treson loste he bothe his eyen.
Tho redde he me, if that I shall not lyen,
725 Of Hercules° and of his Dianire
That caused him to sette himself a-fire.
   "Nothing forgat he the sorwe and wo
That Socrates° hadde with his wives two,
How Xantippa caste pisse upon his heed.
730 This sely man sat stille as he were deed.
He wiped his heed. Namoore dorste he sayn *No more dares*
But, 'Er that thonder stinte, comth a reyn!' *Before thunder stops*
   "Of Phasipha,° that was the queene of Crete,

717–20. For which . . . mankinde: See note to lines 575–84. There is some question about whether these antifeminist lines are Chaucer's own.

721. Sampson: In this story, Sampson makes the mistake of telling Delilah the secret that his strength lies in his hair. She cuts his hair and reports his weakened condition to his enemies, who blind him. See Judges 16. Chaucer tells the story at more length in the Monk's Tale in Fragment VII (Group B² 3205–84). Chaucer apparently took this story and several of the following from Jerome.

725. Hercules: Deianira, Hercules' second wife, without realizing that it will kill him, gives him a shirt dipped in poisoned blood. Rather than let the poison kill him, however, he buries himself in hot coals and dies. Chaucer tells the story at more length in the Monk's Tale, Fragment VII (Group B² 3285–3332).

728. Socrates: Socrates' difficulties with his wife, Xantippe, and his patience in the face of those difficulties, are legendary, but Chaucer derived this incident in which Xantippe dumps a chamber pot on his head from Jerome 48. In Jerome, however, what she dumps is said to be merely "dirty water," not urine.

733. Phasipha: Even bold Alisoun is reluctant to talk openly about Pasiphae, who has a love affair with a bull and later gives birth to the Minotaur.

For shrewednesse him thoughte the tale swete.
735 Fy! Spek namoore — it is a grisly thing —   *horrid*
Of her horrible lust and her liking.   *preference (for a bull)*
"Of Clitermistra,° for her lecherye,
That falsly made her housbonde for to dye,
He redde it with ful good devocioun.   *enthusiasm*
740   "He tolde me eek for what occasioun
Amphiorax° at Thebes loste his lif.
Mine housbonde hadde a legende of his wif,
Eriphilem, that for an ouch of gold   *piece of gold jewelry*
Hath prively unto the Grekes told   *secretly*
745 Wher that her housbonde hidde him in a place
For which he hadde at Thebes sory grace.
"Of Lyvia tolde he me, and of Lucie.
They bothe made hir housbondes for to die,
That oon for love, that oother was for hate.
750 Lyvia° her housbonde, upon an even late,   *evening*
Empoisoned hath for that she was his fo.
Lucia,° likerous, loved her housbonde so   *sexually charged*
That for he sholde alwey upon her thinke
She yaf him swich a manere love-drinke
755 That he was deed er it were by the morwe:
'And thus algates housbondes han sorwe.'
"Thanne tolde he me how oon Latumius°
Compleyned unto his felawe Arrius   *friend*
That in his gardyn growed swich a tree
760 On which he seyde how that his wives three
Hanged hemself for herte despitus.   *out of a spiteful heart*
'O leeve brother,' quod this Arrius,
'Yif me a plante of thilke blissed tree,   *Give me a clipping*
And in my gardyn planted it shall be.'
765   "Of latter date, of wives hath he red
That somme han slayn hir housbondes in hir bed
And lete her lecchour dighte her all the night,   *make love to her*

---

737. **Clitermistra:** Clytemnestra, wife of Agamemnon, commits adultery and eventually murders her husband in his bath.

741. **Amphiorax:** Eriphile betrays her husband Amphiorax's hiding place in exchange for a gold necklace. Because of that betrayal Amphiorax goes to war and dies at Thebes.

750. **Lyvia:** At the suggestion of her lover, Lyvia poisons her husband, Drusus.

752. **Lucia:** Lucilla poisons her husband Lucretius by giving him what she thinks is a love potion.

757. **Latumius:** The story of the precious tree that wives hang themselves from is told in a number of places, including the *Gesta Romanorum* (thirty-third story), but Chaucer is likely to have taken it from Walter Map.

Whan that the corps lay in the floor upright.°   *corpse (of her husband)*
And somme han driven nailes in hir brain   *into their (husbands') brains*
770 Whil that they slepte,° and thus they han hem slain.
Somme han hem yeve poisoun in hir drinke.
     "He spak moore harm than herte may bithinke,
And therwithal he knew of mo proverbes
Than in this world there growen gras or herbes.
775 'Bet is,' quod he, 'thine habitacioun
Be with a leoun or a foul dragoun
Than with a womman using for to chide.'°   *whose habit is to chide*
'Bet is,' quod he, 'hye in the roof abide   *high in the attic*
Than with an angry wif doun in the hous.
780 They been so wikked and contrarious,   *contentious*
They haten that hir housbondes loveth ay.'°   *whatever their husbands like*
He seyde, 'A womman cast her shame away
Whan she cast of her smok.'° And forthermo,   *petticoat*
'A fair womman, but she be chaast also,
785 Is like a gold ring in a sowes nose.'°
     "Who wolde wene or who wolde suppose   *believe*
The wo that in mine herte was, and pyne?   *pain*
And whan I saugh he wolde nevere fyne   *finish*
To reden on this cursed book all night,
790 All sodeynly three leves have I plyght   *plucked*
Out of his book right as he radde, and eke   *read*
I with my fest so took him on the cheke   *struck him on the cheek*
That in oure fire he fil bakward adoun.   *into*
     "And he up stirte as dooth a wood leoun,   *jumped like a mad lion*
795 And with his fest he smoot me on the heed   *fist he punched*
That in the floor I lay as I were deed.   *So that*
And whan he saugh how stille that I lay
He was agast and wolde have fled his way   *away*
Til atte laste out of my swowgh I breyde.   *swoon I awoke*
800 "'O, hastow slain me, false theef?' I seyde,   *false villain*
'And for my land thus hastow mordred me?   *have you murdered*
Er I be deed yet wol I kisse thee.'   *would like to*
     "And neer he cam and kneled faire adoun,   *kneeled gallantly*

766–68. That somme . . . upright: Chaucer probably took this from the story of the widow of Ephesus in John of Salisbury's *Polycraticus* 7:11.
     769–70. And somme . . . slepte: Probably a reference to Jael's murder of Sisera in Judges 14:21, also mentioned in the *Polycraticus* 7:11.
     775–77. Bet is . . . chide: From Ecclesiasticus 25:23, but see also Proverbs 21:19.
     778–81. Bet is . . . ay: See Proverbs 21:9–10.
     782–83. A womman . . . smok: See Jerome 48.
     784–85. A fair . . . nose: See Proverbs 11:22.

And seyde, 'Deere suster Alisoun,°
805 As help me God, I shall thee nevere smite.   *never again*
That I have doon, it is thyself to wyte.°
Foryeve it me, and that I thee biseke.'   *beseech, ask*
      "And yet eftsoones I hitte him on the cheke,   *once again*
And seyde, 'Theef, thus muchel am I wreke.   *much am I revenged*
810 Now wol I die. I may no lenger speke.'
      "But at the laste with muchel care and wo   *in the end*
We fille acorded by usselven two.   *we came to an accord*
He yaf me all the bridel in mine hond,   *bridle (management)*
To han the governance of hous and lond,   *To have*
815 And of his tonge, and of his hond also,
And made him brenne his book anon right tho.   *burn / right then*
      "And whan that I hadde geten unto me   *taken to myself*
By maistrie all the soveraynetee,   *by mastery / dominion*
And that he seyde, 'Mine owene trewe wif,
820 Do as thee lust the terme of all thy lif.   *like for the rest*
Keep thine honour, and keep eek mine estaat,'
After that day we hadden never debaat.   *we never argued*
God helpe me so, I was to him as kinde
As any wif from Denmark unto Inde,   *India*
825 And also trewe, and so was he to me.   *faithful*
I prey to God, that sit in magestee,
So blesse his soule for his mercy deere.   *his (Jankyn's) soul*
Now wol I seye my tale if ye wol heere."

The Frere° lough when he hadde herd all this.
830   "Now dame," quod he, "so have I joye or blis,
This is a long preamble of a tale!"   *introduction to*
And whan the Somonour herde the Frere gale,   *speak out*
      "Lo," quod the Somonour, "Goddes armes two,   *by God's arms*

---

804. Deere suster Alisoun: Dear Alisoun. In this context "sister" is sign of affection, not blood kinship.

806. it is thyself to wyte: It is your own fault (because you struck me first).

829. Frere: The Friar, one of the Canterbury pilgrims. This little interchange involving the Friar, the Summoner, the Host, and the Wife of Bath serves, like the Pardoner's interruption earlier, as a dramatic interlude in Alisoun's long performance. There was a professional rivalry between summoners and friars — both were seeking to make money from the sins of Christians — so the antagonism expressed here would have seemed entirely natural to Chaucer's audience. The argument starting here will flourish in the two tales (not included in this volume) following the Wife of Bath's. The Friar tells a nasty tale about a corrupt summoner, and the Summoner retaliates with a scatological tale about a lecherous and greedy friar. For now, however, the interruption gives us a moment of comic relief before Alisoun begins to tell the narrative portion of her performance. It is noteworthy, of course, that her narrative begins with Alisoun herself picking up on the Summoner's remarks about the interfering work of friars.

A frere wol entremette him everemo.   *stick his nose in always*
835 Lo, goode men, a fly and eek a frere
Wol falle in every dissh and eek mateere.   *other matter*
What spekestow of preambulacioun?   *have you to say of preambling*
What, amble or trotte or pees° or go sit doun!
Thou lettest oure disport in this manere."   *interfere with our fun*
840   "Ye, woltow so, sire Somonour?" quod the Frere,   *will you say so*
"Now, by my feith, I shall er that I go
Telle of a somonour swich a tale or two
That alle the folk shall laughen in this place."
   "Now elles, Frere, I bishrewe thy face,"   *curse your face*
845 Quod this Somonour, "and I bishrewe me   *curse myself as well*
But if I telle tales two or three   *Unless*
Of freres er I come to Sidingborne,°
That I shall make thine herte for to morne,
For well I woot thy pacience is gon."
850 Oure Hoost cride, "Pees, and that anon!"
And seyde, "Lat the womman telle her tale.
Ye fare as folk that dronken ben of ale.
Do, dame, telle forth your tale, and that is best."
   "All redy, sire," quod she, "right as you lest,   *desire*
855 If I have licence of this worthy Frere."   *permission*
"Yis, dame," quod he, "tel forth and I wol heere."

THE WIFE OF BATH'S TALE

In th'olde dayes of the king Arthour,
Of which that Britons° speken greet honour,
All was this land fulfild of fairye.   *filled with fairies*
860 The elf-queene with her joly compaignye   *queen of the fairies*
Daunced ful ofte in many a grene mede.   *meadow*
This was the olde opinion, as I rede —
I speke of many hundred yeres ago.°

838. pees: Pace (walk). The usual gloss of "peace" is unlikely in view of the two previous terms for motion ("amble" and "trot"), and in view of the reference in the preceding line to "perambulacioun" (meaning walk around or stroll), the Summoner's misunderstanding of the Friar's term "preamble."
847. Sidingborne: Sittingborne, a town some forty miles from London, fifteen miles from Canterbury.
858. Britons: Storytellers from Bretony, in northwestern France, a region known for its interest in Arthurian tales and other fictions about imaginative and sometimes magical characters.
857–63. In th'olde . . . ago: Chaucer is careful in these opening seven lines to have the Wife of Bath place her tale far in the past, well before the "now" of line 864 — that is, the fourteenth century. The tale takes place in a time when elf-queens and fairies and magical transformations were common occurrences.

But now kan no man seen none elves mo,	*any elves anymore*
865 For now the grete charitee and prayeres	
Of limitours° and othere hooly freres,	
That serchen every lond and every streem	
As thikke as motes° in the sonne-beem,	
Blessinge halles, chambres, kichenes, boures,	*kitchens, ladies' chambers*
870 Citees, burghes, castels, hye toures,	*boroughs / towers*
Thropes, bernes, shipnes, daieryes.	*villages, barns, stables, dairies*
This maketh that there been no fairyes.°	
For there as wont to walken was an elf	*accustomed to walk*
There walketh now the limitour himself,	
875 In undermeles and in morweninges,	*afternoons / mornings*
And seyth his matins and his hooly thinges	*morning prayers / services*
As he gooth in his limitacioun.	*area where he can beg*
Wommen may go now saufly up and doun.	*safely walk around*
In every bussh or under every tree	
880 There is noon oother incubus° but he,	
And he ne wol doon hem but dishonour.	*will merely dishonor them*
And so bifel that this king Arthour	*it so happened*
Hadde in his hous a lusty bachiler	*lustful young knight*
That on a day came riding fro river,	*from (hawking by) the river*
885 And happed that, allone as he was born,	*it chanced*
He saugh a maide walkinge him biforn,	*walking before him*
Of whiche maide anon, maugree her hed,	*despite her efforts*
By verray force he rafte her maidenhed.	*took her maidenhead*
For which oppressioun was swich clamour	*rape / such an outcry*
890 And swich pursuite unto the king Arthour,	*such an appeal*
That dampned was this knight for to be deed,	*condemned to death*
By cours of lawe, and sholde han lost his heed —	
Paraventure swich was the statut tho —	*It happened that / then*
But that the queene and othere ladies mo	*Except that / more*
895 So longe preyeden the king of grace	*begged the king for clemency*

866. limitours: Friars who are allowed to preach within a certain geographical jurisdiction or "limit."

868. thikke as motes: As thick as dust particles in a sunbeam. One of the standard anticlerical complaints of Chaucer's time was that there were too many friars in the land sticking their noses into matters of no concern to them.

872. This maketh . . . fairyes: In other words, because of all the friars poking around and blessing everything, there are no more fairies in the "modern" world — modern to the Wife of Bath, that is.

880. incubus: An incubus was a demon who made love to women while they were sleeping. The union could result in pregnancy and demonic offspring. Alisoun's point is that the only "incubi" these days are friars, who, having driven off the real ones, give women dishonor rather than offspring or adventure. It is not entirely clear whether the Wife is expressing nostalgia for the good old days or relief that women now need fear only the less dangerous friars.

Til he his lif him graunted in the place,
And yaf him to the queene, all at her wille,   *to do with as she wanted*
To chese wheither she wolde him save or spille.   *slay*
　　The queene thanketh the king with all her might,
900 And after this thus spak she to the knight,
Whan that she saugh her time upon a day:
"Thou standest yet," quod she, "in swich array   *in such a situation*
That of thy lif yet hastow no suretee.   *have you no security*
I graunte thee lif if thou kanst tellen me
905 What thing is it that wommen moost desiren.
Be war and keep thy nekke-boon from iren.   *from (the executioner's) iron*
And if thou kanst not tellen me anon,   *right now*
Yet shall I yeve thee leve for to gon   *freedom to go*
A twelf-month and a day to seche and lere   *seek and learn*
910 An answere suffisant in this matere.
And suretee wol I han, er that thou pace,
Thy body for to yelden in this place."°
　　Wo was this knight and sorwefully he siketh.   *Woeful / sighs*
But what? He may not do all as him liketh.   *So what? / all that he wants*
915 And atte laste he chees him for to wende   *chooses to go*
And come again right at the yeres ende
With swich answere as God wolde him purveye,   *as God will provide him*
And taketh his leve and wendeth forth his weye.   *goes upon*
　　He seketh every hous and every place
920 Where as he hopeth for to finde grace   *help*
To lerne what thing wommen love moost,
But he ne koude arriven in no coost   *at any coast (region)*
Wher as he mighte finde in this matere
Two creatures acordinge in-fere.   *agreeing together*
925 　　Somme seyde wommen loven best richesse,   *wealth*
Somme seyde honour, somme seyde jolynesse,   *jollity*
Somme seyde riche array, somme lust a-bedde,   *fine clothes*
And ofte time to be widwe and wedde.   *widowed and wedded*
Somme seyde that oure herte is moost esed   *satisfied*
930 Whan that we been yflatered and yplesed.   *flattered and attended to*
He gooth ful ny the sothe, I wol not lye.
A man shall winne us best with flaterye,
And with attendance and with bisynesse   *constant attention*
Been we ylimed, bothe moore and lesse.   *caught (as a bird with lime)*
935 And somme sayn that we loven best
For to be free and do right as us lest,   *as we like*

911–12. And suretee . . . place: Before you leave I must have security (presumably a pledge or promise) that you will return and yield up your body to judgment.

And that no man repreve us of oure vice,   *criticize us for our vices*
But seye that we be wise and nothing nyce.   *not at all foolish*
For trewely there is noon of us alle,
940 If any wight wol claw us on the galle,
That we nil kike for he seith us sooth.°   *kick / truth*
Assay, and he shall finde it that so dooth,   *Test it out / happens thus*
For be we never so vicious withinne   *full of vices*
We wol been holden wise and clene of sinne.   *held to be*
945   And somme sayn that greet delit han we   *we take great pleasure*
For to been holden stable, and eek secree,   *in being thought reliable*
And in o purpos stedefastly to dwelle,   *hold to one purpose*
And not biwreye thing that men us telle.   *betray, reveal*
But that tale is not worth a rake-stele.   *opinion / rake handle*
950 Pardee, we wommen konne no thing hele.   *hide, keep to ourselves*
Witnesse on Myda.° Wol ye heere the tale?
Ovide, amonges othere thinges smale,   *anecdotes*
Seyde Myda hadde under his longe heres   *hair*
Growinge upon his heed two asses eres,   *head two ass's ears*
955 The which vice he hidde as he best mighte   *flaw*
Ful subtilly from every mannes sighte,   *subtly, slyly*
That save his wif there wiste of it namo.   *So that / no one knew of it*
He loved her moost and trusted her also.
He preyde her that to no creature
960 She sholde tellen of his disfigure.   *disfigurement*
She swoor him nay. For all this world to winne,   *For all the world*
She nolde do that vileynye or syn   *She would not*
To make her housbonde han so foul a name.   *To give her husband*
She nolde not telle it for her owene shame.
965 But, nathelees, her thoughte that she dyde
That she so longe sholde a conseil hide.°
Her thoughte it swal so soore aboute her herte   *It seemed to swell*
That nedely some word her moste asterte.   *of necessity / must escape her*
And sith she dorste not telle it to no man,   *since she dare*
970 Doun to a maris faste by she ran.   *marsh close by*
Til she cam there her herte was afire.   *burning*

939–41. **For trewely . . . sooth:** Truly, there is not a one of us women who, if someone scratched us on a sore place, would not kick him for telling the truth.

951. **Myda:** Midas. In Book II of the *Metamorphoses* Ovid tells the story of Midas's ears. Midas's barber is the only person who knows that Midas has the ears of an ass under his long hair. He tries to keep the secret but cannot contain himself. He digs a small hole in the ground and whispers the secret there, but the winds blowing over the reeds growing about the hole reveal the secret. Alisoun's version of the story is somewhat different.

965–66. **But, nathelees . . . hide:** But, nevertheless, it seemed to her that she would die to have to keep the secret for so long.

And as a bitore bombleth in the mire, *heron bellows in the mud*
She leyde her mouth unto the water doun:
"Biwreye me not, thou water, with thy soun," *Don't betray me*
975 Quod she. "To thee I telle it and namo. *no more (no one else)*
Mine housbonde hath longe asses eres two.
Now is mine herte all hool, now it is oute.
I mighte no lenger kepe it, out of doute." *could / unquestionably*
Heere may ye see, thogh we a time abide, *can abide for a while*
980 Yet out it moot. We kan no conseil hide. *must / secrets*
The remenant of the tale, if ye wol heere,
Redeth Ovide and there ye may it leere. *learn*
This knight, of which my tale is specially,
Whan that he saugh he mighte not come therby —
985 This is to seye, what wommen loven moost —
Withinne his brest ful sorweful was the goost. *spirit*
But hom he gooth, he mighte not sojourne.°
The day was come that homward moste he tourne.
And in his wey it happed him to ride
990 In all this care under a forest side°
Wher as he saugh upon a daunce go *Where he saw dancing*
Of ladies foure and twenty and yet mo.° *and still more*
Toward the whiche daunce he drow ful yerne, *drew very eagerly*
In hope that some wisdom sholde he lerne.
995 But certeinly, er he came fully there,
Vanisshed was this daunce, he nyste where. *he knew not whereto*
Ne creature saugh he that bar lif *saw / was alive*
Save on the grene he saugh sittinge a wif.° *uglier person / imagine*
A fouler wight there may no man devise.
1000 Agayn the knight this olde wif gan rise, *In front of / stood up*

---

987. he mighte not sojourne: Could not stay away any longer (because his year was nearly up).

990. under a forest side: At the edge of a forest — a place known for supernatural events. See Chaucer's Friar's Tale, D1380, where a summoner meets up with a demon at the "forest side."

991–92. a daunce ... mo: Who these dancers are and why there are over twenty-four of them remains a mystery, but of course it was supposed to be something of a mystery. One clue may be a reference at the very start of the tale's being set in a time when the elf-queen and her "joly compaignye/Daunced ful ofte in many a grene mede" (860–61).

998. a wif: See note to A445. When used with the indefinite article, "wif" could mean simply "woman." When used with one of the possessive pronouns ("his," "thy," "my") it meant "wife." Who this woman is and how she gets there, of course, are among the pleasing mysteries of Chaucer's version of the story. Alisoun has prepared for her presence by telling us earlier that the story takes place back in the days before friars had cast out elves and fairies. Is it possible that we are to imagine that the raped maiden has managed to transform herself into this old woman?

And seyde, "Sire knight, heer forth ne lith no wey.   *the path ends here*
Tel me what that ye seken, by your fey.   *what you seek, by your faith*
Paraventure it may the bettre be.   *Perhaps it may get better*
Thise olde folk kan muchel thing," quod she.   *old folks know a lot*
1005   "My leeve mooder,"° quod this knight, "certeyn
I nam but deed but if that I kan sayn   *I shall die unless / say*
What thing it is that wommen moost desire.
Koude ye me wisse, I wolde well quite your hire."°   *repay you*
   "Plight me thy trouthe heere in mine hand,"° quod she.
1010 "The nexte thing that I requere thee   *ask of you*
Thou shalt it do, if it lie in thy might,   *if you can*
And I wol telle it you er it be night."   *before nightfall*
   "Have heer my trouthe," quod the knight, "I grante."   *I grant it*
   "Thanne," quod she, "I dar me well avante   *say, boast*
1015 Thy lif is sauf. For I wol stonde therby   *saved*
Upon my lif. The queene wol seye as I.   *agree with what I say*
Lat see which is the prouddeste of hem alle
That wereth on a coverchief or a calle
That dar seye nay of that I shall thee teche.°
1020 Lat us go forth withouten lenger speche."   *Let's go find out*
Tho rowned she a pistel in his ere°
And bad him to be glad and have no fere.   *bade / no fear*
   Whan they be comen to the court, this knight   *the (queen's) court*
Seyde he had holde his day as he hadde hight,   *kept the day / promised*
1025 And redy was his answere, as he sayde.
Ful many a noble wif, and many a maide,
And many a widwe — for that they been wise —   *because they are wise*
The queene herself sittinge as justise,   *judge*
Assembled been, his answere for to here.   *hear*
1030 And afterward this knight was bode appere.   *bidden to come forth*
To every wight comanded was silence,   *person*
And that the knight sholde telle in audience   *(commanded) to tell*
What thing that worldly wommen loven best.
   This knight ne stood not stille as doth a best,   *beast (dumb animal)*

1005. My leeve mooder: My dear woman. "Mother" could be a sign of respect for an older woman and need not indicate blood kinship.

1008. Koude ye . . . hire: If you tell me, I will make it worth your while.

1009. Plight me . . . hand: Promise me, shake hands on it. "Plight me your troth" had not yet come to mean "Marry me."

1017–19. Lat see . . . teche: We'll see whether even the proudest of those ladies, whether they wear a handkerchief or a fancy netted headdress, will dare to contradict what I teach you.

1021. Tho rowned . . . ere: Then she whispered an epistle (message) in his ear.

1035 But to his questioun anon answerde	*immediately*
With manly vois that all the court it herde:	
"My lige lady, generally," quod he,	*liege, noble*
"Wommen desire to have sovereynetee°	
As well over her housbond as her love,°	
1040 And for to been in maistrie° him above.	
This is your mooste desire — thogh ye me kille.°	
Dooth as you list. I am heer at your wille."	
In all the court ne was there wif, ne maide,	
Ne widwe that contraried that he sayde,	*contradicted*
1045 But seyden he was worthy han his lif.	*to have his life*
And with that word up stirte the olde wif	*jumped*
Which that the knight saugh sitting on the grene.	
"Mercy," quod she, "my sovereyn lady queene!	
Er that your court departe, do me right.	*let me have justice*
1050 I taughte this answere unto the knight,	
For which he plighte me his trouthe there:	*gave me his promise*
The firste thing I wolde him requere	*require (ask) of him*
He wolde it do, if it lay in his might.	
Before the court thanne preye I thee, sir knight,"	
1055 Quod she, "that thou me take unto thy wif,	*to be your wife*
For well thou woost that I have kept thy lif.	*you know well / saved*
If I seye fals, sey nay, upon thy fey."	*say so, on your faith*
This knight answerde, "Allas and weylawey!	*woe is me*
I woot right well that swich was my biheste.	*know / promise*
1060 For Goddes love as chees a newe requeste.	*choose something else*
Taak all my good and lat my body go."	*worldly goods*
"Nay, thanne," quod she, "I shrewe us bothe two!	*curse us both*
For thogh that I be foul, and oold, and poore,	
I nolde for all the metal ne for oore	*would not / precious metal or ore*
1065 That under erthe is grave or lith above,	*beneath or above ground*

1038. sovereynetee: Sovereignty. The key concept in sovereignty is power, the ability to control not only one's own destiny but the destiny of others. The concept may be related to the notion of courtly love, in which the man serves at the pleasure of his "sovereign lady."

1039. As well . . . love: The line is usually translated to mean that women desire to have sovereign power over both their husbands and their lovers. Perhaps a better reading is that women desire to have over their husbands the same power they have over lovers. Lovers, of course, eagerly serve their women; husbands often do not.

1040. maistrie: Mastery. "Mastery" is almost a synonym for "sovereignty," but "sovereignty" suggests wider power, if only because a sovereign is a king or queen. One might have mastery over a household or a family, but sovereignty over a nation.

1041. This is . . . kille: This is your greatest desire, even though you may kill me for saying it.

But if thy wif I were, and eek thy love."°
　　"My love?" quod he, "nay, my dampnacioun!　　　　*damnation*
Allas, that any of my nacioun　　　　　　　　　　　　*family*
Sholde evere so foule disparaged be."　　　　　*be so foully degraded*
1070 But all for noght; th'ende is this, that he　　*But his complaining was in vain*
Constreyned was, he nedes moste her wedde,　　　*Had no choice*
And taketh his olde wif, and gooth to bedde.
　　　Now wolden some men seye, paraventure,　　　　*perhaps*
That for my necligence I do no cure　　*out of negligence I don't bother*
1075 To tellen you the joye and all th'array
That at the feeste was that ilke day.　　　　*feast that very day*
To which thing shortly answere I shall.
I seye there nas no joye ne feeste at all.
There nas but hevinesse and muche sorwe,　　　*was only dreariness*
1080 For prively he wedded her on morwe.　　　　　*the next day*
And all day after hidde him as an owle,°
So wo was him, his wif looked so foule.　　　　　*woeful*
　　　Greet was the wo the knight hadde in his thoght
Whan he was with his wif abedde ybroght.
1085 He walweth and he turneth to and fro.　　*wallows, tosses to and fro*
His olde wif lay smilinge everemo,
And seyde, "O deere housbonde, benedicitee,　　　*bless you*
Fareth every knight thus with his wif as ye?　　　*Behaves*
Is this the lawe of king Arthures hous?
1090 Is every knight of his thus daungerous?　　　*so standoffish*
I am your owene love and eek your wif.
I am she which that saved hath your lif,
And certes yet ne dide I you nevere unright.　　　*any wrong*
Why fare ye thus with me this firste night?　　*do you behave this way*
1095 Ye faren like a man had lost his wit.　　　*who has gone crazy*
What is my gilt? For Goddes love, tell it,　　*What have I done wrong?*
And it shall been amended, if I may."　　　　*corrected*
　　　"Amended?" quod this knight. "Allas. Nay, nay.
It wol not been amended nevere mo.
1100 Thou art so loothly, and so oold also,　　　　*loathsome*
And therto comen of so lough a kinde,　　*such a low class*
That litel wonder is thogh I walwe and winde.　　*twist and turn*

　　　1062–66. Nay, thanne . . . love: No, then, she said. I would curse us both to hell
in that case. Even though I am ugly and old and poor, I would not, for all the gold and
jewels on earth or buried under it, accept anything else than your taking me as your
wife and your love.
　　　1081. hidde him as an owle: Hid like an owl. Owls, of course, are nocturnal
birds, seldom seen. The knight is so ashamed of his new bride that he refuses to be seen
in public with her.

So wolde God mine herte wolde breste."°

"Is this," quod she, "the cause of your unreste?"

1105　"Ye, certeinly," quod he, "no wonder is."

"Now, sire," quod she, "I koude amende all this,　　*correct*

If that me liste, er it were dayes three,　　　　*If I wanted*

So well ye mighte bere you unto me.　　　　　*If you behave well*

But, for ye speken of swich gentillesse°

1110　As is descended out of old richesse,　　　　　*wealth*

That therfore sholden ye be gentil men —

Swich arrogaunce is not worth an hen.°

"Looke who that is moost vertuous alway,

Privee and apert, and moost entendeth ay

1115　To do the gentil dedes that he kan.°

Taak him for the grettest gentil man —

Crist. Wole we clayme of him oure gentillesse,　　*We should*

Not of oure eldres for hir old richesse.

For thogh they yeve us all her heritage,

1120　For which we claime to been of heigh parage,　　*parentage*

Yet may they not biquethe for no thing　　　　*bequeath*

To noon of us hir vertuous living,

That made hem gentil men ycalled be,°

And bad us folwen hem in swich degree.°　　*bade us / in their gentility*

1125　"Well kan the wise poete of Florence

That highte Dant° speken in this sentence.　　*was called / this moral*

Lo, in swich maner rym is Dantes tale:

'Ful selde up riseth by his branches smale°　　　*seldom*

1103. So wolde . . . breste: I wish to God my heart would burst open (so I would be out of this situation).

1109. gentillesse: Gentility. Here begins the old wife's long disquisition on the nature of true gentility. It may derive in part from Dante's *Convivio* and in part from the *Roman de la Rose*. The Wife of Bath challenges the usual definition that gentility is a matter of birth or wealth. Even an ugly old peasant, she says, can be noble in demeanor and action. This whole speech is both an education for the young knight and an advertisement for herself as an appropriate wife.

1111–12. That therfore . . . hen: That, because you are rich, you are therefore gentle — such arrogance is not worth so much as a hen.

1113–15. Looke who . . . kan: Look at the man who is most virtuous, both in public and privately, and tries to do all the gentle deeds he can.

1119–23. For thogh . . . be: Though our ancestors may give us their worldly heritage, for which we *claim* a high nobility, they can in no way bequeath to us any of the virtues that made them known as truly gentle.

1118–24. Not of . . . degree: Compare *Roman de la Rose*, lines 18620–34.

1126. Dant: Dante Alighieri (1265–1321), Italian poet and author of the *Divine Comedy*. The lines quoted are from the *Purgatorio* 7, 121–23.

1128. by his branches smale: The higher branches of the family tree. The idea here is that our immediate ancestors can give us little. Rather, our important characteristics come from the ultimate or root ancestor, God.

Prowesse of man, for God of his prowesse   *strength, excellence*
1130 Wole that of him we claime oure gentillesse.'   *Wants*
For of oure eldres may we no thing claime
But temporel thing that man may hurte and maime.°
"Eek every wight woot this as well as I.   *every person knows*
If gentillesse were planted natureelly   *transmitted genetically*
1135 Unto a certeyn linage doun the line,
Privee and apert, thanne wolde they nevere fine   *stop (finish)*
To doon of gentillesse the faire office.   *Doing gentle deeds*
They mighte do no vileynye or vice.
"Taak fire and ber it in the derkeste hous
1140 Bitwix this and the mount of Kaukasous,°
And lat men shette the dores and go thenne,   *thence*
Yet wole the fire as faire lie and brenne
As twenty thousand men mighte it biholde.   *As if*
His office natureel ay wol it holde,
1145 Up peril of my lif, til that it dye.°
Heere may ye see well how that genterye   *gentility*
Is not annexed to possessioun,   *connected with*
Sith folk ne doon hir operacioun
Alwey, as dooth the fire, lo, in his kinde.°   *by its own nature*
1150 "For, God it woot, men may well often finde
A lordes sone do shame and vileynye.
And he that wole han pris of his gentrye   *be praised for*
For he was boren of a gentil hous   *Just because he was born*
And hadde his eldres noble and vertuous   *had virtuous ancesters*
1155 And nil himselven do no gentil dedis   *will not himself*
Ne folwen his gentil auncestre that deed is,
He nis not gentil, be he duc or erl,
For vileyns sinful dedes make a cherl.°
"For 'gentillesse' nis but renomee   *reputation*

1131–32. For of . . . maime: From our ancestors we can lay claim only to tempo-
rary things that can be harmed or taken away by other men.
   1140. Kaukasous: A mountain in Russia. Its only importance seems to be that this
mountain is a long way off, making "the darkest house" *really* dark.
   1139–45. Taak fire . . . dye: The point seems to be that just as a fire glows natu-
rally whether or not anyone sees it, so gentility shines forth whether or not anyone rec-
ognizes it. The old woman suggests that even though she is so old and ugly and poor
that no one recognizes her virtue, she nevertheless, like the fire in that darkest of
houses, might glitter with virtues.
   1146–49. Heere may . . . kinde: The idea in this difficult passage seems to be
that, unlike the fire that burns bright all the time, wealthy people only sometimes do
gentle deeds, thus proving that virtue is not a function of wealth.
   1152–58. And he . . . cherl: When a lord's son commits vicious acts, he is a churl,
his noble ancestry being no guarantee that he can act gently.

1160 Of thine auncestres for hir hye bountee,	
Which is a strange thing for thy persone.	*not part of your character*
Thy gentillesse cometh fro God allone.°	
Thanne comth oure verray gentillesse of grace.	*the grace (of God)*
It was no thing biquethe us with oure place.	*with our rank*
1165 Thenketh hou noble, as seith Valerius,°	
Was thilke Tullius Hostillius	
That out of poverte roos to heigh noblese.	
Reed Senek, and redeth eek Boece.°	
There shul ye seen expres that no drede is	*there is no doubt about it*
1170 That he is gentil that dooth gentil dedis.	
And therfore, leeve housbonde, I thus conclude:	*dear husband*
Al were it that mine auncestres were rude,	*Although / of low birth*
Yet may the hye God, and so hope I,	
Graunte me grace to liven vertuously.	
1175 Thanne am I gentil whan that I biginne	
To liven vertuously and weyve sinne.	*abandon sin*
"And there as ye of poverte me repreve,	*reprove me for poverty*
The hye God, on whom that we bileve,	
In wilful poverte chees to live his lif.	*deliberate poverty chose*
1180 And certes every man, maiden, or wif,	
May understonde that Jhesus, hevene-king,	*king of heaven*
Ne wolde not chese a vicious living.	*would not*
Glad poverte is an honeste thing, certeyn.	*Voluntary poverty*
This wole Senek and othere clerkes sayn.	*say*
1185 Whoso that halt him paid of his poverte,	*satisfied with his poverty*
I holde him riche al hadde he not a sherte.	*although he had not even*
He that coveiteth is a povre wight,	
For he wolde han that is not in his might.°	
But he that noght hath, ne coveiteth have,	*neither has nor covets*
1190 Is riche, although ye holde him but a knave.	*peasant*
"Verray poverte, it singeth proprely.	*True poverty sings*
Juvenal° seith of poverte, 'Myrily	*Merrily*

1159–62. For 'gentillesse' . . . allone: "Gentility" as it is usually (but wrongly) referred to is based only on the reputation of your ancestors, but that has nothing to do with your own gentility, which comes from God.
    1165. Valerius: Valerius Maximus described in *Facta et dicta memorabilia* 3:4 how Tullius Hostillius rose from the peasantry to be the third king of Rome and came to enjoy great honor.
    1168. Senek, and . . . Boece: Seneca, Roman philosopher (4 B.C.–A.D. 65). See his *Epistolae* 17. Boethius, a sixth-century philosopher whose *Consolation of Philosophy* Chaucer admired so much that he translated it into Middle English.
    1187–88. He that . . . might: He who covets is a poor man because he wants what is not in his power to get.
    1192. Juvenal: Roman poet (c. A.D. 60–140). See his *Satires* 10, 21–22.

The poure man, whan he goth by the weye,   *walks along*
Before the theves he may singe and pleye.'   *thieves*
1195 Poverte is hateful good and, as I gesse,   *a despised virtue*
A ful greet bringere out of bisynesse,   *encourager of industry*
A greet amendere eek of sapience   *improver also of wisdom*
To him that taketh it in pacience.   *(poverty) patiently*
Poverte is this, although it seme alenge
1200 Possessioun that no wight wol chalenge.°
Poverte ful ofte, whan a man is lowe,
Maketh his God and eek himself to knowe.°
Poverte a spectacle is, as thinketh me,   *magnifying glass*
Thurgh which he may his verray freendes see.°   *see who his true friends are*
1205 And therfore, sire, syn that I noght you greve,   *give you a hard time*
Of my poverte namoore ye me repreve.   *no longer reprove me*
   "Now, sire, of elde ye repreve me.   *old age*
And certes, sire, thogh noon auctoritee   *no authority*
Were in no book, ye gentils of honour   *is written in a book*
1210 Sayn that men an oold wight sholde doon favour   *do favors for an old person*
And clepe him 'fader' for your gentilesse.   *"father" out of respect*
And auctours shall I finden, as I gesse.°
Now there ye seye that I am foul and old,   *Now whereas*
Thanne drede you noght to been a cokewold.   *fear not becoming a cuckold*
1215 For filthe and elde, also moot I thee,   *so may I thrive*
Been grete wardeyns upon chastitee.   *guardians of chastity*
   "But nathelees, syn I knowe your delit,   *since / what you want*
I shall fulfille your worldly appetit.
Chese now," quod she, "oon of thise thinges tweye: *Choose / two*
1220 To han me foul and old til that I deye
And be to you a trewe humble wif,   *faithful and humble*
And nevere you displese in all my lif,
Or elles ye wol han me yong and fair,   *have*
And take your aventure of the repair   *chances about the visitors*
1225 That shall be to your hous by cause of me,   *come / because*
Or in some oother place, may well be.   *perhaps*
Now chese yourselven, wheither that you liketh."   *whichever*

1199–1200. Poverte is . . . chalenge: Although poverty seems to be an unwelcome possession, no one will try to take it away from you.
1201–02. Poverte ful . . . knowe: When a man is low in spirit, poverty often helps him to know both his God and himself.
1203–04. Poverte a . . . see: The notion that we can better see who our friends are when we are poor than when we are rich is commonplace. See, for example, *Roman de la Rose,* lines 4949–56.
1212. auctours shall . . . gesse: I suppose, if I searched, I could find authors to support this position. The old bride is perhaps growing weary of the subject of gentility and decides to stop citing the "authorities."

This knight aviseth him and sore siketh, *considers / sorrowfully sighs*
But atte laste he seyde in this manere:
1230 "My lady, and my love, and wif so deere,
I put me in your wise governaunce. *under your wise control*
Cheseth yourself which may be moost plesaunce *Chose / joyful*
And moost honour to you and me also. *honorable*
I do no fors the wheither of the two, *I don't care which*
1235 For as you liketh it suffiseth me." *suffices for me*
"Thanne have I gete of you maistrie," quod she, *gotten / mastery*
"Syn I may chese and governe as me lest?" *choose / as I like*
"Ye, certes, wif," quod he. "I holde it best."
"Kys me," quod she. "We be no lenger wrothe, *longer at odds*
1240 For, by my trouthe, I wol be to you bothe,
This is to sayn, ye, bothe fair and good. *yes*
I prey to God that I moote sterven wood *may die mad*
But I to you be also good and trewe *Unless*
As evere was wif syn that the world was newe. *since / created*
1245 And but I be tomorn as fair to seene *tomorrow morning*
As any lady, emperice, or queene, *empress*
That is bitwixe the est and eke the west,
Do with my lif and deth right as you lest. *as you like*
Cast up the curtin!° Looke how that it is."
1250 And whan the knight saugh verraily all this, *saw truly*
That she so fair was, and so yong therto,
For joye he hente her in his armes two. *clasped her*
His herte bathed in a bath of blisse, *was bathed in happiness*
A thousand time a-rewe he gan her kisse. *in a row*
1255 And she obeyed him in every thing
That mighte doon him plesance or liking. *give him pleasure*
And thus they live unto hir lives ende
In parfit joye. And Jhesu Crist us sende *perfect*
Housbondes meeke, yonge, and fressh abedde,
1260 And grace t'overbide hem that we wedde. *to outlive*
And eek I pray Jhesu shorte hir lives *shorten*
That wol not be governed by hir wives.
And olde and angry nigardes of dispence, *skinflints*
God sende hem soone verray pestilence! *a veritable plague*

1249. curtin: Curtain. No previous mention has been made of a curtain, but because we know that the two are in bed (line 1084), she presumably means a drapery around the bed that, if raised, would let in enough light that he can see her.

PART TWO

The Wife of Bath:
A Case Study in
Contemporary Criticism

A Critical History
of the Wife of Bath's
Prologue and Tale

Will it do to say anything more about Chaucer? Can any one
hope to say anything, not new, but even fresh, on a topic so
well worn? It may well be doubted. (291)

–JAMES RUSSELL LOWELL, 1870

It must be remembered that very little modern literary theory
has been applied to Chaucer. Just as it was some fifteen years
before New Criticism reached Chaucer in the 1950s, so is it
the case with new literary theorizing, which is now about ripe
to reach Chaucer. (25)

–MORTON W. BLOOMFIELD, 1981

New directions in literary theory and critical practice over the
past twenty years have brought with them a potential for gen-
erating fresh approaches to Chaucer, often by bringing ne-
glected aspects of his works into the foreground of attention.
(56)

–JOHN STEPHENS AND MARCELLA RYAN, 1989

In the century and a quarter since James Russell Lowell wrote the
question and answer that make up the first epigraph, scholars have
found many new and fresh things to say about Chaucer. The "new lit-
erary theorizing" Bloomfield predicted more than fifteen years ago has
hit with refreshing fury, and it has, indeed, as Stephens and Ryan have

noted, brought into critical scrutiny aspects of Chaucer's work scarcely noticed before. The purpose of this history of the criticism of the Wife of Bath's Prologue and Tale is to sketch the broad outlines and the major developments of the published scholarship on the Wife of Bath. That scholarship has been enormous. Indeed, the University of Toronto Press has under contract a book-length annotated bibliography on the scholarship on the Wife of Bath. When complete, that bibliography will probably list somewhere near a thousand individual items. And the University of Oklahoma Press has under contract an extensive "variorum" edition of the Wife of Bath's Prologue and Tale — a scholarly edition with extensive notes and discussion of the critical issues that have surfaced with respect to the Wife of Bath and her performance.

Early commentators tended to make general and highly appreciative statements about Chaucer, statements like Lowell's own that "there is a pervading wholesomeness in the writings of this man" (291). Even when speaking more specifically of the Wife of Bath, they tend to speak in generalities, such as Robert K. Root's 1927 opinion that the Wife's prologue proves Chaucer to be "the first modern man of England" (232) and that her tale is "one of Chaucer's poetic triumphs" (244).

Most of the later criticism on the Wife of Bath has been more focused. In the following pages I shall attempt to hit a balance between coverage and selectivity: coverage of a range of critical positions on the Wife of Bath and selectivity of those that have been particularly influential. I can describe, and then but cursorily, only a handful of the landmark books and several of the articles that later scholars refer to the most, either to reject them or to build on them. Full references to these books and articles appear in the list of Works Cited at the end of this essay.

DATE AND DEVELOPMENT

One of the first tasks of early scholars was to try to figure out when Chaucer wrote his various works. They discovered that we have very little to go on — allusions to contemporary historical, social, or political conditions; references to earlier Chaucerian works; the general "artistic maturity" of the poetry; and so on. John S. P. Tatlock, for example, wrote in his 1907 *Development and Chronology of Chaucer's Works* that in his opinion Chaucer wrote the Wife of Bath materials around 1394. Robert A. Pratt and others, however, suggest that

Chaucer's conception of the Wife of Bath developed over the years. At one point, for example, Chaucer seems to have meant to assign to the Wife of Bath what is now the Shipman's Tale, a comic tale about a wife who sells sexual favors both to her husband and to a visiting monk. If so, then it is possible that this comic tale once followed line 193 of her prologue, after the Pardoner's interruption, and that the autobiographical section about her five husbands was a later addition, as was the Arthurian tale that we all now think of as the Wife of Bath's Tale. But this is speculation. All we can say with assurance is that Chaucer must have been at the height of his powers when he conceived and developed the Wife of Bath and wrote the materials that make up her performance on the pilgrimage to Canterbury.

MANUSCRIPTS AND EDITING

We have no manuscripts that we are sure were written in Chaucer's own hand. Instead, we have a rather large number of manuscripts copied down by scribes or professional makers of books after Chaucer's death. Some of the fundamental early work on the Wife of Bath was necessarily a sorting out of the eighty-odd manuscripts containing parts or all of Chaucer's *Canterbury Tales*. Modern Chaucer textual scholarship may be said to begin in 1940 with the publication of John M. Manly and Edith Rickert's eight-volume *Text of the Canterbury Tales,* which shows the textual variants to virtually all of the words in the work. We learn, for example, that instead of "in wommen vinolent is no defence" in line 467 of the Wife of Bath's Prologue we have in some manuscripts "in wommen violent is no defense." That second reading is almost surely a scribal mistake: clearly the Wife of Bath means to suggest that inebriated women ("vinolent") have little defense against sexual advances, not that violent ones are vulnerable to attack.

The work of Manly and Rickert continues to be widely influential, although scholars have grown less interested in the textual variants of the later manuscripts than in the readings of a select few of the manuscripts, especially the Hengwrt manuscript, the most reliably Chaucerian of the lot. Many scholars now see even the lovely Ellesmere manuscript, copied by the Hengwrt scribe and arranged by a highly intelligent editor, as a distraction rather than an aid to understanding Chaucer's work.

Now that the task of locating and establishing the relationships

among the various manuscripts is mostly done, textual scholars have
been focusing more of their attention on the question of editing
Chaucer. The F. N. Robinson edition, long the modern standard and
the basis of Larry D. Benson's now-standard *Riverside Chaucer*, has
been called into question as being too heavily edited. Paul G. Rug-
giers in his 1984 *Editing Chaucer: The Great Tradition* brings to-
gether a number of essays on the work of some of the most influential
editors of Chaucer. One issue coming under increased scrutiny by edi-
tors is how to punctuate Chaucer. Because punctuation as we know it
had simply not been invented yet in Chaucer's time, virtually every pe-
riod, comma, question mark, apostrophe, exclamation mark, and quo-
tation mark that we see in modern editions — including this one — is
the work not of Chaucer or of a medieval scribe but of a modern edi-
tor. Some scholars, concerned about the influence that the punctua-
tion of modern editions of Chaucer has had on interpreting Chaucer,
are advocating teaching Chaucer in an unpunctuated text, if only to
warn students that punctuated editions exercise a kind of tyranny over
the text by insisting on non-Chaucerian meanings or obscuring
Chaucerian ambiguities.

One issue of particular concern to editors of the Wife of Bath's
Prologue is what to do about five brief passages, amounting to some
32 lines, that have long been considered Chaucerian but may not be.
In 1961 Robert A. Pratt, in his speculative analysis of Chaucer's "de-
velopment" of his conception of the character of the Wife of Bath,
stated that it was "generally agreed that these passages represent late
additions by Chaucer to the text" (71). Some scholars, however, have
recently called that conclusion into question by contending that the
five passages are the work not of Chaucer but of a scribe or editor.
Norman Blake (1985) bases his arguments on the belief that what
does not appear in the Hengwrt manuscript is not Chaucerian. Bev-
erly Kennedy (1995) bases hers on two beliefs: that the passages in
question can scarcely be late additions by Chaucer because the inser-
tion of the lines is clumsy, and that Chaucer would not have wanted
to "disambiguate" his text by putting such openly misogynist asper-
sions into the mouth of the Wife of Bath. If Blake and Kennedy are
right and the five passages are merely scribal, the lines should be elimi-
nated from modern editions, and scholars will have to rethink much of
the scholarly work that has been done on the Wife of Bath. If Blake
and Kennedy are wrong and the five passages represent Chaucer's own
later revision of the prologue, then the lines should remain in modern
editions. No critical consensus has been reached on this question. In

this edition I include the five passages but place them in brackets and comment in the notes on their uncertain authorship.

SOURCE RELATIONSHIPS

In addition to establishing reliable textual editions of the *Canterbury Tales,* scholars have sought to identify the literary sources of Chaucer's work. At first the point of source studies was primarily to try to discover what Chaucer had read and where he got his ideas. In recent years, scholars have wanted to know about Chaucer's sources primarily so that they could look for patterns in his alterations of those sources in an effort to get a better idea both of what was most original in Chaucer and of what themes, characters, and plot elements he was most interested in developing. These scholars wanted to know about John Gower's Tale of Florent so that they could see, by holding side by side the two stories of an ugly old woman transformed on her wedding night into a lovely young woman, what was most distinctively Chaucer's own narrative contribution to the story.

The landmark collection of most of the possible sources of Chaucer's tales appeared in 1941: the Bryan and Dempster *Sources and Analogues of Chaucer's Canterbury Tales.* Bartlett J. Whiting's chapters on the Wife of Bath's Prologue and Tale established the most important probable sources for some of the materials in Alisoun's performance. For the prologue Chaucer almost certainly consulted Saint Jerome's letter *Adversus Jovinianum* and Guillaume de Lorris and Jean de Meun's *Roman de la Rose.* For the tale he might have consulted John Gower's Tale of Florent from the *Confessio Amantis,* but he may also have consulted an early version of a narrative recorded later, the anonymous romance called the Wedding of Sir Gawain and Dame Ragnell. These are included in *Sources and Analogues.* These and other possible sources — Walter Map, Valerius Maximus, Theophrastus, Ovid, John of Salisbury, and of course the Scriptures — are mentioned at the appropriate places in my notes to this edition. *Sources and Analogues,* long a standard resource of Chaucer scholars, is currently being superseded by a planned expanded new edition reflecting recent discoveries about Chaucer's possible source materials and including translations of those materials. Important early discussion of the possible source relationships of the Wife of Bath's Tale are G. H. Maynadier's *The Wife of Bath's Tale: Its Sources and Analogues* (1901) and Sigmund Eisner's *A Tale of Wonder* (1957).

HISTORICAL APPROACHES

For many decades Chaucerians have tried to understand Chaucer better by "contextualizing" him, or viewing his works in the light of the history, culture, science, philosophy, and religious beliefs of his own time. To understand the Wife of Bath, for example, historical critics think that we need to understand the economic situation of English weavers and what it meant for women to go on pilgrimages. To understand her tale we need to understand the legal status of rape in Chaucer's time and before. And we need to consider whether, by having Arthur acquiesce so readily to the desires of his queen, Chaucer may have been sending a subtle message to Richard II about how he should listen to the expressed desires of his subjects. One of the forces stimulating the historical approach is the notion that literary study may not be able to survive in isolation. D. W. Robertson puts it this way in 1974: "If literary studies are divorced from larger concerns of cultural history they will eventually wither away" (75).

One of the most influential historical approaches was to see Chaucer in the context of the scientific principles of his day. The standard early book on the subject is Walter Clyde Curry's 1926 *Chaucer and the Mediaeval Sciences.* On the basis of information Chaucer gives us about the astrological situation at the Wife of Bath's birth, Curry casts her horoscope. On the basis of descriptions of her face (her gap teeth, for example) and person (her large hips, for example), Curry also does an analysis of her character. Although later scholars like Chauncey Wood (1970) and J. D. North (1988) have questioned the details of Curry's analyses, Curry's view of the richly contradictory nature of the Wife of Bath has been widely influential and still informs much of Chaucer scholarship.

In another early kind of historical criticism, John M. Manly, in his 1926 *Some New Light on Chaucer,* tries to discover the "real" personages who may have served as the models for the various pilgrims. Manly suggests that in the General Prologue "Chaucer's character sketches represent not so much types as individuals" (74), real people whom Chaucer's contemporary audiences would have recognized. "Chaucer was not writing for posterity," Manly tells us, "but for a handful of courtiers, gentlemen, churchmen, professional men, officials, and city merchants" (76). Manly suggests that Chaucer's audience might have recognized in Alisoun of Bath a real woman of that name, and he finds in the records of medieval Bath several wives named Alice (or Alisoun): "Curiously enough more than one of these

Alices rejoiced in three or more husbands, though I can find none who had clearly achieved five" (234).

Few scholars take Manly's conclusions seriously or try to replicate his methods. The very fact that Manly was able to locate records of so many historical men and women who *might* have been the real-life counterparts of Chaucer's pilgrims leads us to believe that Chaucer tried to write realistically about his fellow English citizens. And even though most scholars question Manly's specific findings, they are encouraged by his example to see Chaucer as a writer who was very much involved in the affairs and people of his time. Many of these scholars have contributed to the storehouse of information about Chaucer and the world he lived in. Still useful are G. G. Coulton's *Chaucer and His England* (1908) and Edith Rickert's *Chaucer's World* (1948).

Jill Mann's *Chaucer and Medieval Estates Satire* (1973) has been another widely influential work of historical criticism. Mann disagrees with Manly's notion that the pilgrims are meant to represent specific individuals but rather finds that each represents an "estate" — that is, a class or occupation. In Mann's view the Wife of Bath represents less an individual woman than a social type — the secular professional woman. Mann finds in the Wife's portrait, though laced with some individualizing characteristics, a quite traditional antifeminist satire against medieval middle-class women: their absurd dress, their love of pilgrimages, their sexuality. In the end Mann finds Alisoun to be "a typical woman whose feminine weaknesses are her strength as an estates representative" (127). Mann has almost nothing to say about the Wife of Bath's Prologue and Tale; she is interested, rather, in the satiric estates portrait of her in the General Prologue.

Some historical scholarship suggests that Chaucer's tale is a thinly veiled allegory. Some see it as political allegory. Michael Wilks, for example, in 1962 suggested that Chaucer was using the knight's rape of the maiden in the Wife of Bath's Tale and the knight's subsequent conversion to gentility as a direct message to Richard II to stop harming his people and to join in a legitimate "marriage" with them. A related, and much more influential, allegorical approach has come to be known as Christian or patristic exegesis. Scholars who engage in exegetical analysis of literary texts believe that Chaucer's poetry, if properly understood within the religious contexts of its own times, was almost entirely Christian and symbolic.

The landmark exegetical study of Chaucer is D. W. Robertson's 1962 *A Preface to Chaucer*. Robertson insists that the critic's job is to understand Chaucer as his contemporaries would have understood him. Specifically, we must understand that the pilgrims represent certain abstract qualities and that the meaning of their tales is more Christian than it may at first seem to readers who have not steeped themselves in the religious symbolism of the fourteenth century. For Robertson, Chaucer's Wife of Bath "is not a 'character' in the modern sense at all, but an elaborate iconographic figure" (330), "a literary personification of rampant 'femininity' or carnality" (321). Robertson finds it significant that the Wife of Bath has had five — rather than two, three, four, or six — husbands: "The five husbands . . . may be the laws of the first five ages, before the coming of Christ and the New Law" (321). Robertson goes on to say, however, that Alisoun's five husbands may reflect the five husbands of the Samaritan, whose devotion to her five senses in youth suggests that her senses ruled her like husbands. Robertson is explicit in insisting that Chaucer was in no sense a "modern" poet:

> The nature of Chaucer's literary art is thus quite different from that of more recent times. We admire psychological profundity, dramatic intensity, well-rounded characters, realism, and well-structured plot development in our own literature, and we naturally ascribe these same characteristics to Chaucer's narrative art in order to express our admiration for it. But such criteria are basically misleading when used in this way. They are inconsistent with fourteenth-century stylistic conventions. (276)

In the wake of the New Criticism and the assumption that each work of literature is a self-contained work of art that needs no external reference, this kind of historical scholarship fell into disrepute.

NEW CRITICAL APPROACHES

The scholar who has come to be associated more than anyone else with the New Critical view of Chaucer is E. Talbot Donaldson. In the preface to the second edition of *Chaucer's Poetry* (1975), Donaldson specifically challenges the historical critics both for obscuring the beauty of Chaucer's poetry and for deflecting readers' attention away from their enjoyment of that poetry. Donaldson suggests that a proper understanding of Chaucer depends on pleasure: "In reading poetry, understanding is dependent on pleasure and will diminish proportionately as pleasure does." To make that pleasure possible Donaldson insists that "historical considerations must not be permitted to detract from the reader's enjoyment of great poetry." Donaldson gives as succinct a statement of historical "close reading" methods of the New Criticism as we are likely to find: "I have been reluctant to invoke historical data from outside the poem to explain what is in it: [my] criticism is in general based firmly on the text" (iii–iv).

In his brief discussions of the Wife of Bath's Prologue and Tale, Donaldson emphasizes Alisoun's universal humanity rather than her historical womanliness but does so in language that sounds curiously sexist now: "Behind all the masculine forcefulness of the Wife's Prologue there lies a highly feminine sensitivity" (1077). Donaldson emphasizes finally neither her maleness nor her femaleness:

> The Wife ceases to be an enormously funny parody of a woman invented by woman-haters, ceases even to be a woman fascinating for her intense individuality, ceases in a way to be a woman at all, and becomes instead a high and gallant symbol of a humanity in which weakness and fortitude are inextricably mingled. (1076)

This unsexed Wife of Bath is, for Donaldson, a thing of artistic beauty.

Although I cite here only one New Critical scholar, Donaldson stands for a generation of Chaucerians who took it as their task to play down the historical context and to "close read" Chaucerian texts in an effort to discover not how Chaucer reflected the ideas and contexts of his own time and place, but why he rose above his time and speaks to human beings who know almost nothing of medieval ideas and contexts.

NEW HISTORICIST APPROACHES

After decades in which the New Criticism seemed to privilege literature by driving history out of literature classrooms and literary journals, history is now returning with increased vigor in the name of "new historicism." But this new historicism, as its name implies, is not merely the old historicism brought on again but is different. Rather than having us look at history for what light it sheds on literary works, the new historicism attempts to regard as literature texts and approaches traditionally viewed as very much outside of literature: sociological, anthropological, philosophical, and legal documents, for example. Rather than regarding such texts as inferior to literary art, new historicists call for a breaking down of the old barriers between art and other verbal expressions in a general effort to broaden cultural awareness. They call instead for a leveling of all oral and written expressions of an era.

One new historicist approach can be found in Paul Strohm's 1992 *Hochon's Arrow*. Strohm endeavors to break down the distinctions that have traditionally been made among literary, religious, political, and historical texts. He refuses in this book to centralize Chaucer as the special text around which all others are informing handmaidens but insists rather that other kinds of texts are just as interesting — indeed, just as "fictional" — as literary texts. Strohm makes almost no mention of Chaucer in *Hochon's Arrow*. He does have a section on the Wife of Bath, but he puts that section fourth in a chapter on "Treason in the Household." Other texts he discusses in the chapter are a 1352 statute on treason and a 1387 legal case in which a wife murdered her husband. Strohm discusses these texts not because they shed any particular light on the Wife of Bath, but because they are as interesting as Chaucer's text in depicting the treasonous wife. For Strohm, Alisoun is just another example of "an antagonist in a struggle that involved other fourteenth-century women across the middle stata of society who opposed male domination and who sought control of their own land and property" (144).

Another of the Chaucerian new historicists is Lee Patterson. Patterson's *Chaucer and the Subject of History* (1991) explores the "dialectic between an inward sense of selfhood — subjectivity — and the claims of the historical world" (11). The key question for Patterson is less "who is the Wife of Bath" in relationship to her psychological makeup than "what is the Wife of Bath" in relationship to history. Patterson suggests that because Chaucer himself was on the boundaries between several social classes — "not bourgeois, not noble, not clerical, he nonetheless participates in all three of these communities" (39) — he would have been particularly interested in the the Wife of Bath's discovery and definition of self within society. In an essay written for this volume (pp. 133–54), Patterson presents a somewhat different new historicist way of reading the wifehood of the Wife of Bath and the marriage in her tale.

MARXIST APPROACHES

Closely associated with the new historicist impulse in Chaucer criticism is the Marxist approach. Marxist critics would have us focus less on historical "contexts" than on that whole nexus of political, religious, and social views that inform both Chaucer's work and our responses to it. Marxist critics are generally concerned with the power relations among the various classes that make up society. The middle-class Wife of Bath, with her challenge to any authority based on gender, class, or religion, easily invites Marxist analyses. In 1973, for example, Dorothy Colmer calls the Wife a "representative of belligerent individualism among the less privileged classes, who is making this case against knightly pretensions and the whole idea of hereditary rank" (335). In 1975 Sheila Delany notes that the Wife of Bath has "thoroughly internalized the economic function of the bourgeoisie in reducing quintessentially human activity — love and the marriage relation — to commercial enterprise. She understands that as a woman she is both merchant and commodity: her youth and beauty the initial capital investment, and her age — the depreciation of the commodity — a condition against which she must accumulate profit as rapidly and therefore as exploitatively as possible" (105).

In 1986 two books reflecting Marxist approaches to Chaucer appeared. In one, Stephen Knight refers to the Wife of Bath as a "dissenting female industrialist" (103) who manages to escape "patriarchy and clerical oppression" (100). In the other, David Aers reminds us that surviving historical texts reflect almost entirely the dominant classes' version of history: the royal, manorial, governmental, military, urban, and ecclesiastical version. His thesis is that Chaucer in his poetry "works over ruling ideas, conventional pieties and the unexamined norms of official culture in a way that subjects them to processes of criticism" (3). When he speaks specifically of the Wife of Bath, Aers focuses on the economic and the power bases of her five marriages. He shows how "the practice and ethos of the market" (68) defines those marriages. Although she seems to accept the commodification of sex and love by unashamedly trading sex for "economic security" (69), Aers says that she at the same time seeks to overturn the standard dominance of husbands over their wives. Aers finds her to be satirizing the whole class structure that produced the system she has to work within.

In a Marxist reading of the Wife of Bath prepared for this volume (pp. 171–88), Laurie Finke shows that the Wife of Bath reflects the need to "breed capital" — a need that was a fact of life for many women in Chaucer's time. As a breeder of capital the Wife gives evidence to the growing importance of sexuality in the shift from a feudal to a capitalist economy.

PSYCHOLOGICAL APPROACHES

Almost from the beginning readers have tended to see the Wife of Bath as interesting psychologically. She is, after all, a contradictory character. She loves men but hates them. She strives for marriage but sees it as a battleground. She seems to like her fourth husband but is ready for a fifth even before the fourth dies. She loves her fifth husband the best but is more abused by him than by any of the others. She sees one of the purposes of marriage as procreation but seems to have had, in five marriages, no children. She thinks women should have sovereignty but seems not really to want it herself, or at least not for long. She tells a tale that seems both to condemn and to reward rapists. She shows both feminist and antifeminist tendencies and demonstrates characteristics usually associated with both males and females. It is almost impossible to read the Wife of Bath's performance, then, without either condemning Chaucer for portraying Alisoun so inconsistently or praising him for creating in her such a psychologically complex character that the apparent contradictions enrich her. Most psychoanalytic critics, of course, prefer to praise rather than to condemn Chaucer and work to explain the richly complex psychology of Alisoun.

Walter Clyde Curry, viewing the Wife of Bath from the standpoint of medieval science, explained her "dual personality" (91) as the result of her having been born under the conflicting signs of Mars, god of war, and Venus, goddess of love: "Chaucer's Wife of Bath is in some measure the living embodiment, both in form and in character, of mingled but still conflicting astral influences" (107). That more recent scholars have tended to read the Wife of Bath from the standpoint of modern psychological theory is no surprise. To do so is to see Alisoun as a complete human being, a person far more complex than a literary type or an astrological abstraction. From this view the apparent contradictions in her personality are really clues to her psychological complexity.

Some psychoanalytic critics see their work as a specific response to the New Criticism. Norman Holland, for example, rejects New Critical readings as "overly intellectual, even sterile, certainly far removed from the roots of our response" (280). Holland's reading is that the knight's fear of losing his head is actually a fear of symbolic castration and that his revulsion at his old bride is actually a revulsion at the notion of an oedipal union with the mother. The tale "starts with phallic, aggressive sexuality [the rape], regresses to a more primitive relation between taboo mother and passive son [the wedding], and finally progresses to genital mutuality [the wedding night]" (283). In telling such a story, Holland goes on, the Wife of Bath is "compensating for her own missing phallus" (283).

In a 1972 article on Chaucer critics who are in "blunderland," Beryl Rowland treats Alisoun as if she is a "deviate" (393) and her prologue and tale as if they are "a modern case history" (395) of such a person. Rowland speaks of Alisoun's "schizophrenic compulsion" (387), which drives her almost always in two directions at once. She seems to like men and sex and marriage, but "towards the men themselves, she shows only the deepest animosity and malice" (389). Why? Alisoun, says Rowland, had become sexually active by age twelve, and, "according to recent studies, precocious sexual experience may create in a woman a trauma which makes her hate all men, seek to get revenge on them, and try to dominate them" (391). In another article that same year Rowland suggested that "the timely death" of the Wife of Bath's fourth husband was neither accidental nor natural, but homicidal. In a 1978 article Donald B. Sands gives Alisoun a modern psychological label, "sociopath":

> She is not, it would seem, a psychotic, a schizophrenic, or a manic depressive — that is, a person suffering from personality disintegration and loss of contact with reality — but rather someone laboring under a character disorder which makes her acceptable to herself, but productive of conflict with others, a disorder which recent psychiatric tests label a sociopathic personality disturbance, an illness characterized by antisocial reaction, dyssocial reaction, and usually addiction (in Alys's case, probably to alcohol). (171)

Following Rowland, Sands concludes that Alisoun probably conspired with Jankyn to murder her fourth husband.

In an effort to apply the psychologist Carl Jung's theories of the myths that underlie most human experience, Eric D. Brown in 1976 sees the Wife of Bath's Tale as a reflection of "a seasonal myth and of a myth of personal, physical transformation" (303). Specifically, he sees the old woman on the forest green "as representative of the unconscious" and the young girl she is transformed into at the end "as representative of the more desirable conscious." Concurrently, the old woman represents "the dark death of winter and anomalous unconsciousness" and the young girl represents "light, fruitful spring and defined consciousness" (310). In a second article two years later

Brown finds, for example, that the twenty-four dancing women are "projections from the knight's psyche" (212), that the old woman they turn into represents his "inferior side," and that the rape represents "his shadow, the unknown unconsciousness" (214). Two later essays, both appearing in 1980, somewhat differently apply Jungian analysis to the Wife of Bath's performance. Michael Atkinson, using Jung's concept of the anima — the soul or source of life — finds that in the Wife of Bath's Tale "there is a development of femininity within the experience of the knight" (72), and D. W. Fritz finds that the Wife of Bath is possessed by "her masculine soul" and "projects her animus on the men in the world around her. . . . She does wish a marriage with God and the transformation from a loathly lady into a pure and untouched virgin. She desires to be whole" (176).

In an essay written for this volume (pp. 205–20), Louise O. Fradenburg gives a modern psychological reading of the fantasy elements in the Wife of Bath's Prologue and Tale, a reading informed not only by Freud but also by the contemporary French philosopher Jacques Lacan.

THE DRAMATIC THEORY

Closely related to the work of psychoanalytic critics is the work of critics who see the various tales as existing primarily to flesh out the characters of the various tellers. Indeed, one of the most influential critical approaches to the *Canterbury Tales* in the twentieth century is what has come to be called the "dramatic theory." According to this theory the tales are intimately and integrally connected with the various Canterbury tellers. Used in this connection the term "dramatic" refers to the notion that the tales in some sense reflect the personalities of the tellers. Indeed, the tales are to be considered as the speeches, soliloquies, or dramatic monologues of the tellers.

The landmark study advocating the dramatic theory was George Lyman Kittredge's 1915 *Chaucer and His Poetry*. Kittredge extended the notion of suitability of tale to teller to embrace the concept of what he called a "roadside drama." We must not, he said, read the tales as isolated works, any more than we would read a speech by Hamlet outside its dramatic context. And we should not read these tales as Chaucer's any more than we would read Hamlet's soliloquy as Shakespeare's.

The analogy with Shakespeare is pertinent. Kittredge was a well-known Harvard Shakespearean scholar when he wrote his book on Chaucer, so it is perhaps natural that he would read the *Canterbury Tales* as if it is a theatrical work. He calls the pilgrims the "dramatis personae" and the General Prologue the "first act" in Chaucer's "play" (155). Kittredge makes no apologies for seeing Chaucer as a kind of proto-Shakespeare. Indeed, one senses that by reading Chaucer as if he were Shakespeare, Kittredge meant to pay Chaucer the greatest compliment possible: "The stories are merely long speeches expressing, directly or indirectly, the characters of the several persons. They are more or less comparable, in this regard, to the soliloquies of Hamlet or Iago or Macbeth" (155).

The Wife of Bath's Prologue and Tale, then, together constitute for Kittredge a self-revealing soliloquy that expresses the Wife's views on marriage. We can thank Kittredge — or blame him, if we will — for the fact that much of the published scholarship on the Wife of Bath focuses more on her than on her tale, for in the dramatic theory the tale becomes little more than a speech that characterizes her. Furthermore, by suggesting that the prologue and tale constitute the opening contribution to a Marriage Group, Kittredge helped to focus much subsequent critical thinking about the Wife of Bath on her apparent thesis that wives should be dominant over their husbands. Other tellers, Kittredge suggested, then joined the debate. They expressed their disagreement with the Wife of Bath's thesis by telling tales reflecting their own views on marriage. The Clerk, for example, tells a tale showing that happiness results when husbands are dominant, and the Franklin follows with a tale demonstrating that in the ideal marriage husbands and wives must seek to revere, not dominate, one another.

Kittredge's most committed disciple was Robert M. Lumiansky. In his 1955 *Of Sondry Folk,* Lumiansky applied the theory of the dramatic principle not just generally, as Kittredge had, and not just to a few of the tellers where it fit most comfortably, but specifically to every one of the tales. Not surprisingly, for Lumiansky the Wife of Bath's Tale is among the tales most closely related to their tellers on the "movable stage" to Canterbury. It is an "internally motivated and extended self-revelation of which the teller is not fully aware" (248). For Lumiansky the tale of the rapist-turned-husband dramatically expresses the Wife's thesis about the sovereignty of women, but it further characterizes her by expressing views that she herself is unconscious of. Lumiansky finds, for example, that Alisoun's character is so richly complex that by her own behavior with her five husbands she violates the very principles she lays down in the old bride's pillow lecture on gentillesse.

A strong critic of the dramatic theory is Robert M. Jordan. In his 1967 *Chaucer and the Shape of Creation,* Jordan finds that the Wife of Bath, far from being a dramatically consistent character, lacks unity. Even if we look only at her prologue, we see in the Wife of Bath, according to Jordan, no fewer than three different women, each used by Chaucer not to express the feminist viewpoint that the dramatic critics find her to express but, on the contrary, Chaucer's own antifeminist opinions. Disagreeing with Kittredge that in the Wife of Bath "medieval feminism has had its say" (192), Jordan concludes that the Wife of Bath's Prologue is really "a dazzling victory for antifeminism" (226).

David Benson in *Chaucer's Drama of Style* (1986) has confronted most directly the Kittredge-Lumiansky dramatic theory of the relationship between the Canterbury stories and their tellers. Benson does not deny that there is sometimes a minimal and general suitability between tales and tellers, but he sees it as suitability between "social class and kind of tale" (3) rather than as between individual pilgrim and individual tale. Benson categorically rejects the methods and most of the conclusions of what he calls the "dramatic critics." He tries to undermine two fundamental tenets of the dramatic theory: first, that the tales can be interpreted through the personalities of the tellers and, second, that the tellers are characterized by their tales. The problem with the dramatic critics, he says, is their failure to recognize that the *Canterbury Tales* is first a collection of *tales.* Benson insists that the tellers, vivid and interesting though some may be, are of interest to Chaucer, and to us, only secondarily. "Dramatic critics," Benson tells us, "are condemned to pursue what is, at best, a less interesting and more unknowable question — the psychology of the pilgrim instead of the artistry of the tales" (11).

It is unfortunate that Benson says very little about the performance of the Wife of Bath, the character who more than any other seems to support the dramatic theory. He tells us only that her prologue is a "professional" rather than a "personal" confession (11) and that "only the most desperate arguments" can bring Alisoun's stated views on gentility in her tale into "accord with the Wife's portrait in the General Prologue or with the very different values in her own raucous prologue" (12).

Although a growing number of critics share Benson's skepticism about Kittredge's notion that the tales are to be read as dramatic monologues designed primarily to reveal information about their tellers, Benson's insistence on a "drama of style" has won only a limited following. Stated briefly, Benson's central thesis is that the various tales, quite apart from their tellers, not only are unique but offer contrasting poetic styles. Few disagree with that general thesis, but some wonder why Benson, having eliminated the fictional pilgrims as meaningful tellers of the various tales, feels the need to replace them with what he calls "many poets" (20). Benson does not deny that "Chaucer and only Chaucer wrote all of the tales," but he finds that there are as many different Chaucers as there are tales because Chaucer has gone to great lengths "to create a distinct and consistent artistry for each tale." Benson is quite definite about this matter: "Chaucer turns himself into a new poet for each tale" (20–21).

In addition to taking issue with the notion that the tales are designed to characterize the tellers, contemporary critics are increasingly skeptical of Kittredge's notion that the Wife of Bath initiates a Marriage Group including the tales of the Clerk and the Franklin. We still see references to an "argument" or "debate" among these pilgrims. But as textual scholars are emphasizing more and more the fragmentary and unfinished nature of the *Canterbury Tales,* there is growing doubt about whether the "debaters," whose tales appear in three disconnected fragments, would have been sufficiently close to one another in any final sequencing of the projected one hundred twenty tales that any readers would have picked up on the debate. Scholars who seek to make connections between tales are starting to pay attention to the three tales in Fragment III (Group D) — the Wife of Bath's, the Friar's, and the Summoner's. A number of issues connect the three, but domination in marriage is not one of them. See, for example Blake (1982), Wasserman, and Cooper.

THE DRAMATIC THEORY REVIVED

That the dramatic theory is not so much dead as merely altered is shown by several recent books. Some scholars remind us that Chaucer wrote before literacy and printed books made silent reading the standard means for receiving literature. Chaucer read his works aloud, either to the court or to other groups gathered for the purpose of being entertained or edified by story. Some critics are beginning to redefine what the term "dramatic" means in Chaucer studies. Influenced by the ideas of the Russian thinker Mikhail Bakhtin, Laura Kendrick in *Chaucerian Play: Comedy and Control in the Canterbury Tales* (1988)

sees the drama of the *Canterbury Tales* as a kind of "carnival" mixture
of voices that help to give springtime release to the social tensions that
have developed through the year. The Canterbury carnival becomes in
her view a safe way for the lower-class pilgrims to criticize the nobles:
"Chaucer's problem," Kendrick says, "was the instability of late-
fourteenth-century English society. His solution was the play of the
Canterbury Tales, in which a group of pilgrims, representative of
major classes and estates of contemporary society, led by a Lord of
Misrule, engage in a festive, springtime game of storytelling, a game
that temporarily, intermittently subverts the piety of pilgrimage and
the hierarchy of real life and enables many of the churls to express
their aggression and frustrated rivalry against gentles or against other
churls, harmlessly" (128; see also 156). A key word in that passage is
"play," because Kendrick uses it to refer not merely to play as inno-
cent and joyous activity but also, more specifically, to play as drama.
In carnival, after all, we have theater without footlights, theater in
which the audience joins the players in having fun.

In the *Canterbury Tales* the Host is the lord of a playful misrule,
and the pilgrims are both players and audience. The Wife of Bath's
contribution to this Bakhtinian dialogic interchange is, under protec-
tion of the carnivalesque pilgrimage, to preach an "inversion of the
paternal hierarchy" by telling a fiction in which "a female version
of . . . gentility, permanently replaces paternal authority" (124). Al-
isoun's revolutionary ideas are protected by the festive pilgrimage in
which it is, at least temporarily, quite all right for a low-class miller to
challenge the high-class knight and for an oppressed woman to chal-
lenge patriarchy. This "play" is not, of course, quite the "drama" that
Kittredge spoke of, though for both the road to Canterbury becomes
a kind of movable performance area. In Kendrick's thinking the role
of Chaucer is more paramount. She reminds us that Chaucer himself
would have been the reader or "*performer* of the text — that is, the
jongleur who performed it orally or the scribe who performed it in
writing" (136). Kendrick's notion that as Chaucer recited his various
works actors may have simultaneously mimed the actions he was de-
scribing has not been generously received.

In a variation on the dramatic theory, Leonard Michael Koff in his
Chaucer and the Art of Storytelling (1988) reminds us that Chaucer
was a performer, a man who stood and recited or "declaimed" the
Canterbury stories. At times he might have recited them as if they
were his own; at other times he might have taken on the performing
role of one of the Canterbury pilgrims, such as the Wife of Bath. What

we have in such performances, Koff tells us, is not a "roadside drama" or a "moving stage" in which actors are giving speeches but "the coherent and intrusive presence of a live performer presenting his illusion of real-life scenes" (15). Chaucer would have interacted with his audience, played off their silence and laughter, gestured to them with his eyes and arms, modulated his voice.

Koff makes a useful distinction between stage theater and oral performance: "Medieval declamation was not drama, even in a medieval sense. Unlike a play, which can stage our illusions, . . . a live performance, by its very nature, always works against our illusions. However convincing a performer is, he cannot escape our eyes, nor does he try to" (68). The job of the performer, rather than to act as on a stage, is to create through voice, gesture, and story a kind of imaginary stage in the listeners' mind on which they see characters as they hear the story told. Koff finds particularly engaging the notion of Chaucer or some other performer reading the Wife of Bath's Prologue and Tale. He suggests that a male performer reading the piece would do so quite differently from a female performer. And yet, because of her somewhat androgynous sexuality, her puzzling mixture of the feminine and the masculine, we can all, in reading the tale, in imaginatively "performing" it as we read it, find a comfortable place in it: "Chaucer's Wife of Bath seems deeply accessible and awakening. Her sexuality has the kind of androgyny that engages in men and women the constellation of sexual and social signatures we distinguish as masculine and feminine" (134).

A rather different modern-day dramatic approach to the *Canterbury Tales* is to be found in H. Marshall Leicester's *The Disenchanted Self* (1990). Leicester allies himself firmly not only with Kittredge but also with Jacques Derrida, the contemporary French philosopher commonly viewed as the founder of the critical approach known as deconstruction. Leicester puts his own deconstructive spin on the dramatic theory by insisting that we should not look at the portrait of the Wife of Bath in the General Prologue and then see whether her tale supports or deepens the character we find there. Rather, we should seek in the texts of the Wife of Bath information about the "disenchanted self" that is Alisoun.

For Leicester the Wife of Bath is not the enchanted or magical or mystified subject of a work of art but a fully humanized and highly accessible social construction. Kittredge, Leicester argues, got it backwards in saying that the Wife of Bath creates the texts known as her prologue and tale; rather, those texts create her, tell us all that we need to know about her. Of *course* the tale of the young knight and the old woman of the forest fits the Wife of Bath, because she reveals in that text who *she* is. But any other tale would have fit her just as well because in the act of telling it she would have characterized herself as the sort of person who *would* tell it. The point is not that "preexisting persons create language" but that "language creates people" (10). In a fully deconstructive analysis of the Wife of Bath's performance written for this volume (pp. 234–54), Leicester takes us well beyond the issues of dramatic reading I have been discussing here.

FEMINIST APPROACHES

Perhaps the most vibrant of the various contemporary readings of the Wife of Bath and her tale exemplify feminist approaches — plural because no one approach can be identified as *the* feminist way of reading the Wife of Bath's performance. So clearly are the Wife of Bath's Prologue and Tale the products of a female narrator that critics of almost every persuasion make reference either to her "feminism" or to her "antifeminism." But even if we limit ourselves to critics who call themselves feminists or who claim to discuss feminism, there is surprisingly little agreement on anything except that the Wife, her prologue, and her tale are rich, memorable, and enduring.

We must resist the assumption that recent feminist readings of the Wife of Bath's performance automatically find Chaucer to be an antifeminist. In her 1989 *Chaucer's Sexual Poetics,* for example, Carolyn Dinshaw has much to say about "patriarchal thinking" and "reading like a man," but she praises Chaucer for reminding us of the limitations of such thinking and reading: "The Wife thus articulates the happy possibility of reforming the patriarchal and fundamentally misogynistic hermeneutic . . . to make it accommodate the feminine" (116). Although as a medieval male Chaucer inevitably shares many of the masculine views of his age, he at least allows us, through the Wife of Bath, to "imagine" (117) feminine desire, feminist readings, and the reform of patriarchy.

Priscilla Martin in *Chaucer's Women: Nuns, Wives, and Amazons* (1990) celebrates not Chaucer's limitations in portraying women but his success at capturing their richness and diversity. Martin especially likes the Wife of Bath:

> The Wife of Bath shares [Chaucer's] delight in fictional and narrative diversity. . . . Of the pilgrims she is closest to Chaucer. Like her creator, she criticizes through comedy, she weighs authority

against experience and experience against authority, she is aware of the sexuality in textuality and she jollily subverts the conventions of male authorship. (217)

Jill Mann in her 1991 *Geoffrey Chaucer* gives a feminist reading of the work of a male writer. She insists that Chaucer is very much on the side of women. Virtually all of the positive role models he presents in his work are women, and his male characters are notoriously flawed:

> If feminism has a contribution to make to Chaucer studies, it is not because it reveals what Chaucer did not consider or left to one side or was prevented by his historical position from perceiving; it is rather that it enables us to see the full significance of what is already there in his text. It makes it possible, for instance, to register so simple a fact as that the *Canterbury Tales,* for all its rich variety of mode and genre, contains not a single example of the story-type that embodies its ideals in the central figure of a male hero. Instead, the tales that mediate serious ideals are focused on a series of women: Constance, Griselda, Prudence, and Cecilia. (3–4)

In Mann's view the Wife of Bath's Prologue effectively undercuts the antifeminism that Alisoun finds so demeaning, while her tale effectively condemns a knight's rape of a young woman by insisting that the knight must submit to the authority of a woman by the end of the tale.

Even feminist critics who see limitations in Chaucer often tend to apologize for them. In a 1991 article Susan K. Hagen questions why the Wife (or Chaucer) notes the "discrepancy of character that allows an apparently strong-willed female speaker to give a rude, aggressive, and insensitive male character [the rapist] his heart's desire" (106) by rewarding him with a lovely young bride, but she quickly forgives Chaucer for having had, really, no choice. He was, after all, a "fourteenth-century male poet of privilege" (105): "While one might hold Chaucer responsible within his limitations, one ought not blame him for them. Even if his experiment in feminist hermeneutics is inchoate, he was thwarted by limitations that his critics are beginning to grow beyond only now, six hundred years later" (119).

This gentle feminism, however, is answered by a less forgiving feminism in Elaine Tuttle Hansen's 1992 *Chaucer and the Fictions of Gender.* Hansen is distressed that Chaucer allows the Wife of Bath, who seems to want to challenge the medieval antifeminist rejection of women, in the end to accept it. Hansen is troubled that the old woman of the forest green rewards the rapist knight by giving him a young, lovely, and obedient woman for his marriage bed. The Wife of

Bath, Hansen insists, is the product of a male poet who creates "a feminine monstrosity who is the product of the masculine imagination against which she ineffectively and only superficially rebels" (35). As for those who apologize for Chaucer's limitations as a writer about women, Hansen asserts that those apologies grow out of a desire to adulate one of the literary heroes of our culture by refusing to call him what he was — a man who failed to understand and depict fairly half of humanity.

Hansen divides the history of Chaucer criticism on the Wife of Bath into "three political ages: the prefeminist, the feminist, and the postfeminist" (40). The first, prefeminist era, which started in Chaucer's time and endured well into the second half of this century, is "blatantly sexist." It saw the creator of the Wife of Bath as a "literary hero, a great, wise, godlike creator of characters whose human foibles he captures and exposes, be it lovingly or sternly" (41). In the second, or feminist, era, which began in the 1970s, critics began to see Chaucer as a male writer who did not understand women very well and could not, try as he may have done, rise above the antifeminism of his age. The third, or postfeminist, era began in the 1980s. In this third era Hansen sees too many male critics turning away from the issues raised by feminism because they admit that they, being males, cannot really understand those issues. Hansen finds this postfeminist era particularly troubling because she fears that it will further exclude women readers and critics from the Chaucer club — will once again marginalize them, push them off to the side of Chaucer scholarship. That scholarship, she fears, will once again be dominated by male critics celebrating a male author. Hansen fears that "the scholarly community, along with much of the real world, will return easily and quietly to the prefeminist status quo, where there is no place for the woman reader and critic of Chaucer" (46). In an essay written for this volume (pp. 273–89), Hansen elaborates further on her view that the Wife of Bath is the product of a male writer who reproduces and reinforces male attitudes.

I close this brief review of the history of the criticism on the Wife of Bath's performance by stating that I am of several minds about what has happened to scholarship on one of my favorite literary characters. I am distressed that so many complex interpretations are written about a Chaucerian character who had, for all her famous garrulity, relatively little to say herself. For every word she said in her prologue and tale, I estimate that upwards of five hundred words have been written about her in this century. I am delighted, however, that my favorite writer can sustain such a detailed and varied critical scrutiny. I am distressed that so much Chaucer criticism is now scrambling to distance itself from the approaches that were gospel when I began life as a critic. Still, I am delighted that the richness of new approaches suggests that Chaucer wrote so enduringly and for so wide an audience that scholars six hundred years later are still finding new ways to read him. I am puzzled to discover that it is not currently in fashion for scholars to speak of Chaucer's artistry. I am pleased nevertheless to note that a lesser artist than Chaucer would long ago have joined his contemporaries by slipping into obscurity. Chaucer has not slipped into obscurity, and creations like the Wife of Bath suggest that there is no reason to believe he ever will.

Peter G. Beidler

WORKS CITED

Aers, David. *Chaucer.* Atlantic Highlands: Humanities, 1986.

Atkinson, Michael. "Soul's Time and Transformations: The Wife of Bath's Tale." *Southern Review* 13 (1980): 72–78.

Benson, C. David. *Chaucer's Drama of Style: Poetic Variety and Contrast in the Canterbury Tales.* Chapel Hill: U of North Carolina P, 1986.

Benson, Larry D., ed. *The Riverside Chaucer.* 3rd ed. Boston: Houghton, 1987.

Blake, N. F. *The Textual Tradition of the Canterbury Tales.* London: Edward Arnold, 1985.

———. "The Wife of Bath and Her Tale." *Leeds Studies in English* 13 (1982): 42–55.

Bloomfield, Morton W. "Contemporary Literary Theory and Chaucer." *New Perspectives in Chaucer Criticism.* Ed. Donald M. Rose. Norman: Pilgrim, 1981. 23–36.

Brown, Eric D. "Symbols of Transformation: A Specific Archetypal Examination of the *Wife of Bath's Tale.*" *Chaucer Review* 12 (1978): 202–17.

———. "Transformation and the *Wife of Bath's Tale:* A Jungian Discussion." *Chaucer Review* 10 (1976): 303–15.

Bryan, W. F., and Germaine Dempster, eds. *Sources and Analogues of Chaucer's Canterbury Tales.* Chicago: U of Chicago P, 1941. New York: Humanities, 1958.

Colmer, Dorothy. "Character and Class in the *Wife of Bath's Tale*." *Journal of English and Germanic Philology* 72 (1973): 329–39.

Cooper, Helen. "Fragment III(D): The Wife of Bath (twice), Friar, and Summoner." *The Structure of the Canterbury Tales*. London: Duckworth, 1983. 124–34.

Coulton, G. G. *Chaucer and His England*. London: Methuen, 1908.

Curry, Walter Clyde. *Chaucer and the Mediaeval Sciences*. New York: Oxford UP, 1926. New York: Barnes, 1960.

Delany, Sheila. "Sexual Economics, Chaucer's Wife of Bath and *The Book of Margery Kempe*." *Minnesota Review* 5 (1975): 104–15. Rpt. in *Woman Writing*. New York: Schocken, 1983. 76–92.

Dinshaw, Carolyn. *Chaucer's Sexual Poetics*. Madison: U of Wisconsin P, 1989.

Donaldson, E. Talbot, ed. *Chaucer's Poetry: An Anthology for the Modern Reader*. New York: Ronald, 1958 (2nd ed., 1975).

Eisner, Sigmund. *A Tale of Wonder: A Source Study of the Wife of Bath's Tale*. Wexford: John English, 1957.

Fritz, D. W. "The Animus-Possessed Wife of Bath." *Journal of Analytical Psychology* 25 (1980): 163–80.

Hagen, Susan K. "The Wife of Bath: Chaucer's Inchoate Experiment in Feminist Hermeneutics." *Rebels and Rivals: The Contestive Spirit in The Canterbury Tales*. Ed. Susanna Greer Fein, David Raybin, and Peter C. Braeger. Kalamazoo: Medieval Institute, 1991.

Hansen, Elaine Tuttle. *Chaucer and the Fictions of Gender*. Berkeley: U of California P, 1992.

Holland, Norman N. "Meaning as Transformation: The Wife of Bath's Tale." *College English* 28 (1967): 279–90.

Jordan, Robert M. *Chaucer and the Shape of Creation*. Cambridge: Harvard UP, 1967.

Kendrick, Laura. *Chaucerian Play: Comedy and Control in the Canterbury Tales*. Berkeley: U of California P, 1988.

Kennedy, Beverly. "The Variant Passages in the Wife of Bath's Prologue and the Textual Transmission of the *Canterbury Tales*." *Women, the Book and the Worldly*. Ed. Lesley Smith and Jane H. M. Taylor. Cambridge: D. S. Brewer, 1995. 85–101.

Kittredge, George Lyman. *Chaucer and His Poetry*. 1915. Cambridge: Harvard UP, 1963.

Knight, Stephen. *Geoffrey Chaucer*. Oxford: Basil Blackwell, 1986.

Koff, Leonard Michael. *Chaucer and the Art of Storytelling*. Berkeley: U of California P, 1988.

Leicester, H. Marshall, Jr. *The Disenchanted Self: Representing the Subject in the Canterbury Tales.* Berkeley: U of California P, 1990.

Lowell, James Russell. "Chaucer." *The Writings of James Russell Lowell.* Vol. 3. Cambridge: Riverside, 1870. 291–366.

Lumiansky, R. M. *Of Sondry Folk: The Dramatic Principle in the Canterbury Tales.* Austin: U of Texas P, 1955.

Manly, John M. *Some New Light on Chaucer.* New York: Holt, 1926. Gloucester: Peter Smith, 1959.

Manly, John M., and Edith Rickert, eds. *The Text of the Canterbury Tales.* 8 vols. Chicago: U of Chicago P, 1940.

Mann, Jill. *Chaucer and Medieval Estates Satire: The Literature of Social Class and the General Prologue to the Canterbury Tales.* Cambridge: Cambridge UP, 1973.

———. *Geoffrey Chaucer.* Feminist Readings Series. Atlantic Highlands: Humanities, 1991.

Martin, Priscilla. *Chaucer's Women: Nuns, Wives, and Amazons.* Iowa City: U of Iowa P, 1990.

Maynadier, G. H. *The Wife of Bath's Tale: Its Sources and Analogues.* London: D. Nutt, 1901.

North, J. D. *Chaucer's Universe.* Oxford: Clarendon, 1988.

Patterson, Lee. *Chaucer and the Subject of History.* Madison: U of Wisconsin P, 1991.

Pratt, Robert A. "The Development of the Wife of Bath." *Studies in Medieval Literature in Honor of Professor Albert Croll Baugh.* Ed. MacEdward Leach. Philadelphia: U of Pennsylvania P, 1961. 45–79.

Rickert, Edith. *Chaucer's World.* New York: Columbia UP, 1948.

Robertson, D. W., Jr. *A Preface to Chaucer: Studies in Medieval Perspectives.* Princeton: Princeton UP, 1962.

———. "Some Observations on Method in Literary Studies." *New Directions in Literary History.* Ed. Ralph Cohen. Baltimore: Johns Hopkins UP, 1974.

Robinson, F. N., ed. *The Works of Geoffrey Chaucer.* 2nd ed. Boston: Houghton, 1957.

Root, Robert K. *The Poetry of Chaucer: A Guide to Its Study and Appreciation.* Boston: Houghton, 1927. Gloucester: Peter Smith, 1957.

Rowland, Beryl. "Chaucer's Dame Alys: Critics in Blunderland?" *Neuphilologische Mitteilungen* 73 (1972): 381–95.

———. "On the Timely Death of the Wife of Bath's Fourth Husband." *Archiv fur das Studium der Neuren Sprachen und Literaturen* 209 (1972): 273–82.

Ruggiers, Paul G., ed. *Editing Chaucer: The Great Tradition*. Norman: U of Oklahoma P, 1984.

Sands, Donald B. "The Non-Comic, Non-Tragic Wife: Chaucer's Dame Alys as Sociopath." *Chaucer Review* 12 (1978): 171–82.

Stephens, John, and Marcella Ryan. "Metafictional Strategies and the Theme of Sexual Power in the Wife of Bath's and Franklin's Tales." *Nottingham Medieval Studies* 33 (1989): 56–75.

Strohm, Paul. *Hochon's Arrow: The Social Imagination of Fourteenth-Century Texts*. Princeton: Princeton UP, 1992.

Tatlock, John S. P. *The Development and Chronology of Chaucer's Works*. London: Chaucer Society, 1907. Gloucester: Peter Smith, 1963.

Wasserman, Julian N. "The Ideal and the Actual: The Philosophical Unity of the *Canterbury Tales*, MS. Group III." *Allegorica* 7 (1982): 65–99.

Whiting, Bartlett J. "The Wife of Bath's Prologue" and "The Wife of Bath's Tale." *Sources and Analogues of Chaucer's Canterbury Tales*. Ed. W. F. Bryan and Germaine Dempster. Chicago: U of Chicago P, 1941. New York: Humanities, 1958.

Wilks, Michael. "Chaucer and the Mystical Marriage in Medieval Political Thought." *Bulletin of the John Rylands Library* 44 (1962): 489–530.

Wood, Chauncey. *Chaucer and the Country of the Stars*. Princeton: Princeton UP, 1970.

The New Historicism
and
the Wife of Bath

WHAT IS THE NEW HISTORICISM?

The title of Brook Thomas's *The New Historicism and Other Old-Fashioned Topics* (1991) is telling. Whenever an emergent theory, movement, method, approach, or group gets labeled with the adjective "new," trouble is bound to ensue, for what is new today is either established, old, or forgotten tomorrow. Few of you will have heard of the band called The New Kids on the Block. New Age book shops and jewelry may seem "old hat" by the time this introduction is published. The New Criticism, or formalism, is just about the oldest approach to literature and literary study currently being practiced. The new historicism, by contrast, is *not* as old-fashioned as formalism, but it is hardly new, either. The term "new" eventually and inevitably requires some explanation. In the case of the new historicism, the best explanation is historical.

Although a number of influential critics working between 1920 and 1950 wrote about literature from a psychoanalytic perspective, the majority took what might generally be referred to as the historical approach. With the advent of the New Criticism, however, historically oriented critics almost seemed to disappear from the face of the earth. The dominant New Critics, or formalists, tended to treat literary works as if they were self-contained, self-referential objects. Rather than basing their interpretations on parallels between the text and historical contexts (such as the author's life or stated intentions in writing the work), these critics concentrated on the relationships *within* the text that give it its form and meaning. During the heyday of the New Criticism, concern about the interplay between literature and history virtually disappeared from literary discourse. In its place was a concern about intratextual repetition, particularly of images or symbols but also of rhythms and sound effects.

About 1970 the New Criticism came under attack by reader-response critics (who believe that the meaning of a work is not inherent in its internal form but rather is cooperatively produced by the reader and the text) and poststructuralists (who, following the philosophy of Jacques Derrida, argue that texts are inevitably self-contradictory and that we can find form in them only by ignoring or suppressing conflicting details or elements). In retrospect it is clear that, their outspoken opposition to the New Criticism notwithstanding, the reader-response critics and poststructuralists of the 1970s were very much *like* their formalist predecessors in two important respects: for the most part, they ignored the world beyond the text and its reader, and, for the most part, they ignored the historical contexts within which literary works are written and read.

Jerome McGann first articulated this retrospective insight in 1985, writing that "a text-only approach has been so vigorously promoted during the last thirty-five years that most historical critics have been driven from the field, and have raised the flag of their surrender by yielding the title 'critic,' and accepting the title 'scholar' for themselves" (*Inflections* 17). Most, but not all. The American Marxist Fredric Jameson had begun his 1981 book *The Political Unconscious* with the following two-word challenge: "Always historicize!" (9). Beginning about 1980, a form of historical criticism practiced by Louis Montrose and Stephen Greenblatt had transformed the field of Renaissance studies and begun to influence the study of American and English Romantic literature as well. And by the mid-1980s, Brook Thomas was working on an essay in which he suggests that classroom discussions of Keats's "Ode on a Grecian Urn" might begin with questions such as the following: Where would Keats have seen such an urn? How did a Grecian urn end up in a museum in England? Some very important historical and political realities, Thomas suggests, lie behind and inform Keats's definitions of art, truth, beauty, the past, and timelessness.

When McGann lamented the surrender of "most historical critics," he no doubt realized what is now clear to everyone involved in the study of literature. Those who had *not* yet surrendered — had not yet "yield[ed] the title 'critic'" to the formalist, reader-response, and poststructuralist "victors" — were armed with powerful new arguments and intent on winning back long-lost ground. Indeed, at about the same time that McGann was deploring the near-complete dominance of critics advocating the text-only approach, Herbert Lindenberger was sounding a more hopeful note: "It comes as something of a surprise," he wrote in 1984, "to find that history is making a powerful comeback" (16).

We now know that history was indeed making a powerful comeback in the 1980s, although the word is misleading if it causes us to imagine that the historical criticism being practiced in the 1980s by Greenblatt and Montrose, McGann and Thomas, was the same as the historical criticism that had been practiced in the 1930s and 1940s. Indeed, if the word "new" still serves any useful purpose in defining the historical criticism of today, it is in distinguishing it from the old historicism. The new historicism is informed by the poststructuralist and reader-response theory of the 1970s, plus the thinking of feminist, cultural, and Marxist critics whose work was also "new" in the 1980s. New historicist critics are less fact- and event-oriented than historical critics used to be, perhaps because they have come to wonder whether the truth about what really happened can ever be purely and objectively known. They are less likely to see history as linear and progressive, as something developing toward the present or the future ("teleological"), and they are also less likely to think of it in terms of specific eras, each with a definite, persistent, and consistent *Zeitgeist* ("World Spirit"). Consequently, they are unlikely to suggest that a literary text has a single or easily identifiable historical context.

New historicist critics also tend to define the discipline of history more broadly than it was defined before the advent of formalism. They view history as a social science and the social sciences as being properly historical. In *Historical Studies and Literary Criticism* (1985), McGann speaks of the need to make "sociohistorical" subjects and methods central to literary studies; in *The Beauty of Inflections: Literary Investigations in Historical Method and Theory* (1985), he links sociology and the future of historical criticism. "A sociological poetics," he writes, "must be recognized not only as relevant to the analysis of poetry, but in fact as central to the analysis" (62). Lindenberger cites anthropology as particularly useful in the new historical analysis of literature, especially anthropology as practiced by Victor Turner and Clifford Geertz.

Geertz, who has related theatrical traditions in nineteenth-century Bali to forms of political organization that developed during the same period, has influenced some of the most important critics writing the new kind of historical criticism. Due in large part to Geertz's anthropological influence, new historicists such as Greenblatt have asserted that literature is not a sphere apart or distinct from the history that is relevant to it. That is what the old criticism tended to do: present the background information you needed to know before you could fully appreciate the separate world of art. The new historicists have used what Geertz would call "thick description" to blur distinctions, not only between history and the other social sciences but also between background and foreground, historical and literary materials, political and poetical events. They have erased the old boundary line dividing historical and literary materials, showing that the production of one of Shakespeare's historical plays was a political act and a historical event, while at the same time showing that the coronation of Elizabeth I was carried out with the same care for staging and symbol lavished on works of dramatic art.

In addition to breaking down barriers that separate literature and history, history and the social sciences, new historicists have reminded us that it is treacherously difficult to reconstruct the past as it really was, rather than as we have been conditioned by our own place and time to believe that it was. And they know that the job is utterly impossible for those who are unaware of that difficulty and insensitive to the bent or bias of their own historical vantage point. Historical criticism must be "conscious of its status as interpretation," Greenblatt has written (*Renaissance* 4). McGann obviously concurs, writing that "historical criticism can no longer make any part of [its] sweeping picture unselfconsciously, or treat any of its details in an untheorized way" (*Studies* 11).

Unselfconsciously and *untheorized* are the key words in McGann's statement. When new historicist critics of literature describe a historical change, they are highly conscious of, and even likely to discuss, the *theory* of historical change that informs their account. They know that the changes they happen to see and describe are the ones that their theory of change allows or helps them to see and describe. And they know, too, that their theory of change is historically determined. They seek to minimize the distortion inherent in their perceptions and representations by admitting that they see through preconceived notions; in other words, they learn to reveal the color of the lenses in the glasses that they wear.

Nearly everyone who wrote on the new historicism during the 1980s cited the importance of the late Michel Foucault. A French philosophical historian who liked to think of himself as an archaeologist of human knowledge, Foucault brought together incidents and phenomena from areas of inquiry and orders of life that we normally regard as being unconnected. As much as anyone, he encouraged the new historicist critic of literature to redefine the boundaries of historical inquiry.

Foucault's views of history were influenced by the philosopher Friedrich Nietzsche's concept of a *wirkliche* ("real" or "true") history that is neither melioristic (that is, "getting better all the time") nor metaphysical. Like Nietzsche, Foucault didn't see history in terms of a continuous development toward the present. Neither did he view it as an abstraction, idea, or ideal, as something that began "In the beginning" and that will come to THE END, a moment of definite closure, a Day of Judgment. In his own words, Foucault "abandoned [the old history's] attempts to understand events in terms of . . . some great evolutionary process" (*Discipline and Punish* 129). He warned a new generation of historians to be aware of the fact that investigators are themselves "situated." It is difficult, he reminded them, to see present cultural practices critically from within them, and because of the same cultural practices, it is extremely difficult to enter bygone ages. In *Discipline and Punish: The Birth of the Prison* (1975), Foucault admitted that his own interest in the past was fueled by a passion to write the history of the present.

Like Marx, Foucault saw history in terms of power, but his view of power probably owed more to Nietzsche than to Marx. Foucault seldom viewed power as a repressive force. He certainly did not view it as a tool of conspiracy used by one specific individual or institution against another. Rather, power represents a whole web or complex of forces; it is that which produces what happens. Not even a tyrannical aristocrat simply wields power, for the aristocrat is himself formed and empowered by a network of discourses and practices that constitute power. Viewed by Foucault, power is "positive and productive," not "repressive" and "prohibitive" (Smart 63). Furthermore, no historical event, according to Foucault, has a single cause; rather, it is intricately connected with a vast web of economic, social, and political factors.

A brief sketch of one of Foucault's major works may help clarify some of his ideas. *Discipline and Punish* begins with a shocking but accurate description of the public drawing and quartering of a Frenchman who had botched his attempt to assassinate King Louis XV in 1757. Foucault proceeds by describing rules governing the daily life of modern Parisian felons. What happened to torture, to punishment as public spectacle? he asks. What complex network of forces made it disappear? In working toward a picture of this "power," Foucault turns up many interesting puzzle pieces, such as the fact that in the early years of the nineteenth century, crowds would sometimes identify with the prisoner and treat the executioner as if *he* were the guilty party. But Foucault sets forth a related reason for keeping prisoners alive, moving punishment indoors, and changing discipline from physical torture into mental rehabilitation: colonization. In this historical period, people were needed to establish colonies and trade, and prisoners could be used for that purpose. Also, because these were politically unsettled times, governments needed infiltrators and informers. Who better to fill those roles than prisoners pardoned or released early for showing a willingness to be rehabilitated? As for rehabilitation itself, Foucault compares it to the old form of punishment, which began with a torturer extracting a confession. In more modern, "reasonable" times, psychologists probe the minds of prisoners with a scientific rigor that Foucault sees as a different kind of torture, a kind that our modern perspective does not allow us to see as such.

Thus, a change took place, but perhaps not as great a change as we generally assume. It may have been for the better or for the worse; the point is that agents of power didn't make the change because mankind is evolving and, therefore, more prone to perform goodhearted deeds. Rather, different objectives arose, including those of a new class of doctors and scientists bent on studying aberrant examples of the human mind. And where do we stand vis-à-vis the history Foucault tells? We are implicated by it, for the evolution of discipline as punishment into the study of the human mind includes the evolution of the "disciplines" as we now understand that word, including the discipline of history, the discipline of literary study, and now a discipline that is neither and both, a form of historical criticism that from the vantage point of the 1980s looked "new."

Foucault's type of analysis has been practiced by a number of literary critics at the vanguard of the back-to-history movement. One of them is Greenblatt, who along with Montrose was to a great extent responsible for transforming Renaissance studies in the early 1980s and revitalizing historical criticism in the process. Greenblatt follows Foucault's lead in interpreting literary devices as if they were continuous with all other representational devices in a culture; he therefore turns to scholars in other fields in order to better understand the workings of literature. "We wall off literary symbolism from the symbolic structures operative elsewhere," he writes, "as if art alone were a human creation, as if humans themselves were not, in Clifford Geertz's phrase, cultural artifacts" (*Renaissance* 4).

Greenblatt's name, more than anyone else's, is synonymous with the new historicism; his essay entitled "Invisible Bullets" (1981) has been said by Patrick Brantlinger to be "perhaps the most frequently cited example of New Historicist Work" (Brantlinger 45). An English professor at the University of California, Berkeley — the early academic home of the new historicism — Greenblatt was a founding editor of *Representations,* a journal published by the University of California Press that is still considered today to be *the* mouthpiece of the new historicism.

In *Learning to Curse* (1990), Greenblatt cites as central to his own intellectual development his decision to interrupt his literary education at Yale University by accepting a Fulbright fellowship to study in England at Cambridge University. There he came under the influence of the great Marxist cultural critic Raymond Williams, who made Greenblatt realize how much — and what — was missing from his Yale education. "In Williams's lectures," Greenblatt writes, "all that had been carefully excluded from the literary criticism in which I had been trained — who controlled access to the printing press, who owned the land and the factories, whose voices were being repressed as well as represented in literary texts, what social strategies were being served by the aesthetic values we constructed — came pressing back in upon the act of interpretation" (2).

Greenblatt returned to the United States determined not to exclude such matters from his own literary investigations. Blending what he had learned from Williams with poststructuralist thought about the indeterminacy or "undecidability" of meaning, he eventually developed a critical method that he now calls "cultural poetics." More tentative and less overtly political than cultural criticism, it involves what Thomas calls "the technique of montage. Starting with the analysis of a particular historical event, it cuts to the analysis of a particular literary text. The point is not to show that the literary text reflects the historical event but to create a field of energy between the two so that we come to see the event as a social text and the literary text as a social event" ("New Literary Historicism" 490). Alluding to deconstructor Jacques Derrida's assertion that "there is nothing outside the text," Montrose explains that the goal of this new historicist criticism is to show the "historicity of texts and the textuality of history" (Veeser 20).

The relationship between the cultural poetics practiced by a number of new historicists and the cultural criticism associated with Marxism is important, not only because of the proximity of the two approaches but also because one must recognize the difference between the two to understand the new historicism. Still very much a part of the contemporary critical scene, cultural criticism (sometimes called "cultural studies" or "cultural critique") nonetheless involves several tendencies more compatible with the old historicism than with the thinking of new historicists such as Greenblatt. These include the tendency to believe that history is driven by economics; that it is determinable even as it determines the lives of individuals; and that it is progressive, its dialectic one that will bring about justice and equality.

Greenblatt does not privilege economics in his analyses and views individuals as agents possessing considerable productive power. (He says that "the work of art is the product of a negotiation between a creator or class of creators . . . and the institutions and practices of a society" [*Learning* 158]; he also acknowledges that artistic productions are "intensely marked by the private obsessions of individuals," however much they may result from "collective negotiation and exchange" [*Negotiations* vii].) His optimism about the individual, however, should not be confused with optimism about either history's direction or any historian's capacity to foretell it. Like a work of art, a work of history is the negotiated product of a private creator and the public practices of a given society.

This does not mean that Greenblatt does not discern historical change, or that he is uninterested in describing it. Indeed, in works from *Renaissance Self-Fashioning* (1980) to *Shakespearean Negotiations* (1988), he has written about Renaissance changes in the development of both literary characters and real people. But his view of change — like his view of the individual — is more Foucauldian than Marxist. That is to say, it is not melioristic or teleological. And, like Foucault, Greenblatt is careful to point out that any one change is connected with a host of others, no one of which may simply be identified as cause or effect, progressive or regressive, repressive or enabling.

Not all of the critics trying to lead students of literature back to history are as Foucauldian as Greenblatt. Some even owe more to Marx than to Foucault. Others, like Thomas, have clearly been more influenced by Walter Benjamin, best known for essays such as "Theses on the Philosophy of History" and "The Work of Art in the Age of Mechanical Reproduction." Still others — McGann, for example — have followed the lead of Soviet critic M. M. Bakhtin, who viewed literary works in terms of discourses and dialogues between the official, legitimate voices of a society and other, more challenging or critical voices echoing popular or traditional culture. In the "polyphonic" writings of Rabelais, for instance, Bakhtin found that the profane language of Carnival and other popular festivals offsets and parodies the "legitimate" discourses representing the outlook of the king, church, and socially powerful intellectuals of the day.

Moreover, there are other reasons not to consider Foucault the single or even central influence on the new historicism. First, he critiqued the old-style historicism to such an extent that he ended up being antihistorical, or at least ahistorical, in the view of a number of new historicists. Second, his commitment to a radical remapping of the relations of power and influence, cause and effect, may have led him to adopt too cavalier an attitude toward chronology and facts. Finally, the very act of identifying and labeling *any* primary influence goes against the grain of the new historicism. Its practitioners have sought to "decenter" the study of literature, not only by overlapping it with historical studies (broadly defined to include anthropology and sociology) but also by struggling to see history from a decentered perspective. That struggle has involved recognizing (1) that the historian's cultural and historical position may not afford the best purview of a given set of events, and (2) that events seldom have any single or central cause. In keeping with these principles, it may be appropriate to acknowledge Foucault as just one of several powerful, interactive intellectual forces rather than to declare him the single, master influence.

Throughout the 1980s it seemed to many that the ongoing debates about the sources of the new historicist movement, the importance of Marx or Foucault, Walter Benjamin or Mikhail Bakhtin, and the exact locations of all the complex boundaries between the new historicism and other "isms" (Marxism and poststructuralism, to name only two) were historically contingent functions of the new historicism *newness*. In the initial stages of their development, new intellectual movements are difficult to outline clearly because, like partially developed photographic images, they are themselves fuzzy and lacking in definition. They respond to disparate influences and include thinkers who represent a wide range of backgrounds; like movements that are disintegrating, they inevitably include a broad spectrum of opinions and positions.

From the vantage point of the 1990s, however, it seems that the inchoate quality of the new historicism is characteristic rather than a function of newness. The boundaries around the new historicism remain fuzzy, not because it hasn't reached its full maturity but because, if it is to live up to its name, it must always be subject to revision and redefinition as historical circumstances change. The fact that so many critics we label new historicist are working right at the border of Marxist, poststructuralist, cultural, postcolonial, feminist, and now even a new form of reader-response (or at least reader-oriented) criticism is evidence of the new historicism's multiple interests and motivations, rather than of its embryonic state.

New historicists themselves advocate and even stress the need to perpetually redefine categories and boundaries — whether they be disciplinary, generic, national, or racial — not because definitions are unimportant but because they are historically constructed and thus subject to revision. If new historicists like Thomas and reader-oriented critics like Steven Mailloux and Peter Rabinowitz seem to spend most of their time talking over the low wall separating their respective fields, then maybe the wall is in the wrong place. As Catherine Gallagher has suggested, the boundary between new historicists and feminists studying "people and phenomena that once seemed insignificant, indeed outside of history: women, criminals, the insane" often turns out to be shifting or even nonexistent (Veeser 43).

If the fact that new historicists all seem to be working on the border of another school should not be viewed as a symptom of the new historicism's newness (or disintegration), neither should it be viewed as evidence that new historicists are intellectual loners or divisive outsiders who enjoy talking over walls to people in other fields but who share no common views among themselves. Greenblatt, McGann, and Thomas all started with the assumption that works of literature are simultaneously influenced by and influencing reality, broadly defined. Whatever their disagreements, they share a belief in referentiality — a belief that literature refers to and is referred to by things outside itself — stronger than that found in the works of formalist, poststructuralist, and even reader-response critics. They believe with Greenblatt that the "central concerns" of criticism "should prevent it from permanently sealing off one type of discourse from another or decisively separating works of art from the minds and lives of their creators and their audiences" (*Renaissance* 5).

McGann, in his introduction to *Historical Studies and Literary Criticism*, turns referentiality into a rallying cry:

> What will not be found in these essays . . . is the assumption, so common in text-centered studies of every type, that literary works are self-enclosed verbal constructs, or looped intertextual fields of autonomous signifiers and signifieds. In these essays, the question of referentiality is once again brought to the fore. (3)

In "Keats and the Historical Method in Literary Criticism," he suggests a set of basic, scholarly procedures to be followed by those who have rallied to the cry. These procedures, which he claims are "practical derivatives of the Bakhtin school," assume that historicist critics will study a literary work's "point of origin" by studying biography and bibliography. The critic must then consider the expressed intentions of the author, because, if printed, these intentions have also modified the developing history of the work. Next, the new historicist must learn the history of the work's reception, as that body of opinion has become part of the platform on which we are situated when we study the work at our own particular "point of reception." Finally, McGann urges the new historicist critic to point toward the future, toward his or her *own* audience, defining for its members the aims and limits of the critical project and injecting the analysis with a degree of self-consciousness that alone can give it credibility (*Inflections* 62).

In his introduction to a collection of new historical writings on *The New Historicism* (1989), H. Aram Veeser stresses the unity among new historicists, not by focusing on common critical procedures but, rather, by outlining five "key assumptions" that "continually reappear and bind together the avowed practitioners and even some of their critics":

1. that every expressive act is embedded in a network of material practices;
2. that every act of unmasking, critique, and opposition uses the tools it condemns and risks falling prey to the practice it exposes;
3. that literary and nonliterary texts circulate inseparably;
4. that no discourse, imaginative or archival, gives access to unchanging truths nor expresses inalterable human nature;
5. finally, . . . that a critical method and a language adequate to describe culture under capitalism participate in the economy they describe. (xi)

These same assumptions are shared by a group of historians practicing what is now commonly referred to as "the new cultural history." Influenced by *Annales*-school historians in France, post-Althusserian Marxists, and Foucault, these historians share with their new historicist counterparts not only many of the same influences and assumptions but also the following: an interest in anthropological and sociological subjects and methods; a creative way of weaving stories and anecdotes about the past into revealing thick descriptions; a tendency to focus on nontraditional, noncanonical subjects and relations (historian Thomas Laqueur is best known for *Making Sex: Body and Gender from the Greeks to Freud* [1990]); and some of the same journals and projects.

Thus, in addition to being significantly unified by their own interests, assumptions, and procedures, new historicist literary critics have participated in a broader, interdisciplinary movement toward unification virtually unprecedented within and across academic disciplines. Their tendency to work along disciplinary borderlines, far from being evidence of their factious or fractious tendencies, has been precisely what has allowed them to engage historians in a conversation certain to revolutionize the way in which we understand the past, present, and future.

Ross C Murfin

THE NEW HISTORICISM: A SELECTED BIBLIOGRAPHY

The New Historicism: Further Reading

Brantlinger, Patrick. "Cultural Studies vs. the New Historicism." *English Studies/Cultural Studies: Institutionalizing Dissent*. Ed. Isaiah Smithson and Nancy Ruff. Urbana: U of Illinois P, 1994. 43–58.

Cox, Jeffrey N., and Larry J. Reynolds, eds. *New Historical Literary Study*. Princeton: Princeton UP, 1993.

Dimock, Wai-Chee. "Feminism, New Historicism, and the Reader." *American Literature* 63 (1991): 601–22.

Howard, Jean. "The New Historicism in Renaissance Studies." *English Literary Renaissance* 16 (1986): 13–43.

Lindenberger, Herbert. *The History in Literature: On Value, Genre, Institutions*. New York: Columbia UP, 1990.

———. "Toward a New History in Literary Study." *Profession: Selected Articles from the Bulletins of the Association of Departments of En-*

glish and the Association of the Departments of Foreign Languages. New York: MLA, 1984. 16–23.

Liu, Alan. "The Power of Formalism: The New Historicism." *English Literary History* 56 (1989): 721–71.

McGann, Jerome. *The Beauty of Inflections: Literary Investigations in Historical Method and Theory.* Oxford: Clarendon–Oxford UP, 1985.

———. *Historical Studies and Literary Criticism.* Madison: U of Wisconsin P, 1985. See especially the introduction and the essays in the following sections: "Historical Methods and Literary Interpretations" and "Biographical Contexts and the Critical Object."

Montrose, Louis Adrian. "Renaissance Literary Studies and the Subject of History." *English Literary Renaissance* 16 (1986): 5–12.

Morris, Wesley. *Toward a New Historicism.* Princeton: Princeton UP, 1972.

New Literary History 21 (1990). "History and . . ." (Special Issue). See especially the essays by Carolyn Porter, Rena Fraden, Clifford Geertz, and Renato Rosaldo.

Representations. This quarterly journal, printed by the University of California Press, regularly publishes new historicist studies and cultural criticism.

Thomas, Brook. "The Historical Necessity for — and Difficulties with — New Historical Analysis in Introductory Courses." *College English* 49 (1987): 509–22.

———. *The New Historicism and Other Old-Fashioned Topics.* Princeton: Princeton UP, 1991.

———. "The New Literary Historicism." *A Companion to American Thought.* Ed. Richard Wightman Fox and James T. Kloppenberg. New York: Basil Blackwell, 1995.

———. "Walter Benn Michaels and the New Historicism: Where's the Difference?" *Boundary 2* 18 (1991): 118–59.

Veeser, H. Aram, ed. *The New Historicism.* New York: Routledge, 1989. See especially Veeser's introduction, Louis Montrose's "Professing the Renaissance," Catherine Gallagher's "Marxism and the New Historicism," and Frank Lentricchia's "Foucault's Legacy: A New Historicism?"

Wayne, Don E. "Power, Politics, and the Shakespearean Text: Recent Criticism in England and the United States." *Shakespeare Reproduced: The Text in History and Ideology.* Ed. Jean Howard and Marion O'Connor. New York: Methuen, 1987. 47–67.

Winn, James A. "An Old Historian Looks at the New Historicism." *Comparative Studies in Society and History* 35 (1993): 859–70.

The New Historicism: Influential Examples

New historicism has taken its present form less through the elaboration of basic theoretical postulates and more through certain influential examples. The works listed represent some of the most important contributions guiding research in this area.

Bercovitch, Sacvan. *The Rites of Assent: Transformations in the Symbolic Construction of America*. New York: Routledge, 1993.

Brown, Gillian. *Domestic Individualism: Imagining Self in Nineteenth-Century America*. Berkeley: U of California P, 1990.

Dollimore, Jonathan. *Radical Tragedy: Religion, Ideology and Power in the Drama of Shakespeare and His Contemporaries*. Brighton, Eng.: Harvester, 1984.

Dollimore, Jonathan, and Alan Sinfield, eds. *Political Shakespeare: New Essays in Cultural Materialism*. Manchester, Eng.: Manchester UP, 1985. This volume occupies the borderline between new historicist and cultural criticism. See especially the essays by Dollimore, Greenblatt, and Tennenhouse.

Gallagher, Catherine. *The Industrial Reformation of English Fiction*. Chicago: U of Chicago P, 1985.

Goldberg, Jonathan. *James I and the Politics of Literature*. Baltimore: Johns Hopkins UP, 1983.

Greenblatt, Stephen J. *Learning to Curse: Essays in Early Modern Culture*. New York: Routledge, 1990.

———. *Marvelous Possessions: The Wonder of the New World*. Chicago: U of Chicago P, 1991.

———. *Renaissance Self-Fashioning from More to Shakespeare*. Chicago: U of Chicago P, 1980. See chapter 1 and the chapter on *Othello* titled "The Improvisation of Power."

———. *Shakespearean Negotiations: The Circulation of Social Energy in Renaissance England*. Berkeley: U of California P, 1988. See especially "The Circulation of Social Energy" and "Invisible Bullets."

Liu, Alan. *Wordsworth, the Sense of History*. Stanford: Stanford UP, 1989.

Marcus, Leah. *Puzzling Shakespeare: Local Reading and Its Discontents*. Berkeley: U of California P, 1988.

McGann, Jerome. *The Romantic Ideology*. Chicago: U of Chicago P, 1983.

Michaels, Walter Benn. *The Gold Standard and the Logic of Naturalism: American Literature at the Turn of the Century*. Berkeley: U of California P, 1987.

Montrose, Louis Adrian. "'Shaping Fantasies': Figurations of Gender and Power in Elizabethan Culture." *Representations* 2 (1983): 61–94. One of the most influential early new historicist essays.

Mullaney, Steven. *The Place of the Stage: License, Play, and Power in Renaissance England.* Chicago: U of Chicago, 1987.

Orgel, Stephen. *The Illusion of Power: Political Theater in the English Renaissance.* Berkeley: U of California P, 1975.

Sinfield, Alan. *Literature, Politics, and Culture in Postwar Britain.* Berkeley: U of California P, 1989.

Tennenhouse, Leonard. *Power on Display: The Politics of Shakespeare's Genres.* New York: Methuen, 1986.

Foucault and His Influence

As I point out in the introduction to the new historicism, some new historicists would question the "privileging" of Foucault implicit in this section heading ("Foucault and His Influence") and the following one ("Other Writers and Works"). They might cite the greater importance of one of those other writers or point out that to cite a central influence or a definitive cause runs against the very spirit of the movement.

Foucault, Michel. *The Archaeology of Knowledge.* Trans. A. M. Sheridan Smith. New York: Harper, 1972.

———. *Discipline and Punish: The Birth of the Prison.* 1975. Trans. Alan Sheridan. New York: Pantheon, 1978.

———. *The History of Sexuality.* Vol. 1. Trans. Robert Hurley. New York: Pantheon, 1978.

———. *Language, Counter-Memory, Practice.* Ed. Donald F. Bouchard. Trans. Donald F. Bouchard and Sherry Simon. Ithaca: Cornell UP, 1977.

———. *The Order of Things: An Archaeology of the Human Sciences.* New York: Vintage, 1973.

———. *Politics, Philosophy, Culture.* Ed. Lawrence D. Kritzman. Trans. Alan Sheridan et al. New York: Routledge, 1988.

———. *Power/Knowledge.* Ed. Colin Gordon. Trans. Colin Gordon et al. New York: Pantheon, 1980.

———. *Technologies of the Self.* Ed. Luther H. Martin, Huck Gutman, and Patrick H. Hutton. Amherst: U of Massachusetts P, 1988.

Dreyfus, Hubert L., and Paul Rabinow. *Michel Foucault: Beyond Structuralism and Hermeneutics.* Chicago: U of Chicago P, 1983.

Sheridan, Alan. *Michel Foucault: The Will to Truth.* New York: Tavistock, 1980.

Smart, Barry. *Michel Foucault*. New York: Ellis Horwood and Tavis-
    tock, 1985.

Other Writers and Works of Interest
to New Historicist Critics

Bakhtin, M. M. *The Dialogic Imagination: Four Essays*. Ed. Michael
    Holquist. Trans. Caryl Emerson. Austin: U of Texas P, 1981.
    Bakhtin wrote many influential studies on subjects as varied as
    Dostoyevsky, Rabelais, and formalist criticism. But this book, in
    part due to Holquist's helpful introduction, is probably the best
    place to begin reading Bakhtin.
Benjamin, Walter. "The Work of Art in the Age of Mechanical Repro-
    duction." 1936. *Illuminations*. Ed. Hannah Arendt. Trans. Harry
    Zohn. New York: Harcourt, 1968.
Fried, Michael. *Absorption and Theatricality: Painting and Beholder in
    the Works of Diderot*. Berkeley: U of California P, 1980.
Geertz, Clifford. *The Interpretation of Cultures*. New York: Basic,
    1973.
―――. *Negara: The Theatre State in Nineteenth-Century Bali*. Prince-
    ton: Princeton UP, 1980.
Goffman, Erving. *Frame Analysis*. New York: Harper, 1974.
Jameson, Fredric. *The Political Unconscious*. Ithaca: Cornell UP,
    1981.
Koselleck, Reinhart. *Futures Past*. Trans. Keith Tribe. Cambridge:
    MIT P, 1985.
Said, Edward. *Orientalism*. New York: Columbia UP, 1978.
Turner, Victor. *The Ritual Process: Structure and Anti-Structure*.
    Chicago: Aldine, 1969.
Young, Robert. *White Mythologies: Writing History and the West*. New
    York: Routledge, 1990.

New Historicist Approaches to Chaucer and
the Wife of Bath's Prologue and Tale

Amsler, Mark. "The Wife of Bath and Women's Power." *Assays* 4
    (1987): 67–83.
Carruthers, Mary. "The Wife of Bath and the Painting of Lions."
    PMLA 94 (1979): 209–22.
Crane, Susan. "Alison's Incapacity and Poetic Instability in the *Wife
    of Bath's Tale*." *PMLA* 102 (1987): 20–28.

Knapp, Peggy. *Chaucer and the Social Contract*. London: Routledge, 1990.

——. "Varieties of Medieval Historicism." *Chaucer Yearbook* 1 (1992): 157–75.

Knight, Stephen. *Geoffrey Chaucer*. Oxford: Basil Blackwell, 1986.

Margulies, Cecile Stoller. "The Marriages and the Wealth of the Wife of Bath." *Medieval Studies* 34 (1972): 210–16.

Patterson, Lee. *Chaucer and the Subject of History*. Madison: U of Wisconsin P, 1991.

Robertson, D. W., Jr. "'And for my land thus hastow mordred me?': Land Tenure, the Cloth Industry, and the Wife of Bath." *Chaucer Review* 14 (1980): 403–20.

Sheehan, Michael M. "The Wife of Bath and Her Four Sisters: Reflections on a Woman's Life in the Age of Chaucer." *Medievalia et Humanistica* 13 (1985): 23–42.

Strohm, Paul. *Hochon's Arrow: The Social Imagination of Fourteenth-Century Texts*. Princeton: Princeton UP, 1992.

Wilks, Michael. "Chaucer and the Mystical Marriage in Medieval Political Thought." *Bulletin of the John Rylands Library* 44 (1962): 489–530.

A NEW HISTORICIST PERSPECTIVE

In the essay that follows, Lee Patterson gives voice to the new historicist insistence that we must see the Wife of Bath in relation to the economic, political, social, and cultural practices of the fourteenth century, and especially those practices that defined the situation of wives and widows. In the quotation in Patterson's title the Wife of Bath rejects the view that our sexual organs were designed only to provide an easy way to distinguish males from females or as a means to purge urine. Personal experience, she insists — probably with a twinkle in her eye — tells us that "is noght so" (124). Patterson insists that experience with historical texts tells us that much that others have assumed was true about the Wife of Bath "is noght so." According to Patterson, Chaucer presents Alisoun of Bath not primarily as either a business-savvy cloth-maker or a devoutly religious pilgrim, but as a wife — a woman defined by her connection to a series of men with whom she seeks happiness in marriage. In presenting her in this way, Chaucer affords a telling representation of the historical reality of medieval life for many women.

In sympathy with the new historicist notions of Foucault and Greenblatt, Patterson would have us blur the lines between history and art. Chaucer was writing history as well as literature when he created a special kind of wifehood for Alisoun of Bath. She neither accepts marriage as a dehumanizing institution nor rebels against it. Rather, she does what women have traditionally done with marriage: tried to use it to their own private and mostly emotional advantage, despite the fact that they do so in a world in which almost all of the power lies with their husbands. In showing that Chaucer wrote history while writing literature, of course, Patterson himself produces something of a hybrid text: a work of criticism that itself blurs the boundary between historical and literary analysis.

But Patterson's essay exemplifies the new historicist approach in even more important ways. For example, it is careful to avoid giving us the impression that a literary text can provide us with *the* historical truth about its historical subject or its author's historical moment. Patterson reminds us that Chaucer's Wife of Bath is but one of the possible versions of a late-medieval woman, and that the more we learn about the medieval past the less certain it is that anything can be called *the* medieval past. In making such statements, of course, Patterson reminds us that the past exists only as a reconstruction, and that historically minded critics are providing interpretation as much as are critics who use other methods. Thus, just as Chaucer's decision to depict Alisoun primarily as a wife and widow was to some extent determined by his own age and its prevalent discourses, so our modern tendency to see Chaucer as having offered a bold and radical critique of marriage may be similarly determined by our present-day interests and concerns. In what may be Patterson's most daring insight, he argues that the Wife of Bath may be less the means by which Chaucer critiques the medieval notion of marriage than the means by which he promotes what he and others saw as its best features.

LEE PATTERSON

"Experience woot well it is noght so": Marriage and the Pursuit of Happiness in the Wife of Bath's Prologue and Tale

One goal of historical criticism is to reconstruct a text's original meaning. Would Chaucer's contemporaries have seen the Wife of Bath as a protofeminist, launching a no-holds-barred on certain medieval pieties about male supremacy and female subordination? Would they have seen her as a victim of a marital system that condemned girls as young as twelve (and even younger) to marriage with old, rich men, and that naturally corrupted them into then wanting to buy young husbands when they became rich and old? Or would they have seen her as a typical widow on the make, teasing them by revealing her preferred means of winning "maistrie" (1040) but really wanting all along a happy marriage in which, like the old-young bride of her tale, she can obey her husband "in every thing / That mighte doon him plesance or liking" (1255–56)? Although the answers to these questions can never be definitive, historical evidence can provide some guidance. It can help us to understand both what Chaucer included in the text and, even more important, what he chose to leave out. Chaucer's Wife of Bath is only one possible version of a late-medieval Englishwoman, and historical materials can help us to understand her by allowing us to see what other versions were possible.

New historicism is alert to the fact that the past exists only as a reconstruction. These reconstructions are produced by men and women who are subject both to the usual difficulties relevant to any act of interpretation and to the shaping pressure of their own interests and assumptions. But in reconstructing the medieval past, the complications are especially pressing. For one thing, the evidence that survives about how medieval people lived and what they thought is both voluminous in extent and frustratingly silent on many of the questions we most want answered. The records, handwritten mostly in Latin and French, are both difficult to decipher and, when deciphered, often unhelpful as a means of understanding how people thought and felt. For another, the more historians come to understand the medieval past the less certain it becomes that there is *a* medieval past. The Middle Ages is often thought to be a homogeneous and largely uniform culture, an Age of Faith dominated by church dogma and a feudal social system in which the lord's — and the husband's — word was law. But we now know that the reality must have been not only very different from this modern cliché but very different within the Middle Ages itself, depending on time and place. To investigate, for example, the nature of medieval marriage is to discover that marriage practices varied enormously between, say, Italy and England, between the eleventh and the fourteenth centuries in England, between the powerful English gentry and nobility (who constituted only about 1 percent of the population) and their less affluent and less powerful neighbors, and even between the inhabitants of one part of England and those of another. And there is also a substantial gap between marriage theory (which is itself not entirely straightforward) and practice (which is open to an almost infinite range of variations). So we cannot expect "history" simply to provide "the facts" against which a literary representation of those facts can be measured. And just as there is no single institution we can call "medieval marriage," so there is no single person we can call the "medieval reader." This is not to say that there are not patterns to be observed and generalizations to be made, but it is to stress that historicist critics are providing as much an interpretation — rather than a straightforward description — as are critics who use other methods.

I. ALISOUN AS WEAVER AND PILGRIM

A useful place to begin to understand Chaucer's version of a medieval woman is with the Wife of Bath's profession: "Of clooth-making she hadde swich an haunt, / She passed hem of Ypres and of Gaunt" (A447–48). In the late Middle Ages the English economy was heavily dependent on the export of wool, much of which was sent to the Low Countries, where, in towns like Ypres and Ghent, it was turned into cloth. Gradually an English cloth industry began to develop, however, especially in the west country where Bath is located, and by the third decade of the fifteenth century exports of finished cloth surpassed those of raw wool. The Wife is evidently one of those who prospered from the growth of this industry. But what is her role in it? Some scholars have argued that she is not a mere weaver but a cloth-maker or clothier, a woman who organized a business establishment in which the entire complex process by which wool was transformed into cloth took place (Carruthers; Robertson). But for other scholars, the Wife is simply a weaver, and the reference to Ypres and Ghent is an empty boast: cloths from the west country where she resided were in fact criticized for not meeting the standards required for export to Ypres and Ghent (Manly). What is instructive about this dispute is that Chaucer fails to give us sufficient evidence to resolve it: nowhere in the almost 1,300 lines he devotes to her does Alisoun's capacity as either a clothier or a businesswoman find a place (Fradenburg; Delany, "Strategies"; Crane). Nor is there any indication that her wealth comes from weaving; indeed, her profession seems less that of a clothier or a weaver than a wife.

But there is one other reference to textile working. In her prologue the Wife says that "Deceite, weping, spinning God hath yeve / To wommen kindely whil they may live" (401–02). In this passage, as elsewhere, the Wife is invoking medieval stereotypes about women, including the fact that they spin wool into thread. According to a well-known medieval proverb, "When Adam delved and Eve span, / Who was then the gentleman?" — men do agricultural work, women work with cloth. Chaucer makes her a weaver, in other words, not because he is interested in exploring the condition of the independent businesswoman in late-fourteenth-century England but because her weaving fits with the traditional stereotype of woman's generic identity (Mann 121–22). That most medieval women's *domestic* labor was in fact mostly child care, food preparation, and the care and making of clothing supports this point: the most important aspect of Alisoun's social identity for Chaucer is her status as a wife.

In fact, if Chaucer had wanted to present the Wife as an independent businesswoman, plenty of contemporary instances were available for representation. Some women in late-medieval England did participate in such protocapitalist enterprises as cloth manufacture, just as some women were active in virtually every trade, albeit while surmounting significant barriers (Lacey; Barron). In Chaucer's world a woman in business would have been identified as a *femme sole*, a single woman, whether she was married or not. If she was married, assuming the status of a *femme sole* meant that she was an independent legal entity so that her husband would not be responsible for her business dealings (Lacey 48). As a wife, however, a woman was known as a *femme couverte de baron* — literally, as a woman "covered" by her husband. This meant that legally she had no status. As one historian says, "the *femme couverte* in common law, was a condition of virtual nonexistence (especially in economic matters)" (Bennett, "Medieval Women" 153). As just one example of this nonexistence, a *femme couverte* could not make a grant of land to her husband since "the position of a woman . . . in regard to [her husband was] analogous to the position of an underage child or a mentally incompetent person"

(Palmer 62). Regarded as wholly under the authority of their husbands — the legal phrase was *sub virga viri sui*, "under the rod of her man" — wives were far from being considered full members of the society. The sexual implications of the terms *femme couverte de baron* and *sub virga viri sui* suggest that more than questions of property or legal status were at issue in the subordination of wives: husbands wanted to be sure to control the female body, which both contained and elicited sexual desire. Later in this essay I will describe more fully the nature of medieval marriage and the role of sexuality in it, but for the moment we need only note that in representing Alisoun as a wife and widow, rather than as a weaver or clothier, Chaucer is choosing to depend on a timeless literary tradition rather than dealing with the historical specificity of his contemporary world.

Another example of Chaucer's avoidance of contemporary social conditions in preference to a literary (and, in this case, explicitly misogynist) stereotype is his use of Alisoun's habit of going on pilgrimage. In the General Prologue he tells us that Alisoun not only visited Jerusalem three times but traveled to some of the most famous pilgrimage sites on the Continent: Rome in Italy, Boulogne in France, Santiago de Compostela in Spain, Cologne in Germany (A463–66). This is an impressive itinerary, capable of ranking with those of the most energetic of medieval pilgrims (Sumption). The initiative and self-reliance required of a woman to undertake these always arduous and often hazardous journeys were formidable, and they bespeak an intriguing independence. Students interested in seeing how a real medieval woman negotiated these difficult journeys will want to read *The Book of Margery Kempe*. Margery visited Jerusalem, Rome, Compostela, and Wilsnak (in what is now Poland). Yet Alisoun mentions only one of her seven journeys, and then only in passing. Her adulterous fourth husband died "whan I came fro Jerusalem" (495) — perhaps with the implication that she was somehow responsible, either by her absence (if he was sick, why was she not there to nurse him?) or by her return (did her very presence do him in?). And in the General Prologue these pilgrimages are used to make a point familiar throughout the misogynist literature of the Middle Ages: "She koude muchel of wandring by the weye" (A467). Rather than focusing on her enterprise or even her piety, in other words, the narrator implies instead that Alisoun's pilgrimages indicate a moral and probably sexual errancy, that she is unable to keep to the straight and narrow (Mann 123–24).

Throughout her prologue and tale, then, the Wife of Bath is presented not as an independent person, with her own economic, religious, and even recreational life, but specifically *as a wife*, as a woman defined by her relationships — past, present, or future — to men. This is true, interestingly enough, even in her identity as a widow: there were many advantages to a woman in being a widow — a *femme sole* — rather than a wife (Hanawalt, "Remarriage" 141), but these do not attract Alisoun. On the contrary, having gone through five husbands, she has returned to the marriage market. "Welcome the sixte, whan that evere he shall!" (45), she says at the outset of her prologue, and her entire performance can be usefully read as a complicated and provocative offer to the males in her audience. In thus defining her not as an individual (nor even as a woman) but as a wife, Chaucer was reproducing the conventions and, to a large extent, the social realities of his day. In the Middle Ages women were almost entirely denied access to positions of public authority. They could not serve as public officials, whether in the town or in the country, whether in the guild or in the village community. One of the most common ways medieval society imagined itself was through "estates lists," lists of the various *kinds* of people that were present in society. Many of these lists do not include women at all. Those that do include women represent them in terms of either their marital status (maiden, wife, widow) or their religious vocation (nun, prioress). Sometimes marital status is combined with socioeconomic rank as determined by their male relatives. One of the otherwise most progressive political thinkers of the fourteenth century, Marsilius of Padua, defined "the people" as including everybody but children, slaves, aliens — and women (45–46).

This nondefinition entails two consequences. One is that while women were denied access to public authority, their real exclusion came about through a deeper denial, a refusal to think of them as *social* beings — that is, as independent people capable of a variety of life projects. This does not mean that some women did not participate in a wide range of economic and social activities, although probably they were fewer than we sometimes like to think. But it does mean that there was virtually no way in which such careers could be articulated and described, which is one reason why so many late-medieval women found that a religious life — whether in orders or outside — offered opportunities for self-fulfillment that were not available elsewhere. The second consequence is that to women was ascribed what one historian has called an "overwhelmingly private nature" (Hughes 25). If women were denied social definition, went this thinking, did this not mean that the realm of the asocial — of the internal, the emotional, the subjective — was peculiarly theirs? As befitted historical beings, men had social responsibilities; as befitted the socially invisible, women had private lives. For the Middle Ages (and certainly for earlier periods in history, and for many later ones as well), if men had careers, women had characters. The cultural logic at work here means that it was within a relationship with a man that female inwardness was most likely to be explored. And since virtually all medieval women married (Hanawalt [*Ties*] estimates the figure at 92 percent), it was most prominently through the exploration of marriage that women could become a subject for literary attention. This is why, despite her status as a widow, Alisoun is the *Wife* of Bath, and why her conversation is almost entirely about marriage.

Thus if we see Chaucer *evading* a certain kind of history in his decision not to represent the Wife as either a businesswoman or a traveler — or, for that matter, as a widow satisfied with her condition — we can see that his choice of her as a kind of professional wife is itself historically determined, since being a wife was, apart from a religious vocation, the way of life most typically imagined as normal for a woman in late-medieval England. Hardly surprisingly, then, Chaucer reveals himself to be not only a man but a man of his time. A historicist analysis should not stop here, however, but ask two further questions: Given the many versions of marriage available to him, and the many versions of female character, which does Chaucer choose to represent?

II. ALISOUN AS WIFE:
THE LITERARY EVIDENCE

As we should expect, marriage in the Middle Ages embodied many of the patriarchal values that pervaded medieval culture as a whole. Some historicist readings of the Wife of Bath see medieval marriage as a thoroughly inhumane system, "organized by males to serve economic and political ends, with the woman treated as a useful, child-bearing appendage to the land or goods being exchanged" (Aers 143; see also Delany, "Sexual Economics"). If we accept this version of medieval marriage, then we will read the Wife as having internalized the dehumanizing values of her society by reducing what is potentially the most intimate of human relations to a struggle over property. The final meaning of her recital would then be embodied in the chilling advice she offers in the midst of her account of her first three husbands: "And therfore every man this tale I telle: / Win whoso may, for all is for to selle" (413–14). And certainly she constantly returns to this topic. She boasts that her first three husbands gave her their land and treasure (204, 212); she insists that the wealth in their chests is hers as well as theirs (310); she says that she refuses to have sex with them until they paid for it (410–12); she teases them with the thought that she will sell "my bele chose" (447); she admits that now that she is old she can sell only bran rather than the good flour she had when young (477–78); she says that she scanted on her fourth husband's tomb because it was "but wast to burye him preciously" (500); she defines courtship in terms of negotiating at market (520–23); she marries Jankyn "for love and no richesse" (526) but gives him "all the lond and fee / That evere was me yiven therbifore" (630–31), and when Jankyn strikes her she immediately thinks that he has "mordred" (801) her for her land, land that she reclaims after they are reconciled (814). Doesn't all this suggest that commerce is at the center of the Wife's interest, that Chaucer is depicting through her the dehumanizing effects of a marriage system that treats people as property?

The answer to this question has to be "no," for both literary and historical reasons. The literary reason is that understanding the Wife as focused only on money is possible only if we ignore other aspects of her discourse. We must always be aware of the deliberateness of Alisoun's words, of her self-conscious awareness of the effect her words will have on the men to whom she directs them. She says, "mine entente nis but for to pleye" (192), and play she does, in the sense both of comic extravagance and of dramatic performance. (The brief interpretation offered here is available in a fuller version in Patterson 280–321.) Indeed, the fundamentally theatrical nature of her performance, and its orientation toward men, is stressed by the initially puzzling fact that at one point she addresses her advice on how to manipulate husbands to "Ye wise wives" (225; see also 524). Since there are in fact no other wives on the pilgrimage, these words are best understood as part of the Wife's theatrical display of the way the experienced termagant indoctrinates her colleagues into the mysteries of women's ways. In revealing these female mysteries to the male members of the pilgrimage, she is offering them a glimpse into the secret world of women — or at least into what they think such a world is: "Look," she is saying, "this is how we women teach each other how to dominate you men" (see also her sharing of shameful secrets with her "gossip" in lines 531–42). By pretending to reveal the details of a conspiracy of women, the Wife is here, as throughout her prologue, playing on male paranoia. After the Pardoner interrupts and asks her to "teche[n] us yonge men of your praktike" (187), her account of her marital life is such a teaching. Not surprisingly, Chaucer's contemporary audience also seems to have been largely male (Pearsall; Strohm).

The Wife's prologue falls into four parts: a mock sermon on sex and remarriage (1–162); the account of the first three husbands (194–451); the transitional discussion of husband number four and Alisoun's rueful reminiscences of her youth (452–502); and the extended account of Jankyn and the fight over his book of wicked wives (503–828). The denouement of the whole is the couple's ultimate reconciliation:

> After that day we hadden never debaat.
> God helpe me so, I was to him as kinde
> As any wif from Denmark unto Inde,
> And also trewe, and so was he to me. (822–25)

What ties these parts together is the notion of the "wo that is in mariage" (3) that the Wife announces at the outset as her topic. The mock sermon of the first part deals with this woe in terms of a text from the seventh chapter of Paul's First Epistle to the Corinthians, a chapter she cites eight times in the course of the sermon (46–52, 64–65, 79–84, 87, 102–04, 129–30, 147–48, 154–60). The most important of these citations is the last:

> An housbonde wol I have, I wol not lette,
> Which shall be both my dettour and my thral,
> And have his tribulacioun withal
> Upon his flessh whil that I am his wif. (154–57)

What Paul said in I Corinthians 7:28 was that people who married did not sin but would have "tribulation of the flesh" because of marriage. What he meant — at least according to medieval exegetes — was that marriage brought about unwelcome sexual temptations against which married couples would have to struggle. But the Wife utterly reverses the spirit of Paul's teaching: for her, these temptations are not to be endured but enjoyed.

In this sermon the Wife of Bath presents herself as a woman preacher — a highly troubling figure in a society in which women were prevented from officiating in any religious service, much less preaching. It must be noted, however, that during Chaucer's lifetime a growing group of religious reformers known as the Lollards apparently did promote women preachers, and it has been suggested that the Wife's topic and her treatment of it would probably have been seen by a contemporary audience as characteristic of these Lollards (Blamires).

In her sermon the Wife flaunts not only her preaching but her sexuality, confirming the belief of many medieval men that women were creatures of insatiable sexual appetites. But in the second part of the prologue the "wo" of marriage becomes the "tribulacioun" (173) suffered by the three old husbands, a tribulation in which "myself have been the whippe" (175). Here Alisoun uses the language of medieval misogyny to describe herself as a nightmare of the male imagination, presenting herself as the kind of wife every medieval husband most feared. In the first two parts of the prologue, then, Alisoun presents herself as a perfect stereotype of the kind of woman created by male misogyny: a woman on the sexual rampage, obsessed with wealth and contemptuous of the obedience and loyalty preached by authority. In short, she makes herself into exactly what every misogynist said women really were.

But with the account of husband number four her self-representation begins to change. Now the "wo" that is her topic begins to become her own unhappiness. For one thing, her fourth husband causes her "greet despit" (481), and she describes what must have been a bitterly unhappy marriage. For another, she begins to allow us to see that she is a far less hardened and one-dimensional figure than we might have thought, especially in the very important passage in which she remembers her youth but gracefully accepts its passing: "Lat go. Farewell. . . . But yet to be right myrie wol I fonde" (476, 479). And with her account of her marriage with Jankyn, the "wo" of marriage now becomes her own suffering under the barrage of misogyny that he heaps upon her: "Who wolde wene or who wolde suppose / The wo that in mine herte was, and pyne?" (786–87). In telling us about Jankyn, Alisoun discloses a range of previously unacknowledged human feelings that include both a genuine marital affection and a sense of disappointment. In revealing her woe she shows us that she is capable of love as well as desire, that she covets Jankyn's affection as much as his well-turned legs. Hence, at the end, she is willing to abandon the "maistrie" she has regained when she learns that he cares enough about her to grant it. What she desires, in short, is mutuality in marriage, an affection that transcends the constraints of both cultural stereotypes and commercial self-interest.

The Wife's Arthurian tale is a version of the same story. Rather than beginning with a sermon it ends with one — the so-called "pillow lecture" that the old wife delivers to her young husband. And rather than ending with an act of male violence, it begins with one — the knight's rape of the maiden. In between is the same process of reeducation that the prologue enacts. Just as the audience of the prologue — and surely we should imagine the Wife as directing her words to the male members of the pilgrimage — first receives a series of misogynist stereotypes that it must pass beyond in order to find the real Wife of Bath, so must the knight pass beyond the stereotypes of "What thing is it that wommen moost desiren" (905) to find *his* wife. The answers he receives (money, honor, clothing, sexual pleasure, and so on) all derive from the misogynist tradition, and at the end of his quest his old wife presents him with two choices that are themselves misogynistic. She can, she tells him, be either foul and honest or fair and unreliable — the implication being, of course, that only an undesirable woman could be faithful. (A version of this dictum is part of the misogynist lore that the Wife recites in her prologue in lines 253–70.) The important point is that in refusing to choose, in placing himself in his wife's "wise governaunce" (1231), the knight steps outside the misogynist consciousness within which he had been operating since the beginning — a consciousness whose direst effect is not simply prejudice but actual violence. He is able to do this because the old wife has provided him, in her sermon on gentillesse, with a demonstration not only of her wisdom but of his own lack of understanding of what is truly valuable. As in the prologue, then, the tale ends with both a revelation — "Cast up the curtin! Looke how that it is" (1249) — and a reconciliation — "And thus they live unto hir lives ende / In parfit joye" (1257–58).

It can hardly be said, then, that the Wife is an example of the corrupting influence of the medieval marriage system. Nor can she really be presented as rebelling against it. To read her defiance of her three old husbands (who are actually presented rather sympathetically) as her final message is to ignore the totality of Chaucer's poem, and even to accept a misogynist stereotype common to the Middle Ages — that women are insubordinate creatures who resist rational control — as if it were a revolutionary statement. Chaucer's Wife does not want social or political change. Her sermon on gentillesse is itself entirely traditional, being largely derived from a preacher's handbook (Pratt). On the contrary, the traditional order is quite capable of providing the private happiness she desires. She doesn't want to change the system, simply to use it to her *private*, largely *emotional* advantage. This conclusion is, then, entirely consistent with another one of the medieval stereotypes about women, that they are private and emotional creatures.

It can hardly be said, then, that Chaucer uses the Wife as a way of introducing something new and innovative in thinking about marriage. On the contrary, Alisoun is less a new phenomenon in Western thinking about marriage than the means by which Chaucer sorts out the complexities of the contemporary marriage system and promotes what he (and many others, both then and subsequently) have seen as its best features. But he does this, it is important to note, by obscuring certain crucial elements of that system. Once again, then, Chaucer turns away from some of the more difficult marital realities of his time to create a less historically specific, if admittedly kinder, world.

III. ALISOUN AS WIFE:
THE HISTORICAL EVIDENCE

The nuclear family, which overwhelmingly predominated in the English social system, emphasizes the marital couple as a social unit independent of wider kin relationships. In this, England (and, indeed, most of northern Europe) differed from Italy and southern Europe, where marriage remained a matter not of the joining of two individuals but of the alliance of two kin groups. English individualism was further fostered by the teaching of the church on marriage. Beginning in the twelfth century, the church taught that what made a marriage valid was not a church service, or indeed any form of social ritual, but simply the consent of the two parties.

This consent could be given in two ways. It could be accomplished by means of "words of the present" (*per verba de praesenti*), words such as, "I, John, take you Mary [and vice versa] as my lawful wedded wife [husband], and hereto I plight thee my troth." Having exchanged these words, or words like them, the couple were then and there married — period. Numerous cases in the church courts of the time demonstrate not only that these kinds of marriage often took place but that, despite parental and other objections, including objections by one of the partners (usually the man), the church held that they were valid and could not be dissolved. Discussions of these cases, which often give a fascinating insight into the daily lives of medieval people, can be found in Sheehan ("Formation," "Marriage Theory"), Helmholz, Houlbrooke, Ingram, Donohue, and Palmer. Reading this material will give the student a richer sense of the practical reality of medieval marriage than any summary. The second way consent could be given was through "words of the future" (*per verbi de futuro*), a promise of forthcoming marriage, usually dependent on certain conditions (such as gaining parental approval). If the couple then had sexual intercourse, the church would rule the marriage valid. To be sure, the church insisted that certain conditions be met in either case. The most important of these were that neither of the partners was already married, that both partners were of legal age (twelve in the case of girls, fourteen in the case of boys), that consent was not given under compulsion, and that they were not too closely related.

It is clear that this system undermined the authority of both parents and feudal lords to control the marriages of their dependents. A well-known fifteenth-century case — available to us because of the survival of an extraordinary cache of family letters and papers — is that of a young woman named Margery Paston, who at the age of seventeen secretly married Richard Calle, the bailiff of her family's estates. For some three years her family, and especially her mother, fought against this union, keeping the young couple apart. But finally the case came to the court of the Bishop of Norwich, and Margery and Richard's marriage was confirmed. Margery did, however, pay a steep price, for she was excluded from her family and its wealth, a punishment that also caused real pain both to her intransigent mother and her father. Oddly enough, Richard kept his job as family bailiff (Gairdner, 5.21–23, 25–28, 37–40, numbers 710, 713, 721). A darker case of filial disobedience was that of Elizabeth Paston, Margery's aunt, who resisted marriage to a disfigured fifty-year-old man and was beaten into submission — although in fact the marriage negotiations fell through. One scholar has suggested that Elizabeth was simply holding out for a better property deal from her future husband (Dockray).

As Margery Paston's case illustrates, parents did not give up their authority easily, and the church made it quite clear that the preferable form of marriage was one that was fully public. The banns would be read for three weeks prior to the marriage to see if anyone had objections, and then the service would be held at the church door — "in the face of the church" (*in facie ecclesiae*) in the official phrase. Thus when the Wife boasts that she has had five husbands "at chirche dore" (A460, 6), she is asserting that her marriages have not been clandestine but fully and even ostentatiously legitimate, granted the full validity of both church and society.

She is also making another claim, for it was at the church door that the property arrangements for the new couple would be ratified. Today we think it inappropriate and even sordid to allow economic considerations to contaminate the joining of two hearts and minds. But in the Middle Ages, as in fact virtually everywhere outside the contemporary Western world, marriage was considered a social as well as a personal matter, and hence an event in which various people — feudal lords, guild masters, parents, and other members of the community — had a stake. It was also understood that marriage served a number of purposes for the couple themselves: it provided each party with a social colleague and economic associate as well as a sexual partner and affectional companion. In different circumstances each of these elements would be differently stressed. But it is fair to say that only rarely were any of them ignored.

The clear exceptions were the marriages of the children of noble and well-to-do gentry families, those who comprised the top 1 percent of the social order. Here the primary concern was the transmission of the patrimony, and it is at this level of society that we witness the child betrothals that strike modern observers as so inhumane. For a royal or noble heir or heiress to be betrothed while still a child was not uncommon. When Isabella of France was married (by proxy) to Richard II in 1396 she was only seven. But not all such marriages were disastrous. Richard II and Anne of Bohemia were thirteen when they were betrothed and fifteen when they were married, and had never spent any time together, yet Richard seems to have become almost obsessively devoted to his wife. At a much lower social level, the French intellectual and poet Christine de Pisan was "given to" her husband at fifteen and widowed at twenty-five. She never remarried, at least in part because she felt she could not recreate what she called "the sweet company and the departed joy" of her first marriage (Pisan 110–11). One reason for the early betrothals among the landed classes was fear that the father would die before his child was married, which would mean that the child would become a ward of the lord, who would then sell the marriage rights. Whoever bought these rights would then have the future bride or groom move into his or her household. These rights to a child's marriage were often sold and resold. There are even cases of mothers buying custody of their fatherless children and then selling it again (Walker). Certainly this market in wealthy children and their future is the most dehumanizing aspect of the medieval marriage system.

But there is no evidence that the Wife of Bath was part of this system, and given her social status it is most unlikely that she would have been betrothed so young. Although we cannot know for certain the age of marriage of middle-strata people in fourteenth-century England, all indications are that it was relatively late: probably in the late teens for girls, in the twenties for boys (Macfarlane 213–17; Thrupp 192; Hanawalt, *Ties* 95–96). So what are we to make of the Wife's statement that she was first married when she "twelve yeer was of age" (4)? Again, I think we should take this as part of the swagger that characterizes the first two-thirds of her prologue. She was married, she is telling us, as early as it was possible to be married — at the canonical age of twelve. This claim presents her, in other words, not as a victim of the marriage system but as exactly what she claims herself to be — a woman of extraordinary and extensive experience (Hanawalt, *Ties* 98).

Given the dominance of the nuclear family, with its emphasis on the marital couple rather than the wider kin group, we should expect that in England, and especially among the middle strata, there would be concern with the nature of the relations between the couple. And in fact that is just what we find — not least in the work of Geoffrey Chaucer, a member of that middle strata. But what we also find in this literature is a complex if not contradictory set of attitudes toward marriage. There is an alertness to the practicalities of marriage choice, to the need to choose a spouse with careful attention to social and economic advantage. But there is also a strong streak of what can be called romanticism, a belief that marriage can provide an environment in which, with generosity and forbearance, true love can be achieved. A similar complexity can be found in the medieval accounts of the power relations within marriage. One strain of teaching — largely but by no means entirely emanating from the church — describes marriage as a snare that draws men into partnership with the lower creatures women were thought to be, and that similarly subjects both partners, and especially the wife, to the "filth" of human sexuality (Brundage). But if marriage is undertaken at all, so runs this line of thought, then the man must be vigilant to retain his authority: he is intellect and reason to the woman's fleshly irrationality, and he must discipline her natural sensuality into obedience. As one lay author says in a book written for his young wife, "in all matters, in all terms, in all places and in all seasons, you shall do and accomplish without argument all my commandments whatsoever" (Power 143). Yet at the same time, and often even in the same text, medieval men insist that husband and wife are "equal and partners," that they are bound together by the "social love" of mutual friends, and that "the delightful unity" accomplished by sexual intercourse contributes to their friendship (d'Avray and Tausche 114; Kelly 282). As a contemporary of Chaucer's named Thomas Usk said in his *Testament of Love*, with marriage "two that wern firste in a litel maner discordaunt, hygher that oon and lower that other, ben mad evenliche in gree to stonde" (Kelly 67; translation: "two who were at first somewhat discordant, one higher than the other, by marriage come to have an equal status"). And a contemporary French author, Nicholas Oresme, argued both that a husband must insist on wifely obedience and, contradictorily, that marriage is a true friendship between equals in which the husband must constantly strive to deserve his wife's love: "it is the duty of the husband while he lives to reflect and think constantly how he may conduct himself righteously toward his wife" (Oresme 847).

Chaucer has the Wife of Bath survey most of these attitudes. In her diatribe against her three old husbands, and in her rehearsal of Jankyn's misogynist rant, she provides a full panoply of antimatrimonial attitudes. She herself, however, seems undeterred by these barrages and still clings to the ideal of marriage as a relationship of mutual love. We might well ask, then, whether Chaucer is here articulating simply his *own* optimism about the possibilities for love in marriage, and projecting onto the Wife a *male* complacency about the possibilities for happiness in a relationship in which women were severely disadvantaged. This is a difficult question to answer because very little is known about how medieval women actually experienced marriage or about their attitudes toward it. It is true that most women married, but the options outside marriage were neither numerous nor especially appealing. We also know that some young women went to extraordinary lengths to avoid marriage (Bynum 220–27). Probably only about half of all widows remarried, but we can only guess at the reasons for either choice, if choice it was. Indeed, it seems that the most important variable in the remarriage of widows of the middle strata was whether current conditions made economic opportunity easily available to men. If it was, then men tended not to marry widows (Titow; Bennett, *Gender* 146).

But one piece of evidence, itself somewhat contradictory, does suggest that some women were persuaded that marriage could, at least ideally, provide happiness, even if their own experience did not always support such idealism. This is the frequency with which religious women imagined their union with God in terms of an ideal and only barely asexual marriage. The traditional idea of the sanctified woman as the bride of Christ is exploited both by men who preached to women and, so far as we can tell from the texts we have, by women themselves. The visionary union between the female holy woman and her male deity was imagined with remarkable physicality. Christ joins himself with these women mouth to mouth and heart to heart, at times even fusing himself with their bodies. Catherine of Siena, in perhaps the most striking image, says that she married Christ not with a ring of gold or silver but with the ring of his foreskin, his circumcision being a symbol of accepted suffering (Bynum 174–75). In *The Book of Margery Kempe* Margery tells us that Jesus spoke thus to her:

> I must be intimate with you, and lie in your bed with you. Daughter, you greatly desire to see me, and you may boldly, when you are in bed, take me to your wedded husband, as your dear darling, and as your sweet son, for I want to be loved as a son should be loved by the mother, and I want you to love me, daughter, as a good wife ought to love her husband. Therefore you can boldly take me in the arms of your soul and kiss my mouth, my head, and my feet as sweetly as you want. (Kempe 196–97)

Both in its amalgamation of relationships and in its visionary nature, this passage hardly constitutes an endorsement of marriage, especially since Margery found her real marriage, and especially its sexual obligations, intolerable. She has Jesus say to her later in the narrative, "Daughter, if you knew how many wives there are in this world, who would love me and serve me well and duly, if they might be as free from their husbands as you are from yours, you would say that you were very much beholden to me. And yet they are thwarted from their will and suffer very great pain" (253). Yet Margery Kempe — as well as many others in similar texts — testifies to the degree to which even those women who found real marriage most oppressive imagined ultimate happiness in marital terms.

We can say, then, that there is at least some evidence that Alisoun's desire for a marriage of companionate partnership and mutual satisfaction was one shared by at least some of the men *and* women in her world. But it was an ideal, one that only a few thought either possible or desirable. To this extent, then, we are right to see Chaucer as using the Wife to promote a progressive and humane vision of life. And we can see that if in most respects Chaucer operates within the conceptual limits of his time, in other ways he pushes against them.

IV. MARRIAGE PROPERTY
AND WIFEHOOD

To allow this happy conclusion to be the last word would be misleading, however. I have already argued that in presenting Alisoun as simply a wife and widow Chaucer is accepting the notion that a woman is to be understood in her relationship to a man, thus ignoring the possibility of an independent selfhood. (Since virtually all other males in his society did too, we can hardly be surprised.) But Chaucer could have explored his contemporary reality with greater perceptiveness in two other areas and chose not to do so. One has to do with the Wife's acquisition of wealth. The laws and customs governing marital property were quite explicit in fourteenth-century England, and as a married man Chaucer would have known them. The central issues were three. One is the woman's dowry, the wealth which she brought into the marriage with her. We usually think of dowry as the price a woman pays to get a husband, but it is better thought of as a woman's premortem inheritance from her own family (Searle 7). The dowry sometimes consisted of chattels — movable property like money, livestock, household utensils, farm or trade implements, and so on — but it often consisted of land. The husband had control over the dowry while the marriage lasted; if it was chattels, he could sell them, but if it was land, he could not, and the wife received it back if she outlived him. The second issue is dower, which is the wealth with which the husband, or his family, endows the wife. Again, this could consist of either chattels or land. It usually comprised one-third or one-half of the husband's wealth. The husband controlled this dower throughout the marriage, but if the wife outlived him she received it, and the rest of the wealth went to the heirs. In some circumstances, indeed, if the husband died the wife would receive everything and the heirs nothing. And if she remarried, this wealth — including land — would go with her into the control of the new husband. The third issue was jointure, when a husband agreed to hold his land in joint tenancy with his wife, which meant that she would inherit all of it when he died. Women in strong bargaining positions insisted on jointure before marriage; and some husbands granted it to them after the marriage for what we can only imagine to have been emotional reasons — that is, love (McFarlane 65–66).

Oddly enough, Chaucer's account of the property transactions that Alisoun claims are so important to her is remarkably vague. She says that she inveigled her three old husbands into handing over their

"lond and hir tresor" (204), which perhaps refers to a grant of join-
ture. This would then perhaps explain why she later says that she be-
rated them for hiding the keys to their chests because "It is my good
as well as thine" (310). But when she then immediately complains to
them that they shall not be master both of "my body and of my
good" (314), she speaks as if she were in the position of the usual wife
whose husband controls all the family property, as well as the wife's
dowry. With Jankyn the situation is even more confusing. Alisoun says
at the outset that "to him yaf I all the lond and fee / That evere was
me yiven therbifore" (630–31) — which is not impossible for a wife
to do, but actually quite difficult. The law did not approve of a situa-
tion in which women impoverished themselves to the benefit of their
husbands (Palmer). But if she had already given him all her property,
it is very odd that she asks, after he has struck her, "And for my land
thus hastow mordred me?" (801). If he owned it he could dispose of
it regardless of her wishes. And what then are we to make of her final
statement that a repentant Jankyn "yaf me all the bridel in mine hond,
/ To han the governance of hous and lond" (813–14)? Does "gover-
nance" mean possession or just de facto control? Has he ceded back
to her the land she previously gave him — again, a very difficult legal
transaction, since as his wife she had no legal standing?

The point, I think, is that Chaucer is imprecise with the details of
the Wife's property transactions because the transactions themselves
are, for him (and hence for her), largely symbolic. For the Wife, prop-
erty represents less material wealth and the personal security it can buy
than both a way of keeping score in her marital competitions and,
more important, a sign of the respect and affection of her husbands.
Her goal, in short, is less to be wealthy than to be happy. Both her
prologue and her tale show that what she is looking for in husband
number six is someone who can make her feel loved — loved, that is,
to the point of making her feel "so fair . . . and so yong" (1251). In
other words, she wants to be like the "olde wif," the woman in her
tale who is magically transformed when her husband comes to recog-
nize her, even while she is old and ugly, as "My lady, and my love,
and wif so deere" (1230).

We can be pretty sure that the real wives of Chaucer's world
would not have been so casual about property transactions as the Wife
of Bath is, and we can see here where sentiment blurs social reality. A
similar blurring, it must finally be acknowledged, is present in the rep-
resentation of the Wife's widowhood. One would never know from
Chaucer's account that the situation of many widows in the Middle

Ages was harsh indeed. It is quite true that wealthy widows, like the Wife, were considered good catches. Not only was the remarriage of widows entirely legitimate in the eyes of the church — one canon lawyer went so far as to say that not just a widow's second but her thousandth marriage would be legal (Brundage 447) — but it was a familiar event. Three, four, and five marriages were not especially unusual. There is even a record of one woman who was married no fewer than twenty-five times (Macfarlane 234). But probably about half of all widows did not remarry, and we know that many of their lives were far from merry. They would receive on their husband's death only that part of their dowry that was in landed property (which might not have been any at all) and the one-third of his wealth that constituted their dower (which might have been very little). Even a highly placed woman like Christine de Pisan, whose father and husband were both retained by the French king, discovered on her husband's death that not only was she financially straitened, but she had to fight tooth and nail for what did belong to her: "From everywhere," she wrote, "impediments rose before me; and since this is the widows' fare, lawsuits and legal actions surrounded me" (112). And even for the woman who did remarry, what was entailed was not the merging of two families but her departure from one male-dominated household and entrance into another. The remarrying widow in effect passed through a variety of *men's* families without ever really having one of her own. This may well be, for example, the reason the Wife does not mention children. If she had them, they were her husbands' more than hers. Inheriting whatever property did not go to her, they would, unless they were still children, move out of her life when she remarried. As one historian has said,

> Family dynamics . . . were mostly about men: fathers, sons, brothers, and, when better alternatives failed, nephews and cousins. The social role of women was almost never as important as their biological role, and even when an individual woman became the key in the transmission of a patrimony or the preservation of a lineage her individuality was soon subsumed by the males whom she bore to the new patrilineage. (Rosenthal 175)

In his definition of the Wife as a wife, rather than as either mother or widow, this loss of individuality is a reality that Chaucer's account hides from us. A formidable competitor in the medieval marriage market and an admirable champion of her needs as a marriage partner, Alisoun's very success as a wife encourages Chaucer to turn aside from some of the other, less happy realities endured by many women in his contemporary world.

WORKS CITED

Aers, David. *Chaucer, Langland and the Creative Imagination*. London: Routledge, 1980.

Barron, Caroline. "The 'Golden Age' of Women in Medieval London." *Reading Medieval Studies* 15 (1989): 35–58.

Bennett, Judith. "Medieval Women, Modern Women: Across the Great Divide." *Culture and History 1350–1600: Essays on English Communities, Identities and Writing*. Ed. David Aers. London: Harvester, 1992. 147–75.

———. *Women in the Medieval English Countryside: Gender and Household in Brigstock before the Plague*. New York: Oxford UP, 1987.

Blamires, Alcuin. "The Wife of Bath and Lollardy." *Medium Aevum* 58 (1989): 224–42.

Brundage, James A. *Law, Sex, and Christian Society in Medieval Europe*. Chicago: U of Chicago P, 1987.

Bynum, Caroline Walker. *Holy Feast and Holy Fast: The Religious Significance of Food to Medieval Women*. Berkeley: U of California P, 1987.

Carruthers, Mary. "The Wife of Bath and the Painting of Lions." *PMLA* 94 (1979): 209–22.

Crane, Susan. *Gender and Romance in Chaucer's Canterbury Tales*. Princeton: Princeton UP, 1994.

d'Avray, David, and M. Tausche. "Marriage Sermons in *Ad Status* Collections of the Central Middle Ages." *Archives d'Histoire Doctrinale et Littéraire du Moyen Age* 47 (1980): 71–119.

Delany, Sheila. "Sexual Economics, Chaucer's Wife of Bath and *The Book of Margery Kempe*." *Minnesota Review* 5 (1975): 104–15.

———. "Strategies of Silence in the Wife of Bath's Recital." *Exemplaria* 2 (1990): 49–69.

Dockray, Keith. "Why Did Fifteenth-Century English Gentry Marry?: The Pastons, Plumptons and Stonors Reconsidered." *Gentry and Lesser Nobility in Late Medieval Europe*. Ed. Michael Jones. New York: St. Martin's, 1986. 61–80.

Donohue, Charles, Jr. "The Canon Law on the Formation of Marriage and Social Practice in the Later Middle Ages." *Journal of Family History* 8 (1983): 144–58.

Fradenburg, Louise O. "The Wife of Bath's Passing Fancy." *Studies in the Age of Chaucer* 8 (1986): 31–58.

Gairdner, James, ed. *The Paston Letters*. 6 vols. London: Library, 1904.

Hanawalt, Barbara A. "Remarriage as an Option for Urban and Rural Widows in Late Medieval England." *Wife and Widow in Medieval England*. Ed. Sue Sheridan Walker. Ann Arbor: U of Michigan P, 1993. 141–64.

———. *The Ties That Bound: Peasant Families in Medieval England*. New York: Oxford UP, 1986.

Helmholz, Richard. *Marriage Litigation in Medieval England*. Cambridge: Cambridge UP, 1974.

Houlbrooke, Ralph. "The Making of Marriage in Mid-Tudor England: Evidence from the Records of Matrimonial Contract Litigation." *Journal of Family History* 10 (1985): 339–52.

Hughes, Diane Owen. "Invisible Madonnas? The Italian Historiographical Tradition and the Women of Medieval Italy." *Women in Medieval History and Historiography*. Ed. Susan Mosher Stuard. Philadelphia: U of Pennsylvania P, 1987. 25–57.

Ingram, Martin. "Spousal Litigation in the English Ecclesiastical Courts c. 1350–c. 1640." *Marriage and Society: Studies in the Social History of Marriage*. Ed. R. B. Outhwaite. London: Europa, 1982. 35–57.

Kelly, H. A. *Love and Marriage in the Age of Chaucer*. Ithaca: Cornell UP, 1975.

Kempe, Margery. *The Book of Margery Kempe*. Trans. Barry A. Windeatt. Harmondsworth: Penguin, 1985.

Lacey, Kay E. "Women and Work in Fourteenth and Fifteenth Century London." *Women and Work in Pre-Industrial England*. Ed. Lindsey Charles and Lorna Duffin. London: Croom Helm, 1985. 24–82.

Macfarlane, Alan. *Marriage and Love in England: Modes of Reproduction 1300–1840*. Oxford: Basil Blackwell, 1986.

Manly, John M. *Some New Light on Chaucer*. New York: Holt, 1926.

Mann, Jill. *Chaucer and Medieval Estates Satire*. Cambridge: Cambridge UP, 1973.

Marsilius of Padua. *The Defender of the Peace*. Trans. Alan Gewirth. New York: Columbia UP, 1956.

McFarlane, K. B. *The Nobility of Later Medieval England*. Oxford: Clarendon, 1973.

Oresme, Nicholas. *Oeconomica: Le Livre de Yconomique d'Aristote*. Ed.

and trans. Albert Douglas Menut. *Transactions of the American Philosophical Society*, n.s. 47, pt. 5 (1957): 785–853.

Palmer, Robert C. "Contexts of Marriage in Medieval England: Evidence from the King's Court circa 1300." *Speculum* 59 (1984): 42–67.

Patterson, Lee. *Chaucer and the Subject of History*. Madison: U of Wisconsin P, 1991.

Pearsall, Derek. "The *Troilus* Frontispiece and Chaucer's Audience." *Yearbook of English Studies* 7 (1977): 68–74.

Pisan, Christine de. *La vision Christine*. Trans. Glenda K. McLeod. New York: Garland, 1993.

Power, Eileen, trans. *The Goodman of Paris*. London: Routledge, 1928.

Pratt, Robert A. "Chaucer and the Hand that Fed Him." *Speculum* 41 (1966): 619–42.

Robertson, D. W., Jr. "'And for my land thus hastow mordred me?': Land Tenure, the Cloth Industry, and the Wife of Bath." *Chaucer Review* 14 (1980): 403–20.

Rosenthal, Joel T. *Patriarchy and Families of Privilege in Fifteenth-Century England*. Philadelphia: U of Pennsylvania P, 1991.

Searle, Eleanor. "Seigneurial Control of Women's Marriage: The Antecedents and Function of Merchet in England." *Past and Present* 82 (1979): 3–43.

Sheehan, Michael. "The Formation and Stability of Marriage in Fourteenth-Century England: The Evidence of an Ely Register." *Mediaeval Studies* 32 (1971): 228–63.

———. "Marriage Theory and Practice in Conciliar Legislation and Diocesan Statutes of Medieval England." *Mediaeval Studies* 40 (1978): 408–60.

Strohm, Paul. "Chaucer's Audience." *Literature and History* 5 (1977): 26–41.

Sumption, Jonathan. *Pilgrimage: An Image of Medieval Religion*. London: Faber, 1975.

Thrupp, Sylvia. *The Merchant Class of Medieval London*. Ann Arbor: U of Michigan P, 1962.

Titow, J. Z. "Some Differences between Manors and Their Effects on the Condition of the Peasant in the Thirteenth Century." *Agricultural History Review* 10 (1962): 1–13.

Walker, Sue Sheridan. "Widow and Ward: The Feudal Law of Child Custody in Medieval England." *Women in Medieval Society*. Ed. Susan Mosher Stuard. Philadelphia: U of Pennsylvania P, 1976. 159–72.

Marxist Criticism
and
the Wife of Bath

WHAT IS MARXIST CRITICISM?

To the question "What is Marxist criticism?" it may be tempting to respond with another question: "What does it matter?" In light of the rapid and largely unanticipated demise of Soviet-style communism in the former USSR and throughout Eastern Europe, it is understandable to suppose that Marxist literary analysis would disappear too, quickly becoming an anachronism in a world enamored with full market capitalism.

In fact, however, there is no reason why Marxist criticism should weaken, let alone disappear. It is, after all, a phenomenon distinct from Soviet and Eastern European communism, having had its beginnings nearly eighty years before the Bolshevik revolution and having thrived, since the 1940s, mainly in the West — not as a form of communist propaganda but rather as a form of critique, a discourse for interrogating *all* societies and their texts in terms of certain specific issues. Those issues — including race, class, and the attitudes shared within a given culture — are as much with us as ever, not only in contemporary Russia but also in the United States.

The argument could even be made that Marxist criticism has been strengthened by the collapse of Soviet-style communism. There was a time, after all, when few self-respecting Anglo-American journals would use Marxist terms or models, however illuminating, to analyze

Western issues or problems. It smacked of sleeping with the enemy. With the collapse of the Kremlin, however, old taboos began to give way. Even the staid *Wall Street Journal* now seems comfortable using phrases like "worker alienation" to discuss the problems plaguing the American business world.

The assumption that Marxist criticism will die on the vine of a moribund political system rests in part on another mistaken assumption, namely, that Marxist literary analysis is practiced only by people who would like to see society transformed into a Marxist-communist state, one created through land reform, the redistribution of wealth, a tightly and centrally managed economy, the abolition of institutionalized religion, and so on. In fact, it has never been necessary to be a communist political revolutionary to be classified as a Marxist literary critic. (Many of the critics discussed in this introduction actually *fled* communist societies to live in the West.) Nor is it necessary to like only those literary works with a radical social vision or to dislike books that represent or even reinforce a middle-class, capitalist world-view. It is necessary, however, to adopt what most students of literature would consider a radical definition of the purpose and function of literary criticism.

More traditional forms of criticism, according to the Marxist critic Pierre Macherey, "set . . . out to deliver the text from its own silences by coaxing it into giving up its true, latent, or hidden meaning." Inevitably, however, non-Marxist criticism "intrude[s] its own discourse between the reader and the text" (qtd. in Bennett 107). Marxist critics, by contrast, do not attempt to discover hidden meanings in texts. Or, if they do, they do so only after seeing the text, first and foremost, as a material product to be understood in broadly historical terms. That is to say, a literary work is first viewed as a product *of* work (and hence of the realm of production and consumption we call economics). Second, it may be looked upon as a work that *does* identifiable work of its own. At one level, that work is usually to enforce and reinforce the prevailing ideology, that is, the network of conventions, values, and opinions to which the majority of people uncritically subscribe.

This does not mean that Marxist critics merely describe the obvious. Quite the contrary: the relationship that the Marxist critic Terry Eagleton outlines in *Criticism and Ideology* (1978) among the soaring cost of books in the nineteenth century, the growth of lending libraries, the practice of publishing "three-decker" novels (so that three borrowers could be reading the same book at the same time), and the changing *content* of those novels is highly complex in its own way. But the complexity Eagleton finds is not that of the deeply buried meaning of the text. Rather, it is that of the complex web of social and economic relationships that were prerequisite to the work's production. Marxist criticism does not seek to be, in Eagleton's words, "a passage from text to reader." Indeed, "its task is to show the text as it cannot know itself, to manifest those conditions of its making (inscribed in its very letter) about which it is necessarily silent" (43).

As everyone knows, Marxism began with Karl Marx, the nineteenth-century German philosopher best known for writing *Das Kapital*, the seminal work of the communist movement. What everyone doesn't know is that Marx was also the first Marxist literary critic (much as Sigmund Freud, who psychoanalyzed E. T. A. Hoffman's supernatural tale "The Sandman," was the first Freudian literary critic). During the 1830s Marx wrote critical essays on writers such as Goethe and Shakespeare (whose tragic vision of Elizabethan disintegration he praised).

The fact that Marxist literary criticism began with Marx himself is hardly surprising, given Marx's education and early interests. Trained in the classics at the University of Bonn, Marx wrote literary imitations, his own poetry, a failed novel, and a fragment of a tragic drama (*Oulanem*) before turning to contemplative and political philosophy. Even after he met Friedrich Engels in 1843 and began collaborating on works such as *The German Ideology* and *The Communist Manifesto*, Marx maintained a keen interest in literary writers and their works. He and Engels argued about the poetry of Heinrich Heine, admired Hermann Freiligrath (a poet critical of the German aristocracy), and faulted the playwright Ferdinand Lassalle for writing about a reactionary knight in the Peasants' War rather than about more progressive aspects of German history.

As these examples suggest, Marx and Engels would not — indeed, could not — think of aesthetic matters as being distinct and independent from such things as politics, economics, and history. Not surprisingly, they viewed the alienation of the worker in industrialized, capitalist societies as having grave consequences for the arts. How can people mechanically stamping out things that bear no mark of their producer's individuality (people thereby "reified," turned into things themselves) be expected to recognize, produce, or even consume things of beauty? And if there is no one to consume something, there will soon be no one to produce it, especially in an age in which production (even of something like literature) has come to mean *mass* (and therefore profitable) production.

In *The German Ideology* (1846), Marx and Engels expressed their sense of the relationship between the arts, politics, and basic economic reality in terms of a general social theory. Economics, they argued, provides the "base" or "infrastructure" of society, but from that base emerges a "superstructure" consisting of law, politics, philosophy, religion, and art.

Marx later admitted that the relationship between base and superstructure may be indirect and fluid: every change in economics may not be reflected by an immediate change in ethics or literature. In *The Eighteenth Brumaire of Louis Bonaparte* (1852), he came up with the word *homology* to describe the sometimes unbalanced, often delayed, and almost always loose correspondence between base and superstructure. And later in that same decade, while working on an introduction to his *Political Economy,* Marx further relaxed the base-superstructure relationship. Writing on the excellence of ancient Greek art (versus the primitive nature of ancient Greek economics), he conceded that a gap sometimes opens up between base and superstructure — between economic forms and those produced by the creative mind.

Nonetheless, *at* base the old formula was maintained. Economics remained basic and the connection between economics and superstructural elements of society was reaffirmed. Central to Marxism and Marxist literary criticism was and is the following "materialist" insight: consciousness, without which such things as art cannot be produced, is not the source of social forms and economic conditions. It is, rather, their most important product.

Marx and Engels, drawing upon the philosopher G. W. F. Hegel's theories about the dialectical synthesis of ideas out of theses and antitheses, believed that a revolutionary class war (pitting the capitalist class against a proletarian, antithetical class) would lead eventually to the synthesis of a new social and economic order. Placing their faith not in the idealist Hegelian dialectic but, rather, in what they called "dialectical materialism," they looked for a secular and material salvation of humanity — one in, not beyond, history — via revolution and not via divine intervention. And they believed that the communist society eventually established would be one capable of producing new forms of consciousness and belief and therefore, ultimately, great art.

The revolution anticipated by Marx and Engels did not occur in their century, let alone lifetime. When it finally did take place, it didn't happen in places where Marx and Engels had thought it might be successful: the United States, Great Britain, and Germany. It happened, rather, in 1917 Russia, a country long ruled by despotic czars but also enlightened by the works of powerful novelists and playwrights, including Chekhov, Pushkin, Tolstoy, and Dostoyevsky.

Perhaps because of its significant literary tradition, Russia produced revolutionaries like Nikolai Lenin, who shared not only Marx's interest in literature but also his belief in literature's ultimate importance. But it was not without some hesitation that Lenin endorsed the significance of texts written during the reign of the czars. Well before 1917 he had questioned what the relationship should be between a society undergoing a revolution and the great old literature of its bourgeois past.

Lenin attempted to answer that question in a series of essays on Tolstoy that he wrote between 1908 and 1911. Tolstoy — the author of *War and Peace* and *Anna Karenina* — was an important nineteenth-century Russian writer whose views did not accord with all of those of young Marxist revolutionaries. Continuing interest in a writer like Tolstoy may be justified, Lenin reasoned, given the primitive and unenlightened economic order of the society that produced him. Since superstructure usually lags behind base (and is therefore usually *more* primitive), the attitudes of a Tolstoy were relatively progressive when viewed in light of the monarchical and precapitalist society out of which they arose.

Moreover, Lenin also reasoned, the writings of the great Russian realists would *have* to suffice, at least in the short run. Lenin looked forward, in essays like "Party Organization and Party Literature," to the day in which new artistic forms would be produced by progressive writers with revolutionary political views and agendas. But he also knew that a great proletarian literature was unlikely to evolve until a thoroughly literate proletariat had been produced by the educational system.

Lenin was hardly the only revolutionary leader involved in setting up the new Soviet state who took a strong interest in literary matters. In 1924 Leon Trotsky published a book called *Literature and Revolution,* which is still acknowledged as a classic of Marxist literary criticism.

Trotsky worried about the direction in which Marxist aesthetic theory seemed to be going. He responded skeptically to groups like Proletkult, which opposed tolerance toward pre- and nonrevolutionary writers, and which called for the establishment of a new, proletarian culture. Trotsky warned of the danger of cultural sterility and risked unpopularity by pointing out that there is no necessary connection between the quality of a literary work and the quality of its author's politics.

In 1927 Trotsky lost a power struggle with Josef Stalin, a man who believed, among other things, that writers should be "engineers" of "human souls." After Trotsky's expulsion from the Soviet Union, views held by groups like Proletkult and the Left Front of Art (LEF), and by theorists such as Nikolai Bukharin and A. A. Zhdanov, became more prevalent. Speaking at the First Congress of the Union of Soviet Writers in 1934, the Soviet author Maxim Gorky called for writing that would "make labor the principal hero of our books." It was at the same writers' congress that "socialist realism," an art form glorifying workers and the revolutionary State, was made Communist party policy and the official literary form of the USSR.

Of those critics active in the USSR after the expulsion of Trotsky and the unfortunate triumph of Stalin, two critics stand out. One, Mikhail Bakhtin, was a Russian, later a Soviet, critic who spent much of his life in a kind of internal exile. Many of his essays were written in the 1930s and not published in the West or translated until the late 1960s. His work comes out of an engagement with the Marxist intellectual tradition as well as out of an indirect, even hidden, resistance to the Soviet government. It has been important to Marxist critics writing in the West because his theories provide a means to decode submerged social critique, especially in early modern texts. He viewed language — especially literary texts — in terms of discourses and dialogues. Within a novel written in a society in flux, for instance, the narrative may include an official, legitimate discourse, plus another infiltrated by challenging comments and even retorts. In a 1929 book on Dostoyevsky and a 1940 study titled *Rabelais and His World,* Bakhtin examined what he calls "polyphonic" novels, each characterized by a multiplicity of voices or discourses. In Dostoyevsky the independent status of a given character is marked by the difference of his or her language from that of the narrator. (The narrator's voice, too, can in fact be a dialogue.) In works by Rabelais, Bakhtin finds that the (profane) language of the Carnival and of other popular festivals plays against and parodies the more official discourses, that is, of the king, church, or even socially powerful intellectuals. Bakhtin influenced modern cultural criticism by showing, in a sense, that the conflict between "high" and "low" culture takes place not only between classic and popular texts but also between the "dialogic" voices that exist within many books — whether "high" or "low."

The other subtle Marxist critic who managed to survive Stalin's dictatorship and his repressive policies was Georg Lukács. A Hungarian who had begun his career as an "idealist" critic, Lukács had converted to Marxism in 1919; renounced his earlier, Hegelian work shortly thereafter; visited Moscow in 1930–31; and finally emigrated to the USSR in 1933, just one year before the First Congress of the Union of Soviet Writers met. Lukács was far less narrow in his views than the most strident Stalinist Soviet critics of the 1930s and 1940s. He disliked much socialist realism and appreciated prerevolutionary, realistic novels that broadly reflected cultural "totalities" — and were populated with characters representing human "types" of the author's place and time. (Lukács was particularly fond of the historical canvasses painted by the early-nineteenth-century novelist Sir Walter Scott.) But like his more rigid and censorious contemporaries, he drew the line at accepting nonrevolutionary, modernist works like James Joyce's *Ulysses*. He condemned movements like Expressionism and Symbolism, preferring works with "content" over more decadent, experimental works characterized mainly by "form."

With Lukács its most liberal and tolerant critic from the early 1930s until well into the 1960s, the Soviet literary scene degenerated to the point that the works of great writers like Franz Kafka were no longer read, either because they were viewed as decadent, formal experiments or because they "engineered souls" in "nonprogressive" directions. Officially sanctioned works were generally ones in which artistry lagged far behind the politics (no matter how bad the politics were).

Fortunately for the Marxist critical movement, politically radical critics *outside* the Soviet Union were free of its narrow, constricting policies and, consequently, able fruitfully to develop the thinking of Marx, Engels, and Trotsky. It was these non-Soviet Marxists who kept Marxist critical theory alive and useful in discussing all *kinds* of literature, written across the entire historical spectrum.

Perhaps because Lukács was the best of the Soviet communists writing Marxist criticism in the 1930s and 1940s, non-Soviet Marxists tended to develop their ideas by publicly opposing those of Lukács. German dramatist and critic Bertolt Brecht countered Lukács by arguing that art ought to be viewed as a field of production, not as a container of "content." Brecht also criticized Lukács for his attempt to enshrine realism at the expense not only of other "isms" but also of poetry and drama, both of which had been largely ignored by Lukács.

Even more outspoken was Brecht's critical champion Walter Benjamin, a German Marxist who, in the 1930s, attacked those conventional and traditional literary forms conveying a stultifying "aura" of culture. Benjamin praised Dadaism and, more important, new forms of art ushered in by the age of mechanical reproduction. Those forms — including radio and film — offered hope, he felt, for liberation from capitalist culture, for they were too new to be part of its stultifyingly ritualistic traditions.

But of all the anti-Lukácsians outside the USSR who made a contribution to the development of Marxist literary criticism, the most important was probably Théodor Adorno. Leader since the early 1950s of the Frankfurt school of Marxist criticism, Adorno attacked Lukács for his dogmatic rejection of nonrealist modern literature and for his belief in the primacy of content over form. Art does not equal science, Adorno insisted. He went on to argue for art's autonomy from empirical forms of knowledge, and to suggest that the interior monologues of modernist works (by Beckett and Proust) reflect the fact of modern alienation in a way that Marxist criticism ought to find compelling.

In addition to turning against Lukács and his overly constrictive canon, Marxists outside the Soviet Union were able to take advantage of insights generated by non-Marxist critical theories being developed in post–World War II Europe. One of the movements that came to be of interest to non-Soviet Marxists was structuralism, a scientific approach to the study of humankind whose proponents believed that all elements of culture, including literature, could be understood as parts of a system of signs. Using modern linguistics as a model, structuralists like Claude Lévi-Strauss broke the myths of various cultures down into "mythemes" in an attempt to show that there are structural correspondences or homologies between the mythical elements produced by various human communities across time.

Of the European structuralist Marxists, one of the most influential was Lucien Goldmann, a Rumanian critic living in Paris. Goldmann combined structuralist principles with Marx's base-superstructure model in order to show how economics determines the mental structures of social groups, which are reflected in literary texts. Goldmann rejected the idea of individual human genius, choosing to see works, instead, as the "collective" products of "trans-individual" mental structures. In early studies, such as *The Hidden God* (1955), he related seventeenth-century French texts (such as Racine's *Phèdre*) to the ideology of Jansenism. In later works, he applied Marx's base-superstructure model even more strictly, describing a relationship between economic conditions and texts unmediated by an intervening, collective consciousness.

In spite of his rigidity and perhaps because of his affinities with structuralism, Goldmann came to be seen in the 1960s as the proponent of a kind of watered-down, "humanist" Marxism. He was certainly viewed that way by the French Marxist Louis Althusser, a disciple not of Lévi-Strauss and structuralism but rather of the psychoanalytic theorist Jacques Lacan and of the Italian communist Antonio Gramsci, famous for his writings about ideology and "hegemony." (Gramsci used the latter word to refer to the pervasive, weblike system of assumptions and values that shapes the way things look, what they mean, and therefore what reality *is* for the majority of people within a culture.)

Like Gramsci, Althusser viewed literary works primarily in terms of their relationship to ideology, the function of which, he argued, is to (re)produce the existing relations of production in a given society. Dave Laing, in *The Marxist Theory of Art* (1978), has attempted to explain this particular insight of Althusser's by saying that ideologies, through the "ensemble of habits, moralities, and opinions" that can be found in any literary text, "ensure that the work-force (and those responsible for re-producing them in the family, school, etc.) are maintained in their position of subordination to the dominant class" (91). This is not to say that Althusser thought of the masses as a brainless multitude following only the dictates of the prevailing ideology: Althusser followed Gramsci in suggesting that even working-class people have some freedom to struggle against ideology and to change history. Nor is it to say that Althusser saw ideology as being a coherent, consistent force. In fact, he saw it as being riven with contradictions that works of literature sometimes expose and even widen. Thus Althusser followed Marx and Gramsci in believing that although literature must be seen in *relation* to ideology, it — like all social forms — has some degree of autonomy.

Althusser's followers included Pierre Macherey, who in *A Theory of Literary Production* (1966) developed Althusser's concept of the relationship between literature and ideology. A realistic novelist, he argued, attempts to produce a unified, coherent text, but instead ends up producing a work containing lapses, omissions, gaps. This happens because within ideology there are subjects that cannot be covered, things that cannot be said, contradictory views that aren't recognized as contradictory. (The critic's challenge, in this case, is to supply what the text cannot say, thereby making sense of gaps and contradictions.)

But there is another reason why gaps open up and contradictions become evident in texts. Works don't just reflect ideology (which Goldmann had referred to as "myth" and which Macherey refers to as a system of "illusory social beliefs"); they are also "fictions," works of art, *products* of ideology that have what Goldmann would call a "world-view" to offer. What kind of product, Macherey implicitly asks, is identical to the thing that produced it? It is hardly surprising, then, that Balzac's fiction shows French peasants in two different lights, only one of which is critical and judgmental, only one of which is baldly ideological. Writing approvingly on Macherey and Macherey's mentor Althusser in *Marxism and Literary Criticism* (1976), Terry Eagleton says: "It is by giving ideology a determinate form, fixing it within certain fictional limits, that art is able to distance itself from [ideology], thus revealing . . . [its] limits" (19).

A follower of Althusser, Macherey is sometimes referred to as a "post-Althusserian Marxist." Eagleton, too, is often described that way, as is his American contemporary Fredric Jameson. Jameson and Eagleton, as well as being post-Althusserians, are also among the few Anglo-American critics who have closely followed and significantly developed Marxist thought.

Before them, Marxist interpretation in English was limited to the work of a handful of critics: Christopher Caudwell, Christopher Hill, Arnold Kettle, E. P. Thompson, and Raymond Williams. Of these, Williams was perhaps least Marxist in orientation: he felt that Marxist critics, ironically, tended too much to isolate economics from culture; that they overlooked the individualism of people, opting instead to see them as "masses"; and that even more ironically, they had become an elitist group. But if the least Marxist of the British Marxists, Williams was also by far the most influential. Preferring to talk about "culture" instead of ideology, Williams argued in works such as *Culture and Society 1780–1950* (1958) that culture is "lived experience" and, as such, an interconnected set of social properties, each and all grounded in and influencing history.

Terry Eagleton's *Criticism and Ideology* (1978) is in many ways a response to the work of Williams. Responding to Williams's statement, in *Culture and Society*, that "there are in fact no masses; there are only ways of seeing people as masses" (289), Eagleton writes: "That men and women really are now unique individuals was Williams's (unexceptionable) insistence; but it was a proposition bought at the expense of perceiving the fact that they must mass and fight to achieve their full individual humanity. One has only to adapt Williams's statement to 'There are in fact no classes; there are only ways of seeing people as classes' to expose its theoretical paucity" (*Criticism* 29).

Eagleton goes on, in *Criticism and Ideology*, to propose an elaborate theory about how history — in the form of "general," "authorial," and "aesthetic" ideology — enters texts, which in turn may revivify, open up, or critique those same ideologies, thereby setting in motion a process that may alter history. He shows how texts by Jane Austen, Matthew Arnold, Charles Dickens, George Eliot, Joseph Conrad, and T. S. Eliot deal with and transmute conflicts at the heart of the general and authorial ideologies behind them: conflicts between morality and individualism, individualism and social organicism and utilitarianism.

As all this emphasis on ideology and conflict suggests, a modern British Marxist like Eagleton, even while acknowledging the work of a British Marxist predecessor like Williams, is more nearly developing the ideas of continental Marxists like Althusser and Macherey. That holds, as well, for modern American Marxists like Fredric Jameson. For although he makes occasional, sympathetic references to the works of Williams, Thompson, and Hill, Jameson makes far more *use* of Lukács, Adorno, and Althusser as well as non-Marxist structuralist, psychoanalytic, and poststructuralist critics.

In the first of several influential works, *Marxism and Form* (1971), Jameson takes up the question of form and content, arguing that the former is "but the working out" of the latter "in the realm of superstructure" (329). (In making such a statement Jameson opposes not only the tenets of Russian Formalists, for whom content had merely been the fleshing out of form, but also those of so-called vulgar Marxists, who tended to define form as mere ornamentation or window-dressing.) In his later work *The Political Unconscious* (1981), Jameson uses what in *Marxism and Form* he had called "dialectical criticism" to synthesize out of structuralism and poststructuralism, Freud and Lacan, Althusser and Adorno, a set of complex arguments that can only be summarized reductively.

The fractured state of societies and the isolated condition of individuals, he argues, may be seen as indications that there originally existed an unfallen state of something that may be called "primitive communism." History — which records the subsequent divisions and alienations — limits awareness of its own contradictions and of that lost, Better State, via ideologies and their manifestation in texts, whose strategies essentially contain and repress desire, especially revolutionary desire, into the collective unconscious. (In Conrad's *Lord Jim*, Jameson shows, the knowledge that governing classes don't *deserve* their power is contained and repressed by an ending that metaphysically blames Nature for the tragedy and that melodramatically blames wicked Gentleman Brown.)

As demonstrated by Jameson in analyses like the one mentioned above, textual strategies of containment and concealment may be discovered by the critic, but only by the critic practicing dialectical criticism, that is to say, a criticism aware, among other things, of its *own* status as ideology. All thought, Jameson concludes, is ideological; only through ideological thought that knows itself as such can ideologies be seen through and eventually transcended.

Ross C Murfin

MARXIST CRITICISM:
A SELECTED BIBLIOGRAPHY

Marx, Engels, Lenin, and Trotsky

Engels, Friedrich. *The Condition of the Working Class in England*. Ed. and trans. W. O. Henderson and W. H. Chaloner. Stanford: Stanford UP, 1968.

Lenin, V. I. *On Literature and Art*. Moscow: Progress, 1967.

Marx, Karl. *Selected Writings*. Ed. David McLellan. Oxford: Oxford UP, 1977.

Trotsky, Leon. *Literature and Revolution*. New York: Russell, 1967.

General Introductions to and Reflections on Marxist Criticism

Bennett, Tony. *Formalism and Marxism*. London: Methuen, 1979.

Demetz, Peter. *Marx, Engels, and the Poets*. Chicago: U of Chicago P, 1967.

Eagleton, Terry. *Literary Theory: An Introduction*. Minneapolis: U of Minnesota P, 1983. See chapter on Marxism.

———. *Marxism and Literary Criticism*. Berkeley: U of California P, 1976.

Elster, Jon. *An Introduction to Karl Marx*. Cambridge: Cambridge UP, 1985.

————. *Nuts and Bolts for the Social Sciences.* Cambridge: Cambridge UP, 1989.

Fokkema, D. W., and Elrud Kunne-Ibsch. *Theories of Literature in the Twentieth Century: Structuralism, Marxism, Aesthetics of Reception, Semiotics.* New York: St. Martin's, 1977. See ch. 4, "Marxist Theories of Literature."

Frow, John. *Marxism and Literary History.* Cambridge: Harvard UP, 1986.

Jefferson, Ann, and David Robey. *Modern Literary Theory: A Critical Introduction.* Totowa: Barnes, 1982. See the essay "Marxist Literary Theories," by David Forgacs.

Laing, Dave. *The Marxist Theory of Art.* Brighton, Eng.: Harvester, 1978.

Selden, Raman. *A Readers' Guide to Contemporary Literary Theory.* Lexington: U of Kentucky P, 1985. See ch. 2, "Marxist Theories."

Slaughter, Cliff. *Marxism, Ideology and Literature.* Atlantic Highlands: Humanities, 1980.

Some Classic Marxist Studies and Statements

Adorno, Théodor. *Prisms: Cultural Criticism and Society.* Trans. Samuel Weber and Sherry Weber. Cambridge: MIT P, 1982.

Althusser, Louis. *For Marx.* Trans. Ben Brewster. New York: Pantheon, 1969.

Althusser, Louis, and Etienne Balibar. *Reading Capital.* Trans. Ben Brewster. New York: Pantheon, 1971.

Bakhtin, Mikhail. *The Dialogic Imagination: Four Essays.* Ed. Michael Holquist. Trans. Caryl Emerson. Austin: U of Texas P, 1981.

————. *Rabelais and His World.* Trans. Hélène Iswolsky. Cambridge: MIT P, 1968.

Benjamin, Walter. *Illuminations.* Ed. with introd. by Hannah Arendt. Trans. H. Zohn. New York: Harcourt, 1968.

Caudwell, Christopher. *Illusion and Reality.* 1935. New York: Russell, 1955.

————. *Studies in a Dying Culture.* London: Lawrence, 1938.

Goldmann, Lucien. *The Hidden God.* New York: Humanities, 1964.

————. *Towards a Sociology of the Novel.* London: Tavistock, 1975.

Gramsci, Antonio. *Selections from the Prison Notebooks.* Ed. Quintin Hoare and Geoffrey Nowell Smith. New York: International, 1971.

Kettle, Arnold. *An Introduction to the English Novel.* New York: Harper, 1960.

Lukács, Georg. *The Historical Novel.* Trans. H. Mitchell and S. Mitchell. Boston: Beacon, 1963.

———. *Studies in European Realism.* New York: Grosset, 1964.

———. *The Theory of the Novel.* Cambridge: MIT P, 1971.

Marcuse, Herbert. *One-Dimensional Man.* Boston: Beacon, 1964.

Thompson, E. P. *The Making of the English Working Class.* New York: Pantheon, 1964.

———. *William Morris: Romantic to Revolutionary.* New York: Pantheon, 1977.

Williams, Raymond. *Culture and Society 1780–1950.* New York: Harper, 1958.

———. *The Long Revolution.* New York: Columbia UP, 1961.

———. *Marxism and Literature.* Oxford: Oxford UP, 1977.

Wilson, Edmund. *To the Finland Station.* Garden City: Doubleday, 1953.

Studies by and of Post-Althusserian Marxists

Dowling, William C. *Jameson, Althusser, Marx: An Introduction to "The Political Unconscious."* Ithaca: Cornell UP, 1984.

Eagleton, Terry. *Criticism and Ideology: A Study in Marxist Literary Theory.* London: Verso, 1978.

———. *Exiles and Émigrés.* New York: Schocken, 1970.

Goux, Jean-Joseph. *Symbolic Economies After Marx and Freud.* Trans. Jennifer Curtiss Gage. Ithaca: Cornell UP, 1990.

Jameson, Fredric. *Marxism and Form: Twentieth-Century Dialectical Theories of Literature.* Princeton: Princeton UP, 1971.

———. *The Political Unconscious: Narrative as a Socially Symbolic Act.* Ithaca: Cornell UP, 1981.

Macherey, Pierre. *A Theory of Literary Production.* Trans. G. Wall. London: Routledge, 1978.

Marxist Approaches to Chaucer and the Wife of Bath's Prologue and Tale

Aers, David. *Chaucer* [Harvester New Readings Series]. Atlantic Highlands: Humanities, 1986.

———. *Chaucer, Langland, and the Creative Imagination.* London: Routledge, 1980.

———. *Culture and History, 1350–1600: Essays on English Communities, Identities, and Writing.* Detroit: Wayne State UP, 1992.

Burton, T. L. "'Al is for to selle': Chaucer, Marx, and the New Historicism." *Southern Review* 20 (1987): 192–98.

Colmer, Dorothy. "Character and Class in the *Wife of Bath's Tale.*" *Journal of English and Germanic Philology* 72 (1973): 329–39.

Cook, Jon. "Carnival and the *Canterbury Tales:* 'Only Equals May Laugh.'" *Medieval Literature: Criticism, Ideology, and History.* Ed. David Aers. New York: St. Martin's, 1986. 169–91.

Delany, Sheila. *Medieval Literary Politics: Shapes of Ideology.* New York: Manchester UP, 1990.

——. "Sexual Economics, Chaucer's Wife of Bath, and *The Book of Margery Kempe.*" *Minnesota Review* 5 (1975): 104–15. Rpt. in *Writing Woman.* New York: Schocken, 1983. 76–92.

——. "Strategies of Silence in the Wife of Bath's Recital." *Exemplaria* 2 (1990): 49–69.

Ganim, John M. *Chaucerian Theatricality.* Princeton: Princeton UP, 1990.

Haller, Robert S. "The Wife of Bath and the Three Estates." *Annuale Mediaevale* 6 (1965): 47–64.

Knight, Stephen. *Geoffrey Chaucer.* Oxford: Basil Blackwell, 1986.

——. "Politics and Chaucer's Poetry." *The Radical Reader.* Ed. Stephen Knight and Michael Wilding. Sydney: Wild and Woolley, 1977. 169–92.

——. "The Social Function of Middle English Romances." *Medieval Literature: Criticism, Ideology, and History.* Ed. David Aers. New York: St. Martin's, 1986. 99–122.

Robertson, D. W., Jr. "Simple Signs from Everyday Life in Chaucer." *Signs and Symbols in Chaucer's Poetry.* Ed. John P. Herman and John J. Burke. University: U of Alabama P, 1981. 12–26.

Shoaf, R. A. *Dante, Chaucer, and the Currency of the Word: Money, Images, and Reference in Late Medieval Poetry.* Norman: Pilgrim, 1983.

A MARXIST PERSPECTIVE

In the essay that follows, Laurie Finke views the Wife of Bath's Prologue and Tale in terms of the hegemony — the set of values, practices, and beliefs that constitute lived experience — of the culture in which Chaucer worked. Following Marx, she views literature as a "superstructure" built upon the economic "base" or foundation of the society in which it was produced. Yet, like a more modern Marxist, she also shows how the text can help us see through the economic and related ideological systems of the day. Under Marxist analysis, for instance, Chaucer reveals that the accumulation of wealth that enabled the transition from feudalism to capitalism depended, in large part, on the link among sexuality, marriage, and monetary gain that governs the Wife of Bath's way of thinking, acting, and storytelling. Building on the thought of E. P. Thompson and Raymond Williams, Finke discusses Chaucer's text in terms of the death of feudalism and the rise of capitalism. Her focus is on the new middle class of which Chaucer, like the Wife of Bath, was a member and, more important, on an emerging individual and class consciousness.

Finke shows that Alisoun of Bath is a sexual being, yes, but also an economic being who marries her first three husbands to gain the financial independence that will later put her in a favorable bargaining position for her fourth, fifth, and possibly sixth husbands. Instead of breeding children as a result of her repeated marriages, the Wife of Bath "breeds capital." In doing so, Finke argues, the Wife gives expression to an aspect of the rise of capitalism that Marx all but ignored in his discussion of the history of capitalism: the role of sexuality and marriage in enabling the transition from feudalism to capitalism. The Wife of Bath's autobiographical account of her various relationships is eloquent testimony to her — and of course Chaucer's — awareness of the economic basis of marriage, and of the Wife's challenging of the usual terms of male-female relationships.

It is inevitable that in the tale Chaucer assigns to the Wife of Bath we find a further challenge to the feudal basis of male-female relationships. When the young knight forces his will on a maiden by raping her, he sets in motion a system of justice controlled by women: King Arthur's queen, the women of her court, the women the knight asks in his year's grace, and the old woman on the forest green. Finke argues that the various transformations in the tale — fairies to friars, old woman to lovely young bride, oppressive knight to obedient husband — reflect and reinforce the transformation of marriage to serve a money economy rather than a land-based one. It is significant that, for "payment" for the correct answer to the question of what women most desire, the old woman requests not the worldly goods that he desperately offers, but marriage, the only commodity she really wants. Of particular interest is Finke's discussion of the old woman's pillow lecture on gentillesse. In that lecture the new bride argues that true gentility is a matter not of birth or wealth or possessions or landholdings, but of deeds — a sentiment that Marx, had he read the tale, would have found prophetic.

LAURIE FINKE

"All is for to selle":
Breeding Capital
in the Wife of Bath's Prologue and Tale

It has become a critical commonplace in Chaucer scholarship to remark that the Wife of Bath's five marriages produced no children. At least the Wife does not mention any offspring in recounting her experiences of the "wo that is in mariage" (3). Alisoun's apparent childlessness would seem to run counter to the economic importance placed on the production of heirs in the Middle Ages as well as to the religious significance of procreation as the only legitimate justification for sex in marriage; as the Wife herself notes, "God bad us for to wexe and multiplye. / That gentil text kan I wel understonde!" (28–29). In her apparent barrenness, Alisoun presents a marked contrast to her "real-life" (or historically verifiable) counterpart, Margery Kempe, another late-fourteenth-century wife and businesswoman who appears to have had the leisure and wealth to travel extensively. Margery's account of her life tells us that her single marriage to John Kempe produced no fewer than fourteen children (Kempe 114).

What are we to make then of Alisoun's childlessness? A conventional reading might well see the Wife's sterility as symbolic of the barrenness of her life, of her single-minded pursuit of profit. Such a reading would find support in the medieval church's injunctions against usury, which it characterized as "monstrous and unnatural that an unfruitful thing should bear, that a thing specifically sterile, such as money, should bear fruit and multiply of itself" (Oresme 25). In the Wife of Bath's Prologue, however, this metaphoric characterization of profit as the "breeding" of money out of money shifts our attention from women's reproductive role within marriage to their productive role, at least within the class to which Alisoun claimed membership. It enables us to examine an arena in which the Wife's marriages have been extremely fruitful — in "breeding" capital.

I have taken the phrase "breeding capital" from the second chapter (61–100) of Richard Halpern's 1991 *The Poetics of Primitive Accumulation*. In that chapter Halpern examines what Marx called the "pre-history of capital." In *Capital*, Marx critiques the use of the term "primitive accumulation" to describe the processes by which, during the period between the fourteenth and sixteenth centuries, the conditions for capitalism were forcibly created. Both Marx and Halpern examine such necessary preconditions of capitalism as the formation of merchant's capital (capital produced through the activities of trading) and the forcible separation of workers from the ownership of the means of production. For Marx, beliefs about the mechanisms of primitive accumulation from the Middle Ages onward play the same role in political economy that the doctrine of original sin does in theology: both explain how "man" was condemned to "eat his bread in the sweat of his brow" (*Capital* 873). What Marx's account leaves out is woman's relegation in both theological and economic doctrine to the sphere of reproduction, how she was condemned to "bring forth children in sorrow" (Genesis 3:16). I hope in this essay to provide a more literal reading of Halpern's metaphor of "breeding" capital. The Wife of Bath has used marriage not to procreate, but to increase her wealth and to accumulate property and income:

> I wolde no lenger in the bed abide
> If that I felte his arm over my side
> Til he had maad his raunceon unto me.
> Thanne wolde I suffre him do his nicetee. (409–12)

This link between sexuality and monetary gain is the key to the sexual economy of the Wife's performance — she produces not children but money. In this manner, she ensures that her husbands "me yiven hir lond and hir tresoor" (204) with the result that the Wife is at the time of the Canterbury pilgrimage a wealthy cloth-maker whose work and wealth exceed even "hem of Ypres and of Gaunt" (A448). The Wife of Bath's Prologue and Tale, read in conjunction with Marx's account of primitive accumulation, restores to Marx's narrative of capital's prehistory a dimension that is notably missing — that is the role of sexuality and marriage in the accumulation of wealth that enabled the transition from feudalism to capitalism.

I. COMMODIFICATION, MARRIAGE, PROFIT

It would be a mistake to read the Wife of Bath as representative of some generic notion of womanhood, to see her either as the mouthpiece of patriarchal oppression or as its victim, although the temptation to do so is nearly overwhelming given the catalog of misogynist — that is, woman-hating — commonplaces that make up the bulk of her prologue. As Howard Bloch has noted, the sheer repetitiousness of misogynistic invective reduces women to an unchanging essence — Woman — and removes her from history (5). In the decontextualized, textual space in which medieval misogyny generally circulated, detached from its reference to any specific women, such invective could rely on strategies that took women out of time, out of history. It could reduce the heterogeneity and diversity of "women" to the essential "Woman." But Chaucer created a woman who — however fictional — represents a particular class at a particular moment in time. Putting those misogynist commonplaces into her mouth, he recontextualizes them. In this new textual space, such misogynist commonplaces enter into a dialogue with the material and historical conditions of existence for a late-fourteenth-century wife of the merchant class.

Mary Carruthers describes Alisoun as a "capitalist entrepreneur" (210), while Sheila Delany regards her as a "member of petty bourgeoisie, a middle sized fish in a small pond" (77), who could not hope to compete with the great textile magnates of her time. But perhaps it is not necessary to deduce the Wife's annual income or the extent of her economic power to locate her occupation of cloth manufacture within the mercantilism of late-fourteenth-century England. By the thirteenth century, the textile trade had come to dominate the English economy and the international trade. Thanks to protective legislation, English cloth-makers had, in fact, surpassed "hem of Ypres and of Gaunt" (A448), that is, the formerly dominant textile merchants of Flanders (Postan and Miller 174–75).

Despite the increasing wealth of English textile merchants, of course, it is not technically possible to speak of the Wife as representing any "class" strictly speaking if we define class, as E. P. Thompson has done, not as a reified entity, as a fixed and preexistent "thing," but as the consciousness of relationships of shared interest and struggle:

> Classes do not exist as separate entities, look around, find an
> enemy class, and then start to struggle. On the contrary, people
> find themselves in a society structured in determined ways. . . .
> They identify points of antagonistic interest, they commence to
> struggle around those issues and in the process of struggling they
> discover themselves as classes, they come to know this discovery as
> class consciousness. (149)

In the late fourteenth century, it is not likely that the growing "middle strata" (the term is Thrupp's, 288) of English society — of which Chaucer himself was a member — thought of themselves as a class. Despite the increasing importance of merchant capital in the medieval economy and despite the breakdown of traditional feudal relations based on vassalage, land tenure, and military service, the merchants, esquires, citizens, burgesses, guildsmen, and royal retainers who provided specialized services to a growing state bureaucracy were barely — usually only obliquely or confusedly — recognized in the system of assumptions, meanings, values, and practices that made up the medieval hegemony. (A hegemony constitutes the lived experience of most people within a social formation, what we often call "common sense.")

The dominant but increasingly besieged hegemony of feudalism could recognize only three classes of society. According to Georges Duby, they are those who prayed (*oratores*), those who fought (*bellatores*), and those who worked the land (*labores*). Increasingly that order was coming into conflict with an emergent hegemony in which wealth was based not on land, as in feudalism, but on money. The conflict between these two orders, dominant and emergent, is captured in the General Prologue to the *Canterbury Tales*. Three of the pilgrims represent the feudal orders: the Parson, the Knight, and the Plowman. Side by side with those idealized representatives of feudalism, however, and largely overshadowing them, are a much more lively, chaotic, and heterogeneous group of pilgrims — physicians, guildsmen, sergeants-at-law, friars, franklins, cooks, shipmen, reeves, millers, and merchant wives — who seem to fit within no easily charted hierarchy of medieval life. They would appear to belong to Thrupp's "middle strata" of English society, but that middle covers a very wide ground indeed.

The conflict I am describing here is not simply what might be characterized in Marxist terms as a discrepancy between the economic base of medieval society and its superstructure, that is, the discourses about beliefs and values that make up religion, philosophy, literature, and art. The failure of the medieval ideology of the three orders to encompass the diversity of fourteenth-century urban life is not simply the result of a lag between base and superstructure. That the fourteenth century saw the beginning of the transition from a feudal economic order to a capitalist one is obvious only with the benefit of hindsight. During this period of transition when the outcome was anything but certain, the economic base of feudalism coexisted, and was often in conflict, with an emergent capitalist one. Fiefs were still awarded to vassals, rents were still collected, and peasants were still tied to the land at the same time that goods were being exchanged for profit, interest was being charged on money, and serfs were leaving their manors to become workers in the towns. The conflicts within medieval life that the *Canterbury Tales* enacts occur not simply at the level of ideology — that is, as an abstract and imposed set of ideas — nor as the result of a lag between economic base and ideological superstructure. Rather, these conflicts between residual and emergent hegemonies, between two mutually exclusive means of organizing social and economic life, are lived, not simply contemplated as ideas. They constitute the substance and limit of consciousness, of common sense, of the "natural" (Williams 38). In the model I am describing, superstructure does not merely follow from the economic realities of the base; rather, base and superstructure describe a system in process whose main terms are mutually constitutive, each producing the other.

The institution of marriage as it is presented in the Wife of Bath's Prologue is a good example of a Marxist concept of hegemony as lived experience in which base and superstructure are mutually constitutive. In feudalism, wealth is tied to the land. As a form of wealth, land has certain economic characteristics. It is not easily portable. Those who possess the land and those who work it need to be tied to it and to one another, a need satisfactorily met by the rituals of vassalage, which were sanctified by oath. Furthermore, because it cannot reproduce itself, land is not partible. When it is divided up — as a form of inheritance, for example — each generation will receive an increasingly smaller portion than the last. In England in the Middle Ages, this problem was largely solved among the aristocracy by the custom of primogeniture, a system in which the eldest son in the family inherited the family estate intact. The estate was not usually divided up. Primogeniture requires a specific marital strategy. The legitimacy of the heir must be assured at any cost, and the cost is invariably the wife's sexual liberty. The wife who will produce the heir must be a virgin at marriage and she must have only one sexual partner throughout the marriage. Legally, the customs of aristocratic marriage (codified by common law and canon law) tended to limit the wife's economic freedom as well. After marriage the husband controlled any property his wife brought to the marriage. As if to underscore the connection, the language of marriage and romance in the Middle Ages drew heavily on the political discourse of feudalism. Both vassals and lovers, for instance, "plight their troth."

Money is a very different kind of wealth. It is eminently portable and so, unlike land, tends to free individuals from the old ties both to the land and to other people. This new social mobility is perhaps evidenced by Chaucer's announcement in the General Prologue that the wife "koude muchel of wandring by the weye" (A467). Money is also partible. A monetary inheritance divided up among several heirs does not impoverish them in the same way that the partition of land does because money can, despite the church's insistence on its unnaturalness (Oresme 25), breed more money. In such an economy, very different marital strategies might emerge. In a money economy, one can hold wealth in one's own right, not as the representative of a family. Merchants might place less emphasis on the production of an heir than on the maximization of family labor: a wife and children serve less as conduits of family power than as a cheap and easily exploitable labor pool. Because wealth is detached from land and family, heirs might even prove to be a liability in subsequent marriages. Furthermore, money could be settled on a woman through the practice of jointure and, on marrying, a woman could keep her wealth in her own name and even maintain her own businesses, as Margery Kempe did, when she started both a brewery and a milling business as separate enterprises from those of her husband (Kempe 9–10). It is clear that she has an independent income when she pays his debts in exchange for his permission to go on a pilgrimage to Jerusalem (Kempe 24). Even the old feudal privilege of wardship, in which the custody of a marriageable person is granted to a vassal, can participate in the commodification of relationships bourgeois marriage entails, as Chaucer well knew. In 1375, in his position as king's esquire, Chaucer was given custody of the lands and marriages of the heirs of Edmund de Staplegate, a Canterbury merchant. The grant was worth ten pounds, which Sheila Delany estimates would translate to about $25,000 in the late twentieth century (Delany 79).

In such an economy, one can imagine marriage as profitable in its own right, apart from the production of heirs; that is, both men and women can, as the Wife does, marry for money. The virtues that for the Wife make her first three husbands "goode" are that they are "riche, and olde" (197). Virtually every critic who has written about the Wife of Bath has remarked on the language of commodification the Wife employs to "speke of wo that is in mariage" (3). That language sometimes quite literally represents marriage as a financial transaction, as a form of economic exchange. The Wife barters her body:

> They had me yiven hir lond and hir tresoor. (204)
> For winning wolde I all his lust endure. (416)
> The flour is goon. There is namoore to telle.
> The bren, as I best kan, now moste I selle. (477–78)

Elsewhere the connection between marriage and economics is a more metaphoric one, as when Alisoun calls upon Saint Paul's epistles as proof of her view of marriage:

> Why sholde men elles in her bookes sette
> That man shal yelde to his wif her dette?
> Now wherwith sholde he make his paiement,
> If he ne used his sely instrument? (129–32)

Ultimately, however, the distinction between metaphoric and literal "paiement" is insupportable:

> But sith I hadde hem hoolly in mine hond,
> And sith they hadde yiven me al hir lond,
> What sholde I take kepe hem for to plese
> But it were for my profit and mine ese? (211–14)

> Blessed be God that I have wedded five.
> Of whiche I have picked out the beste
> Bothe of hir nether purs and of hir cheste. (44–44b)

Does "profit" in line 214 refer to further financial gains Alisoun expects, or does it refer only to her sexual pleasure since her husbands have already given her "hir lond and hir tresoor" (204)? Is "nether purs" in line 44b only an obscene pun? Or has the text's ability to distinguish monetary gain and sexual pleasure simply collapsed on itself under the weight of the comparison?

These ambiguities point to one of the most significant characteristics of money and its mode of symbolism: money can act — almost like a metaphor — to transform one thing into something else, to enable an exchange among dissimilar things. As "an idealized standard and measure of values" that gives value to commodities in the economic sphere, money functions as a "general symbolic equivalent" that stands apart from other commodities in a double relationship of privilege and exclusion (Goux 18, 10). As symbolic equivalent, money allows exchange, transformation, substitution, and supplementarity. Both Alisoun's prologue and her tale make extensive use of these processes of transformation and substitution; indeed they constitute the most characteristic features of the Wife's narrative. This pattern is established from the first line of her prologue. Alisoun begins by stating that

> Experience, though noon auctoritee
> Were in this world, is right ynogh for me
> To speke of wo that is in mariage. (1–3)

Immediately, however, her "experience" gives way to — is transformed into — a recitation of the various religious authorities on marriage from the Bible, both Old and New Testament, and from the Church Fathers and classical writers like Ptolemy. The speed with which one citation is replaced by the next tends to flatten out the differences among them. They become atomized and fragmented citations (dare I say "sound bytes"?), detached from their original contexts and reusable more or less interchangeably.

As she describes her five marriages, Alisoun renders her husbands virtually indistinguishable; they function as a chain of substitutions, her desire to accumulate wealth reducing them to so many interchangeable commodities. This is particularly true of the first three husbands, who are so indistinguishable that they are treated as one: "The three men were goode, and riche, and olde" (197). Because they are not significant beyond the wealth they enabled Alisoun to accumulate, they do not merit individual narratives. The fourth and fifth husbands are given slightly more characterization. The fourth is a womanizer who dies. The fifth simply reverses the pattern without substantially altering it: the young Jankyn who reads to Alisoun from his "book of wikked wives" (685) marries the no-longer-young but wealthy Alisoun, and she in turn hands over to him all that she has won from her first husbands: "And to him yaf I all the lond and fee / That evere was me yiven therbifore" (630–31). But the pattern of substitution by which the prologue advances and the promise of its continuity is established early on: "Blessed be God that I have wedded five. / Welcome the sixte, whan that evere he shall!" (44–45).

II. RAPE, ROMANCE, GENTLE DEEDS

Like her prologue, the Wife's tale is structured around substitution and transformation at every level. Alisoun chooses to tell (or Chaucer chooses to have her tell) a tale in the genre of romance, nostalgically invoking "th'olde dayes of the king Arthour" (857). But in doing so, she invokes not simply another time "many hundred yeres ago" (863), but a different class experience as well, one that appears to be quickly fading. In those old days, "All was this land fulfild of fairye" (859). But now all that has changed:

> But now kan no man seen none elves mo,
> For now the grete charitee and prayeres
> Of limitours and othere hooly freres,

That serchen every lond and every streem
As thikke as motes in the sonne-beem,
Blessinge halles, chambres, kichenes, boures,
Citees, burghes, castels, hye toures,
Thropes, bernes, shipnes, daieryes.
This maketh that there been no fairyes.
For there as wont to walken was an elf
There walketh now the limitour himself. (864–74)

Wommen may go now saufly up and doun.
In every bussh or under every tree
There is noon oother incubus but he,
And he ne wol doon hem but dishonour. (878–81)

These passages contain in small the elements of substitution that the
tale exploits on a larger scale. Fairies are instantly transformed into fri-
ars. The mystifications of aristocratic absolutism — the romantic illu-
sions represented by fairies and King Arthur — are dismissed in a few
lines along with the ideologies of chivalry that belong to the genre
and are replaced by the peripatetic friar who is not tied to any specific
location but wanders up and down the countryside. His blessings fall
indiscriminately on bowers and barns, castles and kitchens, flattening
out the economic and class distinctions these spaces would embody.

The choice of the friar is not without significance beyond the
chance to poke yet another satirical jab at corrupt clergymen. The friar
bespeaks the dislocation created by primitive accumulation. One of
the preconditions for capitalism in Marx's analysis of the transition
from feudalism to capitalism is that the workers must become "free"
to dispose of their own labor, and to do so they must not be bound to
the soil. But of course during the historical process of "freeing" work-
ers from this bond, the economy could not possibly absorb all those
who had been dispossessed from the land. Many could not adapt to
the new economic conditions, and during the two centuries after
Chaucer's death (a period during which Chaucer's works were circu-
lating both in manuscript and in printed books), if the increasingly
more severe and violent legislation passed to control them is any indi-
cation, the number of beggars, robbers, and vagabonds would con-
tinue to attest to the growing pains of nascent capitalism (*Capital*
877–90). Friars, although not strictly speaking such vagabonds, are in
some ways at least symbolic of this new dislocation. Indeed, as R. A.
Shoaf has argued, the life of Saint Francis of Assisi — the founder of
the mendicant orders — would be unimaginable outside the context
of a money economy: "his repudiation of his father's mercantile

values . . . [and] the events and consequences of his words and deeds are inextricably involved with money" (Shoaf 7). What anxieties about masterless men, we might ask, are obliquely registered in the transformation of the incubus — that demon-rapist — into a wandering "limitour" from whom women need fear only dishonor?

The Wife of Bath's Tale transforms the elements of the aristocratic genre of romance, undercutting their mystifications but, at the same time, adapting them to embody the ideologies required of the changing economic conditions. The knight-errant becomes a knight-erring. The damsel in distress becomes a loathly old woman who must save the knight in distress. What purpose, we might ask, does such transformation serve? As I have suggested above, the new economic conditions of primitive accumulation would require some change in the sexual labor (both productive and reproductive) required of marriage. I would argue that the primary function of the transformations that structure the Wife's tale is to mystify the sexual violence required as marriage is transformed to serve a money economy rather than a land-based one. Marx's contribution to economic history in *Capital* was not simply to identify the mechanisms by which the conditions of capitalism were created; he also exposed the violence required to bring about these conditions. He rejected previous economic histories that rendered the emergence of capital an innocent and inevitable outcome: "In the tender annals of political economy, the idyllic reigns from time immemorial. Right and 'labour' were from the beginning of time the sole means of enrichment." Rather, he contended that "the methods of primitive accumulation are anything but idyllic. . . . In actual history, it is a notorious fact that conquest, enslavement, robbery, murder, in short, force, play the greatest part" in the creation of property (*Capital* 874). The sexual economy that accompanied primitive accumulation was in its own way violent, relying on forced marriage, wife-beating, and even rape to accomplish its end. Ironically it was Marx's insight as well as his blindness to identify at least metaphorically the link between sexuality and the violence of primitive accumulation when he wrote that "Force is the midwife of every old society which is pregnant with a new one" (*Capital* 916).

In the Wife's prologue the sexual violence of forced marriage and wife-beating are transformed by fictions of equal power. If Alisoun is "beten for a book" (712), she is also represented as powerful enough to be herself an aggressor:

And whan I saugh he wolde nevere fyne
To reden on this cursed book all night,
All sodeynly three leves have I plyght
Out of his book right as he radde, and eke
I with my fest so took him on the cheke
That in oure fir he fil bakward adoun.
    And he up stirte as dooth a wood leoun,
And with his fest he smoot me on the heed
That in the floor I lay as I were deed. (788–96)

The prologue transforms this ugly incident by reasserting the comic motif of the shrewish, overbearing wife and henpecked husband. Alisoun does not hesitate to extract revenge: "And yet eftsoones I hitte him on the cheke, / And seyde, 'Theef, thus muchel am I wreke'" (808–09). The prologue mystifies the sexual violence of marriage by resolving the conflict in mutual "governance" and "maistrie," pretending it is possible to empower all as governors without enslaving any. Even after the Wife's prologue has laid bare the economic calculation of medieval merchant marriages, its ending attempts to pull its readers back into the illusion of romantic love. That illusion, however, is not seamless. There is a moment in which Alisoun attributes calculated and mercenary motives, rather than simple anger, to Jankyn's blow: "'O, hastow slain me, false theef?' I seyde, / 'And for my land thus hastow mordred me?'" (800–02). Such moments remind us of what the romantic mystifications are designed to disguise: that marriage for a woman of Alisoun's means involves economic calculation as much as love.

The Wife's tale also exploits a transformation of sexual violence, this time in the form of rape. The hero, a "lusty bachiler,"

saugh a maide walkinge him biforn,
Of whiche maide anon, maugree her hed,
By verray force he rafte her maidenhed. (886–88)

The rape is sketchily described in only three lines, compressed into its most significant feature represented by the verb "rafte" in line 888, a word whose associations are primarily with property theft (from "reave," "to commit spoliation or robbery; to plunder, pillage" — *OED*). But if rape sets in motion the events of the tale, it also initiates a series of transformations that seem designed to shift our attention away from the rape, to resolve it by denying its violence, displacing it into ritual and game:

> For which oppressioun was swich clamour
> And swich pursuite unto the king Arthour,
> That dampned was this knight for to be deed,
> By cours of lawe, and sholde han lost his heed —
> Paraventure swich was the statut tho —
> But that the queene and othere ladies mo
> So longe preyeden the king of grace
> Til he his lif him graunted in the place,
> And yaf him to the queene, all at her wille,
> To chese wheither she wolde him save or spille. (889–98)

The punishment that we expect to befall the rapist by "cours of lawe," by appeal to the juridical apparatus of the state, is almost instantaneously transformed into a courtly game for the amusement of the ladies of Arthur's court who lay on the knight the quest of discovering the thing "that wommen moost desiren" (905). The court of law is replaced by a court of ladies and the violence of state-sanctioned criminal punishment by the rituals of the game. The brutality of rape vanishes with hardly a trace.

From this point on, the knight's fate is governed not by a rational or even juridical sequence of cause and effect but by the rules of a game that is quickly revealed to be a supernatural — and a mystifying — one. The game's most basic rule is transformation and substitution; nothing can remain what it appears. A second transformation occurs when in the execution of his quest to find out what women most desire, the knight comes upon a dance "of ladies foure and twenty and yet mo" (992):

> But certeinly, er he came fully there,
> Vanisshed was this daunce, he nyste where.
> Ne creature saugh he that bar lif,
> Save on the grene he saugh sittinge a wif.
> A fouler wight there may no man devise. (995–99)

The old woman turns out to be the one person with the knowledge — the wisdom — to answer the question that will save the knight's life, but she extracts a high price for her wisdom: to repay the debt he must marry her.

Despite the tale's emphasis on the old woman's age and ugliness — "A fouler wight there may no man devise" (999) — and her own suggestion that he will reject her because she is foul and old and poor, a reading of the tale's language suggests that the knight's primary objection to his impending marriage has less to do either with age or looks than with the class difference between them, as he himself suggests: "'Allas, that any of my nacioun / Sholde evere so foule disparaged be'" (1068–69). In these lines we should take "nacioun" to refer not to the knight's nationality but to his birth, his "naissance." The knight appeals to the ideology of aristocracy, to the notion that birth equals worth. This ideology naturalizes the class distinctions that underwrote the feudal economic order.

To the knight's challenge that she is "comen of so lough a kinde" (1101), the old woman responds with the famous pillow lecture on gentillesse. It is difficult not to read this lecture, even in a non-Marxist context, as a commentary on class struggle. The old woman focuses her response not so much on the charge that she is old and ugly as on the issue of inherited worth. In response to the notion that gentility must be inherited, she argues that

If gentillesse were planted natureelly
Unto a certeyn linage doun the line,
Privee and apert, thanne wolde they nevere fine
To doon of gentillesse the faire office.
They mighte do no vileynye or vice. (1134–38)

The word *gentillesse* is itself class-marked. Like *courtesy*, it originally referred to the behavior required of those who were of gentle birth (or at court), just as *villainous* or *churlish* (terms we might be tempted to apply to the knight's behavior) were originally defined as the behavior expected of a villain or churl, members of the lower classes: "For vileyns sinful dedes make a cherl" (1158). Only under the pressure of redefinition by a middle class struggling to assert its cultural power against that of the aristocracy were the semantic ranges of these words expanded.

The cultural work that the Wife of Bath's Tale must perform, then, is to transform this aristocratic ideology in which virtue is heritable — a possession only of those of "heigh parage" (1120) — by constructing a counterideology in which virtue can only be known by its deeds. Against "old richesse" (1110), "heritage" (1119), and "heigh parage"(1120) the old woman ranges "gentil dedes" (1115) and "vertuous living" (1122). A person of high birth can be just as villainous as someone of low birth:

Heere may ye see well how that genterye
Is not annexed to possessioun. (1146–47)
For, God it woot, men may well often finde
A lordes sone do shame and vileynye.

> And he that wole han pris of his gentrye
> For he was boren of a gentil hous
> And hadde his eldres noble and vertuous
> And nil himselven do no gentil dedis
> Ne folwen his gentil auncestre that deed is,
> He nis not gentil, be he duc or erl. (1150–57)

After rejecting the aristocratic definition of virtue as high birth, the old woman goes on to define gentillese, somewhat vaguely, by deeds: "he is gentil that dooth gentil dedis" (1170):

> Looke who that is moost vertuous alway,
> Privee and apert, and moost entendeth ay
> To do the gentil dedes that he kan.
> Taak him for the grettest gentil man. (1113–16)

While the sentiments expressed in the old woman's speech — "gen-terye / Is not annexed to possessioun" — might strike us from our historical perspective as self-evident and even clichéd (perhaps because of our own ideological commitments to what George Bernard Shaw called "middle-class morality"), this speech literally redefines for the benefit of Chaucer's audience the meanings of its key words: "gentillesse" and "vileynye."

Such redefinition would be crucial to the development of the sort of class consciousness to which E. P. Thompson alludes. The superstructure for this consciousness seems to have been in place long before capitalism had fully replaced feudalism in the economic base. Indeed, the sentiments expressed by the woman are largely drawn from Dante, and very similar sentiments turn up in collections of moral proverbs such as that compiled by the early-fifteenth-century poet Christine de Pisan.

What is new in the old woman's pillow lecture, then, is not that she expresses such sentiments — after all, she admits she is quoting Dante — but that these ideas appear in the superstructure — in literature — long before they have come to dominate the economic base. The middle class's legitimation of its cultural hegemony during the following centuries would rest on exactly this set of interlocking claims about the benefits of its industriousness, its hardworking devotion to the enrichment of the country as a whole, its prudence, moderation, common sense, temperance, stability — in short, its virtue and its moral superiority to both the profligate aristocracy and to the lazy underclasses. This is the "political idyll" to which Marx refers when he exposes in *Capital* the political fiction by which capitalism claims economic domination:

> Long ago there were two sorts of people; one, the diligent, intelligent and above all frugal elite; the other, lazy rascals, spending their substance, and more in riotous living. . . . Thus it came to pass that the former sort accumulated wealth, and the latter sort finally had nothing to sell except their own skins. And from this original sin dates the poverty of the great majority who, despite all their labour, have up to now nothing to sell but themselves, and the wealth of the few that increases constantly, although they have long ceased to work. (*Capital* 873)

In the Wife's tale, the old woman expresses ideas about virtue and gentility that, while now almost clichéd in the saying, appear to precede and hence influence the formation of a new economic system.

In the final transformation the old woman is turned into a beautiful woman "as fair to seene / As any lady, emperice, or queene" (1245–46; note in these lines the conflation of beauty to class). This transformation resolves the series of events that began with the rape by covering over altogether whatever traces remain of the violence that drives the sexual economy of courtship and marriage. This transformation is framed as a choice, presented to the knight-rapist now turned husband:

> "Chese now," quod she, "oon of thise thinges tweye:
> To han me foul and old til that I deye
> And be to you a trewe humble wif,
> And nevere you displese in all my lif,
> Or elles ye wol han me yong and fair,
> And take your aventure of the repair
> That shall be to your hous by cause of me,
> Or in some oother place, may well be." (1219–26)

The knight's choice between having a chaste wife and having a beautiful one reveals the contradictions inherent in the ideological manipulation of female sexuality. Female sexuality is conceived of as a man's personal possession to be jealously guarded from the encroachments of other men. At the same time, female beauty is worthless if it is not on display; a hidden beauty is really no beauty at all, so that fidelity without beauty is of no value. This point may be more fully illuminated by comparing the knight-rapist's choice in the Wife's tale with the one framed in one of the tale's analogues, the Wedding of Sir

Gawain and Dame Ragnell. (This poem appears in Bodleian MS
Rawlinson c.86, a fifteenth-century manuscript, but I quote from the
edition in Bryan and Dempster.) There is no rape in this version; the
hero, Gawain, is not depicted as a rapist, but as excessively courteous;
he marries the old woman without complaint out of loyalty to
Arthur. And in this version, Gawain's choice is framed somewhat dif-
ferently:

> "Syr," she sayd, "thus shalle ye me haue,
> Chese of the one, so god me saue,
> My beawty wolle nott hold;
> Wheder ye wolle haue me fayre on nyghtes,
> And as foulle on days to alle men sightes,
> Or els to haue me fayre on days,
> And on nyghtes on the fowlyst wyfe." (656–62)

Gawain, of course, finds it impossible to choose:

> To haue you fayre on nyghtes and no more,
> That wold greve me hartt ryghte sore,
> And my worshypp shold I lese. (670–72)

Gawain's choice to have Ragnell beautiful by day and ugly by night,
or vice versa, is impossible because in the culture of primitive accumu-
lation, possessing perfect beauty without the ability to display it would
rob the owner of "worshypp," of the status that accrues from the pos-
session of a beautiful wife. In both tales, despite rather significant dif-
ferences in plot, the choice between physical beauty or ugliness reveals
the contradictions implicit in the sexual economies of primitive accu-
mulation.

I do not mean to imply in my analysis of the Wife of Bath's perfor-
mance that Chaucer intended to write a critique of the sexual econ-
omy of primitive accumulation. Such an intentionalist argument
would, of course, be anachronistic and, at any rate, unnecessary. The
ultimate dominance of capitalism, after all, is obvious only with the
benefit of hindsight. Rather, I argue that, given the circles to which
Chaucer belonged and in which his texts were read, Chaucer could
not help but replicate in his writing the sexual economies — with all
their conflict, contradiction, and struggle — of his time. If, as Marx
suggests, the transformation from a feudal to a capitalist economy re-
quired violence, and if that violence was later mystified through the
creation of a "political idyll," the Wife of Bath's Tale suggests some of

the mechanisms of transformation that created that idyll. Beginning in sexual violence and rape, it ends, as a good fairy tale must, with the knight-rapist and his old wife miraculously transformed into that heterosexual idyll — the romantic couple who live happily ever after, she obeying him "in every thing / That mighte doon him plesance or liking" (1255–56). Other tales told on the road to Canterbury expose the sexual violence implicit in that ending.

WORKS CITED

Bloch, Howard. *Medieval Misogyny and the Invention of Western Romantic Love.* Chicago: U of Chicago P, 1991.

Bryan, W. F., and Germaine Dempster. *Sources and Analogues of the Canterbury Tales.* Chicago: U of Chicago P, 1941.

Carruthers, Mary. "The Wife of Bath and the Painting of Lions." *PMLA* 94 (1979): 209–22.

Delany, Sheila. *Writing Woman: Women Writers and Women in Literature, Medieval to Modern.* New York: Schocken, 1983.

Duby, Georges. *The Three Orders: Feudal Society Imagined.* Trans. Arthur Goldhammer. Chicago: U of Chicago P, 1980.

Goux, Jean-Joseph. *Symbolic Economies After Marx and Freud.* Trans. Jennifer Curtiss Gage. Ithaca: Cornell UP, 1990.

Halpern, Richard. *The Poetics of Primitive Accumulation: English Renaissance Culture and the Genealogy of Capital.* Ithaca: Cornell UP, 1991.

Kempe, Margery. *The Book of Margery Kempe.* Ed. Sanford Brown Meech and Hope Emily Allen. London: Early English Text Society, 1940.

Marx, Karl. *Capital.* Vol. 1. Trans. Ben Fowkes. New York: Penguin, 1976.

Oresme, Nicholas. *De moneta.* Ed. and trans. Charles Johnson. London: Thomas Nelson, 1956.

Pisan, Christine de. *The Moral Proverbs of Christine de Pisan.* Trans. Earl Rivers. Rpt. from 1428 edition by William Caxton, with introductory remarks by William Blades. London, 1859.

Postan, M. M., and Edward Miller. *Cambridge Economic History of Europe.* Vol. 2. Cambridge: Cambridge UP, 1987.

Shoaf, R. A. *Dante, Chaucer, and the Currency of the Word: Money, Images, and Reference in Late Medieval Poetry.* Norman: Pilgrim, 1983.

Thompson, E. P. "Eighteenth-Century English Society: Class
    Struggle Without Class?" *Social History* 3 (1978): 133–65.

Thrupp, Sylvia L. *The Merchant Class of Medieval London: 1300–1500.*
    Chicago: U of Chicago P, 1948.

Williams, Raymond. *Problems in Materialism and Culture.* London:
    Verso, 1980.

Psychoanalytic Criticism
and
the Wife of Bath

WHAT IS PSYCHOANALYTIC CRITICISM?

It seems natural to think about literature in terms of dreams. Like dreams, literary works are fictions, inventions of the mind that, although based on reality, are by definition not literally true. Like a literary work, a dream may have some truth to tell, but, like a literary work, it may need to be interpreted before that truth can be grasped. We can live vicariously through romantic fictions, much as we can through daydreams. Terrifying novels and nightmares affect us in much the same way, plunging us into an atmosphere that continues to cling, even after the last chapter has been read — or the alarm clock has sounded.

The notion that dreams allow such psychic explorations, of course, like the analogy between literary works and dreams, owes a great deal to the thinking of Sigmund Freud, the famous Austrian psychoanalyst who in 1900 published a seminal study, *The Interpretation of Dreams*. But is the reader who feels that Emily Brontë's *Wuthering Heights* is dreamlike — who feels that Mary Shelley's *Frankenstein* is nightmarish — necessarily a Freudian literary critic? To some extent the answer has to be yes. We are all Freudians, really, whether or not we have read a single work by Freud. At one time or another, most of us have referred to ego, libido, complexes, unconscious desires, and sexual repression. The premises of Freud's thought have changed the way the Western world thinks about itself.

Psychoanalytic criticism has influenced the teachers our teachers studied with, the works of scholarship and criticism they read, and the critical and creative writers *we* read as well.

What Freud did was develop a language that described, a model that explained, a theory that encompassed human psychology. Many of the elements of psychology he sought to describe and explain are present in the literary works of various ages and cultures, from Sophocles' *Oedipus Rex* to Shakespeare's *Hamlet* to works being written in our own day. When the great novel of the twenty-first century is written, many of these same elements of psychology will probably inform its discourse as well. If, by understanding human psychology according to Freud, we can appreciate literature on a new level, then we should acquaint ourselves with his insights.

Freud's theories are either directly or indirectly concerned with the nature of the unconscious mind. Freud didn't invent the notion of the unconscious; others before him had suggested that even the supposedly "sane" human mind was conscious and rational only at times, and even then at possibly only one level. But Freud went further, suggesting that the powers motivating men and women are *mainly* and *normally* unconscious.

Freud, then, powerfully developed an old idea: that the human mind is essentially dual in nature. He called the predominantly passional, irrational, unknown, and unconscious part of the psyche the *id,* or "it." The *ego,* or "I," was his term for the predominantly rational, logical, orderly, conscious part. Another aspect of the psyche, which he called the *superego,* is really a projection of the ego. The superego almost seems to be outside of the self, making moral judgments, telling us to make sacrifices for good causes even though self-sacrifice may not be quite logical or rational. And, in a sense, the superego *is* "outside," since much of what it tells us to do or think we have learned from our parents, our schools, or our religious institutions.

What the ego and superego tell us *not* to do or think is repressed, forced into the unconscious mind. One of Freud's most important contributions to the study of the psyche, the theory of repression, goes something like this: much of what lies in the unconscious mind has been put there by consciousness, which acts as a censor, driving underground unconscious or conscious thoughts or instincts that it deems unacceptable. Censored materials often involve infantile sexual desires, Freud postulated. Repressed to an unconscious state, they emerge only in disguised forms: in dreams, in language (so-called

Freudian slips), in creative activity that may produce art (including literature), and in neurotic behavior.

According to Freud, all of us have repressed wishes and fears; we all have dreams in which repressed feelings and memories emerge disguised, and thus we are all potential candidates for dream analysis. One of the unconscious desires most commonly repressed is the childhood wish to displace the parent of our own sex and take his or her place in the affections of the parent of the opposite sex. This desire really involves a number of different but related wishes and fears. (A boy — and it should be remarked in passing that Freud here concerns himself mainly with the male — may fear that his father will castrate him, and he may wish that his mother would return to nursing him.) Freud referred to the whole complex of feelings by the word "oedipal," naming the complex after the Greek tragic hero Oedipus, who unwittingly killed his father and married his mother.

Why are oedipal wishes and fears repressed by the conscious side of the mind? And what happens to them after they have been censored? As Roy P. Basler puts it in *Sex, Symbolism, and Psychology in Literature* (1975), "from the beginning of recorded history such wishes have been restrained by the most powerful religious and social taboos, and as a result have come to be regarded as 'unnatural,'" even though "Freud found that such wishes are more or less characteristic of normal human development":

> In dreams, particularly, Freud found ample evidence that such wishes persisted. . . . Hence he conceived that natural urges, when identified as "wrong," may be repressed but not obliterated. . . . In the unconscious, these urges take on symbolic garb, regarded as nonsense by the waking mind that does not recognize their significance. (14)

Freud's belief in the significance of dreams, of course, was no more original than his belief that there is an unconscious side to the psyche. Again, it was the extent to which he developed a theory of how dreams work — and the extent to which that theory helped him, by analogy, to understand far more than just dreams — that made him unusual, important, and influential beyond the perimeters of medical schools and psychiatrists' offices.

The psychoanalytic approach to literature not only rests on the theories of Freud; it may even be said to have *begun* with Freud, who was interested in writers, especially those who relied heavily on symbols. Such writers regularly cloak or mystify ideas in figures that make sense only when interpreted, much as the unconscious mind of a neurotic disguises secret thoughts in dream stories or bizarre actions that need to be interpreted by an analyst. Freud's interest in literary artists led him to make some unfortunate generalizations about creativity; for example, in the twenty-third lecture in *Introductory Lectures on Psycho-Analysis* (1922), he defined the artist as "one urged on by instinctive needs that are too clamorous" (314). But it also led him to write creative literary criticism of his own, including an influential essay on "The Relation of a Poet to Daydreaming" (1908) and "The Uncanny" (1919), a provocative psychoanalytic reading of E. T. A. Hoffmann's supernatural tale "The Sandman."

Freud's application of psychoanalytic theory to literature quickly caught on. In 1909, only a year after Freud had published "The Relation of a Poet to Daydreaming," the psychoanalyst Otto Rank published *The Myth of the Birth of the Hero*. In that work, Rank subscribes to the notion that the artist turns a powerful, secret wish into a literary fantasy, and he uses Freud's notion about the oedipal complex to explain why the popular stories of so many heroes in literature are so similar. A year after Rank had published his psychoanalytic account of heroic texts, Ernest Jones, Freud's student and eventual biographer, turned his attention to a tragic text: Shakespeare's *Hamlet*. In an essay first published in the *American Journal of Psychology*, Jones, like Rank, makes use of the oedipal concept: he suggests that Hamlet is a victim of strong feelings toward his mother, the queen.

Between 1909 and 1949 numerous other critics decided that psychological and psychoanalytic theory could assist in the understanding of literature. I. A. Richards, Kenneth Burke, and Edmund Wilson were among the most influential to become interested in the new approach. Not all of the early critics were committed to the approach; neither were all of them Freudians. Some followed Alfred Adler, who believed that writers wrote out of inferiority complexes, and others applied the ideas of Carl Gustav Jung, who had broken with Freud over Freud's emphasis on sex and who had developed a theory of the *collective* unconscious. According to Jungian theory, a great work of literature is not a disguised expression of its author's personal, repressed wishes; rather, it is a manifestation of desires once held by the whole human race but now repressed because of the advent of civilization.

It is important to point out that among those who relied on Freud's models were a number of critics who were poets and novelists as well. Conrad Aiken wrote a Freudian study of American literature, and poets such as Robert Graves and W. H. Auden applied Freudian insights when writing critical prose. William Faulkner, Henry James, James Joyce, D. H. Lawrence, Marcel Proust, and Toni Morrison are only a few of the novelists who have either written criticism influenced by Freud or who have written novels that conceive of character, conflict, and creative writing itself in Freudian terms. The poet H. D. (Hilda Doolittle) was actually a patient of Freud's and provided an account of her analysis in her book *Tribute to Freud*. By giving Freudian theory credibility among students of literature that only they could bestow, such writers helped to endow earlier psychoanalytic criticism with a largely Freudian orientation that has only begun to be challenged in the last two decades.

The willingness, even eagerness, of writers to use Freudian models in producing literature and criticism of their own consummated a relationship that, to Freud and other pioneering psychoanalytic theorists, had seemed fated from the beginning; after all, therapy involves the close analysis of language. René Wellek and Austin Warren included "psychological" criticism as one of the five "extrinsic" approaches to literature described in their influential book, *Theory of Literature* (1942). Psychological criticism, they suggest, typically attempts to do at least one of the following: provide a psychological study of an individual writer; explore the nature of the creative process; generalize about "types and laws present within works of literature"; or theorize about the psychological "effects of literature upon its readers" (81). Entire books on psychoanalytic criticism began to appear, such as Frederick J. Hoffman's *Freudianism and the Literary Mind* (1945).

Probably because of Freud's characterization of the creative mind as "clamorous" if not ill, psychoanalytic criticism written before 1950 tended to psychoanalyze the individual author. Poems were read as fantasies that allowed authors to indulge repressed wishes, to protect themselves from deep-seated anxieties, or both. A perfect example of author analysis would be Marie Bonaparte's 1933 study of Edgar Allan Poe. Bonaparte found Poe to be so fixated on his mother that his repressed longing emerges in his stories in images such as the white spot on a black cat's breast, said to represent mother's milk.

A later generation of psychoanalytic critics often paused to analyze the characters in novels and plays before proceeding to their authors — but not for long, since characters, both evil and good, tended to be seen by these critics as the author's potential selves or projections of various repressed aspects of his or her psyche. For instance, in *A Psychoanalytic Study of the Double in Literature* (1970), Robert Rogers begins with the view that human beings are double or multiple in nature. Using this assumption, along with the psychoanalytic concept of "dissociation" (best known by its result, the dual or multiple personality), Rogers concludes that writers reveal instinctual or repressed selves in their books, often without realizing that they have done so.

In the view of critics attempting to arrive at more psychological insights into an author than biographical materials can provide, a work of literature is a fantasy or a dream — or at least so analogous to daydream or dream that Freudian analysis can help explain the nature of the mind that produced it. The author's purpose in writing is to gratify secretly some forbidden wish, in particular an infantile wish or desire that has been repressed into the unconscious mind. To discover what the wish is, the psychoanalytic critic employs many of the terms and procedures developed by Freud to analyze dreams.

The literal surface of a work is sometimes spoken of as its "manifest content" and treated as a "manifest dream" or "dream story" by a Freudian analyst. Just as the analyst tries to figure out the "dream thought" behind the dream story — that is, the latent or hidden content of the manifest dream — so the psychoanalytic literary critic tries to expose the latent, underlying content of a work. Freud used the words *condensation* and *displacement* to explain two of the mental processes whereby the mind disguises its wishes and fears in dream stories. In condensation several thoughts or persons may be condensed into a single manifestation or image in a dream story; in displacement, an anxiety, a wish, or a person may be displaced onto the image of another, with which or whom it is loosely connected through a string of associations that only an analyst can untangle. Psychoanalytic critics treat metaphors as if they were dream condensations; they treat metonyms — figures of speech based on extremely loose, arbitrary associations — as if they were dream displacements. Thus figurative literary language in general is treated as something that evolves as the writer's conscious mind resists what the unconscious tells it to picture or describe. A symbol is, in Daniel Weiss's words, "a meaningful concealment of truth as the truth promises to emerge as some frightening or forbidden idea" (20).

In a 1970 article entitled "The 'Unconscious' of Literature," Norman Holland, a literary critic trained in psychoanalysis, succinctly sums up the attitudes held by critics who would psychoanalyze authors, but without quite saying that it is the *author* that is being analyzed by the psychoanalytic critic. "When one looks at a poem psychoanalytically," he writes, "one considers it as though it were a dream or as though some ideal patient [were speaking] from the couch in iambic pentameter." One "looks for the general level or levels of fantasy associated with the language. By level I mean the familiar stages of childhood development — oral [when desires for nourishment and infantile sexual desires overlap], anal [when infants receive their primary pleasure from defecation], urethral [when urinary functions are the locus of sexual pleasure], phallic [when the penis or, in girls, some penis substitute is of primary interest], oedipal." Holland continues by analyzing not Robert Frost but Frost's poem "Mending Wall" as a specifically oral fantasy that is not unique to its author. "Mending Wall" is "about breaking down the wall which marks the separated or individuated self so as to return to a state of closeness to some Other" — including and perhaps essentially the nursing mother ("Unconscious" 136, 139).

While not denying the idea that the unconscious plays a role in creativity, psychoanalytic critics such as Holland began to focus more on the ways in which authors create works that appeal to *our* repressed wishes and fantasies. Consequently, they shifted their focus away from the psyche of the author and toward the psychology of the reader and the text. Holland's theories, which have concerned themselves more with the reader than with the text, have helped to establish another school of critical theory: reader-response criticism. Elizabeth Wright explains Holland's brand of modern psychoanalytic criticism in this way: "What draws us as readers to a text is the secret expression of what we desire to hear, much as we protest we do not. The disguise must be good enough to fool the censor into thinking that the text is respectable, but bad enough to allow the unconscious to glimpse the unrespectable" (117).

Holland is one of dozens of critics who have revised Freud significantly in the process of revitalizing psychoanalytic criticism. Another such critic is R. D. Laing, whose controversial and often poetical writings about personality, repression, masks, and the double or "schizoid" self have (re)blurred the boundary between creative writing and psychoanalytic discourse. Yet another is D. W. Winnicott, an "object-relations" theorist who has had a significant impact on literary criticism. Critics influenced by Winnicott and his school have questioned the tendency to see reader/text as an either/or construct; instead, they have seen reader and text (or audience and play) in terms of a *relationship* taking place in what Winnicott calls a "transitional" or "potential space" — space in which binary terms like real and illusory, objective and subjective, have little or no meaning.

Psychoanalytic theorists influenced by Winnicott see the transitional or potential reader/text (or audience/play) space as being *like* the space entered into by psychoanalyst and patient. More important, they also see it as being similar to the space between mother and infant: a space characterized by trust in which categorizing terms such as *knowing* and *feeling* mix and merge and have little meaning apart from one another.

Whereas Freud saw the mother-son relationship in terms of the son and his repressed oedipal complex (and saw the analyst-patient relationship in terms of the patient and the repressed "truth" that the analyst could scientifically extract), object-relations analysts see both relationships as *dyadic* — that is, as being dynamic in both directions. Consequently, they don't depersonalize analysis or their analyses. It is hardly surprising, therefore, that contemporary literary critics who apply object-relations theory to the texts they discuss don't depersonalize critics or categorize their interpretations as "truthful," at least, not in any objective or scientific sense. In the view of such critics, interpretations are made of language — itself a transitional object — and are themselves the mediating terms or transitional objects of a relationship.

Like critics of the Winnicottian school, the French structuralist theorist Jacques Lacan focuses on language and language-related issues. He treats the unconscious *as* a language and, consequently, views the dream not as Freud did (that is, as a form and symptom of repression) but rather as a form of discourse. Thus we may study dreams psychoanalytically in order to learn about literature, even as we may study literature in order to learn more about the unconscious. In Lacan's seminar on Poe's "The Purloined Letter," a pattern of repetition like that used by psychoanalysts in their analyses is used to arrive at a reading of the story. According to Wright, "the new psychoanalytic structural approach to literature" employs "analogies from psychoanalysis . . . to explain the workings of the text as distinct from the workings of a particular author's, character's, or even reader's mind" (125).

Lacan, however, did far more than extend Freud's theory of dreams, literature, and the interpretation of both. More significantly, he took Freud's whole theory of psyche and gender and added to it a crucial third term — that of language. In the process, he both used and significantly developed Freud's ideas about the oedipal stage and complex.

Lacan points out that the pre-oedipal stage, in which the child at first does not even recognize its independence from its mother, is also a pre*verbal* stage, one in which the child communicates without the medium of language, or — if we insist on calling the child's communications a language — in a language that can only be called *literal.* ("Coos," certainly, cannot be said to be figurative or symbolic.) Then, while still in the pre-oedipal stage, the child enters the *mirror* stage.

During the mirror period, the child comes to view itself and its mother, later other people as well, *as* independent selves. This is the stage in which the child is first able to fear the aggressions of another, to desire what is recognizably beyond the self (initially the mother), and, finally, to want to compete with another for the same, desired object. This is also the stage at which the child first becomes able to feel sympathy with another being who is being hurt by a third, to cry when another cries. All of these developments, of course, involve projecting beyond the self and, by extension, constructing one's own self (or "ego" or "I") as others view one — that is, as *another.* Such constructions, according to Lacan, are just that: constructs, products, artifacts — fictions of coherence that in fact hide what Lacan calls the "absence" or "lack" of being.

The mirror stage, which Lacan also refers to as the *imaginary* stage, is fairly quickly succeeded by the oedipal stage. As in Freud, this stage begins when the child, having come to view itself as self and the father and mother as separate selves, perceives gender and gender differences between its parents and between itself and one of its parents. For boys, gender awareness involves another, more powerful recognition, for the recognition of the father's phallus as the mark of his difference from the mother involves, at the same time, the recognition that his older and more powerful father is also his rival. That, in turn, leads to the understanding that what once seemed wholly his and even indistinguishable from himself is in fact someone else's: something properly desired only at a distance and in the form of socially acceptable *substitutes.*

The fact that the oedipal stage roughly coincides with the entry of the child into language is extremely important for Lacan. For the linguistic order is essentially a figurative or "Symbolic order"; words are not the things they stand for but are, rather, stand-ins or substitutes for those things. Hence boys, who in the most critical period of their development have had to submit to what Lacan calls the "Law of the Father" — a law that prohibits direct desire for and communicative intimacy with what has been the boy's whole world — enter more easily into the realm of language and the Symbolic order than do girls, who have never really had to renounce that which once seemed continuous with the self: the mother. The gap that has been opened up for boys, which includes the gap between signs and what they substitute — the gap marked by the phallus and encoded with the boy's sense of his maleness — has not opened up for girls, or has not opened up in the same way, to the same degree.

For Lacan, the father need not be present to trigger the oedipal stage; nor does his phallus have to be seen to catalyze the boy's (easier) transition into the Symbolic order. Rather, Lacan argues, a child's recognition of its gender is intricately tied up with a growing recognition of the system of names and naming, part of the larger system of substitutions we call language. A child has little doubt about who its mother is, but who is its father, and how would one know? The father's claim rests on the mother's *word* that he is in fact the father; the father's relationship to the child is thus established through language and a system of marriage and kinship — names — that in turn is basic to rules of everything from property to law. The name of the father (*nom du père,* which in French sounds like *non du père*) involves, in a sense, nothing of the father — nothing, that is, except his word or name.

Lacan's development of Freud has had several important results. First, his sexist-seeming association of maleness with the Symbolic order, together with his claim that women cannot therefore enter easily into the order, has prompted feminists not to reject his theory out of hand but, rather, to look more closely at the relation between language and gender, language and women's inequality. Some feminists have gone so far as to suggest that the social and political relationships between male and female will not be fundamentally altered until language itself has been radically changed. (That change might begin dialectically, with the development of some kind of "feminine language" grounded in the presymbolic, literal-to-imaginary, communication between mother and child.)

Second, Lacan's theory has proved of interest to deconstructors and other poststructuralists, in part because it holds that the ego (which in Freud's view is as necessary as it is natural) is a product or construct. The ego-artifact, produced during the mirror stage, *seems* at once unified, consistent, and organized around a determinate center. But the unified self, or ego, is a fiction, according to Lacan. The yoking together of fragments and destructively dissimilar elements takes its psychic toll, and it is the job of the Lacanian psychoanalyst to "deconstruct," as it were, the ego, to show its continuities to be contradictions as well.

Ross C Murfin

PSYCHOANALYTIC CRITICISM: A SELECTED BIBLIOGRAPHY

Some Short Introductions to Psychological and Psychoanalytic Criticism

Holland, Norman. "The 'Unconscious' of Literature." *Contemporary Criticism.* Ed. Norman Bradbury and David Palmer. Stratford-upon-Avon Series 12. New York: St. Martin's, 1970. 131–54.

Natoli, Joseph, and Frederik L. Rusch, comps. *Psychocriticism: An Annotated Bibliography.* Westport: Greenwood, 1984.

Scott, Wilbur. *Five Approaches to Literary Criticism.* London: Collier-Macmillan, 1962. See the essays by Burke and Gorer as well as Scott's introduction to the section "The Psychological Approach: Literature in the Light of Psychological Theory."

Wellek, René, and Austin Warren. *Theory of Literature.* New York: Harcourt, 1942. See the chapter "Literature and Psychology" in pt. 3, "The Extrinsic Approach to the Study of Literature."

Wright, Elizabeth. "Modern Psychoanalytic Criticism." *Modern Literary Theory: A Comparative Introduction.* Ed. Ann Jefferson and David Robey. Totowa: Barnes, 1982. 113–33.

Freud, Lacan, and Their Influence

Basler, Roy P. *Sex, Symbolism, and Psychology in Literature.* New York: Octagon, 1975. See especially 13–19.

Clément, Catherine. *The Lives and Legends of Jacques Lacan.* Trans. Arthur Goldhammer. New York: Columbia UP, 1983.

Freud, Sigmund. *Introductory Lectures on Psycho-Analysis.* Trans. Joan Riviere. London: Allen, 1922.

Gallop, Jane. *Reading Lacan.* Ithaca: Cornell UP, 1985.

Hoffman, Frederick J. *Freudianism and the Literary Mind.* Baton Rouge: Louisiana State UP, 1945.

Hogan, Patrick Colm, and Lalita Pandit, eds. *Lacan and Criticism: Essays and Dialogue on Language, Structure, and the Unconscious.* Athens: U of Georgia P, 1990.

Kazin, Alfred. "Freud and His Consequences." *Contemporaries.* Boston: Little, 1962. 351–93.

Lacan, Jacques. *Écrits: A Selection.* Trans. Alan Sheridan. New York: Norton, 1977.

———. *Feminine Sexuality: Lacan and the École Freudienne.* Ed. Juliet Mitchell and Jacqueline Rose. Trans. Rose. New York: Norton, 1982.

———. *The Four Fundamental Concepts of Psychoanalysis.* Trans. Alan Sheridan. London: Penguin, 1980.

Macey, David. *Lacan in Contexts.* New York: Verso, 1988.

Meisel, Perry, ed. *Freud: A Collection of Critical Essays.* Englewood Cliffs: Prentice, 1981.

Muller, John P., and William J. Richardson. *Lacan and Language: A Reader's Guide to "Écrits."* New York: International, 1982.

Porter, Laurence M. *"The Interpretation of Dreams": Freud's Theories Revisited.* Twayne's Masterwork Studies Series. Boston: G. K. Hall, 1986.

Reppen, Joseph, and Maurice Charney. *The Psychoanalytic Study of Literature.* Hillsdale: Analytic, 1985.

Schneiderman, Stuart. *Jacques Lacan: The Death of an Intellectual Hero.* Cambridge: Harvard UP, 1983.

———. *Returning to Freud: Clinical Psychoanalysis in the School of Lacan.* New Haven: Yale UP, 1980.

Selden, Raman. *A Reader's Guide to Contemporary Literary Theory.* 2nd ed. Lexington: U of Kentucky P, 1989. See "Jacques Lacan: Language and the Unconscious."

Sullivan, Ellie Ragland. *Jacques Lacan and the Philosophy of Psychoanalysis.* Champaign: U of Illinois P, 1986.

Sullivan, Ellie Ragland, and Mark Bracher, eds. *Lacan and the Subject of Language.* New York: Routledge, 1991.

Trilling, Lionel. "Art and Neurosis." *The Liberal Imagination.* New York: Scribner's, 1950. 160–80.

Wilden, Anthony. "Lacan and the Discourse of the Other." Lacan, *Speech and Language in Psychoanalysis.* Trans. Wilden. Baltimore: Johns Hopkins UP, 1981. (Published as *The Language of the Self* in 1968.) 159–311.

Psychoanalysis, Feminism, and Literature

Chodorow, Nancy. *The Reproduction of Mothering: Psychoanalysis and the Sociology of Gender.* Berkeley: U of California P, 1978.

Gallop, Jane. *The Daughter's Seduction: Feminism and Psychoanalysis.* Ithaca: Cornell UP, 1982.

Garner, Shirley Nelson, Claire Kahane, and Madelon Sprengnether. *The (M)other Tongue: Essays in Feminist Psychoanalytic Interpretation.* Ithaca: Cornell UP, 1985.

Irigaray, Luce. *The Speculum of the Other Woman.* Trans. Gillian C. Gill. Ithaca: Cornell UP, 1985.

———. *This Sex Which Is Not One*. Trans. Catherine Porter. Ithaca: Cornell UP, 1985.

Jacobus, Mary. "Is There a Woman in This Text?" *New Literary History* 14 (1982): 117–41.

Kristeva, Julia. *The Kristeva Reader*. Ed. Toril Moi. New York: Columbia UP, 1986. See especially the selection from *Revolution in Poetic Language*, 89–136.

Mitchell, Juliet. *Psychoanalysis and Feminism*. New York: Random, 1974.

Mitchell, Juliet, and Jacqueline Rose. "Introduction I" and "Introduction II." Lacan, *Feminine Sexuality: Jacques Lacan and the École Freudienne*. New York: Norton, 1985. 1–26, 27–57.

Sprengnether, Madelon. *The Spectral Mother: Freud, Feminism, and Psychoanalysis*. Ithaca: Cornell UP, 1990.

Psychological and Psychoanalytic Studies of Literature

Bettelheim, Bruno. *The Uses of Enchantment: The Meaning and Importance of Fairy Tales*. New York: Knopf, 1976. Although this book is about fairy tales instead of literary works written for publication, it offers model Freudian readings of well-known stories.

Crews, Frederick C. *Out of My System: Psychoanalysis, Ideology, and Critical Method*. New York: Oxford UP, 1975.

———. *Relations of Literary Study*. New York: MLA, 1967. See the chapter "Literature and Psychology."

Diehl, Joanne Feit. "Re-Reading *The Letter*: Hawthorne, the Fetish, and the (Family) Romance." *Nathaniel Hawthorne, "The Scarlet Letter."* Ed. Ross C Murfin. Case Studies in Contemporary Criticism Series. Ed. Ross C Murfin. Boston: Bedford–St. Martin's, 1991. 235–51.

Hallman, Ralph. *Psychology of Literature: A Study of Alienation and Tragedy*. New York: Philosophical Library, 1961.

Hartman, Geoffrey, ed. *Psychoanalysis and the Question of the Text*. Baltimore: Johns Hopkins UP, 1978. See especially the essays by Hartman, Johnson, Nelson, and Schwartz.

Hertz, Neil. *The End of the Line: Essays on Psychoanalysis and the Sublime*. New York: Columbia UP, 1985.

Holland, Norman N. *Dynamics of Literary Response*. New York: Oxford UP, 1968.

———. *Poems in Persons: An Introduction to the Psychoanalysis of Literature*. New York: Norton, 1973.

Kris, Ernest. *Psychoanalytic Explorations in Art*. New York: International, 1952.

Lucas, F. L. *Literature and Psychology*. London: Cassell, 1951.

Natoli, Joseph, ed. *Psychological Perspectives on Literature: Freudian Dissidents and Non-Freudians: A Casebook*. Hamden: Archon Books–Shoe String, 1984.

Phillips, William, ed. *Art and Psychoanalysis*. New York: Columbia UP, 1977.

Rogers, Robert. *A Psychoanalytic Study of the Double in Literature*. Detroit: Wayne State UP, 1970.

Skura, Meredith. *The Literary Use of the Psychoanalytic Process*. New Haven: Yale UP, 1981.

Strelka, Joseph P. *Literary Criticism and Psychology*. University Park: Pennsylvania State UP, 1976. See especially the essays by Lerner and Peckham.

Weiss, Daniel. *The Critic Agonistes: Psychology, Myth, and the Art of Fiction*. Ed. Eric Solomon and Stephen Arkin. Seattle: U of Washington P, 1985.

Lacanian Psychoanalytic Studies of Literature

Collings, David. "The Monster and the Imaginary Mother: A Lacanian Reading of *Frankenstein*." *Mary Shelley, "Frankenstein."* Ed. Johanna M. Smith. Case Studies in Contemporary Criticism Series. Ed. Ross C Murfin. Boston: Bedford–St. Martin's, 1992. 245–58.

Davis, Robert Con, ed. *The Fictional Father: Lacanian Readings of the Text*. Amherst: U of Massachusetts P, 1981.

———. "Lacan and Narration." *Modern Language Notes* 5 (1983): 843–1063.

Felman, Shoshana, ed. *Jacques Lacan and the Adventure of Insight: Psychoanalysis in Contemporary Culture*. Cambridge: Harvard UP, 1987.

———, ed. *Literature and Psychoanalysis: The Question of Reading: Otherwise*. Baltimore: Johns Hopkins UP, 1982.

Froula, Christine. "When Eve Reads Milton: Undoing the Canonical Economy." *Canons*. Ed. Robert von Hallberg. Chicago: U of Chicago P, 1984. 149–75.

Homans, Margaret. *Bearing the Word: Language and Female Experience in Nineteenth-Century Women's Writing*. Chicago: U of Chicago P, 1986.

Muller, John P., and William J. Richardson, eds. *The Purloined Poe: Lacan, Derrida, and Psychoanalytic Reading*. Baltimore: Johns

Hopkins UP, 1988. Includes Lacan's seminar on Poe's "The Purloined Letter."

Psychoanalytic Approaches to Chaucer and the Wife of Bath's Prologue and Tale

Atkinson, Michael. "Soul's Time and Transformations: The Wife of Bath's Tale." *Southern Review* 13 (1980): 72–78.

Brown, Eric D. "Symbols of Transformation: A Specific Archetypal Examination of the *Wife of Bath's Tale." Chaucer Review* 12 (1978): 202–17.

———. "Transformation and the *Wife of Bath's Tale:* A Jungian Discussion." *Chaucer Review* 10 (1976): 303–15.

Fradenburg, Louise O. "The Wife of Bath's Passing Fancy." *Studies in the Age of Chaucer* 8 (1986): 31–58.

Fritz, D. W. "The Animus-Possessed Wife of Bath." *Journal of Analytical Psychology* 25 (1980): 163–80.

Holland, Norman N. "Meaning as Transformation: The Wife of Bath's Tale." *College English* 28 (1967): 279–90.

Leicester, H. Marshall, Jr. *The Disenchanted Self: Representing the Subject in the Canterbury Tales.* Berkeley: U of California P, 1990.

Palomo, Dolores, "The Fate of the Wife of Bath's 'Bad Husbands.'" *Chaucer Review* 9 (1975): 303–19.

Renoir, Alain. "The Impossible Dream: An Underside to the Wife of Bath." *Moderna Språk* 70 (1976): 311–22.

Rowland, Beryl. "Chaucer's Dame Alys: Critics in Blunderland?" *Neuphilologische Mitteilungen* 73 (1972): 381–95.

Steinberg, Aaron. "The Wife of Bath's Tale and Her Fantasy of Fulfillment." *College English* 26 (1964): 187–91.

A PSYCHOANALYTIC PERSPECTIVE

Louise O. Fradenburg uses psychoanalytic techniques to help us understand the Wife of Bath, who is both a character in a literary work and the fictional author of an autobiography and a romance. In doing so Fradenburg combines two of the uses of psychoanalysis as it relates to literature: its use as a key to understanding the dynamic of a work of literature, and its use as a key to understanding an author.

For Sigmund Freud, the founder of psychoanalysis and psychoanalytic criticism, dreams often expressed in disguised form the fantasies, fears, and desires we learned in childhood to repress or at least discipline. In her discussion of the Wife's interest in romance, a genre that allows us to imagine a world in which we are not constrained by growing old and dying, Fradenburg takes us into the Wife of Bath's imaginary world, in which desires are satisfied, fears allayed, wishes fulfilled. Medieval romances were magical stories, usually about knights of old who in serving their kings or their ladies encounter unforeseen dangers and supernatural happenings. Although these romances lost their high literary authority after the Renaissance, the genre, in its modern forms, has remained very popular. Romances express in any age a longing for a world in which the boredom of day-to-day living is supplanted by passion and adventure, a world free of the constraints of ordinary mortality.

Fradenburg makes significant use of Sigmund Freud, particularly his discussion of the way familiar scenes in dramas by Sophocles and Shakespeare play out the fantasy that we can choose not only death but also to *avoid* death. That fantasy, she argues, underlies to a great extent the Wife of Bath's Prologue and Tale. In addition, her essay is conversant with post-Freudian psychoanalytic theory, specifically the work of Jacques Lacan. Using Lacan's theory that the stable "subject" or self is not natural but, rather, a construction shaped by language and by kinship and power relations, Fradenburg suggests that the Wife's recollections of lost pleasure may be read as desire for freedom from the construction and regulation of subjectivity.

Fradenburg invites us to see that psychoanalysis and autobiography are similar experiences: in both activities people use language to reveal their appetites, pleasures, pains, and losses. Psychoanalysis would see the Wife of Bath's Prologue as the elegiac history of pleasures now lost, but it would also see in her prologue and tale the wish for a better life to come. Fradenburg shows us that the Wife of Bath laments the passing of a land "fulfild of fairye" (859), but also that the Wife uses her romance to show that fantasy, by imagining "reality" as otherwise, can remake it.

LOUISE O. FRADENBURG

"Fulfild of fairye": The Social Meaning of Fantasy in the Wife of Bath's Prologue and Tale

The Wife of Bath has captivated, and sometimes offended, readers of the *Canterbury Tales* in very special ways. She has been considered astonishingly "lively" and realistic — so much so that she is more commonly spoken of as a person than as a literary character. To many readers she has seemed more "modern" than Chaucer's other pilgrims — especially "alive" to us, especially able to speak to our contemporary moment. A critic named D. W. Robertson has even suggested that the Wife is typically "feminine" (330). But other critics, including Robertson himself, have seen the Wife as only deceptively modern and vital. These critics argue that Chaucer did not mean the Wife to be a vivacious modern "character" (Robertson 330). Instead, they suggest, the Wife is meant to embody a profoundly medieval idea, that of "carnal understanding" (Robertson 330) — of pleasurable, but lethal, abuses of reason, which lead to the kinds of mistaken understandings of Scripture the Wife proposes in her prologue.

Critics have argued over whether the Wife is medieval or modern; over whether her prologue is an exemplification of bad readings of Scripture or an autobiography. I am interested in why the question of the Wife's modernity has been so important to literary critics. I am also interested in why the question of the Wife's modernity is so often linked to the Wife's pursuit of carnal pleasure. The Wife impresses some readers as lively, as modern, as a "personality," in part because she defends bodily pleasure, and in part because she tells us the story of her life. For other readers, she only *impresses* us as full of life, and is really a very old figure, a medieval way of imaging carnal misunderstanding. For such readers the Wife is so far from being full of life as to be dangerous to life, or desperate for it. In her critical tradition, then, she appears a little bit like the old woman of her tale: now young (or at least full of energy), now old; now a frightening reminder of death and the limits of human knowledge, now a beneficent donor of life and happiness. Why have critics argued so much over what we might call the Wife of Bath's "temporality" — over whether, when, and how she lives and addresses us?

In this essay I will explain some of the ways in which anxieties about mortality have shaped criticism of the Wife of Bath's Prologue and Tale. I will also show how concerns about the mortal body and its pleasures are at work in the prologue and tale themselves. First, it will be helpful to understand how the problem of pleasure is linked to that of mortality. The body is often understood to be the part of us that dies, even if we believe that the body will ultimately be resurrected. Moreover, the vulnerability of our bodies to time can make them seem frightening to us. Distrust of the body's pleasures and appetites has been a long tradition in Western thought, perhaps because our appetites remind us so forcefully of how material our bodies are. When we feel hunger, for example, and can think of little other than satisfying our hunger as pleasantly as possible, we are very much aware that we are embodied creatures, not pure spirit. And when our appetites remind us of our corporeality, they remind us also of our bodies' vulnerability to time: we know that all flesh is grass.

In discussing how awareness of mortality shapes the Wife's prologue and tale, I will be exploring a long-standing association of the romance genre with fantasy. Fantasy inspires anxieties similar to those linked with the mortal body and its pleasures. For example, most of us are familiar with the idea that supermarket romance novels are escapist fantasy. We fear fantasy will be so pleasurable that it will separate us from truth or reality, and thereby endanger us. We fear that, by isolating us from reality, fantasy can leave us vulnerable to the perils of reality, among which are aging and death. For example, we often speak of people who live in "a world of their own." Such people can seem "out of touch with reality." Although these figures can be enormously charismatic — gurus, dreamers, saints — we often hesitate to adopt their example. We fear that if we live in a world of our own, we may not notice that the world around us is changing, and making different demands on us. We may not adapt to those demands, and may thus lose friends, lovers, money, life. So fantasy, like bodily appetite and pleasure, can make us anxious, partly because we fear that fantasy may become *too* pleasurable, a preferable alternative to reality.

Class and gender are also important to my argument in this essay. I will not be discussing class and gender as explicitly as some of the other topics I've already mentioned, since my chief task in this essay is to explore psychoanalytic methods of reading. But critical methods rarely work in isolation, and it will be helpful to readers of this essay to understand some of the ways in which class and gender relate to my concerns about mortality and pleasure.

In medieval as well as modern culture, women are sometimes associated with death, pleasure, and fantasy. Women are sometimes thought to be especially dangerous to life, especially sensual, or especially rebellious with respect to the demands of reality and truth. Perhaps the most obvious example is the myth of Eve's desire for the apple and her consequent responsibility for bringing death into the world. Another example would be the damsel-in-distress story, in which the hero must risk his life to save a woman who has gotten into trouble through her stubbornness or helplessness. These plots are as popular now — for example, in action and adventure movies and in supermarket romances — as they were during the Middle Ages.

The idea that the Wife of Bath commits "carnal misunderstanding" likewise associates the Wife with danger and with an unwillingness to accept truth. According to some critics, the Wife interprets Scripture the way she wants to — according to her fantasies or wishes — instead of the way theologians say it should be read. These critics suggest that when the Wife argues that Scripture encourages sex, she is arguing a point of view that could endanger her spiritual life, and the spiritual lives of her audience. Moreover, her desire to dominate her husbands seems to many commentators a clear inversion of what, in the Middle Ages, were supposed to be the proper relations between husband and wife: the husband was to rule the wife, just as reason ought to rule the appetites. If this structure of rule was upset, then the proper order of things was upset, with dangerous consequences for all.

The Wife's class position is also relevant to the ways in which she can seem dangerous. The Wife is a wealthy commoner. She is successful in cloth-making, one of the most active sectors of the late-medieval English economy, and she is an able manipulator of the ways the late-medieval marriage market could also be a financial market. Critics have argued over the significance of the Wife's class and economic positioning, but most agree that her sexual appetite is somehow connected to her economic appetite: she seems to want property as much as she wants carnal pleasure or rule over husbands. Some critics have seen her as astray because she regards her own sexuality *as* a commodity. To these critics, she seems to accept the idea that women can be turned into objects of exchange in the marriage market. Other critics have regarded her economic enterprise as a clear sign of her dedication to false idols, analogous to her pursuit of love in all the wrong places. It is certainly easy to conclude from her prologue that the Wife is ambitiously determined to do well for herself in a number of ways, as a woman but also as a businesswoman. She thus might seem to threaten not only medieval gender hierarchies, in which husbands were ideally to rule wives, but social hierarchies as well — in which the lower classes were also ideally to stay in their "place."

The central thesis of my argument is that the Wife of Bath's Prologue and Tale ask us to analyze and undo these associations among women, commoners, death, pleasure, and fantasy. In particular, I will argue that the Wife of Bath's Prologue and Tale ask us to reevaluate fantasy. In the Wife's prologue and tale, Chaucer asks us to consider the possibility that fantasies do not simply separate us from reality. Instead, Chaucer suggests, fantasies can have the power to remake the social realities in which we live and desire. This means not that fantasies are inevitably benign, but that, far from being illusions powerless to affect reality, fantasies affect the way people and societies feel and act.

I. TRUE ROMANCE

By way of beginning to think about how psychoanalysis can help us address the questions about fantasy raised in the Wife of Bath's Prologue and Tale, we might turn to Freud's "The Theme of the Three Caskets," an essay concerned partly with Shakespeare's *The Merchant of Venice* and *King Lear*. In *The Merchant of Venice*, three suitors vying for the hand of Portia must choose among three caskets — one of lead, one of silver, and one of gold. The successful suitor, Bassanio, chooses the lead casket — the least valuable and beautiful of the three. In *King Lear*, Lear asks his three daughters to declare their love for him, so that he can evaluate which of them loves him most. On the basis of their declarations, he will decide how much of his kingdom each will inherit. Cordelia, the youngest, gives the plainest speech, and is disinherited; but she is eventually revealed to be Lear's only truly faithful and loving daughter.

Freud suggests that these literary examples can be related to a mythic scene whose workings he detects in a wide variety of stories and beliefs: "a scene of choosing between three women, of whom the youngest is the best, the supreme one" (65). Freud argues, however, that in this scene the youngest and most beautiful of the three women represents death; to choose her is to choose death, or, to put it another way, is to accept the fact of death, to accept the fact that all living things must die. For most of us, the thought of our own death is a sad, even horrible, one. Indeed, Freud argues that unconsciously we cannot believe we will die. But the scene he analyzes in "Three Caskets" makes Death appear fair, not horrible. It depicts the masculine hero as choosing death, rather than fantastically refusing to believe in this powerful fact of life. Through a defensive reversal — "replacement by the opposite" — death appears as the "fairest, best, most desirable and the most lovable among women" (72).

For Freud, the purpose of this scene of choice is twofold. The scene "warns man that he too is a part of nature and therefore subject to the immutable law of death" (72). But the scene also eases, makes palatable, the terror and sense of unfreedom produced by this warning. It does so by representing the hero as *choosing* death rather than simply submitting to its necessity. Indeed, the scene makes the choice of death seem a free and heroic one, one that will bring good fortune, at least of a certain kind. The element of choice transforms unfreedom (no one can escape death) into an experience of freedom (the hero chooses to recognize the truth that he will not escape death). Thus the element of choice transforms warning and terror into pleasure. As Freud puts it:

> Choice stands in the place of necessity, of destiny. Thus man overcomes death, which in thought he has acknowledged. No greater triumph of wish-fulfillment is conceivable. Just where in reality he obeys compulsion, he exercises choice; and that which he chooses is not a thing of horror, but the fairest and most desirable thing in life. (73)

How might we make use of this passage in interpreting the Wife's tale? First, the nameless knight commits the crime of rape and is sentenced to death. But instead of losing his life, he is rewarded with "the most lovable among women" — the ideal wife, who is both beautiful and faithful. At the end of the tale, his power and freedom are restored: "And she obeyed him in every thing / That mighte doon him plesance or liking" (1255–56). But, as in Freud's scene, this transformation is accomplished through the knight's *submission*. At the beginning of the tale, the knight is mortally ignorant of what women want. We might say that he is out of touch with certain realities. His experiences in the world of "fairye," however, offer him a magical, redemptive knowledge that turns multifarious and confusing data about women's preferences into a single truth about a species. That truth is women's wish for sovereignty — which, if the knight willingly submits to it, will be transformed into his freedom. Thus a death sentence is transformed into its reverse, a new lease on life, and necessity is transformed into its reverse, freedom of choice. The obligation to submit to reality, once met, turns magically into new powers and freedoms.

These reversals of necessity into freedom and of mortality into the promise of enduring life are also at work in the relations between the Wife's prologue and her tale. Most critics accept the idea that the old woman beside the forest is a figure for the Wife of Bath herself, or at least of some part of her. The Wife describes herself in her prologue as a troublesomely appetitive woman who is willing to scheme against and injure her husbands to get what she wants. In her tale, however, she transforms herself into a loving rescuer of man.

The kind of time that characterizes the prologue is also transformed, even reversed, in the tale. In the prologue we are made aware of the passage of time as the Wife laments the loss of her beauty brought on by the aging process. But the tale is characterized by the magical timing of "fairye," in which bodies can choose their age — can choose to be young again. The transition from prologue to tale converts sex and violence into loving rescue, a movement repeated within the tale itself. Interestingly, Freud interprets rescue fantasies as renegotiations of mortality: the fantasy is that if we can save someone, we might perhaps have power over life and death (see his essay "A Special Type of Object Choice Made by Men"). Moreover, in the transition from prologue to tale vulnerability to the passing of time is changed into magical power *over* time. Despite these conversions of sex and violence into a fantasy of rescue, however, the Wife's tale ends with her curse and with a reminder of the fact (dwelt on in her prologue, but forgotten until the end of her tale) that men grow old: "And olde and angry nigardes of dispence, / God sende hem soone verray pestilence!" (1263–64). It would seem from this ending that the enchantment of romance — its promise of wish fulfillment — is fragile and transitory; the Wife's curse seems designed to make us feel that we are back in the real world and that we had better be aware of its power conflicts if we are going to survive in it. The Wife's performance appears to suggest, then, that romance fantasy is distinct from, even opposed to, the real world. This idea is also commonly expressed in scholarly and critical writing on the romance.

The romance genre has often been associated with the marvelous and has been contrasted to genres, like history writing or the novel, that seem more committed to the truthful depiction of reality. In one of the most influential twentieth-century accounts of the romance genre, Eric Auerbach argues that "the courtly romance is not reality shaped and set forth by art, but an escape into fable and fairy tale" which has a "restrictive" effect on the development of "literary realism" (138). Bishop Richard Hurd also contrasts the romance with more truthful kinds of discourse. He wrote his *Letters on Chivalry and Romance* in the later eighteenth century, at a time when English literary culture was taking a certain pride in throwing off what it regarded as the superstitions and unreasonable fancies of older literary forms like the romance. Hurd's own estimation of the romance is ambivalent. He seems nostalgic for it. He writes, "we have lost . . . a world of fine fabling" (120). But he identifies the "*lying wonders*" of romance with the female figure of "Fancy." And he writes that Fancy, who "had wantoned it so long in the world of fiction," was "now constrained . . . to ally herself with strict truth, if she would gain admittance into reasonable company" (120).

Like Bassanio in *The Merchant of Venice*, who chooses the lead rather than the gold or silver casket, critics of romance seem perpetually to be preferring plain truth, however dull, to glitter. And in order to present themselves as preferring plain truth to glitter, they must first insist on the distinction between truth and glitter. They must convince us, and themselves, that there is a huge difference between reality and fantasy. What do they gain by doing so? The simple answer is, in Hurd's words, "strict truth" — now in the form of critical or scholarly wisdom. And the truths revered by this "reasonable company" of scholars promise new life just as much as the truth offered by the old woman of the Wife's tale. Hurd, for example, implies that anyone in the eighteenth century who preferred romance to strict truth would have been regarded as hopelessly old-fashioned. But, as we have seen, the idea that we will be rewarded with a better life if we "choose" reality is an idea with which the romance genre is very much at home. Critics of romance shake their heads over the alluring frivolities of the genre and admit that after all reality is a better thing: Bassanio gives up the gold casket, and the knight in the Wife's tale chooses to obey his elderly but wise wife.

So although critics of romance may think they are analyzing the genre's fantastic failings at realism, they may really be repeating the very wish that romance promises to fulfill: that necessity could be turned into choice, death into a better life. This tells us that romance is not just wish-fulfillment fantasy; it is instead a genre that helps, in a variety of ways, to persuade its readers that submitting to necessity might be almost as pleasant as a dream — maybe even more pleasant. Sometimes romance lets us dream that we might live happily ever after in fairyland. One medieval romance, *Launfal*, actually lets its hero vanish into fairyland, never returning to the real world. More often, though, romance fulfills a slightly different wish: the wish that, by renouncing fairyland, we will live better lives in a world we can securely believe is reality. The romance can thus be a very powerful agent in persuading us to accept our lives as they are, rather than as they might be.

Like Eric Auerbach and Bishop Hurd, the Wife of Bath also tells a story about the demise of romance. But she tells this story in a way that nonetheless suggests the continuing relevance of the romance to her real world of bickering and brokering. What can we learn further about the romance, and about the Wife's romance, from the way psychoanalysis itself narrates the loss of a "world of fine fabling"? In the section following I will show a few ways psychoanalysis can help us to understand the timing of sexuality and death, and the relation of such timing to historical and autobiographical narration, in the Wife's prologue and tale.

II. MORTALITY AND THE SUBJECT

One of the chief intellectual contributions of psychoanalytic theory has been its approach to the way human subjectivity takes shape in time. From the perspective of psychoanalysis, human subjectivity is profoundly historical and mortal. It is also structured by, and seeks structural change through, language. In psychoanalytic therapy, every subject has her own story to tell. Every subject explains herself by telling a story about the past. It is through the process of speaking, listening to, and transforming this kind of historical narrative that psychoanalysis aims to restore the subject to happiness. Moreover, for Freud — and for one of his most influential followers, Jacques Lacan — the subject learns, through telling her story, that she *has* a history, even that she *is* her history. The subject learns to recognize the ego's fantastic structure, its limitations, its mortality. In some strains of psychoanalysis this lesson can unfortunately take the form of a normalization; that is, some psychoanalysts, just like romance critics, would like us to believe that we must accept the truth of death if we are to be realistic, normal people. But psychoanalytic theory has also offered a different, much more interesting formulation: by telling the story of her pleasures and pains, her living and dying, as a mortal creature, the subject can remake her chances for happiness in this world and in the body. In doing so the subject does not so much accept reality as come to recognize that there are different definitions and experiences of reality, some of which are indeed unacceptable.

One of the narratives that psychoanalysis itself uses to explain the formation of the subject is the story of the subject's movement from the "polymorphous perverse" of infancy to the regulated sexual and emotional styles of later years. The term "polymorphous perverse" refers to the notion that in infancy our pleasures are varied because we do not yet have a sense of the "normal" way to experience pleasure. We are born without an identity, an ego; the infant enjoys, and suffers from, a multiple and shifting array of wishes, pleasures, and pains. Only later will these pleasures and pains be organized into an "I" who feels separate from its own sensations and the objects of its desires — an "I" who wants "this" and not "that." This multifarious play of desires is shaped through repression and other processes into an "I" who eats socially approved foods at socially approved times, spends wisely, and engages in genital sexuality. Or, conversely, it may be shaped into an "I" who has eating "disorders," or gambles "compulsively," or engages in sexual "perversion." Incidentally, while the term "perversion" has too often been used as a disciplinary or derogatory term, Freud's work argues that the desires at stake in "perversion" are common to us all, because we have all experienced the polymorphous pleasures of infancy.

Whether a given identity has been styled in such a way as to produce genital sexuality or perversion, eating disorders or balanced meals, psychoanalysis contends that all such identities mourn the loss of pleasures and experiences they have learned to forget. All identities are haunted by the traces of memories of proscribed pleasures. And because of such psychic losses, none of us will find happiness easy to achieve. Both the multifariousness of human pleasures and their fragility are registered in the Wife of Bath's performance. She remarks:

I ne loved nevere by no descrecioun,
But evere folwede mine appetit,
All were he short, or long, or blak, or whit.
I took no kepe, so that he liked me,
How poore he was, ne eek of what degree. (622–26)

The Wife's language here suggests something of the range and mobility of desire as psychoanalysis understands it. This "appetite" that refuses "discretion" cares little for considerations of class, wealth, shape, complexion. But even as the Wife of Bath speaks of her transgressive appetite and searches for her next husband, she is telling the story, the history, of her pleasures and pains, and she speaks of her loves as past loves — as fond memories from a past quite separate from her uncertain present and future. Psychoanalysis helps us understand why this sense of loss is registered at the very moment the Wife of Bath declares the range and extent of her appetite: she says "I ne loved nevere by no descrecioun" in the past tense.

The Wife's sensitivity to the passage of time is expressed perhaps most strongly in the following lines of her prologue:

> But, Lord Crist, whan that it remembreth me
> Upon my youthe and on my jolitee,
> It tikleth me aboute mine herte roote.
> Unto this day it dooth mine herte boote
> That I have had my world as in my time.
>   But age, allas, that all wole envenyme,
> Hath me biraft my beautee and my pith.
> Lat go. Farewell. The devel go therwith! (469–76)

The haunting, recognized by psychoanalysis, of our moments of greatest happiness by the memory of something lost is one way of accounting for the frequently elegiac tone of the Wife of Bath's exuberant defense of embodied pleasures. The importance of loss and pleasure to questions of identity, to the very question of what identity is, is enacted in the prominence of the "I" in the Wife of Bath's Prologue, and in the extraordinary length and complexity of its autobiographical mode. The Wife of Bath's Prologue is *about* the historical nature of the subject and the shaping of the subject's identity through the history of its losses and pleasures.

If the subject is historical she is also always social. Psychoanalytic theory recognizes that the individual subject's feelings are always mediated by the structures of the family and the larger social world. Freud's notion of the Oedipus complex is perhaps the most famous instance of the idea that the family works to manage the desire of the subject. Freud named the Oedipus complex after the protagonist of the Greek play *Oedipus Rex*, by Sophocles, in which Oedipus, abandoned at birth, later mistakenly kills his father and marries his mother (discussed in Freud's essay "A Special Type of Object Choice Made by Men"). Through the Oedipus complex, the subject's complicated networks of desire are triangulated into the relations among father, mother, and child. The various ways in which the parents feel, perform, and embody desire in front of the child and for the child help to shape how, what, and whom she desires. In turn, the parents' desires include traces of the histories and communities that shaped them, traces that will be felt and relayed by their children and their children's children.

Not all these desires are conscious, and this fact has important implications for psychoanalytic understandings of the social nature of desire. As theorized by Freud and Lacan, the unconscious is not only that most private of places where the individual ego keeps its most shameful and exciting secrets; it is also a part of the subject that the subject does not know precisely because the unconscious is social. For example, some of the unconscious desires that shape the subject are secrets transmitted unknowingly from one generation to another. Lacanian psychoanalysis in particular has emphasized that the subject participates in an unconscious social structuring of desires and demands, sometimes called the symbolic order. The symbolic order is the network of language, kinship, and power that names and identifies us as "I," as "you," as a "person" with a proper name, and so on. We are not fully conscious of our dependence on and participation in these networks.

At this point it might seem that the subject is carefully structured indeed — shaped and disciplined by family, by family history, and by the symbolic order more generally. But the social nature of desire also means that desire is unpredictable. So much information comes from so many different directions, and terms can shift their meanings so readily, that the subject's desire can never be managed completely. For example, the Oedipus complex seems often designed to produce the transgression of its own careful structures. The child might wish to explode her parents' marriage by murdering one member and carrying off the other. Or the child might give up on both parents as hopeless or lethal or inaccessible, and seek pleasure elsewhere — although often from an elsewhere powerfully reminiscent of these past loves and hatreds. One way in which the Wife of Bath's Prologue suggests both the weaknesses and disciplinary power of family and social structures is through the account the Wife gives of her marital history. Her marital statistics — the way they reflect, but also exaggerate, the frequency of multiple marriage in the Middle Ages — would suggest to a psychoanalytic critic that the role of the family in structuring, and failing to structure, desire is being addressed in the Wife of Bath's Prologue and Tale.

Having recognized the openness of the social structuring of the subject's desire, we must also remind ourselves that the subject's desire is *never* not social. The moment the subject is born, with all the apparent freedom of her polymorphous perversities, the subject is already plunged into the social relationships that will shape her desire. But the social nature of the subject's desire is often itself repressed. The idea that the child simply wants things that she must learn, for her own safety, not to want defends against recognition of the broad social function of the family as transmitter of desire and loss through and across generations. To misrecognize the unconscious as individual rather than social is part of the workings of a repression that tries to locate infantile pleasure safely in the past and to equate maturity with increasing respect for reality — as though the subject's acquaintance with social realities had not always been at stake in its desire.

Freud's notion of the relationship between the pleasure principle and the reality principle can be interpreted as just such a misrecognition. Infancy is seen as a time when the search for pleasure is so dominant that the infant will seek satisfaction in fantastic and, possibly, injurious scenarios when it encounters the obstacles posed by reality. As the subject is shaped and regulated through those very encounters, the subject learns to submit to the discipline of reality, seeking pleasure by more roundabout and safer means. This narrative has much in common with the romance structures discussed above. It makes the following assumptions: reality is a given, and pleasure is not itself a way of knowing or shaping reality; pleasure blocks, rather than results from, maturation; pleasure, not reality, can be dangerous, partly because it is insufficiently aware of death. But psychoanalysis also complicates these assumptions. It insists that desire is always social — always interacting with reality — *and* that past pleasures never leave us. For Freud, the past is always with us. And Freud insists that if we are to remake ourselves and our world for happiness, an embrace of the past (and of its continuing presence) is essential. In the next section I will show how the Wife of Bath's Tale offers a similar insight. While the Wife's tale depicts the power of the romance wish that we could better our lives by choosing to submit to reality, it does something else as well, something more interesting: it proposes that we might contend with necessity by changing it.

III. FANTASY MAKES THE WORLD

The Wife of Bath's Tale begins by lamenting the passing of the days of King Arthur and "fairye." The opening lines also lament the disenchanted nature of modern times, when the only fairies to be found are friars hiding behind bushes, waiting to assault the objects of their desire:

In th'olde dayes of the king Arthour,
Of which that Britons speken greet honour,
All was this land fulfild of fairye.
The elf-queene with her joly compaignye
Daunced ful ofte in many a grene mede.
This was the olde opinion, as I rede —
I speke of many hundred yeres ago.
But now kan no man seen none elves mo. (857–64)

In this passage, the Wife recounts a history of Britain by developing a contrast between past and present, between the "olde dayes" (857) and "now" (864). This past and present, moreover, are different not just because they represent different times; they are distinct worlds.

The old world — which the Wife knows about only through "olde opinion" (862) — is spoken of with respect, is "fulfild of fairye" (859) and of "joly" women (860). It is a world in which pleasure and women are not opposed to truth or honor, but are rather their insepa-rable companions or even embodiments. The romance genre is thus presented from the very beginning of the Wife of Bath's Tale as the trace of a lost world, strange now but once very familiar, indeed once reality itself, the archaic reality of England. The passage thus reminds us that one person's fantasy may once have been another person's re-ality. Reality shifts over time and space, and what can seem the very touchstone of reality in one context will seem an elaborate dream in another.

Any power structure will find it useful to be able to represent *as past* (for example, as "primitive") kinds of people, pleasures, or view-points that are threatening. Social realities persuade us that they are real, that they are all there is, by distinguishing themselves from lost, absent pleasures, from a fantastic past. But the ability to *offer* pleasure is equally crucial to power. Medieval archaisms often function in this way for contemporary U.S. culture. Medieval or Renaissance banquets and fairs, medieval motifs in movies and theme parks (*Braveheart*, Cinderella's castle) and in family hotels in Las Vegas (Excalibur), Dungeons and Dragons, and Goth fashion are examples of how ar-chaisms can be used to signify pleasurable alternatives to the weary disenchantments of modern life.

The Wife of Bath shows us that associating the past with happiness and wish fulfillment was also a medieval practice. She moves us sharply away from fairyland to her modern world, fulfilled not of "fairye" but of the inventoried objects of a disenchanted reality:

> For now the grete charitee and prayeres
> Of limitours and othere hooly freres,
> That serchen every lond and every streem
> As thikke as motes in the sonne-beem,
> Blessinge halles, chambres, kichenes, boures,
> Citees, burghes, castels, hye toures,
> Thropes, bernes, shipnes, dairyes.
> This maketh that there been no fairyes.
> For there as wont to walken was an elf
> There walketh now the limitour himself. (865–74)

The Wife laments that women are now safe from those pleasurable elves of old, and that their replacements, the friars, give women dishonor, not excitement:

> Wommen may go now saufly up and doun.
> In every bussh or under every tree
> Ther is noon oother incubus but he,
> And he ne wol doon hem but dishonour. (878–81)

This world has been thoroughly demystified. There is no time for reflection — no time, literally, for old-fashioned visions, for stories, for the elf queen and her "joly compaignye." We are made to feel that this new world is intensely realistic in contrast to its predecessor. Chaucer achieves this feeling partly by a technique of proliferation; instead of "a grene mede" the new world is full of proliferating man-made structures like "halles, chambres, kichenes, boures" and "citees, burghes, castels, hye toures" and "thropes, bernes, shipnes, dairyes" (869–71). The rhythm and tumble of these lines suggest that this new world is all moving too fast. For the Wife of Bath, the world of "now" (864, 865, 874, 878) measures its distance from the past by evoking, through a kind of material chaos, the loss of archaic beauty. In the welter of all that man-made hustle and bustle, who could possibly see an elf?

Through such masterful strokes as the rhyming of "dairyes / fairyes" (871–72), the Wife calls attention to the incommensurability of the marvelous and the everyday. Her prologue also evokes a world that feels concrete and everyday and "now" to the reader because it is full of scarlet cloth, moths, books, slaps, wine, money, calculation. But this world gives way to the romance and "th'olde dayes of the king Arthour" (857). Chaucer seems to distinguish sharply between prologue and tale, between transitory and lasting happiness, between the everyday world of time and work and the romance world.

But the Wife of Bath's performance calls attention to the *dependence* of the everyday on the marvelous. This insight is similar to psychoanalytic formulations of the way reality and desire transform one another. For example, the Wife's tale seems clearly to be produced by the desires and anxieties registered in the prologue. This implies that romance fantasy is for the Wife a contemporary practice. The Wife might be dreaming of the good old days, but we see that she is doing so *because* her modern world is troublesome.

Moreover, "fairye" turns out in the end to be absolutely central to the tale's ambitious politics, not an escape from them. The old woman's magical changeability works to reassure the knight — and by extension, the aristocracy — that it can mingle, even in marriage, with the common (poor, ugly) body without losing its own identity. Thus alliances between commoners and aristocrats are made to look not only safe, but desirable. Magical transformations of the common people into fairy-tale brides serve to reassure the aristocracy of its immortality. Crucial to this reassurance are the oscillations between fantasy and harsh reality *within* the romance. The knight rides

> In all this care under a forest side
> Wher as he saugh upon a daunce go
> Of ladyes foure and twenty and yet mo.
> Toward the whiche daunce he drow ful yerne,
> In hope that some wisdom sholde he lerne.
> But certeinly, er he came fully there,
> Vanisshed was this daunce, he nyste where.
> Ne creature saugh he that bar lif,
> Save on the grene he saugh sittinge a wif.
> A fouler wight there may no man devise. (990–99)

The twenty-four ladies whom the old woman replaces clearly offer a vision of happiness. Their disappearance, in turn, offers a vision of the fragility of happiness, of its tendency to vanish. Thus the promise of happiness is transformed, through a rude awakening, into an ugly truth about aging and death: "a fouler wight there may no man devise" (999). Romance has become a mere dream. And yet the ugly truth that replaces it — think, for example, of the old woman's truth-telling powers (the answer to the knight's quest, and the sermon on gentillesse) — is itself a marvel, an ugly old woman who can turn herself into a youthful, beautiful blessing for her noble knight.

Given the Wife's own social circumstances — a rebellious sexual ideologue, a successful participant in one of the most aggressive sectors of the late-fourteenth-century English economy — one might have expected from her a tale more obviously critical of powerful male aristocrats. But, at least when considered in tandem with psychoanalytic understandings of fantasy, the Wife's performance offers something more subtle: a reading of how social change is made possible by fantasy. It's true that, through the old woman's transfiguration, the threat of change represented by the Wife herself is domesticated: "love in a cottage" will be enough. An image of death is made into an image of life when the tale promises that the aristocracy will be able to keep its fabulous body of perpetual youth and beauty, its entitlement to privilege, so long as it is willing to forge alliances with the wealth and knowledge of the commons. And the tale promises that, in the process, the social and sexual threat posed by aging and ambitious women will be completely controlled and tamed. But the Wife's closing curse suggests the extent to which this promise is indeed a fairy tale. And her tale registers an even more powerful message: that the transformation and preservation of relations of power depend on the fantastic pleasure of imagining the world otherwise.

WORKS CITED

Auerbach, Eric. *Mimesis: The Representation of Reality in Western Literature*. 1953. Trans. Willard R. Trask. Princeton: Princeton UP, 1968, 1974.

Freud, Sigmund. *On Creativity and the Unconscious: Papers on the Psychology of Art, Literature, Love, Religion*. Ed. Benjamin Nelson. New York: Harper, 1958.

———. "A Special Type of Object Choice Made by Men." *On Creativity* 162–72.

———. "The Theme of the Three Caskets." *On Creativity* 63–75.

Hurd, Bishop Richard. *Letters on Chivalry and Romance* 1762. Ed. Hoyt Trowbridge. Los Angeles: Augustan Reprint Society / Clark Memorial Library, 1963.

Robertson, D. W. *A Preface to Chaucer: Studies in Medieval Perspectives*. Princeton: Princeton UP, 1962.

Deconstruction
and
the Wife of Bath

WHAT IS DECONSTRUCTION?

Deconstruction has a reputation for being the most complex and forbidding of contemporary critical approaches to literature, but in fact almost all of us have, at one time, either deconstructed a text or badly wanted to deconstruct one. Sometimes when we hear a lecturer effectively marshal evidence to show that a book means primarily one thing, we long to interrupt and ask what he or she would make of other, conveniently overlooked passages, passages that seem to contradict the lecturer's thesis. Sometimes, after reading a provocative critical article that *almost* convinces us that a familiar work means the opposite of what we assumed it meant, we may wish to make an equally convincing case for our former reading of the text. We may not think that the poem or novel in question better supports our interpretation, but we may recognize that the text can be used to support *both* readings. And sometimes we simply want to make that point: texts can be used to support seemingly irreconcilable positions.

To reach this conclusion is to feel the deconstructive itch. J. Hillis Miller, the preeminent American deconstructor, puts it this way: "Deconstruction is not a dismantling of the structure of a text, but a demonstration that it has already dismantled itself. Its apparently solid ground is no rock but thin air" ("Stevens' Rock" 341). To deconstruct a text isn't to show that all the high old themes aren't there to be found in it. Rather, it is to show that a text — not unlike DNA with its double helix — can have intertwined, opposite "discourses" — strands of narrative, threads of meaning.

Ultimately, of course, deconstruction refers to a larger and more complex enterprise than the practice of demonstrating that a text means contradictory things. The term refers to a way of reading texts practiced by critics who have been influenced by the writings of the French philosopher Jacques Derrida. It is important to gain some understanding of Derrida's project and of the historical backgrounds of his work before reading the deconstruction that follows, let alone attempting to deconstruct a text. But it is important, too, to approach deconstruction with anything but a scholar's sober and almost worshipful respect for knowledge and truth. Deconstruction offers a playful alternative to traditional scholarship, a confidently adversarial alternative, and deserves to be approached in the spirit that animates it.

Derrida, a philosopher of language who coined the term "deconstruction," argues that we tend to think and express our thoughts in terms of opposites. Something is black but not white, masculine and therefore not feminine, a cause rather than an effect, and so forth. These mutually exclusive pairs or dichotomies are too numerous to list but would include beginning/end, conscious/unconscious, presence/absence, speech/writing, and construction/destruction (the last being the opposition that Derrida's word *deconstruction* tries to contain and subvert). If we think hard about these dichotomies, Derrida suggests, we will realize that they are not simply oppositions; they are also hierarchies in miniature. In other words, they contain one term that our culture views as being superior and one term viewed as negative or inferior. Sometimes the superior term seems only subtly superior (*speech, masculine, cause*), whereas sometimes we know immediately which term is culturally preferable (*presence* and *beginning* and *consciousness* are easy choices). But the hierarchy always exists.

Of particular interest to Derrida, perhaps because it involves the language in which all the other dichotomies are expressed, is the hierarchical opposition speech/writing. Derrida argues that the "privileging" of speech, that is, the tendency to regard speech in positive terms and writing in negative terms, cannot be disentangled from the privileging of presence. (Postcards are written by absent friends; we read Plato because he cannot speak from beyond the grave.) Furthermore, according to Derrida, the tendency to privilege both speech and presence is part of the Western tradition of *logocentrism*, the belief that in some ideal beginning were creative *spoken* words, words such as "Let there be light," spoken by an ideal, *present* God. According to logocentric tradition, these words can now only be represented in unoriginal speech or writing (such as the written phrase in quotation marks above). Derrida doesn't seek to reverse the hierarchized opposition between speech and writing, or presence and absence, or early and late, for to do so would be to fall into a trap of perpetuating the same forms of thought and expression that he seeks to deconstruct. Rather, his goal is to erase the boundary between oppositions such as speech and writing, and to do so in such a way as to throw the order and values implied by the opposition into question.

Returning to the theories of Ferdinand de Saussure, who invented the modern science of linguistics, Derrida reminds us that the association of speech with present, obvious, and ideal meaning and writing with absent, merely pictured, and therefore less reliable meaning is suspect, to say the least. As Saussure demonstrated, words are *not* the things they name and, indeed, they are only arbitrarily associated with those things. Neither spoken nor written words have present, positive, identifiable attributes themselves; they have meaning only by virtue of their difference from other words *(red, read, reed)*. In a sense, meanings emerge from the gaps or spaces between them. Take *read* as an example. To know whether it is the present or past tense of the verb — whether it rhymes with *red* or *reed* — we need to see it in relation to some other word (for example, *yesterday*).

Because the meanings of words lie in the differences between them and in the differences between them and the things they name, Derrida suggests that all language is constituted by *différance,* a word he has coined that puns on two French words meaning "to differ" and "to defer": words are the deferred presences of the things they "mean," and their meaning is grounded in difference. Derrida, by the way, changes the *e* in the French word *différence* to an *a* in his neologism *différance;* the change, which can be seen in writing but cannot be heard in spoken French, is itself a playful, witty challenge to the notion that writing is inferior or "fallen" speech.

In *De la grammatologie* [*Of Grammatology*] (1967) and *Dissemination* (1972), Derrida begins to redefine writing by deconstructing some old definitions. In *Dissemination,* he traces logocentrism back to Plato, who in the *Phaedrus* has Socrates condemn writing and who, in all the great dialogues, powerfully postulates that metaphysical longing for origins and ideals that permeates Western thought. "What Derrida does in his reading of Plato," Barbara Johnson points out, "is to unfold dimensions of Plato's *text* that work against the grain of

(Plato's own) Platonism" (xxiv). Remember: that is what deconstruction does according to Miller; it shows a text dismantling itself.

In *Of Grammatology,* Derrida turns to the *Confessions* of Jean-Jacques Rousseau and exposes a grain running against the grain. Rousseau, another great Western idealist and believer in innocent, noble origins, on one hand condemned writing as mere representation, a corruption of the more natural, childlike, direct, and therefore undevious speech. On the other hand, Rousseau admitted his own tendency to lose self-presence and blurt out exactly the wrong thing in public. He confesses that, by writing at a distance from his audience, he often expressed himself better: "If I were present, one would never know what I was worth," Rousseau admitted (Derrida, *Of Grammatology* 142). Thus, writing is a *supplement* to speech that is at the same time *necessary.* Barbara Johnson, sounding like Derrida, puts it this way: "Recourse to writing . . . is necessary to recapture a presence whose lack has not been preceded by any fullness" (Derrida, *Dissemination* xii). Thus, Derrida shows that one strand of Rousseau's discourse made writing seem a secondary, even treacherous supplement, whereas another made it seem necessary to communication.

Have Derrida's deconstructions of *Confessions* and the *Phaedrus* explained these texts, interpreted them, opened them up and shown us what they mean? Not in any traditional sense. Derrida would say that anyone attempting to find a single, correct meaning in a text is simply imprisoned by that structure of thought that would oppose two readings and declare one to be right and not wrong, correct rather than incorrect. In fact, any work of literature that we interpret defies the laws of Western logic, the laws of opposition and noncontradiction. In the views of poststructuralist critics, texts don't say "A and not B." They say "A and not-A," as do texts written by literary critics, who are also involved in producing creative writing.

Miller has written that the purpose of deconstruction is to show "the existence in literature of structures of language which contradict the law of noncontradiction." Why find the grain that runs against the grain? To restore what Miller has called "the strangeness of literature," to reveal the "capacity of each work to surprise the reader," to demonstrate that "literature continually exceeds any formula or theory with which the critic is prepared to encompass it" (Miller, *Fiction* 5).

Although its ultimate aim may be to critique Western idealism and logic, deconstruction began as a response to structuralism and to formalism, another structure-oriented theory of reading. (Deconstruction, which is really only one kind of a poststructuralist criticism, is sometimes referred to as poststructuralist criticism, or even as poststructuralism.)

Structuralism, Robert Scholes tells us, may now be seen as a reaction to modernist alienation and despair (3). Using Saussure's theory as Derrida was to do later, European structuralists attempted to create a *semiology*, or science of signs, that would give humankind at once a scientific and a holistic way of studying the world and its human inhabitants. Roland Barthes, a structuralist who later shifted toward poststructuralism, hoped to recover literary language from the isolation in which it had been studied and to show that the laws that govern it govern all signs, from road signs to articles of clothing. Claude Lévi-Strauss, a structural anthropologist who studied everything from village structure to the structure of myths, found in myths what he called *mythemes*, or building blocks, such as basic plot elements. Recognizing that the same mythemes occur in similar myths from different cultures, he suggested that all myths may be elements of one great myth being written by the collective human mind.

Derrida could not accept the notion that structuralist thought might someday explain the laws governing human signification and thus provide the key to understanding the form and meaning of everything from an African village to a Greek myth to Rousseau's *Confessions*. In his view, the scientific search by structural anthropologists for what unifies humankind amounts to a new version of the old search for the lost ideal, whether that ideal be Plato's bright realm of the Idea or the Paradise of Genesis or Rousseau's unspoiled Nature. As for the structuralist belief that texts have "centers" of meaning, in Derrida's view that derives from the logocentric belief that there is a reading of the text that accords with "the book as seen by God." Jonathan Culler, who thus translates a difficult phrase from Derrida's *L'Écriture et la différance* [*Writing and Difference*] (1967) in his book *Structuralist Poetics* (1975), goes on to explain what Derrida objects to in structuralist literary criticism:

> [When] one speaks of the structure of a literary work, one does so from a certain vantage point: one starts with notions of the meaning or effects of a poem and tries to identify the structures responsible for those effects. Possible configurations or patterns that make no contribution are rejected as irrelevant. That is to say, an intuitive understanding of the poem functions as the "centre". . . : it is both a starting point and a limiting principle. (244)

For these reasons, Derrida and his poststructuralist followers reject the very notion of "linguistic competence" introduced by Noam Chomsky, a structural linguist. The idea that there is a competent reading "gives a privileged status to a particular set of rules of reading, . . . granting preeminence to certain conventions and excluding from the realm of language all the truly creative and productive violations of those rules" (Culler, *Structuralist Poetics* 241).

Poststructuralism calls into question assumptions made about literature by formalist, as well as by structuralist, critics. Formalism, or the New Criticism as it was once commonly called, assumes a work of literature to be a freestanding, self-contained object, its meanings found in the complex network of relations that constitute its parts (images, sounds, rhythms, allusions, and so on). To be sure, deconstruction is somewhat like formalism in several ways. Both the formalist and the deconstructor focus on the literary text; neither is likely to interpret a poem or a novel by relating it to events in the author's life, letters, historical period, or even culture. And formalists, long before deconstructors, discovered counterpatterns of meaning in the same text. Formalists find ambiguity and irony, deconstructors find contradiction and undecidability.

Undecidability, as Paul de Man came to define it, is a complex notion easily misunderstood. There is a tendency to assume it refers to readers who, when forced to decide between two or more equally plausible and conflicting readings motivated by the same text, throw up their hands and decide that the choice can't be made. But undecidability in fact debunks this whole notion of reading as a decision-making process carried out on texts by readers. To say we are forced to choose or decide — or that we are unable to do so — is to locate the problem of undecidability falsely outside ourselves, and to make it reside within a text to which we come as an Other. The poststructuralist concept of undecidability, we might say, deconstructs the either/or type distinction or opposition that structuralists and formalists have made between reader and text. It entails what de Man calls the "mutual obliteration" not only of propositions apparently opposed but also of the subject/object relation.

Undecidability is thus rather different from ambiguity, as understood by formalists. Formalists believe a complete understanding of a literary work is possible, an understanding in which even the ambiguities will fulfill a definite, meaningful function. Deconstructors confront the apparently limitless possibilities for the production of meaning that develop when the language of the critic enters the language of the text. They cannot accept the formalist view that a work of literary art has organic unity (therefore, structuralists would say, a "center"), if only we could find it. The formalist critic ultimately makes sense of ambiguity; undecidability, by contrast, is never reduced, let alone resolved, by deconstructive reading.

Poststructuralists break with formalists, too, over an issue they have debated with structuralists. The issue involves metaphor and metonymy, two terms for different kinds of rhetorical *tropes,* or figures of speech. *Metonymy* refers to a figure that is chosen to stand for something that it is commonly associated with, or with which it happens to be contiguous or juxtaposed. When said to a waitress, "I'll have the cold plate today" is a metonymic figure of speech for "I'll eat the cold food you're serving today." We refer to the food we want as a plate simply because plates are what food happens to be served on and because everyone understands that by *plate* we mean food. A *metaphor*, on the other hand, is a figure of speech that involves a special, intrinsic, nonarbitrary relationship with what it represents. When you say you are blue, if you believe that there is an intrinsic, timeless likeness between that color and melancholy feeling — a likeness that just doesn't exist between sadness and yellow — then you are using the word *blue* metaphorically.

Although both formalists and structuralists make much of the difference between metaphor and metonymy, Derrida, Miller, and de Man have contended with the distinction deconstructively. They have questioned not only the distinction but also, and perhaps especially, the privilege we grant to metaphor, which we tend to view as the positive and superior figure of speech. De Man, in *Allegories of Reading* (1979), analyzes a passage from Proust's *Swann's Way,* arguing that it is about the nondistinction between metaphor and metonymy — and that it makes its claim metonymically. In *Fiction and Repetition: Seven English Novels* (1982), Miller connects the belief in metaphorical correspondences with other metaphysical beliefs, such as those in origins, endings, transcendence, and underlying truths. Isn't it likely, deconstructors keep implicitly asking, that every metaphor was once a metonym, but that we have simply forgotten what arbitrary juxtaposition or contiguity gave rise to the association that now seems mysteriously special?

The hypothesis that what we call metaphors are really old metonyms may perhaps be made clearer by the following example. We used the word *Watergate* as a metonym to refer to a political scandal that began in the Watergate building complex. Recently, we have used

part of the building's name (*gate*) to refer to more recent scandals
(*Irangate*). However, already there are people who use and "under-
stand" these terms who are unaware that Watergate is the name of
a building. In the future, isn't it possible that *gate*, which began as
part of a simple metonym, will seem like the perfect metaphor for
scandal — a word that suggests corruption and wrongdoing with a
strange and inexplicable rightness?

This is how deconstruction works: by showing that what was prior
and privileged in the old hierarchy (for instance, metaphor and
speech) can just as easily seem secondary, the deconstructor causes the
formerly privileged term to exchange properties with the formerly de-
valued one. Causes become effects and (d)evolutions become origins,
but the result is neither the destruction of the old order or hierarchy
nor the construction of a new one. It is, rather, *deconstruction*. In
Robert Scholes's words, "If either cause or effect can occupy the posi-
tion of an origin, then origin is no longer originary; it loses its
metaphorical privilege" (88).

Once deconstructed, literal and figurative can exchange proper-
ties, so that the prioritizing between them is erased: all words, even
dog and *cat,* are understood to be figures. It's just that we have used
some of them so long that we have forgotten how arbitrary and
metonymic they are. And, just as literal and figurative can exchange
properties, criticism can exchange properties with literature, in the
process coming to be seen not merely as a supplement — the second,
negative, and inferior term in the binary opposition creative writing/
literary criticism — but rather as an equally creative form of work.
Would we write if there were not critics — intelligent readers moti-
vated and able to make sense of what is written? Who, then, depends
on whom?

"It is not difficult to see the attractions" of deconstructive reading,
Jonathan Culler has commented. "Given that there is no ultimate or
absolute justification for any system or for the interpretations from it,"
the critic is free to value "the activity of interpretation itself, . . . rather
than any results which might be obtained" (*Structuralist Poetics* 248).
Not everyone, however, has so readily seen the attractions of decon-
struction. Two eminent critics, M. H. Abrams and Wayne Booth, have
observed that a deconstructive reading "is plainly and simply parasiti-
cal" on what Abrams calls "the obvious or univocal meaning"
(Abrams 457–58). In other words, there would be no deconstructors
if critics did not already exist who can see and show central and defi-

nite meanings in texts. Miller responded in an essay entitled "The Critic as Host," in which he deconstructed not only the oppositional hierarchy (host/parasite) but also the two terms themselves, showing that each derives from two definitions meaning nearly opposite things. *Host* means "hospitable welcomer" and "military horde." *Parasite* originally had a positive connotation; in Greek, *parasitos* meant "beside the grain" and referred to a friendly guest. Finally, Miller suggests, the words *parasite* and *host* are inseparable, depending on one another for their meaning in a given work, much as do hosts and parasites, authors and critics, structuralists and poststructuralists.

Ross C Murfin

DECONSTRUCTION: A SELECTED BIBLIOGRAPHY

Deconstruction, Poststructuralism, and Structuralism: Introductions, Guides, and Surveys

Arac, Jonathan, Wlad Godzich, and Wallace Martin, eds. *The Yale Critics: Deconstruction in America.* Minneapolis: U of Minnesota P, 1983. See especially the essays by Bové, Godzich, Pease, and Corngold.

Berman, Art. *From the New Criticism to Deconstruction: The Reception of Structuralism and Post-Structuralism.* Urbana: U of Illinois P, 1988.

Butler, Christopher. *Interpretation, Deconstruction, and Ideology: An Introduction to Some Current Issues in Literary Theory.* Oxford: Oxford UP, 1984.

Cain, William E. "Deconstruction in America: The Recent Literary Criticism of J. Hillis Miller." *College English* 41 (1979): 367–82.

Culler, Jonathan. *On Deconstruction: Theory and Criticism After Structuralism.* Ithaca: Cornell UP, 1982.

———. *Structuralist Poetics: Structuralism, Linguistics, and the Study of Literature.* Ithaca: Cornell UP, 1975. See especially ch. 10.

Esch, Deborah. "Deconstruction." *Redrawing the Boundaries: The Transformation of English and American Literary Studies.* Ed. Stephen Greenblatt and Giles Gunn. New York: MLA, 1992. 374–91.

Gasché, Rodolphe. "Deconstruction as Criticism." *Glyph* 6 (1979): 177–215.

Jay, Gregory. *America the Scrivener: Deconstruction and the Subject of Literary History*. Ithaca: Cornell UP, 1990.

Jefferson, Ann. "Structuralism and Post Structuralism." *Modern Literary Theory: A Comparative Introduction*. Totowa, NJ: Barnes, 1982. 84–112.

Leitch, Vincent B. *American Literary Criticism from the Thirties to the Eighties*. New York: Columbia UP, 1988. See especially ch. 10, "Deconstructive Criticism."

———. *Deconstructive Criticism: An Advanced Introduction and Survey*. New York: Columbia UP, 1983.

Lentricchia, Frank. *After the New Criticism*. Chicago: U of Chicago P, 1981.

Melville, Stephen W. *Philosophy Beside Itself: On Deconstruction and Modernism*. Vol. 27 of *Theory and History of Literature*. Minneapolis: U of Minnesota P, 1986.

Norris, Christopher. *Deconstruction and the Interests of Theory*. Vol. 4 of *Oklahoma Project for Discourse and Theory*. Norman: U of Oklahoma P, 1989.

———. *Deconstruction: Theory and Practice*. London: Methuen, 1982. Rev. ed. London: Routledge, 1991.

Raval, Suresh. *Metacriticism*. Athens: U of Georgia P, 1981.

Scholes, Robert. *Structuralism in Literature: An Introduction*. New Haven: Yale UP, 1974.

Sturrock, John. *Structuralism and Since*. New York: Oxford UP, 1975.

Selected Works by Jacques Derrida and Paul de Man

de Man, Paul. *Allegories of Reading*. New Haven: Yale UP, 1979. See especially ch. 1, "Semiology and Rhetoric."

———. *Blindness and Insight*. New York: Oxford UP, 1971. Minneapolis: U of Minnesota P, 1983. The 1983 edition contains important essays not included in the original edition.

———. *The Resistance to Theory*. Minneapolis: U of Minnesota P, 1986.

Derrida, Jacques. *Acts of Literature*. Ed. Derek Attridge. New York: Routledge, 1992. Includes a helpful editor's introduction on Derrida and literature.

———. *Dissemination*. 1972. Trans. Barbara Johnson. Chicago: U of Chicago P, 1981. See especially the concise, incisive "Translator's Introduction," which provides a useful point of entry into this work and others by Derrida.

———. *Margins of Philosophy*. Trans. Alan Bass. Chicago: U of Chicago P, 1982.

——. *Of Grammatology.* 1967. Trans. Gayatri C. Spivak. Baltimore: Johns Hopkins UP, 1976.

——. *The Postcard: From Socrates to Freud and Beyond.* Trans. with intro. Alan Bass. Chicago: U of Chicago P, 1987.

——. *Writing and Difference.* 1967. Trans. Alan Bass. Chicago: U of Chicago P, 1978.

Essays in Deconstruction and Poststructuralism

Barthes, Roland. *S/Z.* Trans. Richard Miller. New York: Hill, 1974. In this influential work, Barthes turns from a structuralist to a post-structuralist approach.

Bloom, Harold, et al., eds. *Deconstruction and Criticism.* New York: Seabury, 1979. Includes essays by Bloom, de Man, Derrida, Miller, and Hartman.

Chase, Cynthia. *Decomposing Figures.* Baltimore: Johns Hopkins UP, 1986.

Harari, Josué, ed. *Textual Strategies: Perspectives in Post-Structuralist Criticism.* Ithaca: Cornell UP, 1979.

Johnson, Barbara. *The Critical Difference: Essays in the Contemporary Rhetoric of Reading.* Baltimore: Johns Hopkins UP, 1980.

——. *A World of Difference.* Baltimore: Johns Hopkins UP, 1987.

Krupnick, Mark, ed. *Displacement: Derrida and After.* Bloomington: Indiana UP, 1987.

Miller, J. Hillis. *Ariadne's Thread: Story Lines.* New Haven: Yale UP, 1992.

——. *The Ethics of Reading: Kant, de Man, Eliot, Trollope, James, and Benjamin.* New York: Columbia UP, 1987.

——. *Fiction and Repetition: Seven English Novels.* Cambridge: Harvard UP, 1982.

——. *Hawthorne and History, Defacing It.* Cambridge: Basil Blackwell, 1991. Contains a bibliography of Miller's work from 1955 to 1990.

——. "Stevens' Rock and Criticism as Cure." *Georgia Review* 30 (1976): 5–31, 330–48.

Ulmer, Gregory L. *Applied Grammatology.* Baltimore: Johns Hopkins UP, 1985.

Other Work Referred to in "What Is Deconstruction?"

Abrams, M. H. "Rationality and the Imagination in Cultural History." *Critical Inquiry* 2 (1976): 447–64.

Deconstructionist Approaches to Chaucer and the Wife of Bath's Prologue and Tale

Ferster, Judith. "Reading the Self: The Wife of Bath." *Chaucer on Interpretation*. Cambridge: Cambridge UP, 1985. 122–38.

Fineman, Joel. "The Structure of Allegorical Desire." *The Subjectivity Effect in Western Literary Tradition: Essays Toward the Release of Shakespeare's Will*. Cambridge: MIT, 1991. 3–31.

Hahn, Thomas. "Teaching the Resistant Woman: The Wife of Bath and the Academy." *Exemplaria* 4 (1992): 431–40.

Knapp, Peggy A. "Deconstructing the *Canterbury Tales:* Pro." *Studies in the Age of Chaucer* 2 (1987): 73–81. Rpt. in *Critical Essays on Chaucer's Canterbury Tales*. Ed. Malcolm Andrew. Toronto: U of Toronto P, 1991. 214–21.

———. "'Wandrynge by the Weye': On Alisoun and Augustine." *Medieval Texts and Contemporary Readers*. Ed. Laurie A. Finke and Martin B. Schictman. Ithaca: Cornell UP, 1987. 142–57.

Lawler, Traugott. "Deconstructing the *Canterbury Tales:* Con." *Studies in the Age of Chaucer* 2 (1987): 83–91. Rpt. in *Critical Essays on Chaucer's Canterbury Tales*. Ed. Malcolm Andrew. Toronto: U of Toronto P, 1991. 222–29.

Leicester, H. Marshall, Jr. *The Disenchanted Self: Representing the Subject in the Canterbury Tales*. Berkeley: U of California P, 1990.

———. "'Oure Tonges *Différance*': Textuality and Deconstruction in Chaucer." *Medieval Texts and Contemporary Readers*. Ed. Laurie A. Finke and Martin B. Schictman. Ithaca: Cornell UP, 1987. 15–26.

Martin, Priscilla. "Chaucer and Feminism: A Magpie View." *A Wyf Ther Was*. Ed. Juliette Dor. Liege: U of Liege, 1992.

Schibanoff, Susan. "Taking the Gold Out of Egypt: The Art of Reading as a Woman." *Gender and Reading: Essays on Readers, Texts, and Contexts*. Ed. Elizabeth A. Flynn and Patrocinio P. Schweickart. Baltimore: Johns Hopkins UP, 1986. 83–106.

Straus, Barrie Ruth. "The Subversive Discourse of the Wife of Bath: Phallocentric Discourse and the Imprisonment of Criticism." *ELH* 55 (1988): 527–54.

A DECONSTRUCTIONIST PERSPECTIVE

By the nature of their very approach to literature and interpretation, deconstructive critics resist being pinned down to arguing in favor of any one single meaning. Reading their work, then, is sometimes frustrating because no sooner do they seem to say something than they seem to back away and unsay it or qualify or contradict it. In doing so they are often having fun, playing with ideas and readings and even words that other critics take more grimly.

In the essay that follows, H. Marshall Leicester, Jr. reads deconstructively several elements of the Wife of Bath's performance. In doing so he repeatedly plays with the notion of interruption. Just as the Wife of Bath continually interrupts the train of her discourse by derailing herself and then rerailing herself in a way that has amused audiences for centuries, so Leicester interrupts himself almost before he has started, and then returns to his old outline again. Like the Wife of Bath, he has an abundance of useful things to say along the way. Particularly useful is his discussion of the meanings of some of the terms deconstructionists use — "subject," "voice," "reification," and "disenchantment." Using a distinction Derrida drew in *Of Grammatology*, Leicester argues that we should not confuse "voice" with "presence" or "self," the latter of which imply the existence of something or someone outside the text. In discussing reification Leicester makes clear why deconstruction resists the efforts of literary critics to make the abstract concrete, and he urges that we resist efforts to reify the Wife of Bath by trying to assign "determinate" or definite meanings to almost anything she says in her prologue or tale.

Leicester deconstructs the dream that the Wife of Bath tells us she tells Jankyn — of his killing her in her bed, such that "all my bed was ful of verray blood" (579). The Wife also tells us that she lied to him: "all was false" (582). All this seems definite and determinate: the Wife tells us that she made up the dream, so we know at least one thing about her: that she is a liar. Fine. We can pin that fact down. But wait. If she is a liar, Leicester asks, how can we be sure that she is not lying about telling a lie? Perhaps she really did have that dream after all, but has reasons of her own for wanting to conceal that frightening fact from the rest of us, and perhaps even from herself. If so, then that might explain why she interrupts herself immediately after describing the dream to tell us, "Ah ha! By God, I have my tale ageyn" (586). Leicester would have us believe *neither* that the Wife of Bath is lying *nor* that she is telling the truth about the bloody dream. Nor would he have us believe that she is *both* lying and telling the truth about the dream. His point, rather, is that we cannot decide.

In a typically deconstructive move, Leicester shows how the complex and conflicting etymologies of individual words prevent us from assigning them single, stable meanings. Deconstructing Chaucer's word *paraventure,* Leicester launches into a fascinating discussion of the rape of the maiden at the start of the Wife of Bath's Tale. He considers that crime in relation to the statutes of the time, arguing that they may — or again, may not! — have stipulated the death penalty for rape. But it is time for me to interrupt this introduction and let Leicester speak for "himself" — that is, his edited self.

H. MARSHALL LEICESTER, JR.

"My bed was ful of verray blood": Subject, Dream, and Rape in the Wife of Bath's Prologue and Tale

As the representative of deconstructive criticism in this book, I will begin with a discussion of certain assumptions I make about the relationship of the Wife of Bath to her tale, about the relationship between the Wife of Bath as self and as subject, and about the nature of the disenchantment she voices. Then I will take a deconstructive look at the "false" dream that the Wife discusses in her prologue, and finally I will attempt to show how the Wife of Bath deconstructs, and is herself deconstructed by, the rape in her tale.

But first I will interrupt myself.

Like most people, I resist labels because I do not want others to assume things about me that may not be true. I want to be free to define myself, not to be defined by labels. I want to give voice to my own authentic views, rather than being heard to say something just because others with that label may have said it. I want, that is, to be free to deconstruct the labels — even the label "deconstructionist" — to mean not just the one thing the label implies, but also its opposite, or even something quite different. Therefore, in what follows, I acknowledge my debt to the deconstructive attitude to literature, but also to other approaches. The most obvious of these perspectives is psychoanalysis, but I am also interested in the relations between gender and power in a text in the way a feminist critic might be, I am something of a historicist in wanting to understand the Wife of Bath in the context of the fourteenth century, and I am a quasi-Marxist materialist in my interest in the text's representation of economic issues.

As it happens, in this I am something like the Wife of Bath in her prologue and tale, since she too seems to want to define herself in terms of her own experience without being pinned down by prior labels, although she also seems to want to be free to appropriate the methods of others, even of those misogynist writers she does battle with, when it suits her convenience. Thus, when Saint Paul is incautious enough to grant her the kind of power over her husband's body that the husband is also supposed to have over hers, she seizes on it as permission to do battle for the advantage: "I have the power duringe all my lif / Upon his propre body, and noght he. . . . / All this sentence me liketh every deel!" (158–59, 162). Like me, perhaps, sometimes the Wife wants to make use of established labels — which is to say of determinate, stable meanings — and sometimes she wants to escape them.

Thus perhaps, if we share nothing else, the Wife and I share something of a common attitude to determinate meanings, and our common ambivalence suggests that together the Wife and I might add up to a generalization. In any case, as it happens, when you read deconstructive criticism you can't escape without a little theoretical lecture on meaning, and here is ours:

In general, "deconstruction" names the place of a certain "wait-a-minute" attitude to meaning, a continually affirmed negative or pure suspension that denies to meaning any completeness, closure, or determinacy. As such, a *purely* "deconstructive approach" runs the risk of becoming reductive, and all deconstructions (despite the particularity of terms in each deconstruction) run the risk of looking the same. Indeed, such a result seems almost inevitable if the aim is primarily to demonstrate the negative and affirm the attitude, since the desired outcome will be defined as always ending up in the same place of indeterminacy. In doing "deconstructive criticism," it is more fruitful to think of deconstruction not as a final outcome but as a moment in an ongoing process of *doing and undoing meaning* (of detextualizing and retextualizing a text). Psychologically, historically, and politically interesting are the various particular deployments of the possibility and impossibility of determinate meaning in particular texts and situations, how the "place of deconstruction" can be *used*, within and without the text.

I. SOME HISTORY AND SOME TERMS

In 1915 Harvard professor George Lyman Kittredge published his groundbreaking *Chaucer and His Poetry*. In that book he praised Chaucer for creating tales that were nicely suited to their fictional tellers on the road to Canterbury. Instead of assigning tales to tellers randomly, Kittredge said, Chaucer selected for them tales that matched their station and personality: Chaucer gives the moral Knight a stately romance of warriors and dukes and fair damsels; the immoral Miller a lowlife tale of sex, infidelity, and raucous bad taste; and the Wife of Bath a fairy-tale romance that reflects her view that women want and deserve the upper hand in marriage. Forty years later, Robert M. Lumiansky, in *Of Sondry Folk*, carried Kittredge's notion further forward by arguing that the linkages between the tales and their tellers were far more intricate than previous scholars had imagined. In Lumiansky's view, for example, Chaucer has the Wife of Bath reveal "certain unfavorable aspects of her character which she does not intend to reveal; she no doubt would look upon such revelation as a source of embarrassment" (119).

The general response to Kittredge's "roadside drama" view — the notion that the various tales are to be read almost as if they were soliloquies or self-characterizing stage-speeches of their tellers — has been largely positive. Lumiansky's more detailed insistence that the tales reflect the personalities and unconscious revelations of their tellers has met with more resistance, despite the distinguished example of such a method in E. Talbot Donaldson's *Chaucer's Poetry*, of 1958. In 1988, for instance, C. David Benson, in *Chaucer's Drama of Style*, argued with some force that the Kittredge-Lumiansky school had focused so narrowly on improbable connections between tales and tellers as to neglect the far more important, and far more dramatic, differences in the literary styles of the various tales, although it has to be said that in choosing his ground for his own case, Benson all but ignored the Wife of Bath, one of the centerpiece exhibits of the Kittredgeans.

In my 1990 *The Disenchanted Self* I set forth — in more detail than I can here — my own view that although the dramatic-speaker critics were generally right in their desire to recognize the close connections between Chaucerian tales and tellers, they had put the dramatic horse before the narrative cart. Too often they had looked first outside the tale — in the General Prologue and in the links between tales — for supposedly factual information about the various tellers, and had then read the tales to see how they fit those preestablished figures. In contrast, my view is that the character and personality of a pilgrim are not to be inferred from what is found outside the tale and measured against what is in it, but rather that the tale is the most important indication of what the teller is like.

Drawing on deconstructive texts like "Writing Before the Letter" in Part I of Jacques Derrida's *Of Grammatology*, I suggested that we must not confuse "voice," a grammatical category, with "presence," a property of things. At the time I was writing, virtually all the critics who attempted to assess the relationship between Chaucerian tales and tellers sought to trace the voice of a tale to a person or "self" who exists as a living presence outside the tale, prior to and apart from the text of his or her story. But I think it is crucial to remember that there is *never* anyone there; a text is *always* the absence of a person. Since the text is the only presence we have, the voice that matters is that of the language of the tale. For one thing, there is a lot more of it. The Plowman of the General Prologue, who tells no tale, is almost nothing, a shadowy and unmemorable absence rather than a vibrant and speaking one.

The point, then, is not that the teller produces a tale but that a text produces a teller. The Wife of Bath is not a living presence or self who creates a prologue about her views on marriage and her experience with five husbands, and then a tale about a rapist who learns what women most desire. Rather, the Wife is a "subject" (another grammatical term) — a *virtual* woman whose very existence is determined by the Chaucerian texts she is made to tell. In my view, then, it is misleading even to suggest that the Wife of Bath's Prologue and Tale are unsuitable to their teller, because she barely exists outside of her prologue and tale. They are not spoken in her voice or outside her voice; they *are* her voice. I can thus agree in part with Benson that previous dramatic criticism neglected the drama of style without giving up my adherence to the idea of the importance of the teller (or voice) of a tale. As I see it, the style of a given tale — its genre, its decorum or lack of it, its formulas and stock situations — is just as much a feature of the teller who chose to tell *that* kind of tale rather than another as any other fact of the text's language such as the grammatical gender of its pronouns. It should be remembered that none of the Canterbury pilgrims tells an original tale, in the modern sense of a story made up by the teller that did not exist before she or he told it. If these tellers argue with one another, they do it by adopting — choosing to adopt — conflicting positions already embodied in the stories they tell. Note that this position does not prevent a teller from *proposing*, as part of the telling, that a tale is in some sense unsuitable to him or her, that is, from criticizing what he or she tells while telling it. This is, as it happens, what the Wife does with her tale.

Modern critics sometimes use the verb *reify* — to make into a *res*, or thing — to mean attempting to render real something that is abstract, to give an idea a body. My view is that many modern Chaucer critics have assumed that the task of criticism is to reify the Wife of Bath, to read and analyze her in such a way as to give her a self. Inevitably, they have imposed on her their own notion of what that self is: a schizophrenic personality caught between the contradictory pulls of Mars and Venus, a liberated woman who puts men in their places, a nostalgic sentimentalist who yearns for the days of her youth when men valued her for her sexuality, and so on. But insofar as these characterizations reflect genuine features of the text, we could as easily say that they are the result of the Wife of Bath's attempts to reify herself, to define her own true nature by telling us her history and her tale. Reification is thus associated with those moments in the prologue and tale when the speaker purports to tell us who she is, what happened, and what it means, to *lay down the law* about herself: "For certes, I am all Venerien / In feelinge" (609–10); "And all was fals. I dremed of it right naught" (582); "Wommen desire to have sovereynetee" (1038). In this context, *reification* is another word for the act of legislating determinate meaning, and settling on a self — a history and a body — that persist outside the text.

In the poem, the Wife of Bath's drive to reification is in tension with a countertendency, which, drawing on the work of the sociologist Max Weber, I call "disenchantment." In general, disenchantment is the perception that features of the world that had previously been ascribed by culture or individuals to nonhuman forces like God or nature are actually the product of concealed human making. In Chaucer's time many long-standing social institutions were being challenged as never before in this way. In the Wife's case, the clearest evidence of her participation in this historical tendency is her challenge to the male-dominated institutions that have in effect "enchanted" men and women alike into accepting as "natural" the socially imposed moral, physical, and social inferiority of women. When she argues, for example, that the accounts of women's inferiority of which Jankyn's book is full are the productions of clerks who write such things only when they are too old to be sexually involved with women anymore (707–10), the Wife of Bath is pointing to the human motives that have *constructed* those supposedly authoritative accounts, and by showing that such pronouncements *are* constructed, she *deconstructs* them. Insofar as she operates as a "disenchanted self," the Wife of Bath is herself a deconstructionist.

Thus, insofar as she wants to criticize traditional male-dominated accounts of female nature, the "deconstructionist" Wife is engaged in a project of undoing established prior meanings. Insofar as she wants to base a new version of women on a new idea of herself — to convert her own "experience" into a new "auctoritee" — the reifying Wife is engaged in a counterproject of establishing new meanings on the basis of a new self. But this latter project is somewhat unstable, not only because so much male power is arrayed against her, but also because it is hard to keep the disenchanted criticism the Wife of Bath levels against male constructions from reflecting back on her own constructive activity. The question of motives — and the constructions they lead to — cannot, once it has been raised, be easily kept away from her own "authoritative" pronouncements. For this reason among others, it is important to reserve the term "subject" for whatever it is in the text that we posit as lying behind *both* of these activities, the indeterminate agency who is *neither* the traditional construction of woman that she resists, *nor* the equally constructed version of femininity she strives to put in its place. Many of the apparent (and often real) contradictions of her telling, and of her subjectivity, arise from the way her text shuttles back and forth between these contrary impulses of doing and undoing meaning.

II. UNDECIDABLY FALSE DREAMING

As part of her program to make herself into a new self the Wife of Bath gives a long account of her marriages. The first three husbands she groups together as if they were one (since to her as she narrates now they might just as well have been), a good example of her reifying side: she presents them as men whose meaning, like their sexuality, is fixed, used up, over and done with. The fourth husband she individualizes more because he was an individual to her and she still remembers him that way. The fifth husband, Jankyn, she individualizes most because, as she tells us, she loved him most and pursued him with the most vigor. Part of her pursuit of Jankyn involved telling him about a dream she had:

> And eek I seyde I mette of him all night,
> He wolde han slayn me as I lay upright,
> And all my bed was ful of verray blood.
> But yet I hope that he shall do me good,
> For blood bitokeneth gold, as me was taught.
> And all was fals. I dremed of it right naught. (577–82)

I am aware that this passage is not in the supposedly authoritative Hengwrt manuscript on which this edition is (mostly) based, and that it is possible — although rather unlikely — that its addition may have been made by someone other than Chaucer. For the view that the strongest likelihood is probably that these five passages represent Chaucer's revisions, see Hanna. But what the "authority" of Hengwrt really means from a disenchanted perspective is that certain people with names and histories and agendas of their own — one of them is named N. F. Blake — have carried out their persuasion that Hengwrt has better readings than any other manuscript. Other people — I for one — are persuaded that for this tale at least another manuscript called Ellesmere, which includes these lines about the dream, has at least some better readings, and here I too am acting accordingly.

The fact of disagreement itself, however, is relevant to my project in this essay. It shows how a disagreement about persons — in this case not only who the Wife of Bath is but who Chaucer himself is — is in the last analysis a debate not about a person but about a text. If "Chaucer," whoever he was, did not, somebody shortly after his death certainly wanted to suggest that the Wife of Bath learned from her mother that she should lie and tell a man she was attracted to that she dreamed that he tried to murder her in her bed, and that the blood might be a sign of money. And whoever thought that also thought that "Chaucer" *should* have suggested it too, or they wouldn't have claimed to be the poet when they smuggled it in. To recognize that what is given to you here as "Chaucer's poem" is the result not of a single authoritative text that actually exists somewhere, but of a complex set of human decisions, disagreements, and actions in *constructing* the text at both the beginning and the current end of its temporal existence, is to be initiated into a disenchanted, deconstructionist view of it. In such a view there is no authoritative, original text of Chaucer, only a mass of indeterminate textual material that has continually to be made and remade into editions like the one in this volume.

But perhaps I have interrupted myself.

As it happens, the paraphrase of the Wife's account of the dream that I gave a moment ago already contains several reifying interpretations of the Wife: that she is a liar, that she learns female wiles from her mother, that she uses gold as a come-on to Jankyn, and so on. Despite the fact that all these statements are ones the Wife, at this point in the text, seems to want to make about herself, a deconstructor might question every one of them, and make room for other, potentially contradictory ones. We do not have the Wife's actual life in front of us, but only a text that is an account of her memory of it or, more exactly, an editor's text that purports to be Chaucer's account of the Wife of Bath's account of her memory of it. The Wife, therefore, can easily be thought of as a kind of editor of the text of herself, whose motives for making that text look one way or another would need to be questioned, especially since she herself admits more than once (here, for example) that she lies about herself when she has a reason to. What if, for example, the Wife of Bath were not lying, but really did have such a dream? If she would lie to Jankyn about having such a dream, then she might lie to her audience about not having it. That is, she might lie about lying, or about learning that bit of falsehood from her mother, and so on. It may be that the dream had (and still has) such a powerful meaning for her that she is unwilling to admit openly to having had it, and so seeks to deny it. If the memory is thus powerful, it might explain why her account of the dream is immediately followed by one of the most striking of the places in the poem where she has to interrupt herself because she has lost her place in the narrative: "But now, sire, lat me see, what I shall sayn? / A ha! By God, I have my tale ageyn" (585–86).

The point is not to insist that the Wife of Bath did or did not have the dream, but to point to those conditions in the text that make it fundamentally impossible to know for sure whether or not she did, the conditions that make the truth about the dream undecidable. As mediated as it is, little about what the Wife tells her fellow pilgrims about her dream can be taken unproblematically as fact *outside* the text. Therefore, whatever may have happened as real personal experience in the past, our attention has to shift to the way the passage, and the dream, function *now*, that is, in the text we have, if we are to have much more to say about it. If we do shift our attention in this way, the dream turns out to have considerable importance as a focus of certain fundamental themes of the prologue and tale, whether or not it actually happened.

To begin with, what we might call the unstated "subtext" of the dream is a counterstatement to the commodity view of sexuality that informs both the Wife's announced reasons for telling the prologue and the framing of the dream itself as a deception aimed at gaining an advantage over Jankyn. The Wife of Bath has argued openly and consistently the disenchanted view that marriage as she has known it is an economic matter in which sexual attractiveness is an asset to be sold to the highest bidder for whatever advantages in money or power it will bring, and that in this context affection — real love — is a weakness to

be avoided in oneself and pressed for advantage in another. This view
of love and marriage is compactly summed up here in the Wife's asser-
tion that "blood bitokeneth gold" (581). On one level the statement
is a reminder to Jankyn that he stands to gain monetarily by marrying
her, since she is richer than he is. Further details of the dream bear out
this reading, as Doris Palomo has noted in her discussion of "He
wolde han slayn me as I lay upright, / And all my bed was ful of ver-
ray blood" (578–79). Palomo stresses that this image takes on special
meaning as an evocation of the virgin blood lost on the wedding
night: "The Wife invents a dream for Jankyn's benefit in which she
imagines herself slain at night, her bed full of blood. She interprets
this dream according to her mother's precepts: 'blood bitokeneth
gold.' Such words to a young girl on the verge of marriage inform her
that in exchange for the bloody rupture of the hymen the girl will ac-
quire wealth" (305). And that, of course, is apparently the trade that
the young Alisoun made, at the tender age of twelve, when she ac-
cepted her first husband. The Wife of Bath has every reason to under-
stand that for young virgins, as well as for men like Jankyn, blood can
bring gold, and her own explicit reading of the dream here presents
both of them as commodities in the system of marital exchange.

But the association of blood with bodily invasion — the rupturing
of the hymen figured as a murderous attack — allows its other,
noneconomic implication of *violence* to emerge fully in the dream,
which is, after all, a dream of assault. One might say it is a dream of
marriage *as* assault. This aspect of the theme is picked up at other mo-
ments in the prologue, such as the time the Wife asks Jankyn during
their row in front of the fire, "O, hastow slain me, false theef? . . . And
for my land thus hastow mordred me?" (800–01). Like any other
commodity in an exchange, the value of sexuality is fully convertible:
if blood betokens gold and gold betokens sex, then sex — and there-
fore marriage — betokens not only loss of virginity, but death. This
convergence of gold, sex, and death in the dream is powerful, and it
makes even more problematical the prospect of limiting the meanings
of that supposedly false dream. What the Wife of Bath presents as an
example of how to get ahead in a world dominated by commodifica-
tion can also be read as her conscious portraying — and decrying —
of the commodification of sex in the institution of marriage. The sac-
rifice of pleasure, spontaneity, independence, and affection (even con-
sidered as goods) that the convertibility of blood and gold entails is a
bad bargain ("to greet cheep is holde at litel pris" [523]), not least
because by encouraging a woman to accept the valuation the system

places on her, it encourages her as well to acquiesce in her own dehumanization. But of course she does not stop here, because the loss of those things is a more than monetary loss — it is also a kind of death. The Wife's text embodies her insight that marriage, represented by the men who have married her, has been trying all her life (like Jankyn in the dream) to kill her.

Nor should we stop here in pursuing the strands of meaning that run into and out of the text of the dream. In portraying Jankyn as a violent attacker, the language of the dream connects with aspects of the rest of the text that emphasize a view of him as potentially like all the other men in the Wife's marital life so far, the agent of a murderous system. Those aspects of the dream that present it as a scene of defloration, however, connect with a different set of elements in the prologue and tale that allow us to read it also as her *desire*, that is, as a wish. From this point of view, the imagery of the dream marks her desire to start over, to become a virgin again for this man and give herself for love, without taint of the commodification that had up to now marked sexuality for the Wife. To imagine herself a virgin again is to imagine transfiguring the system; then the "lond and fee" (630) become something that she gives as if they were a new part of herself unbroken by the system, not as things, but as the body of her love.

Surely it is clear that I do not argue for any one of these three readings of the dream — of the wife as commodity, as victim, and as desiring subject — as the only or even the best one. I hope it is also clear that I do not argue that the dream is "ambiguous," in the older sense that all these readings are valid in such a way as to form a synthesis, to which characterizations like "organic unity" or "living tapestry" (or even "authorial text") might be applied. One could construct such a unity only by abstracting the compatible features of each of the three readings and laying them over one another. Insofar as this procedure would deny the claims of each individual reading to account for the whole text, it would create a set of leftover meanings — which deconstruction customarily calls "supplements" — from which yet another series of meanings could be constructed, and so on. The analogy with textual editing, which deals with the readings of a given line in different manuscripts and often puts the questionable readings in some special but available category, like the brackets that this version's editor, Peter Beidler, uses for the passages I discuss, is worth bearing in mind. The text here generates readings — demonstrable connections to other parts of itself — that produce the Wife of Bath and Jankyn as simultaneously but incompatibly commodities, deadly enemies, and lovers. It is important not to allow the fundamental strangeness of the text in this regard to be diffused or displaced, even or especially if we also insist that the text represents a subjectivity, that is, has a voice. One might think of the Wife's dream as the navel of the prologue, somewhat in the way Freud speaks of "the dream's navel, the spot where it reaches down into the unknown. The dream-thoughts to which we are led by interpretation cannot, from the nature of things, have any definite endings; they are bound to branch out in every direction into the intricate network of our world of thought" (564). Looked at this way, the dream represents such a site of multiple indeterminacy just as much for the Wife of Bath as for us. As it happens, the condition of being a multiplicity of this kind which is both absolutely particular, embodied, desiring and feeling as a person, and also absolutely textual, self-estranged, made into a thing that always escapes itself, is a condition that surfaces elsewhere in the Wife's language. It appears, for example, in one of her common euphemisms for her sexuality, "bele chose," beautiful thing. But one might argue that this condition is particularly close to the surface of the text in this passage. This is particularly the case because the passage, with its interruption of an interruption at the end, stresses so strongly its location in the Wife's present of remembering and narrating. That is, the break in continuity points up the extent to which the contradictory meanings that run through the text have not been resolved by time, but remain as unresolved as ever long after the events purportedly narrated are over. Such a thesis, at any rate, would provide another explanation for the "interruption effect" that has led everybody from editors to the Wife herself — "A ha! By God . . ." (586) — to sense gaps and breaks in the text here that are in need of comment, explanation, and repair. Perhaps this is one of the places where the Wife displays most openly the indeterminate text out of which she makes her own multiple editions of her life. Perhaps it is a place where she encounters most richly, and passes on most forcefully, the textual stuff that makes her.

III. STATUTORY RAPE, OR THE FORLORN MAID

At the beginning of her tale, the Wife of Bath momentarily interrupts herself in her account of the rape that founds the tale's action:

And so bifel that this king Arthour
Hadde in his hous a lusty bachiler

That on a day came riding fro river,
And happed that, allone as he was born,
He saugh a maide walkinge him biforn,
Of whiche maide anon, maugree her hed,
By verray force he rafte her maidenhed.
For which oppressioun was swich clamour
And swich pursuite unto the king Arthour,
That dampned was this knight for to be deed,
By cours of lawe, and sholde han lost his heed —
Paraventure swich was the statut tho —
But that the queene and othere ladies mo
So longe preyeden the king of grace
Til he his lif him graunted in the place,
And yaf him to the queene, all at her wille,
To chese wheither she wolde him save or spille.
                         (882–98; emphasis added)

The interruption creates a slight break in a narrative that otherwise proceeds smoothly and assumptively from the masculine law to female sovereignty: doomed to die by a male authority (King Arthur's) as savage and relentless as his own act, the knight is rescued by female supplication in the queen's prayer, only to find his sentence stretched out into a program. He is required to chasten his own virile desire by subjecting himself to the discipline of discovering that of the feminine Other, "What thing is it that wommen moost desiren" (905). He embarks on a quest that will end, as it happens, with his internalization of the Wife's message about the need for female sovereignty in marriage as the key to satisfactory (and civilized) relations between the sexes. One might say that the overall drift of the tale is to subordinate the violation and its punishment to a larger process of rehabilitation, of making whole and making lawful. This smoothing over is perhaps clearest if we reflect that whatever we think of what happens to the knight and the old woman, the raped maid apparently receives no compensation in blood *or* gold for her violation, is not consulted about the rescue of the knight, and is never heard of again in the tale. Who is this maid, and what is her relation to the law?

For a moment, the primal, taken-for-granted quality of this initial scene — rape is rape, and the penalty for it is death — is ruffled by the Wife of Bath's odd comment on the penalty: "Paraventure swich was the statut tho" (893). Beidler's gloss on "paraventure" (modern "per-adventure") takes it in the first of the meanings the *Oxford English Dictionary* (*OED*) gives: "it happened that" such was the law then.

(*Peradventure*, adv., sense B.1: In a statement of fact: By chance, by accident; as it chanced, befell, or happened.) So taken, the line notes a factual condition: it was the case that the penalty for rape at that time was death, perhaps with the disenchanted implication that this is no longer (always) so. The same authority, however, establishes that *peradventure* can also mean "perhaps": "maybe" that was the law in those days (*OED*, sense B.3: In a hypothetical or contingent statement; and hence, making a statement contingent: Perchance, haply, maybe, perhaps, not improbably, belike). The question of whether or not something actually happened is not uninteresting in discussing a phenomenon, rape, whose legal treatment in modern times, like that of sexual harassment, is often concerned with establishing what are called "the actual facts." One might instance here the Anita Hill–Clarence Thomas case, which, although surely not about legal rape, was certainly treated, by the congressional committee and the press, as about whether or not the "facts" of the case constituted a violation, statutory or not, sufficient to disqualify Thomas from taking office. Equally important here, however, is what the slight wobble in *peradventure* puts in question, namely, *statute*: "a law or decree made by a sovereign or a legislative authority . . . at one time, and expressed in a formal document" (*OED*, I conflate senses 1 and 2 above. Note the presence in the definition of two of the words central to the Wife of Bath's Tale, *sovereign* and *authority*). The word is best glossed by the definition of its contrary: "*Common law*. The unwritten law of England, administered by the King's courts, which purports to be derived from ancient and universal usage, and is embodied in the older commentaries and the reports of adjudged cases. In this sense opposed to *statute law*" (*OED*, sense 2).

A statute is thus a specifically promulgated act with a specific author and a particular historical location. The Wife uses the word correctly at 198–99: "Unnethe mighte they [her first three husbands] the statut holde / In which that they were bounden unto me"; that is, they could scarcely pay the sexual debt they owed her as a result of the law (not natural law but a statute instituted along with the sacrament of Christian marriage) promulgated by Saint Paul in 1 Corinthians. When the Wife says of those same husbands "I governed hem so well, after my lawe" (219), the self-originated "law" of husbandly obedience is also in effect a statute. Typically, statutes address a particular set of historical circumstances, and, in contrast to the give-and-take of cases, customary practices, precedents, and argument that makes common law a continually developing process, a statute attempts to *lay down the law* once and for all, and to settle the issue it addresses in a definitive way. A statute is the legal equivalent of reification: it tries to give a determinate meaning to a state of affairs ("the penalty for rape is death") and to specify procedures and penalties for ensuring that that meaning is sustained. The Wife's own marriages "at chirche dore" (A460, 6) have all been statutory in this way because they involved specific ceremonies and agreements regulating the exchange of land and possessions as well as bodies, as opposed to "oother compaignye in youthe" (A461), a looser and less regulated form of sexual and personal connection that, if it involves cohabitation, is still called "common-law marriage." Insofar as this rape, which, as the violation not just of a woman's body but of her "maidenhed," constitutes a breach in the fabric of orderly social meanings and of what might be called "the law of the father" about lawful sexual access to women and the property they represent, King Arthur's statute is an attempt to repair that breach, uphold that law, and restore those meanings by treating rape as an *exception* to the normal course of events that can be rectified by establishing proper penalties. One might also speak of the rape as an error in the social text that is in need of emendation and repair. Stephanie Jed has pointed out that from earliest times the process of textual editing has been referred to as the "castigation," or making chaste, of the text, as if it were an operation performed on the body of a woman. It is perhaps worth noting that both King Arthur's statute (if it exists) and the queen's abrogation of it in order to rehabilitate the knight actually have the same reparatory aim, and that both constitute, in different ways, defenses of marriage.

Line 893 might be variously followed up from the point of view of history — for example, an investigation of actual statutes defining rape and dictating its penalties, perhaps with reference to the notorious document in which Cecilia Chaumpaigne releases Chaucer of any responsibility in her "raptus" — or of the economic entailments of rape in relation to marriage, or of a psychoanalytic study of the resolution of a problematic relation to the paternal law, which is usually called the resolution of the Oedipus complex. But from a deconstructive point of view, what the indeterminacy of "paraventure" does to "statut" here is to pose an unanswerable question about the relation of the crime of rape to lawful marriage, in a way that resonates from this relatively marginal interruption in the tale backward and forward to a number of its central concerns.

To ask whether the punishment of death for rape is a matter of statute or of common law is, as I have just suggested, to put in question the place of rape in relation to the normal course of events: is its place so firmly embedded in normal understanding that the crime and its punishment follow naturally from one another as cause and effect, or is the punishment for the crime (that is, the understanding of what sort of crime it is) sufficiently indeterminate to require a statutory interruption of the normal course, a special setting of penalties? Once this uncertainty has been allowed to arise, the "special case" of rape immediately becomes inextricably entangled with all the other, more central, instances of the consequences and entailments of a breach of bodily integrity that inform the tale from beginning to end. The easiest way to see this is to carry the issue back to the dream in the prologue, where, we remember, marriage itself is experienced and projected by the Wife as a form of institutionalized rape, one, moreover, whose statutory consequences include the lawful transfer of property to the advantage, in her case, of the violated party. One might put it that in the Wife's experience as her text represents it, the most legal version and the most transgressive version of such a breach coalesce in such a way that rape is simultaneously an interruption of the normal course of events and itself the normal course of events. To trace fully the implications and extensions of this situation would require far more space, and a far more intricate argument, than are available here, but I will conclude by suggesting a few of its consequences for the subjectivity of the Wife of Bath.

In the dream, violence and love, loss and profit, are undecidably signified by the same set of images as simultaneously both a rape and the voluntary giving of oneself. That is, each of these paired sets of terms is simultaneously and convertibly all of the others — love is at once violence, profit, loss, rape, giving, and so on with all the others. The Wife's experience as she narrates it in the prologue reproduces this contradiction in subjective terms not only in her early marriages but, as the dream implies, in the last and most successful of the relationships she narrates, her marriage to Jankyn. At the beginning of her discussion of that marriage she reports that Jankyn used to beat her so badly that she feels it yet, but that he was so fresh in bed and so persuasive in his "glosing" (509) that he could always win her love — and her "bele chose" (510) — again. It is perhaps worth insisting that she nowhere says or implies, as critics occasionally do, that what she liked sexually was the violence, although she clearly sees that the two things are connected and continually recur together. What is at stake here is not a simple psychological nature like masochism, but a structural situation that constrains the very possibilities under which desire

can exist, a situation the Wife tries to account for at this point in her
story by a sort of economic psychology, a typical mixture of desire and
profit-and-loss calculation: "I trowe I loved him best for that he /
Was of his love daungerous to me" (513–14). At the end of the pro-
logue she recounts a violent physical battle between herself and
Jankyn, which, she says, led him to burn his book, give her the sover-
eignty, and allow them to live happily ever after. As I argue at length
in *The Disenchanted Self*, the vividness with which she remembers this
combat and what led up to it has the effect of putting in question her
"happy ending" account, at least to the extent of suggesting that she
continues in the present of narrating to be exercised by Jankyn's be-
havior, including the material in his book and the way he used it. As
scholars have shown in detail, almost all the antifeminist material —
stories, examples, proverbs — in the poem, from beginning to end,
can be traced to what the Wife says was in Jankyn's book, which, as
the whole of the prologue shows, she has virtually memorized. If, as I
have already argued, the Wife of Bath may be said to be an editor of
herself, her edition is an edition of Jankyn's book, a set of choices on
her part about what in that text to keep and what to reject, what to
enact and what to fight. In my own book, I stress how this detailed
internalization of her fifth husband's discourse and style functions as a
way of continuing to care about him, of keeping him and their battles
alive and fresh in memory. It must be obvious, however, that this kind
of caring does not always extend to the content of the things he said,
especially when somebody else says them, as all too many men con-
tinue to do. This difference between a psychological and personal
living-out of a set of deep institutional contradictions under condi-
tions of intimacy, or of confronting the same contradictions publicly
and at an institutional level, can provide a guide to the reading of the
tale proper.

I have noted already that the queen's project in the tale to rehabil-
itate the knight is in a certain sense in complicity with King Arthur's
law as a defense of lawful marriage. Perhaps I should have said it *turns
out* to be complicit in this way once the old woman of the tale has got
hold of it, and makes marrying her a condition of providing the
knight with the redeeming knowledge of women's desire he needs, a
condition she enforces with utter ruthlessness in public and in private
and in the teeth of the knight's objections, up to almost the last mo-
ment of the tale. The Old Wife thus becomes an obvious surrogate for
the Wife of Bath herself in that version of herself that has played the
marriage game successfully for profit of various kinds since she was

twelve, taking advantage of whatever leverage the situation offered to reap a variety of rewards in money, sex, affection, revenge, and doubtless much more. But the end of the tale, in magically granting the knight a beautiful wife as well as a wise one, replays a certain version of the dream, because it also grants the wish that dream expresses to become young and beautiful again so as to take full advantage of a marriage more to one's liking than the first ones were. Of course, it is not so clear that the sullen rapist of the tale is really as good a candidate for a genuinely successful marriage as Jankyn seems to have been, even now that the wife who has been forced on him is more attractive, and the way the "happy ending" is shaded by this suspicion that it may simply reproduce the unsatisfactory beginnings of the whole enterprise in the Wife of Bath's life, helps to account for some of the tones of the tale's actual conclusion.

In particular, I and others have noticed the brief but pointed coda that follows the supposedly happy ending:

> And thus they live unto hir lives ende
> In parfit joye. And Jhesu Crist us sende
> Housbondes meeke, yonge, and fressh abedde,
> And grace t'overbide hem that we wedde.
> And eek I pray Jhesu shorte hir lives
> That wol not be governed by hir wives.
> And olde and angry nigardes of dispence,
> God sende hem soone verray pestilence! (1257–64)

Elsewhere I have interpreted the change to a more abrasive and combative tone here as a reflection of the Wife's sense of the difference between a fictional fantasy and real life. She can enjoy the fantasy of living happily ever after, but she knows such things need to be protected by a readiness to resume combat at any time with a hostile and uncaring world of male domination. I still believe this reading, but I see that the passage can also — that is, in addition — be read as a kind of supplement of leftover hostility to the complicitous act of coming to terms with marriage as an institution that the rest of the prologue and tale have been working through. From this perspective, these lines could be taken to represent something like the voice of the ravished maid, who is also, after all, a part of the Wife of Bath both in her history and in her present subjectivity. Given such things as the Wife's account of the dissatisfactions of her youth, the aspect of her ambiguous dream that makes it an image of a rape that never healed, and the conspicuous silencing of the maiden in the tale, it is not hard to hear

an unabated anger at what was done to her in her youth and an un-
quenched passion for justice and for revenge echoing in the way these
lines revisit the characters and the issues of those earliest moments.
This is especially true, I think, if we reflect on how the poem continu-
ally shows in its deepest structure that those concerns were never con-
fined to a set of specific moments and events in specific times and
places, but were and are carried on through her life and her text as a
set of continuing, irresolvable tensions in the institutions that have
constituted the Wife as a subject, and in the very language that has
formulated those institutions and made subjectivity itself possible,
since long before the Wife or the poet ever encountered them.

IV. INTERRUPTED SUBJECTIVITIES

My reading of this text, however sketchy, has suggested that there
is something fundamentally incompatible between the condition of
textuality that all of us inhabit by virtue of our necessary being in lan-
guage, and the stability and continuity of the self we all desire and try
to project. Certainly this is true of my own voice in this essay, which
has, in one sense at least, been interrupted from the outset by what
might look like a set of particular and exceptional circumstances. Be-
cause of unusual pressures on my own time and attention, the editor
of the volume, Peter Beidler, was kind enough to draft the first part of
the essay (through the discussion of the dream) as a summary of my
previous work on subjectivity and on the Wife of Bath, drawing on his
reading of my earlier texts. What he wrote, of course, was written in
his version of my voice, and in the light of what I told him of my feel-
ings and plans about the essay. When I came to write, I was therefore
in the position of adapting and correcting — of editing, in fact — a
rather complex version of myself. In doing so, I changed some and
kept some of what he wrote that I wrote, working at a level of detail
sufficiently fine that I can no longer say with certainty about many
sentences in the early parts of the essay whether they were written by
one of us or both, to say nothing of the question whether an unre-
vised sentence surrounded by two new ones is still the "same" sen-
tence as before. I would call attention in particular to the third para-
graph of the essay, beginning "Like most people, I resist labels . . . ,"
which as a deconstructionist I can neither agree with nor entirely dis-
avow. Perhaps I can still say that I would want to give voice to my
own authentic views if I could be sure that the ones voiced here be-

longed entirely to me, or that the "I" created by their voicing is (or is not) authentically me.

But it seems that I will have to be content (and so will Beidler, and so will you) with being inauthentically myself, especially since the contingencies that have produced a situation in which I have been edited before I write as well as afterward (by Beidler, and Murfin, and the copyeditors at Bedford Books) do not fundamentally affect the more basic situation of writing. No one who has published anything and been copyedited can seriously believe that she or he owns his or her language in an uncontested way — and in any case all writing can exist only on the condition that it may have been, or could still be, edited. No reader or writer can escape this possibility, regardless of what happens in any given case. What is also true and not trivial is that language itself, which exists before and constrains any given user of it, is by that fact alone, in a phrase deconstructionists are fond of, *always already* a form of editing. Language cannot be used at all without putting someone else's words in your mouth and under your pen; everyone is always edited before writing.

But again I have interrupted myself, and although I think it does no harm if the authority of my own text is made more questionable, the interruption is of little interest or significance, even to me, except insofar as it sheds a little more light on the Wife of Bath and her text. As I have already suggested, the peculiar relation of the Wife to Jankyn's text as an instance of the prior constructions of woman (the vast array of antifeminist discourses, examples, and clichés) that she entered into long before she met him ensures that she too was edited before ever she began to speak, that all she can do in her speaking (and it's a lot) is to reedit how she has already been written. And what *that* says, it seems to me, is that my fears about the sameness of all deconstructions may have been excessive. Some indeterminacies *are* more interesting and more significant — historically, situationally, and politically — at a given time and place than others, depending on who wants to use them and for what. The indeterminacy I have been tracing in the latter part of this essay stretches between the two selves, old woman and ravished maid, whose incompatible linkage unites and divides the subjectivity of the Wife of Bath, in such a way as to give a very precise and very complex account of the subjective conditions and consequences of a certain historical set of social and legal arrangements vis-à-vis desire and the body. Although it is probably a historical universal that the body is always experienced (represented in language) as simultaneously integral and violated, a condition that

Derrida has investigated under the rubric, apt enough in the circumstances, of the term *hymen*, this poem enacts a precise and particular working-out of that logic in historical, material, gender, and psychological terms (so there, all the rest of you contributors!).

Finally, however, it is also worth remembering that those two self-positions do not encompass or account for the whole of the text. In the course of his quest, and in moving from embracing one of those women to being embraced by the other, the knight is arrested for a moment by a vision:

> And in his wey it happed him to ride
> In all this care under a forest side
> Wher as he saugh upon a daunce go
> Of ladies foure and twenty and yet mo.
> Toward the whiche daunce he drow ful yerne,
> In hope that some wisdom sholde he lerne.
> But certeinly, er he cam fully there,
> Vanisshed was this daunce, he nyste where.
> Ne creature saugh he that bar lif
> Save on the grene he saugh sittinge a wif. (989–98)

The dancing ladies settle down into the closest and most compendious of the Wife of Bath's surrogate selves in the tale, the old woman, as if she somehow contained them all, and so she does, if we understand "contained" in the sense that a text (and its reading) contains its elements without fully controlling them. That is, the dance of ladies functions, perhaps, as a brief, potential, supplemental catalog of all the women who are left out of the knight's story, of the Wife's tale, and, as it happens, of this reading of mine. After all, the Wife of Bath's Prologue and Tale are, like Jankyn's book on which they are based, composed of nothing else but memories of women, versions of women, and texts about women. If the Wife and I have traced a few connections between a couple of those women here — and what else is a critical reading, whether mine or the Wife's, if not an attempt to speak in the voice of the text and to get the text to speak with one's own voice? — there are at least four-and-twenty more to be permuted and combined from any number of other points of view and places to start. As it happens, the Wife herself seems aware of this effect, insofar as the catalog takes its place alongside a number of other gestures (like the break in tone at the end) that articulate her reluctance to settle fully on a final, determinate meaning. Perhaps we still share an attitude about that, since I want to end by suggesting that, far from al-

ways producing the same result in any text, a deconstructive under-
standing of text itself as the space of indeterminacies is more produc-
tive of different *determinate* effects in the same text and outside it
than any search for a final determinate meaning could provide.

WORKS CITED

Benson, C. David. *Chaucer's Drama of Style: Poetic Variety and Con-
trast in the Canterbury Tales.* Chapel Hill: U of North Carolina P,
1988.

Blake, N. F. *The Textual Tradition of the Canterbury Tales.* London:
Arnold, 1985.

Derrida, Jacques. "Hymen." *Margins of Philosophy.* Trans. with addi-
tional notes by Alan Bass. Chicago: U of Chicago P, 1982.

———. *Of Grammatology.* Trans. Gayatri Chakravorty Spivak. Balti-
more: Johns Hopkins UP, 1976.

Donaldson, E. Talbot, ed. *Chaucer's Poetry: An Anthology for the
Modern Reader.* 1958. New York: Ronald, 1975.

Freud, Sigmund. *The Interpretation of Dreams.* Ed. and trans. James
Strachey. New York: Avon, 1965.

Hanna, Ralph III. "The Hengwrt Manuscript and the Canon of the
Canterbury Tales." *English Manuscript Studies 1100–1700* 1
(1989): 64–84.

Jed, Stephanie H. *Chaste Thinking: The Rape of Lucretia and the Birth
of Humanism.* Bloomington: Indiana UP, 1989.

Kittredge, George L. *Chaucer and His Poetry.* Cambridge: Harvard
UP, 1915.

Leicester, H. Marshall, Jr. *The Disenchanted Self: Representing the Sub-
ject in the Canterbury Tales.* Berkeley: U of California P, 1990.

Lumiansky, Robert M. *Of Sondry Folk: The Dramatic Principle in the
Canterbury Tales.* Austin: U of Texas P, 1955.

Palomo, Doris. "The Fate of the Wife of Bath's 'Bad Husbands.'"
Chaucer Review 9 (1975): 303–19.

Weber, Max. "Science as a Vocation." *From Max Weber: Essays in So-
ciology.* Ed. H. H. Gerth and C. Wright Mills. New York: Oxford
UP, 1946. 129–56.

Feminist Criticism
and
the Wife of Bath

WHAT IS FEMINIST CRITICISM?

Feminist criticism comes in many forms, and feminist critics have a variety of goals. Some have been interested in rediscovering the works of women writers overlooked by a masculine-dominated culture. Others have revisited books by male authors and reviewed them from a woman's point of view to understand how they both reflect and shape the attitudes that have held women back. A number of contemporary feminists have turned to topics as various as women in postcolonial societies, women's autobiographical writings, lesbians and literature, womanliness as masquerade, and the role of film and other popular media in the construction of the feminine gender.

Until a few years ago, however, feminist thought tended to be classified not according to topic but, rather, according to country of origin. This practice reflected the fact that, during the 1970s and early 1980s, French, American, and British feminists wrote from somewhat different perspectives.

French feminists tended to focus their attention on language, analyzing the ways in which meaning is produced. They concluded that language as we commonly think of it is a decidedly male realm. Drawing on the ideas of the psychoanalytic philosopher Jacques Lacan, they reminded us that language is a realm of public discourse. A child enters the linguistic realm just as it comes to grasp its separateness from its mother, just about the time that boys identify with their father, the family representative of culture. The language learned reflects a binary logic that opposes such terms as active/passive, masculine/feminine, sun/moon, father/mother, head/heart, son/daughter, intelligent/sensitive, brother/sister, form/matter, phallus/vagina, reason/emotion. Because this logic tends to group with masculinity such qualities as light, thought, and activity, French feminists said that the structure of language is phallocentric: it privileges the phallus and, more generally, masculinity by associating them with things and values more appreciated by the (masculine-dominated) culture. Moreover, French feminists suggested, "masculine desire dominates speech and posits woman as an idealized fantasy-fulfillment for the incurable emotional lack caused by separation from the mother" (Jones, "Writing" 83).

French feminists associated language with separation from the mother. Its distinctions, they argued, represent the world from the male point of view. Language systematically forces women to choose: either they can imagine and represent themselves as men imagine and represent them (in which case they may speak, but will speak as men) or they can choose "silence," becoming in the process "the invisible and unheard sex" (Jones, "Writing" 83).

But some influential French feminists maintained that language only *seems* to give women such a narrow range of choices. There is another possibility, namely that women can develop a *feminine* language. In various ways, early French feminists such as Annie Leclerc, Xavière Gauthier, and Marguerite Duras suggested that there is something that may be called *l'écriture féminine:* women's writing. More recently, Julia Kristeva has said that feminine language is "semiotic," not "symbolic." Rather than rigidly opposing and ranking elements of reality, rather than symbolizing one thing but not another in terms of a third, feminine language is rhythmic and unifying. If from the male perspective it seems fluid to the point of being chaotic, that is a fault of the male perspective.

According to Kristeva, feminine language is derived from the pre-oedipal period of fusion between mother and child. Associated with the maternal, feminine language is not only a threat to culture, which is patriarchal, but also a medium through which women may be creative in new ways. But Kristeva paired her central, liberating claim — that truly feminist innovation in all fields requires an understanding of the relation between maternity and feminine creation — with a warning. A feminist language that refuses to participate in "masculine" discourse, that places its future entirely in a feminine, semiotic discourse, risks being politically marginalized by men. That is to say, it risks being relegated to the outskirts (pun intended) of what is considered socially and politically significant.

Kristeva, who associated feminine writing with the female body, was joined in her views by other leading French feminists. Hélène Cixous, for instance, also posited an essential connection between the woman's body, whose sexual pleasure has been repressed and denied expression, and women's writing. "Write your self. Your body must be heard," Cixous urged; once they learn to write their bodies, women will not only realize their sexuality but enter history and move toward a future based on a "feminine" economy of giving rather than the "masculine" economy of hoarding (Cixous 880). For Luce Irigaray, women's sexual pleasure (*jouissance*) cannot be expressed by the dominant, ordered, "logical," masculine language. Irigaray explored the connection between women's sexuality and women's language through the following analogy: as women's *jouissance* is more multiple than men's unitary, phallic pleasure ("woman has sex organs just about everywhere"), so "feminine" language is more diffusive than its "masculine" counterpart. ("That is undoubtedly the reason . . . her language . . . goes off in all directions and . . . he is unable to discern the coherence," Irigaray writes [*This Sex* 101–03].)

Cixous's and Irigaray's emphasis on feminine writing as an expression of the female body drew criticism from other French feminists. Many argued that an emphasis on the body either reduces "the feminine" to a biological essence or elevates it in a way that shifts the valuation of masculine and feminine but retains the binary categories. For Christine Fauré, Irigaray's celebration of women's difference failed to address the issue of masculine dominance, and a Marxist-feminist, Catherine Clément, warned that "poetic" descriptions of what constitutes the feminine will not challenge that dominance in the realm of production. The boys will still make the toys and decide who gets to use them. In her effort to redefine women as political rather than as sexual beings, Monique Wittig called for the abolition of the sexual categories that Cixous and Irigaray retained and revalued as they celebrated women's writing.

American feminist critics of the 1970s and early 1980s shared with French critics both an interest in and a cautious distrust of the concept of feminine writing. Annette Kolodny, for instance, worried that the "richness and variety of women's writing" will be missed if we see in it only its "feminine mode" or "style" ("Some Notes" 78). And yet

Kolodny herself proceeded, in the same essay, to point out that women *have* had their own style, which includes reflexive constructions ("she found herself crying") and particular, recurring themes (clothing and self-fashioning are mentioned by Kolodny; other American feminists have focused on madness, disease, and the demonic).

Interested as they became in the "French" subject of feminine style, American feminist critics began by analyzing literary texts rather than philosophizing abstractly about language. Many reviewed the great works by male writers, embarking on a revisionist rereading of literary tradition. These critics examined the portrayals of women characters, exposing the patriarchal ideology implicit in such works and showing how clearly this tradition of systematic masculine dominance is inscribed in our literary tradition. Kate Millett, Carolyn Heilbrun, and Judith Fetterley, among many others, created this model for American feminist criticism, a model that Elaine Showalter came to call "the feminist critique" of "male-constructed literary history" ("Poetics" 128).

Meanwhile another group of critics including Sandra Gilbert, Susan Gubar, Patricia Meyer Spacks, and Showalter herself created a somewhat different model. Whereas feminists writing "feminist critique" analyzed works by men, practitioners of what Showalter used to refer to as "gynocriticism" studied the writings of those women who, against all odds, produced what she calls "a literature of their own." In *The Female Imagination* (1975), Spacks examined the female literary tradition to find out how great women writers across the ages have felt, perceived themselves, and imagined reality. Gilbert and Gubar, in *The Madwoman in the Attic* (1979), concerned themselves with well-known women writers of the nineteenth century, but they too found that general concerns, images, and themes recur, because the authors that they wrote about lived "in a culture whose fundamental definitions of literary authority were both overtly and covertly patriarchal" (45).

If one of the purposes of gynocriticism was to (re)study well-known women authors, another was to rediscover women's history and culture, particularly women's communities that nurtured female creativity. Still another related purpose was to discover neglected or forgotten women writers and thus to forge an alternative literary tradition, a canon that better represents the female perspective by better representing the literary works that have been written by women. Showalter, in *A Literature of Their Own* (1977), admirably began to fulfill this purpose, providing a remarkably comprehensive overview of women's writing through three of its phases. She defined these as the "Feminine, Feminist, and Female" phases, phases during which women first imitated a masculine tradition (1840–80), then protested against its standards and values (1880–1920), and finally advocated their own autonomous, female perspective (1920 to the present).

With the recovery of a body of women's texts, attention returned to a question raised in 1978 by Lillian Robinson: Shouldn't feminist criticism need to formulate a theory of its own practice? Won't reliance on theoretical assumptions, categories, and strategies developed by men and associated with nonfeminist schools of thought prevent feminism from being accepted as equivalent to these other critical discourses? Not all American feminists came to believe that a special or unifying theory of feminist practice was urgently needed; Showalter's historical approach to women's culture allowed a feminist critic to use theories based on nonfeminist disciplines. Kolodny advocated a "playful pluralism" that encompasses a variety of critical schools and methods. But Jane Marcus and others responded that if feminists adopt too wide a range of approaches, they may relax the tensions between feminists and the educational establishment necessary for political activism.

The question of whether feminism weakens or fortifies itself by emphasizing its separateness — and by developing unity through separateness — was one of several areas of debate within American feminism during the 1970s and early 1980s. Another area of disagreement touched on earlier, between feminists who stress universal feminine attributes (the feminine imagination, feminine writing) and those who focus on the political conditions experienced by certain groups of women at certain times in history, paralleled a larger distinction between American feminist critics and their British counterparts.

While it gradually became customary to refer to an Anglo-American tradition of feminist criticism, British feminists tended to distinguish themselves from what they saw as an American overemphasis on texts linking women across boundaries and decades and an underemphasis on popular art and culture. They regarded their own critical practice as more political than that of North American feminists, whom they sometimes faulted for being uninterested in historical detail. They joined such American critics as Myra Jehlen in suggesting that a continuing preoccupation with women writers may bring about the dangerous result of placing women's texts outside the history that conditions them.

British feminists felt that the American opposition to male stereotypes that denigrate women often leads to counterstereotypes of feminine virtue that ignore real differences of race, class, and culture

among women. In addition, they argued that American celebrations
of individual heroines falsely suggest that powerful individuals may be
immune to repressive conditions and may even imply that *any* individ-
ual can go through life unconditioned by the culture and ideology in
which she or he lives.

Similarly, the American endeavor to recover women's history —
for example, by emphasizing that women developed their own strate-
gies to gain power within their sphere — was seen by British feminists
like Judith Newton and Deborah Rosenfelt as an endeavor that "mys-
tifies" male oppression, disguising it as something that has created for
women a special world of opportunities. More important from the
British standpoint, the universalizing and "essentializing" tendencies
in both American practice and French theory disguise women's op-
pression by highlighting sexual difference, suggesting that a dominant
system is impervious to political change. By contrast, British feminist
theory emphasized an engagement with historical process in order to
promote social change.

By now the French, American, and British approaches have so
thoroughly critiqued, influenced, and assimilated one another that the
work of most Western practitioners is no longer easily identifiable
along national boundary lines. Instead, it tends to be characterized ac-
cording to whether the category of *woman* is the major focus in the
exploration of gender and gender oppression or, alternatively, whether
the interest in sexual difference encompasses an interest in other dif-
ferences that also define identity. The latter paradigm encompasses the
work of feminists of color, Third World (preferably called postcolo-
nial) feminists, and lesbian feminists, many of whom have asked
whether the universal category of woman constructed by certain
French and North American predecessors is appropriate to describe
women in minority groups or non-Western cultures.

These feminists stress that, while all women are female, they are
something else as well (such as African American, lesbian, Muslim
Pakistani). This "something else" is precisely what makes them, their
problems, and their goals different from those of other women. As
Armit Wilson has pointed out, Asian women living in Britain are ex-
pected by their families and communities to preserve Asian cultural
traditions; thus, the expression of personal identity through clothing
involves a much more serious infraction of cultural rules than it does
for a Western woman. Gloria Anzaldúa has spoken personally and elo-
quently about the experience of many women on the margins of Eu-

rocentric North American culture. "I am a border woman," she writes in *Borderlands: La Frontera = The New Mestiza* (1987). "I grew up between two cultures, the Mexican (with a heavy Indian influence) and the Anglo. . . . Living on the borders and in margins, keeping intact one's shifting and multiple identity and integrity is like trying to swim in a new element, an 'alien' element" (i).

Instead of being divisive and isolating, this evolution of feminism into femin*isms* has fostered a more inclusive, global perspective. The era of recovering women's texts — especially texts by white Western women — has been succeeded by a new era in which the goal is to recover entire cultures of women. Two important figures of this new era are Trinh T. Minh-ha and Gayatri Spivak. Spivak, in works such as *In Other Worlds: Essays in Cultural Politics* (1987) and *Outside in the Teaching Machine* (1993), has shown how political independence (generally looked upon by metropolitan Westerners as a simple and beneficial historical and political reversal) has complex implications for "subaltern" or subproletarian women.

The understanding of woman not as a single, deterministic category but rather as the nexus of diverse experiences has led some white, Western, "majority" feminists like Jane Tompkins and Nancy K. Miller to advocate and practice "personal" or "autobiographical" criticism. Once reluctant to inject themselves into their analyses for fear of being labeled idiosyncratic, impressionistic, and subjective by men, some feminists are now openly skeptical of the claims to reason, logic, and objectivity that have been made in the past by male critics. With the advent of more personal feminist critical styles has come a powerful new interest in women's autobiographical writings.

Shari Benstock, who has written personal criticism in her book *Textualizing the Feminine* (1991), was one of the first feminists to argue that traditional autobiography is a gendered, "masculinist" genre. Its established conventions, feminists have recently pointed out, call for a life-plot that turns on action, triumph through conflict, intellectual self-discovery, and often public renown. The body, reproduction, children, and intimate interpersonal relationships are generally well in the background and often absent. Arguing that the lived experiences of women and men differ — women's lives, for instance, are often characterized by interruption and deferral — Leigh Gilmore has developed a theory of women's self-representation in her book *Autobiographics: A Feminist Theory of Self-Representation* (1994).

Autobiographics and personal criticism are only two of a number of recent developments in contemporary feminist criticism. Others alluded to in the first paragraph of this introduction — lesbian studies, performance or "masquerade" theory, and studies of the role played by film and various other "technologies" in shaping gender today — are also prominent in contemporary *gender* criticism, whose practitioners investigate categories of gender (masculinity as well as femininity) and sexuality (gay male sexuality as well as lesbianism) insofar as they inform not only the writing of literary texts but also the ways in which they are read. In speaking of the overlap between feminist and gender criticism, however, it is important to be clear about one thing: gender criticism *began* as feminist criticism; it could never have developed as it has without the precedents set by feminist theorists. When Simone de Beauvoir proclaimed, in *The Second Sex* (1949), that "one is not born a woman, one becomes one" (301), she helped make possible a panoply of investigations into the ways in which we all are engendered, whether as women or men, not only by literary texts but also through a host of other discourses and practices.

Ross C Murfin

FEMINIST CRITICISM: A SELECTED BIBLIOGRAPHY

French Feminist Theory

Cixous, Hélène. "The Laugh of the Medusa." Trans. Keith Cohen and Paula Cohen. *Signs* 1 (1976): 875–93.

Cixous, Hélène, and Catherine Clément. *The Newly Born Woman.* Trans. Betsy Wing. Minneapolis: U of Minnesota P, 1986.

Feminist Readings: French Texts/American Contexts. Special issue, *Yale French Studies* 62 (1981).

French Feminist Theory. Special issue, *Signs* 7.1 (1981).

Irigaray, Luce. *An Ethics of Sexual Difference.* Trans. Carolyn Burke and Gillian C. Gill. Ithaca: Cornell UP, 1993.

———. *This Sex Which Is Not One.* Trans. Catherine Porter. Ithaca: Cornell UP, 1985.

Jardine, Alice A. *Gynesis: Configurations of Woman and Modernity.* Ithaca: Cornell UP, 1985.

Jenson, Deborah, ed. *"Coming to Writing" and Other Essays* (essays by Hélène Cixous). Trans. Sarah Cornell. Cambridge: Harvard UP, 1991.

Jones, Ann Rosalind. "Writing the Body: Toward an Understanding of *L'Écriture féminine.*" *The New Feminist Criticism.* Ed. Elaine Showalter. New York: Pantheon, 1985. 361–77.

Kristeva, Julia. *Desire in Language: A Semiotic Approach to Literature and Art.* Ed. Leon S. Roudiez. Trans. Thomas Gora, Alice Jardine, and Roudiez. New York: Columbia UP, 1980.

Marks, Elaine, and Isabelle de Courtivron, eds. *New French Feminisms: An Anthology.* Amherst: U of Massachusetts P, 1980.

Moi, Toril, ed. *French Feminist Thought: A Reader.* Oxford: Basil Blackwell, 1987.

Spivak, Gayatri Chakravorty. "French Feminism in an International Frame." *Yale French Studies* 62 (1981): 154–84.

Stanton, Domna C. "Language and Revolution: The Franco-American Dis-Connection." *The Future of Difference.* Ed. Hester Eisenstein and Alice Jardine. Boston: G. K. Hall, 1980.

Wittig, Monique. *Les Guérillères.* 1969. Trans. David Le Vay. New York: Avon, 1973.

Feminist Theory: Classic Texts, General Approaches, Collections

Abel, Elizabeth, and Emily K. Abel, eds. *The "Signs" Reader: Women, Gender, and Scholarship.* Chicago: U of Chicago P, 1983.

Barrett, Michèle, and Anne Phillips. *Destabilizing Theory: Contemporary Feminist Debates.* Stanford: Stanford UP, 1992.

Beauvoir, Simone de. *The Second Sex.* 1949. Trans. and ed. H. M. Parshley. New York: Vintage, 1974.

Benstock, Shari, ed. *Feminist Issues in Literary Scholarship.* Bloomington: Indiana UP, 1987.

de Lauretis, Teresa, ed. *Feminist Studies/Critical Studies.* Bloomington: Indiana UP, 1986.

Fetterley, Judith. *The Resisting Reader: A Feminist Approach to American Fiction.* Bloomington: Indiana UP, 1978.

Fuss, Diana. *Essentially Speaking: Feminism, Nature and Difference.* New York: Routledge, 1989.

Gallop, Jane. *Around 1981: Academic Feminist Critical Theory.* New York: Routledge, 1992.

Greer, Germaine. *The Female Eunuch.* New York: McGraw, 1971.

Herndl, Diana Price, and Robyn Warhol, eds. *Feminisms: An Anthology of Literary Theory and Criticism.* New Brunswick: Rutgers UP, 1991.

hooks, bell. *Feminist Theory: From Margin to Center.* Boston: South End P, 1984.

Keohane, Nannerl O., Michelle Z. Rosaldo, and Barbara C. Gelpi, eds. *Feminist Theory: A Critique of Ideology*. Chicago: U of Chicago P, 1982.

Kolodny, Annette. "Dancing Through the Minefield: Some Observations on the Theory, Practice, and Politics of a Feminist Literary Criticism." *The New Feminist Criticism*. Ed. Elaine Showalter. New York: Pantheon, 1985. 144–67.

Lovell, Terry, ed. *British Feminist Thought: A Reader*. Oxford: Basil Blackwell, 1990.

Malson, Micheline, et al., eds. *Feminist Theory in Practice and Process*. Chicago: U of Chicago P, 1986.

Meese, Elizabeth. *Crossing the Double-Cross: The Practice of Feminist Criticism*. Chapel Hill: U of North Carolina P, 1986.

Millett, Kate. *Sexual Politics*. Garden City: Doubleday, 1970.

Rich, Adrienne. *On Lies, Secrets, and Silence: Selected Prose, 1966–1979*. New York: Norton, 1979.

Showalter, Elaine, ed. *The New Feminist Criticism: Essays on Women, Literature, and Theory*. New York: Pantheon, 1985.

———. "Women's Time, Women's Space: Writing the History of Feminist Criticism." *Tulsa Studies in Women's Literature* 3 (1984): 29–43. Rpt. in Benstock, *Feminist Issues in Literary Scholarship*.

Stimpson, Catherine R. "Feminist Criticism." *Redrawing the Boundaries: The Transformation of English and American Literary Studies*. Ed. Stephen Greenblatt and Giles Gunn. New York: MLA, 1992. 251–70.

———. *Where the Meanings Are: Feminism and Cultural Spaces*. New York: Methuen, 1988.

Weed, Elizabeth, ed. *Coming to Terms: Feminism, Theory, Politics*. New York: Routledge, 1989.

Woolf, Virginia. *A Room of One's Own*. New York: Harcourt, 1929.

Women's Writing and Creativity

Abel, Elizabeth, ed. *Writing and Sexual Difference*. Chicago: U of Chicago P, 1982.

Abel, Elizabeth, Marianne Hirsch, and Elizabeth Langland, eds. *The Voyage In: Fictions of Female Development*. Hanover: UP of New England, 1983.

Auerbach, Nina. *Communities of Women: An Idea in Fiction*. Cambridge: Harvard UP, 1978.

Benstock, Shari. "Reading the Signs of Women's Writing." *Tulsa Studies in Women's Literature* 4 (1985): 5–15.

Berg, Temma F., ed., and Anna Shannon Elfenbein, Jeanne Larsen, and Elisa K. Sparks, co-eds. *Engendering the Word: Feminist Essays in Psychosexual Poetics.* Urbana: U of Illinois P, 1989.

Diehl, Joanne Feit. "Come Slowly Eden: An Exploration of Women Writers and Their Muse." *Signs* 3 (1978): 572–87.

DuPlessis, Rachel Blau. *The Pink Guitar: Writing as Feminist Practice.* New York: Routledge, 1990.

Finke, Laurie. *Feminist Theory, Women's Writing.* Ithaca: Cornell UP, 1992.

Gilbert, Sandra M., and Susan Gubar. *The Madwoman in the Attic: The Woman Writer and the Nineteenth-Century Literary Imagination.* New Haven: Yale UP, 1979.

Homans, Margaret. *Bearing the Word: Language and Female Experience in Nineteenth-Century Women's Writing.* Chicago: U of Chicago P, 1986.

Jacobus, Mary, ed. *Women Writing and Writing About Women.* New York: Barnes, 1979.

Miller, Nancy K., ed. *The Poetics of Gender.* New York: Columbia UP, 1986.

———. *Subject to Change: Reading Feminist Writing.* New York: Columbia UP, 1988.

Montefiore, Janet. "Feminine Identity and the Poetic Tradition." *Feminist Review* 13 (1983): 69–84.

Newton, Judith Lowder. *Women, Power and Subversion: Social Strategies in British Fiction, 1778–1860.* Athens: U of Georgia P, 1981.

Poovey, Mary. *The Proper Lady and the Woman Writer: Ideology as Style in the Works of Mary Wollstonecraft, Mary Shelley, and Jane Austen.* Chicago: U of Chicago P, 1984.

Showalter, Elaine. *Daughters of Decadence: Women Writers of the Fin de Siècle.* New Brunswick: Rutgers UP, 1993.

———. *A Literature of Their Own: British Women Novelists from Brontë to Lessing.* Princeton: Princeton UP, 1977.

———. "Women Who Write Are Women." *New York Times Book Review* I (December 16, 1984): 31–33.

Women's History/Women's Studies

Bridenthal, Renate, and Claudia Koonz, eds. *Becoming Visible: Women in European History.* Boston: Houghton, 1977.

Donovan, Josephine. "Feminism and Aesthetics." *Critical Inquiry* 3 (1977): 605–08.

Farnham, Christie, ed. *The Impact of Feminist Research in the Academy.* Bloomington: Indiana UP, 1987.

Kelly, Joan. *Women, History and Theory: The Essays of Joan Kelly.* Chicago: U of Chicago P, 1984.

McConnell-Ginet, Sally, et al., eds. *Woman and Language in Literature and Society.* New York: Praeger, 1980.

Mitchell, Juliet, and Ann Oakley, eds. *The Rights and Wrongs of Women.* London: Penguin, 1976.

Riley, Denise. *"Am I That Name?": Feminism and the Category of "Women" in History.* Minneapolis: U of Minnesota P, 1988.

Rowbotham, Sheila. *Woman's Consciousness, Man's World.* Harmondsworth: Penguin, 1973.

Feminisms and Sexualities

Snitow, Ann, Christine Stansell, and Sharon Thompson, eds. *Powers of Desire: The Politics of Sexuality.* New York: Monthly Review P, 1983.

Vance, Carole S., ed. *Pleasure and Danger: Exploring Female Sexuality.* Boston: Routledge, 1984.

Feminism, Race, Class, and Nationality

Anzaldúa, Gloria. *Borderlands: La Frontera = The New Mestiza.* San Francisco: Spinsters/Aunt Lute, 1987.

Christian, Barbara. *Black Feminist Criticism: Perspectives on Black Women Writers.* New York: Pergamon, 1985.

Collins, Patricia Hill. *Black Feminist Thought: Knowledge, Consciousness, and the Politics of Empowerment.* Boston: Hyman, 1990.

hooks, bell. *Ain't I a Woman?: Black Women and Feminism.* Boston: South End P, 1981.

———. *Black Looks: Race and Representation.* Boston: South End P, 1992.

Mitchell, Juliet. *Woman's Estate.* New York: Pantheon, 1971.

Moraga, Cherríe, and Gloria Anzaldúa. *This Bridge Called My Back: Writings by Radical Women of Color.* New York: Kitchen Table, 1981.

Newton, Judith, and Deborah Rosenfelt, eds. *Feminist Criticism and Social Change: Sex, Class, and Race in Literature and Culture.* New York: Methuen, 1985.

Newton, Judith L., et al., eds. *Sex and Class in Women's History.* London: Routledge, 1983.

Pryse, Marjorie, and Hortense Spillers, eds. *Conjuring: Black Women, Fiction, and Literary Tradition.* Bloomington: Indiana UP, 1985.

Robinson, Lillian S. *Sex, Class, and Culture.* 1978. New York: Methuen, 1986.

Smith, Barbara. "Towards a Black Feminist Criticism." *The New Feminist Criticism.* Ed. Elaine Showalter. New York: Pantheon, 1985. 168–85.

Feminism and Postcoloniality

Emberley, Julia. *Thresholds of Difference: Feminist Critique, Native Women's Writings, Postcolonial Theory.* Toronto: U of Toronto P, 1993.

Mohanty, Chandra Talpade, Ann Russo, and Lourdes Torres, eds. *Third World Women and the Politics of Feminism.* Bloomington: Indiana UP, 1991.

Schipper, Mineke, ed. *Unheard Words: Women and Literature in Africa, the Arab World, Asia, the Caribbean, and Latin America.* London: Allison, 1985.

Spivak, Gayatri Chakravorty. *In Other Worlds: Essays in Cultural Politics.* New York: Methuen, 1987.

———. *Outside in the Teaching Machine.* New York: Routledge, 1993.

Trinh T. Minh-ha. *Woman, Native, Other: Writing Postcoloniality and Feminism.* Bloomington: Indiana UP, 1989.

Wilson, Armit. *Finding a Voice: Asian Women in Britain.* 1979. London: Virago, 1980.

Women's Self-Representation and Personal Criticism

Benstock, Shari, ed. *The Private Self: Theory and Practice of Women's Autobiographical Writings.* Chapel Hill: U of North Carolina P, 1988.

Gilmore, Leigh. *Autobiographics: A Feminist Theory of Self-Representation.* Ithaca: Cornell UP, 1994.

Martin, Biddy, and Chandra Talpade Mohanty. "Feminist Politics: What's Home Got to Do with It?" *Life/Lines: Theorizing Women's Autobiography.* Ed. Bella Brodski and Celeste Schenck. Ithaca: Cornell UP, 1988.

Miller, Nancy K. *Getting Personal: Feminist Occasions and Other Autobiographical Acts.* New York: Routledge, 1991.

Feminism and Other Critical Approaches

Armstrong, Nancy, ed. *Literature as Women's History I*. Special issue, *Genre* 19–20 (1986–87).

Barrett, Michèle. *Women's Oppression Today: Problems in Marxist Feminist Analysis*. London: Verso, 1980.

Belsey, Catherine, and Jane Moore, eds. *The Feminist Reader: Essays in Gender and the Politics of Literary Criticism*. New York: Basil Blackwell, 1989.

Benjamin, Jessica. *The Bonds of Love: Psychoanalysis, Feminism, and the Problem of Domination*. New York: Pantheon, 1988.

Benstock, Shari. *Textualizing the Feminine: On the Limits of Genre*. Norman: U of Oklahoma P, 1991.

Butler, Judith, and Joan W. Scott, eds. *Feminists Theorize the Political*. New York: Routledge, 1992.

de Lauretis, Teresa. *Alice Doesn't: Feminism, Semiotics, Cinema*. Bloomington: Indiana UP, 1986.

de Lauretis, Teresa, and Stephen Heath. *The Cinematic Apparatus*. London: Macmillan, 1980.

Delphy, Christine. *Close to Home: A Materialist Analysis of Women's Oppression*. Trans. and ed. Diana Leonard. Amherst: U of Massachusetts P, 1984.

Dimock, Wai-chee. "Feminism, New Historicism, and the Reader." *American Literature* 63 (1991): 601–22.

Doane, Mary Ann. *Re-vision: Essays in Feminist Film Criticism*. Frederick: University Publications of America, 1984.

Felman, Shoshana, ed. *Literature and Psychoanalysis: The Question of Reading: Otherwise*. Baltimore: Johns Hopkins UP, 1982.

———. "Women and Madness: The Critical Fallacy." *Diacritics* 5 (1975): 2–10.

Feminist Studies 14 (1988). Special issue on feminism and deconstruction.

Gallop, Jane. *The Daughter's Seduction: Feminism and Psychoanalysis*. Ithaca: Cornell UP, 1982.

Gilligan, Carol. *In a Different Voice: Psychological Theory and Women's Development*. Cambridge: Harvard UP, 1982.

Hartsock, Nancy C. M. *Money, Sex, and Power: Toward a Feminist Historical Materialism*. Boston: Northeastern UP, 1985.

Kaplan, Cora. *Sea Changes: Essays on Culture and Feminism*. London: Verso, 1986.

Meese, Elizabeth, and Alice Parker, eds. *The Difference Within: Feminism and Critical Theory*. Philadelphia: John Benjamins, 1989.

Modleski, Tania. *Feminism Without Women: Culture and Criticism in a "Postfeminist" Age.* New York: Routledge, 1991.

Mulvey, Laura. *Visual and Other Pleasures.* Bloomington: Indiana UP, 1989.

Newton, Judith Lowder. "History as Usual? Feminism and the New Historicism." *The New Historicism.* Ed. H. Aram Veeser. New York: Routledge, 1989. 152–67.

Nicholson, Linda J., ed. *Feminism/Postmodernism.* New York: Routledge, 1990.

Penley, Constance, ed. *Feminism and Film Theory.* New York: Routledge, 1988.

Riviere, Joan. "Womanliness as a Masquerade." *International Journal of Psycho-Analysis* 10 (1929): 303–13. Rpt. in *Formations of Fantasy.* Ed. Victor Burgin, James Donald, and Cora Kaplan. New York: Methuen, 1986.

Rose, Jacqueline. "Introduction II." *Feminine Sexuality: Jacques Lacan and the École Freudienne.* Ed. Juliet Mitchell and Rose. Trans. Rose. New York: Norton, 1983.

Sargent, Lydia, ed. *Women and Revolution: A Discussion of the Unhappy Marriage of Marxism and Feminism.* Montreal: Black Rose, 1981.

Weedon, Chris. *Feminist Practice and Poststructuralist Theory.* New York: Basil Blackwell, 1987.

Feminist Approaches to Chaucer and the Wife of Bath's Prologue and Tale

Bolton, W. F. "The Wife of Bath: Narrator as Victim." *Gender and Literary Voice.* Ed. Janet Todd. New York: Holmes and Meier, 1980. 54–65.

Carruthers, Mary. "The Wife of Bath and the Painting of Lions." *PMLA* 94 (1979): 209–22.

Chance, Jane. *The Mythographic Chaucer: The Fabulation of Sexual Politics.* Minneapolis: U of Minnesota P, 1995.

Cooper, Helen. "The Shape-Shiftings of the Wife of Bath, 1395–1670." *Chaucer Traditions: Essays in Honour of Derek Brewer.* Ed. Ruth Morse and Barry Windeatt. Cambridge: Cambridge UP, 1990. 168–84.

Delany, Sheila. "Strategies of Silence in the Wife of Bath's Recital." *Exemplaria* 2 (1990): 49–69.

Diamond, Arlyn. "Chaucer's Women and Women's Chaucer." *The*

Authority of Experience. Ed. Arlyn Diamond and Lee Edwards. Amherst: U of Massachusetts P, 1977. 60–83.

Dickson, Lynne. "Deflection in the Mirror: Feminine Discourse in *The Wife of Bath's Prologue* and *Tale*." *Studies in the Age of Chaucer* 15 (1993): 61–90.

Dinshaw, Carolyn. *Chaucer's Sexual Poetics*. Madison: U of Wisconsin P, 1989.

Disbrow, Sarah. "The Wife of Bath's Old Wives' Tale." *Studies in the Age of Chaucer* 8 (1986): 59–71.

Fradenburg, Louise O. "The Wife of Bath's Passing Fancy." *Studies in the Age of Chaucer* 8 (1986): 31–58.

Hagen, Susan K. "The Wife of Bath: Chaucer's Inchoate Experiment in Feminist Hermeneutics." *Rebels and Rivals: The Contestive Spirit in the Canterbury Tales*. Ed. Susanna Greer Fein, David Raybin, and Peter C. Braeger. Kalamazoo: Medieval Institute, 1991. 105–24.

———. "The Wife of Bath, the Lion, and the Critics." *The Worlds of Medieval Women: Creativity, Influence, and Imagination*. Ed. Constance H. Berman et al. Morgantown: U of West Virginia P, 1985. 130–38.

Hanning, Robert W. "From Eva and Ave to Eglentyne and Alisoun: Chaucer's Insight into the Roles Women Play." *Signs* 2 (1977): 580–99.

Ireland, Colin A. "'A Coverchief or a Calle': The Ultimate End of the Wife of Bath's Search for Sovereignty." *Neophilologus* 75 (1991): 150–59.

Justman, Stewart. "Trade as Pudendum: Chaucer's Wife of Bath." *Chaucer Review* 28 (1994): 344–52.

Knapp, Peggy. "Alisoun Looms." *Chaucer and the Social Contest*. New York: Routledge, 1990. 114–28.

Leicester, H. Marshall, Jr. "Of a Fire in the Dark: Public and Private Feminism in the *Wife of Bath's Tale*." *Women's Studies* 11 (1984): 157–78.

Lindley, Arthur. "'Vanysshed Was this Daunce, He Nyste Where': Alisoun's Absence in the *Wife of Bath's Prologue and Tale*." *ELH* 59 (1992): 1–21.

Malvern, Marjorie M. "'Who peyntede the leon, tel me who?' Rhetorical and Didactic Roles Played by an Aesopic Fable in the *Wife of Bath's Prologue*." *Studies in Philology* 80 (1983): 238–52.

Mann, Jill. *Geoffrey Chaucer* [Feminist Readings Series]. Atlantic Highlands: Humanities, 1991.

Martin, Priscilla. *Chaucer's Women: Nuns, Wives, and Amazons.* Iowa City: U of Iowa P, 1990.

Oberembt, Kenneth. "Chaucer's Anti-misogynist Wife of Bath." *Chaucer Review* 10 (1976): 287–302.

Schauber, Ellen, and Ellen Spolsky. "The Consolation of Alison: The Speech Acts of the Wife of Bath." *Centrum* 5 (1977): 20–34.

Schibanoff, Susan. "Taking the Gold out of Egypt: The Art of Reading as a Woman." *Gender and Reading: Essays on Readers, Texts, and Contexts.* Ed. Elizabeth A. Flynn and Patrocinio P. Schweickart. Baltimore: Johns Hopkins UP, 1986. 83–106.

Spisak, James. "Anti-feminism Bridled: Two Rhetorical Contexts." *Neuphilologische Mitteilungen* 81 (1980): 150–60.

Stephens, John, and Marcella Ryan. "Metafictional Strategies and the Theme of Sexual Power in the Wife of Bath's and Franklin's Tales." *Nottingham Medieval Studies* 33 (1989): 56–75.

Straus, Barrie Ruth. "The Subversive Discourse of the Wife of Bath: Phallocentric Discourse and the Imprisonment of Criticism." *ELH* 55 (1988): 527–54.

Weissman, Hope Phyllis. "Antifeminism and Chaucer's Characterizations of Woman." *Geoffrey Chaucer: A Collection of Original Articles.* Ed. George D. Economou. New York: McGraw, 1975. 93–110.

Wilson, Katharina M., and Elizabeth M. Makowski. "Wykked Wyves: A Tradition Reasserted in *De conjuge non ducenda, Quinze joies de mariage,* and the Wife of Bath's Prologue." *Wykked Wyves and the Woes of Marriage: Misogamous Literature from Juvenal to Chaucer.* Ed. Katharina M. Wilson and Elizabeth M. Makowski. Albany: State U of New York P, 1990. 123–62.

A FEMINIST PERSPECTIVE

In her essay Elaine Tuttle Hansen prefaces her own reading of the Wife of Bath's Prologue and Tale with a helpful discussion of the complexity and variety of other feminist approaches to the amazing literary creation known as Alisoun of Bath. Hansen begins her essay by referring to the work of Gilbert and Gubar, groundbreaking feminists who chose to see the Wife of Bath as a kind of feminist poet and, therefore, her author, Chaucer, as protofeminist. In the approach of such feminists the Wife of Bath becomes one of the first truly liberated women in literature, a woman who boldly stands up for the individual, sexual, and marital rights of women in a society dominated by men

and the interests of men. At the same time that the Wife accepts —
even demands — a series of relationships with men, she also insists on
herself as a more-than-equal partner in those relationships.

Another approach discussed by Hansen sees the Wife of Bath's
Prologue and Tale as "subversively" presenting Alisoun as a pathetic
or monstrous victim of a misogynist culture and calling for a change in
the social and political situation of women. According to this feminist
approach, Chaucer's contemporary audience, and later audiences as
well, are envisioned as having their consciousness raised about women
and sex and romance, and joining with Alisoun in a call for more ma-
ture relations between the sexes based on equality and mutuality.

Questioning both of these approaches, Hansen identifies problems
in reading either the Wife of Bath or Chaucer as feminist. She dis-
cusses domestic violence and the way it is normalized and trivialized
by both the Wife of Bath's Prologue and Tale. She calls particular at-
tention to the Wife's fifth husband's love as being "daungerous"
(514) — an adjective that can mean distant, domineering, or danger-
ous. What we have in the Wife of Bath's remarkable performance, fi-
nally, is not a woman speaking but a man creating a voice for a
woman. For all of Alisoun's talk about gentility and equality, what this
nonwoman woman really seems to want is to be the kind of lovely and
submissively feminine woman that *men* crave. What we see here, ac-
cording to Hansen, then, is neither a feminist woman speaking nor a
call for reform. Rather, we see a male writer who reproduces and rein-
forces male attitudes (sometimes called "patriarchal") that tend to
hold women back.

Instead of insisting on one single or reductive feminist reading,
however, Hansen acknowledges the complexity of all matters relating
to gender and finds it misguided to demand or provide final answers
to the question of Chaucer's sexual politics. Considering the construc-
tion not only of femininity but also of masculinity, she suggests that
Chaucer may have been "feminized" by his roles as poet, but that he
appropriates to himself powers that might be associated with a subver-
sive feminine position, powers that are in fact denied to women like
the Wife of Bath, who remains locked in quintessential femininity.

ELAINE TUTTLE HANSEN

"Of his love daungerous to me": Liberation, Subversion, and Domestic Violence in the Wife of Bath's Prologue and Tale

The first thing to say about feminist criticism of the Wife of Bath's Prologue and Tale is that its value can hardly be disputed. Questions of gender, language, and power are not merely appropriate but indispensable if we seek to understand this beleaguered but indomitable female speaker as she takes on standard antimarriage and antifeminist rhetoric and tells the story of a man who will die if he does not find out what women really want. The second thing to say about feminist criticism of the Wife of Bath's Prologue and Tale is that it has not led — and I think will not and should not lead — to consensus about the meaning of this text. Prefeminist critics debated whether the Wife was a monster or a joke, whether Chaucer in the last analysis meant us (where "we" were predominantly male readers) to deplore her behavior or find it amusing, even titillating. With the rise of feminist reading in the last few decades, more interesting and nuanced but equally divergent opinions about the significance of the Wife and her contribution to the *Canterbury Tales* have emerged.

I. THE WIFE AS FEMINIST

In the earliest days of this new approach, when feminist literary critics and historians first undertook the search for images and voices of strong, active, outspoken women, there was the Wife. Purporting to speak so frankly and extensively about women's experience, she was available to pioneering scholars like Sandra Gilbert and Susan Gubar. In *The Madwoman in the Attic* (see especially 11–12, 16, and 78–79) Gilbert and Gubar cite the Wife of Bath's fictional words as an instance of authentic female speech and take her as a direct spokeswoman for the perceptive protofeminism of Chaucer. Similarly, attempting to reconstruct a historical tradition for feminist literary criticism, Lawrence Lipking identifies a powerful line of real women writers from Sappho to Simone de Beauvoir and then tacks on at the end of his list another three who possibly transcend fictional or mythic status: "and perhaps the Authoress of the *Odyssey*, the White Goddess, and the Wife of Bath" (77). In keeping with this seemingly irresistible urge to see the Wife as the kind of female speaker and actor we so rarely find in early texts, much feminist debate has centered (and still does) on the Wife as a psychologically realistic woman whose behavior has to be judged as liberated or not.

At one end of the spectrum of opinion, some have insisted that the Wife is to be seen as a victim of the antifeminism so rampant in her day, ironically trapped in the misogynist culture she explicitly names as the enemy and blind to the ways in which her tactics further embed her in the assumptions she tries in vain to defy. In her efforts to refute antifeminist claims, she spends most of her time quoting, and misquoting, what they say. Cleverly, she seeks to turn the principles of masculine authority inside out, as for instance when she insists that "sith a man is moore resonable / Than womman is" (441–42), her husbands ought to be patient with her tantrums. But however ironically, she thereby endorses the misogynist view that women are naturally irrational. The deafness attributed to her in the General Prologue (A446) is a sign of how she, like many women in her culture, has been literally maimed by the barrage of antifeminist doctrine she has endured; fighting back, given the weapons she must use, only makes her situation worse.

At the other end of the spectrum, many have argued that the Wife knows that she is doing all this and therefore represents an independent, strong woman, a historically plausible counter to the idealized or demonized female characters found in both religious and secular writings throughout the Middle Ages. Given women's supposed position in culture and language, the Wife chooses perhaps the best option for a woman who would resist subordination: she attacks, impersonates, and parodies the words and voices that seek to control her. So exaggerated are her citations of antifeminist rhetoric that we see how silly it really is. She may indeed become a monster, and her awareness of that fact may surface in her tale. Many readers have seen the mysterious and surpassingly ugly old woman the knight encounters in the woods — "A fouler wight there may no man devise" (999) — as an image of the Wife's deepest self. But in the monstrosity of her domineering, demanding self, she also reveals the real threat that female anger poses. When she repeatedly addresses herself, in part at least, to a female audience — "Ye wise wives, that kan understonde" (225) — she further suggests to some feminist readers that actual women were not utterly marginalized and silenced, but could play a role in fourteenth-century textual communities. She also lays claim to bodily desire, something that women were usually said not to have, or to have in an excess that must be proscribed. She seems at the same time to long for a different, better order, one in which men and women could live harmoniously and respectfully together. To some readers, the ending of both her prologue and her tale gesture toward what may be still only a utopian dream, but one that has subversive potential, the possibility of mutuality in heterosexual relationships.

Such conflicting evaluations bring a feminist slant to the older division between readers who thought the Wife was to be pitied for her errors of understanding (that is, seen as a victim) and readers who believed she was meant to be scorned for upsetting a divinely ordained system of gender relations (that is, seen as a real revolutionary). In a feminist debate, this division recalls, without resolving it, an early and ongoing twentieth-century question about women and power: Should women imitate men and attempt to seize what the Wife calls "maistrie," the power to control someone else's behavior and will, in which case we might hail the Wife as a survivor who turns the tables? Or should women reject this traditional definition of power as one-upmanship and affirm some alternative set of values, in which case we might see the Wife as a male-identified woman, a gull, and a failure?

Somewhat more recently, as many feminist readers of Chaucer have become concerned with understanding and deconstructing the ways in which "woman" as a category has been constituted and constrained by centuries of misogyny, the Wife of Bath has been available in another way, as a prime example of a female character who is nothing more or less than a projection of collective male fear, conventionally masculine desire, and a male-dominated linguistic order. As she herself reminds us, even as she appears to tell her own story, women have *not* told their stories. A figure like the Wife is the product of a long and complicated tradition of clerkly writing *about* women by men whose faith extols celibacy and reviles the flesh, not the direct or authentic spokesperson of something we can comfortably identify as a woman's point of view or a mirror of embodied female experience. Many scholars have continued, then, to document and compare the verbal sources, both secular and religious, out of which the Wife is compounded. Her prototypes range from a character in an influential French poem by Guillaume de Lorris and Jean de Meun, *The Romance of the Rose* (see especially sections 58–64), to the uncooperative and outspoken Mrs. Noah, a popular comic figure in late-medieval English religious dramatic renditions of the story of the Flood. In style and content, her prologue has been analyzed as a type of sermon, a compendium of satire, and a mode of confession, and her tale has been seen to participate in and critique the conventions and cultural work of secular romances. (See, for example, Galloway, Hanna, Patterson, Root, Sanders, and Storm in my Works Cited.)

Almost nothing the Wife says or does is, it seems, what we would think of as original or unprecedented, without one or more prior textual or oral ancestors. Even from such a perspective, of course, the Wife's performance may still support a strong feminist position, embodying, for example, the French feminist claim that "woman" does not exist, at least not in ways we can know through ordinary, "phallocentric" language. By such a view, perhaps the Wife signifies "femininity" at its most subversive, ironically, because "she," insofar as we can speak of her as the facsimile of a unique, unified individual, is unknowable. This "she" is identified with silence, radical absence, and "undecidability" — a key deconstructive notion associated with contradictions that disrupt logical thinking, defy the separation of truth and nontruth, and resist being interpreted, analyzed, defined, and thereby controlled.

II. DOMESTIC VIOLENCE, RAPE, AND (HAPPY?) ENDINGS

Efforts to identify "woman" with a position outside the constraints of conventional language and to celebrate the Wife as an avatar of playful, postmodern notions of identity can remind us that women need not see themselves or be seen only as victims, that within the very logic of so-called patriarchal thinking there can be a space for disruption and difference. Insofar as the Wife's prologue and tale can in this way clearly help us think about femininity as something created by men and their words, oral and written — and therefore subject to change, since language is a constantly evolving system — it serves certain feminist purposes well. I want, however, to sound two cautionary notes to this kind of reading. In this section I look at some instances in the text that strike me as problematic in any effort to construe the Wife as feminist in our present-day, political senses of the term. In the final section I turn to the equally problematic question of Chaucer's sexual politics.

There are many moments in the Wife of Bath's Prologue and Tale that readers need to wrestle with, moments that do not easily lend themselves to clear answers to the questions that feminists insist on asking about power, desire, gender politics, and language. As I noted earlier, the Wife is often praised for her "liberated" attitude toward sexuality. But in fact we cannot be altogether certain that she enjoys the sexual experience she boasts so liberally of having and using. There are contradictions here, as in many other regards, in the self-professed character of the Wife. Speaking of how cleverly she bargained with her body in her first three marriages, she tells us something about the history of the faked orgasm and denies that there was any pleasure in it for her:

> For winning wolde I all his lust endure
> And make me a feyned appetit.
> And yet in bacon hadde I nevere delit. (416–18)

Modern editors are not sure exactly how to annotate the last line: Is "bacon" a euphemism for penis or sexual intercourse, or does it refer to old men, like her first three husbands (see note to line 418 in this edition)? The latter explanation would seem to be consistent with other points at which she speaks of her sexual experiences as if her desire were genuine. But even in these moments there is room for doubt. In telling us about her fourth husband, the Wife speaks of her love of wine and then confesses that "after wine on Venus moste I thinke / . . . A likerous mouth moste han a likerous tail" (464, 466). That statement is usually read as a frank admission of Alison's lusty nature; it might even be a subtle invitation to some of her drunken male companions on the pilgrimage. But in light of the earlier comment, might it not also suggest that she needs to be under the influence to take "delit" in sex?

A few lines later in a reference to Jankyn, her fifth husband, the Wife reveals something even more disturbing and important about her sexual practices and preferences:

> Now of my fifthe housbonde wol I telle.
> God let his soule nevere come in helle.
> And yet was he to me the mooste shrewe.
> That feel I on my ribbes al by rewe,
> And evere shall unto mine ending-day.
> But in oure bed he was so fresshe and gay,
> And therwithal so well koude he me glose,
> Whan that he wolde han my bele chose,
> That thogh he hadde me bet on every bon,
> He koude winne agayn my love anon.
> I trowe I loved him best for that he
> Was of his love daungerous to me. (503–14)

The Wife speaks first here of the felt, lasting pain in her body that her husband, God bless him, inflicted. While "but" in line 508 and "thogh" in line 511 logically imply that he could get away with beating her up because "in oure bed" he was such a great lover, the last few lines may also indicate something very different: male violence is not just offset by good sex, but male violence and female pain are mutually constitutive elements of female desire. "Daungerous" in line 514 is usually glossed as "aloof" or "distant," but given the likelihood of puns and double entendres in any Chaucerian text, it is impossible not to hear the other meanings of the word, also current in the Middle English lexicon: "domineering, overbearing" and "fraught with danger; hazardous, risky, dangerous" (*Middle English Dictionary*, Part D, 847–48).

The message seems to be clear here: whatever sexual pleasure the Wife may enjoy, sober or not, has a considerable element of what we might identify as masochism. The Wife is apparently a woman who enjoys being beaten up by her young husband. As she reveals that this is so, the radical late-twentieth-century feminist argument that sex is violence — not to mention the fact that speaking up for herself can be dangerous to a woman's health — begins to look like old news. In the lines that immediately follow, moreover, the Wife insists that in this way, like others, her experience is not idiosyncratic but representative of a generic female trait. Attraction to a "daungerous" man, the aloof, domineering, violent hero of any standard romance, is a "queynte fantasye" (516; pun intended) that every woman shares and smart women understand: "This knoweth every womman that is wis" (524). The allegedly intimate and stereotypically gendered connection between pleasure and danger, between (hetero) sexuality and violence, is all the more important in that it resurfaces at the end of the prologue and again at the beginning of the tale, so that the move from autobiographical confession to fictional story entails the escalation of abuse, from a beating to a rape. Both of these structurally prominent moments are frequently discussed, but with little or no attention to the question of the sexual violence they simultaneously imagine and gloss over.

For many readers, the story told at the end of the prologue about the Wife of Bath's last physical battle and subsequent reconciliation with Jankyn is the most hopeful thing about this poem. It suggests that the Wife, interpreted as a lifelike character with drives and motives that correspond to those of real people, wants what many of her modern readers want too, a model of gender and heterosexual relationships based on equality and mutuality. Although her physical violence and moral disobedience may still be seen by some as proof of her lack of several proper Christian virtues, it is easier for most readers today to applaud the Wife for standing up to Jankyn when he does what she falsely accused her first three husbands of doing: trying to control her transgressive behavior by preaching stock antifeminism. In this case the antifeminism takes the form of his reading to her from a misogynist collection of stories and sayings. At another level, it is both funny and aesthetically satisfying to see that the prologue closes with this literalization of the strategies the character has used throughout, as the Wife brings to life the cliché that has governed her "preamble" by actually tearing a page out of the clerk-husband's book of wicked wives.

Or is it three pages? Reading more suspiciously, we might ask whether the minor discrepancy between line 667, where she says she tore "a leef" out of the book, and line 790, where she says she ripped out "three leves," casts doubt on the accuracy of her testimony. Is the Wife making this whole story up, or at least lying about some parts of it? We will never know for sure, and the uncertainty itself can underscore what is far more important here: as fact or fantasy, or more plausibly a mix of both, Jankyn's and the Wife's fight, summed up by her claim that she "was beten for a book" (712), represents what modern feminist critics have repeatedly alleged, the real power of mere words and stories to do material damage to women. This episode could even speak in a timely way to our own concerns about the connection between domestic violence against women and present-day forms of entertainment that may be as deeply misogynist as Jankyn's reading matter. What about the connection between televised sports, for example, in which men are the more engaged spectators, and the real abuse of women at home that they reportedly can occasion?

If we pursue this line of reasoning, the sudden denouement of this episode of domestic violence may be less reassuring and hopeful, more unconvincing and unsettling. It suggests the persistence of those self-deluding hopes of reconciliation that battered wives so often express. Jankyn's sudden repentance and surrender, together with the unnarrated story of how this marriage was saved — "But at the laste with muchel care and wo / We fille acorded by usseleven two" (811–12) — resolves the problems the prologue has exposed by ignoring or forgetting them. The Wife's alleged submission, once she has things under control again, seems at first glance totally out of character. If women desire a "daungerous" man, what fun could Jankyn be after they both become "kinde" and "trewe" to each other? But on closer scrutiny, in the added context of the tale she proceeds to tell, it may reveal that underneath the tough skin of this savvy, satirical, pushy woman beats the heart of a good girl, a proper wife who not only enjoys being beaten up but who is also an incurable romantic. The Wife's marital experiences are grounded in domestic and sexual violence against women, and yet repeatedly her narrative serves two purposes: (1) it normalizes this violence by suggesting that men who are really attractive to women are just violent by nature, and anyhow women actually enjoy it; and (2) it erases this violence by suggesting that Jankyn actually loved her and stopped hurting her after that last big fight. Women are erotically aroused by the injuries done to them, according to the Wife, but the good news is that an abusive husband can be reformed if the blow he strikes is finally hard enough to deafen his spouse for life. What does it mean that the only female character who is allowed to speak of her own putative experience has this particular story to tell?

As if this were the only story women tell, moreover, the same contradictory message that we find in the autobiographical prologue is underscored in the Wife's subsequent tale. Feminist concerns oblige us to pay particular attention to a fact barely mentioned in prefeminist scholarship: that the central action in this favorite tale is precipitated by an even more extreme example of violence against women, a clear-cut case of rape. In the space of seven lines (882–88), we are introduced to a "lusty bachiler" of King Arthur's court, riding alone, who happens to see an unnamed maiden and, in the same sentence, sexually attacks her. The grammar of the passage couples the random encounter of a powerful man and an unprotected woman with rape as if they were everyday cause and effect, action and reaction. The swiftness of the telling itself suggests the unthinking, unpremeditated, and unstoppable nature of the knight's assault. The rape is called "oppressioun," and there is reportedly "clamour" and "pursuite" (889–90) by unspecified parties. Does it come from the maiden herself, whom we never meet? Her family? Other virtuous knights or citizens?

Everyone, it seems, deplores this unexceptional knightly behavior — but who, exactly, is responsible for seeing why it might happen or for preventing it before it does happen, or before it happens again? In any event, without due process the knight is quickly sentenced to death. But the apparent seriousness of the crime conveyed by this punishment is thoroughly undercut by the breathless, offhand manner in which it is reported. The Wife's pause to explain the capital sentence — "Paraventure swich was the statut tho" (893) — suggests that her contemporary readers would not otherwise understand why the penalty for sexual assault was so high. Normalized in all these ways, the rape is just as quickly erased: the knight is reprieved as swiftly as he was condemned, thanks to the intervention of the queen and her ladies. Their response seems to confirm what the Wife alleged in her prologue, that women really love a violent man. The only women who have any say in the action are complicit in the effort to downplay the criminality of the rapist and focus attention on *his* need for sympathy and education, not on his invisible victim and *her* needs.

The knight is not only spared and reformed but eventually rewarded, it seems, for his crime. The ending of the tale first inverts and then repeats the ending of the prologue. The knight submits to an apparently unsatirical pillow lecture from the ugly old wife he was forced to marry, who reiterates the borrowed wisdom of male clerics just as Jankyn did. Can the Wife fail to see that these are the same clerics whose philosophy of "gentillesse" is grounded in the logic of domination that oppresses her? Overwhelmed by the old woman's orthodox, male-authored brilliance, the knight is able to swallow the disgust he feels for her aging female body and grant her the "maistrie" she is said to want. This turn of the plot presupposes that his initial loathing is natural; only a woman with both a man's superior mind and a fairy's supernatural powers could counter (and then magically transform) the offense of sagging female flesh. In return for the knight's new sensitivity, the old woman gives "maistrie" back to her new husband and becomes the fair and virtuous young wife all men are said to dream of. As implausibly as the Wife and Jankyn, these two can then settle forever after into a proper relationship in which "she obeyed him in every thing" (1255).

This second, matching happy ending, however, is not quite the Wife's last word, and the fact that she turns around and curses men who will not be "governed by hir wives" (1262) could suggest that she has not been fooled by her own fairy tales into believing that husbands will so easily accept the lesson, contradictory as it is, that she claims to want to teach. There are further implications of her curse, moreover, that qualify the extent to which we might want to celebrate the Wife's use or theory of language as a model of feminist subversion. Someone who curses in the way she does here implies exactly what the prologue assumes and demonstrates: words have real power to do harm. Like sticks and stones, they can break bones, shorten lives, bring pestilence. In cursing, this power comes not from the speaker's own agency, however, but from the external force of some higher power — God or fate. A curse, moreover, closes off rather than opens up dialogue. Unlike most other speech acts, it makes no assumption about the presence or understanding of other persons. If the curse is effective, it need not be heard by anyone, including the people it directly seeks to affect. After the curse, there is nothing left to say.

The curse assumes a model of language, then, that a woman like the Wife might well have learned from the antifeminist words that have brought her into being. Encapsulating the spirit of prologue and tale, her parting shot undercuts the notion that as a woman the wife might use language to escape antifeminist constructions and suggests that her only actual alternative to speech may be a violent blow or a cry of outrage. While one feminist response to this displacement of women, as I have noted, might be to applaud the possibility of a femininity located "elsewhere," outside of language and culture, I would stress here the cost of such a location. Among other things, it seems to be a position from which little can be done to prevent or even speak out against the violence to female bodies that pervades and actually instigates the kind of narratives the Wife tells. Such violence is said to be welcomed and repeatedly forgiven or forgotten by women, alluded to as if an everyday event, neither denied nor condemned, but seemingly brought up only to be explained away or triumphed over. As Diana Fuss puts it in her discussion of feminism and deconstruction, "positing woman as a figure of displacement risks, in its effects, continually displacing real material women" (14).

III. WHO PAINTED THE LION?

While violence against women has not been a subject for prefeminist scholarly concern, a less immediately disturbing aspect of the Wife's contradictory performance has been of long-standing interest: her seemingly paradoxical allegation that no wife has been the author of her own story. The Wife's comment reinforces the conventional notion that literacy has been reserved chiefly for unmarried men, and the corollary follows that if women could speak, they would tell even worse stories about men than men have told about them. She makes this point by alluding to Aesop's fable about the lion who observed a picture of a man defeating a lion. The lion noted that it must have been painted by a man, because if a lion had painted it he would have reversed the outcome:

> Who peyntede the leon, tel me who?
> By God, if wommen hadde writen stories,
> As clerkes han withinne hir oratories,
> They wolde han writen of men moore wikkednesse
> Than all the mark of Adam may redresse. (692–96)

This characteristically ironic moment presumes the same model of language that the Wife's parting curse implies. Words are powerful and determine reality. Those who lack the power to talk, the marginalized and oppressed (such as women and lions), would do reciprocal verbal violence if they could, but given their material and discursive position, they can express resistance only in angry, nonverbal, subhuman behavior. The paradoxical element here — the woman or the lion speaking to tell us that they are not allowed to enter the symbolic order — also serves to raise the question of who exactly is painting the picture here. Isn't it finally *not* a woman, indeed, but "Chaucer," the name we give to the man whom we assume composed this poem and created (or at least patched together) the Wife?

Many feminist readings of the Wife, whether they take her as an authentic female voice or a figure of the impossibility of female speech, assume that Chaucer is in charge and directly or indirectly address the further question of this male author's intentions. For some, particularly those who understand the Wife as a victim in some sense, unable to escape the system that oppresses her and not really representing anything like a viable female role or feminine position, Chaucer, as the source of the Wife's meaning, is not perhaps to be blamed for the antifeminist sins of his era, but is not exempt, either, from our disapproval of them. For many others, however, whether the Wife knows it or not, whether she manages at any level to escape her situation, her text allows us to analyze the workings of antifeminism. And so it must be the case that Chaucer was at least sensitive, if not openly opposed, to the ways in which women are oppressed by the dominant authorities and cultural conventions of his day. Even to readers who discount her status as authentic female speaker, the Wife may be, as I have said, either a figure of parody, showing us such an extreme version of all the stereotypical notions about women that we can only see how unnatural they are, or a bundle of contradictions, reflecting the ways in which any effort to attain "maistrie" paradoxically entails the oppressor's dependence on and fear of the oppressed. In either case Chaucer, who imagined her into existence, is subversive, fully cognizant of the implications of his characters' complexities.

At the same time, still other recent readings that are responsive to feminist concerns implicitly or explicitly avoid the question of authorial intentions by arguing that individual authors have less control than we might think over the assumptions and operations inherent in language and literary conventions, or, somewhat conversely, that if no utterance is the property of one person, any text will consist of competing or "dialogic" voices, some of which will always speak resistance against any supposedly dominant authority. By this view, Chaucer's intentions, knowable and reliable or not, are beside the point. I tend to agree with the view that Chaucer's intentions ought to be somewhat beside the point of literary criticism as I understand it, but it is for that very reason that I have previously argued (see *Chaucer and the Fictions of Gender*) strongly against ongoing efforts either to prove or to leave unchallenged the various, often contradictory, but always flattering and fundamentally self-serving claims that modern critics have typically made about Chaucer: that this male author is uniquely sympathetic to women; subversive, insofar as that term implies active political resistance; or so artistically great that questions of politics are simply irrelevant and undoubtedly biased. Here I can summarize only a few of the reasons why I think the long-standing tradition of adulating the male author, which is inherent in readings of Chaucer as either a transcendent Father of English poetry *or* a feminist, is antithetical to the aims of feminist criticism.

What has interested me most about the image of the poet that we see in Chaucer's writing is indeed what has looked to others like his sympathy or empathy or even identification with women: that is, the similarities, both evident and more subtle, between him and many of his female characters. At the most obvious level, we find such resemblances in the poet's fictional self-presentation in the tales and elsewhere. The apparently high-testosterone Host, who "of manhod . . . lakkede right naught" (A756), makes fun of shy Chaucer the pilgrim and calls him a "popet" (B²1891), a term defined by the *Middle English Dictionary* as "A youth, young girl; a babe" (Part P, 5). In many of the earlier dream visions, the persona of the poet is subject to the challenge or domination of other manly figures and often projects himself, frequently in dreams, into female characters. Thinking about what we know of the historical position of the court poet in the late fourteenth century, we might recall R. F. Green's claim that the male poet is something of an outsider who must be careful not to speak in ways that offend men of higher rank. He must seek to please those who have power over him, both as patrons and as interpreters of his art (see esp. Green's chapter 4). As I have suggested, we might see the male author then as "feminized" by his culture — put sometimes in positions much like the positions women are in, treated as women are often treated. Yet the courtly poet also has to compete *with* other men by writing poems *about* women in which he asserts a conventional masculine desire *for* women.

To negotiate these difficult relationships, there is a tendency to indirection, obliqueness, and self-effacement in the persona of the late-medieval court poet. Nowhere is this more evident than in the slippery figure of Chaucer, known best for his irony and evasiveness and playfulness. In the *Canterbury Tales*, such slipperiness is exacerbated by the fact that each story is told as the fictional offering of a fictional character. It is always practically difficult if not theoretically impossible to determine who is speaking, whose intentions are in control, whose unconscious is registering its hidden force, or where meaning and reference might be grounded. In this regard, again, the poet and his most famous female character, the Wife of Bath, have particularly salient traits in common. Both are figures of ambiguity and undecidability. Both avoid too much self-revelation, and thereby imply their possession of private selves, by speaking through other voices: the larger part of the Wife's utterances are citations from the words of dead men, and Chaucer is heard chiefly in the characters whose stories he imagines. Both play up the parts they are assigned in such a way as to seem to hide something behind the exaggerated performance, and at the same time in doing so both expose just how much of (gendered) behavior *is* performance of prescripted parts.

Despite their obvious love of speaking and their fluency with words, paradoxically, both Chaucer and the Wife also seem to share a fantasy of silent submission to higher forces. As we have seen, the happy endings of the Wife's prologue and tale, however undercut by their failure to seem fully consistent with other aspects of her performance, reveal a romantic willingness to become what most men are said to want women to be. The *Canterbury Tales* ends with a sermon in the Parson's Tale, followed by the so-called Retraction, in which Chaucer says he wants to take back anything he has ever written that might not lead to the love of God. The apparently unironic Parson's Tale, told by one of the few pilgrims presented unsatirically, is full of prescriptions that seem to condemn the Wife on many counts, like this one: "a womman sholde be subget to hire housbonde . . . and discreet in alle hire wordes and hire dedes" (1929, 935). The Retraction, found in several good manuscripts of the *Canterbury Tales*, asks that readers "preye for me that Crist have mercy on me and foryeve me my giltes" (11084). Biographical explanations have assumed that the Retraction was written when Chaucer knew death was approaching and hoped for forgiveness. My point is that, like the Wife, Chaucer seems after all to want to be good and obedient, in thoroughly orthodox terms, and he prays for the intervention of a power greater than that of his own mind and his own poetry.

But here we may also observe a key difference between the poet and the woman as represented in the Wife of Bath. While nothing undoes the poet's curious Retraction, the Wife's cursing of men who will not be governed by their wives seems to undercut both her romantic fantasy, for which humanists have admired her, and her ironically subversive silence, for which deconstructionists have celebrated her. It suggests the Wife's belief in a certain self-canceling model of language; and it also evinces her desire, consistent with what we see throughout the prologue and tale, to perpetuate a war between the sexes in which she pits herself as quintessential female against men, the enemy with whom she also wants to sleep. She is not allowed to escape from the role of authentic, essential, vengeful woman to a position in which her gender would be less marked, where heterosexuality could be less violent or less normative and compulsory, and where she might appear neutral or transcendent, as Chaucer so readily and frequently does. Instead she is fixed in the position of rigid sexual difference implied by the topic her tale turns on — the thing that "wommen moost desiren" (905). The question of what women want is one that subsequent male thinkers like Freud and Lacan have also asked, and at first glance it seems to imply a concern for women's rights and feelings. But as feminists observe, it may also be a particularly problematic question, insofar as it presupposes that women are a unified category, defined by nothing more or less than their mysterious need for something that they do not have. And here it is Chaucer who appropriates those powers of ambiguity and mystery that are often projected onto woman in this question. His works typically claim for the poet alone a position above or outside of the alleged war between the sexes, a position potentially figured by but finally unavailable to any of his female characters (or, for that matter, most of his male characters), and especially forbidden to the character most often taken as the archetype of femininity, his Wife of Bath.

Chaucer's apparent understanding of the potential tyranny of linguistic and literary conventions and the limits of self-expression and verbal agency may readily appear, especially when we are focusing on his portraits of women, to be in sympathy with female characters and with their so-called feminine bind: trying to speak in a language that is conventionally used to silence them, to define them as not-men, as lacking and absent. The very form of the *Canterbury Tales* — multi-voiced, dialogical, open-ended — may seem to undermine what we sometimes think of as a "masculine" style, insofar as masculinity is often too simplistically defined and associated with the quest for fixed origins and single truths. The poet's refusal to take an authoritative stance may seem to subvert authority, so that we can read Chaucer's indeterminacy and invisibility, the way Virginia Woolf reads Shake-speare's, as a sign of the great artist's aloofness from politics and prej-udice: "his grudges and spites and antipathies are hidden from us. . . . Therefore his poetry flows from him free and unimpeded" (Woolf 58–59). But one of the most important contributions of con-tinued feminist debate about the complexities of the Wife of Bath's Prologue and Tale is to make us pause when anyone claims to have found a free and unimpeded place from which to speak, a position safely beyond the constraints of cultural rules like those that govern gender and sexual difference or exempt from the responsibility of tak-ing a stance on troubling issues like those I focused on earlier, the problems of rape and domestic violence.

There is new evidence (see the Cannon article) that the historical Chaucer was once sued for raping a woman named Cecilia Chaumpaigne. This would seem to make it even more tempting for feminists, who see the way rape is covered up in the Wife's tale, to press the critique of Chaucer further. Colleagues and students have sometimes assumed that this was either what I meant or what I ought to do, and they have urged me to indict Chaucer's sexual politics more firmly and clearly, even to "do him in." Instead I want to close by suggesting why I think it is important to entertain this urge up to a point — the point where, as I have said, we no longer accept a sani-tized or neutralized image of Chaucer or his artistry — and then let it go. The task of feminist criticism is complicated, and feminist readings of the Wife's prologue and tale are particularly valuable because they highlight many of the most important complications. Feminist cri-tique of the Wife requires us to consider, for example, the direct and indirect mechanisms by which women are both victims and survivors of physical and verbal violence, to talk about when it is better to stress the things women have in common and when it is better to recognize differences, and to judge the often fine and strategic lines between complicity with and resistance to oppression. As is almost always the case in thinking about the past and the marginalized, a feminist approach to the Wife also requires us to seek out the experience of women in what has been said about them and thereby to understand more about the overlap between so-called experience and so-called authority.

But here we can be distracted from our main goal by a poet as fascinating and skillful and "daungerous," in all senses of the term I noted above, as Chaucer. The quest to determine what the master of irony really meant can still take our minds off our worries about women, as it has for so many centuries. It is critical to remember that it is Chaucer as male poet, not the Wife as female character, who simultaneously escapes the constraints of gender and enjoys the privileges of maleness. If Chaucer is the Father of English poetry, we should not wonder that it has been so difficult, over the centuries, for his daughters to write. But if we remain focused on Chaucer's intentions, for good or bad, we repeat the fundamentally antifeminist move made possible by the Wife's narratives. We center our attention still on the dangerous male (poet or rapist); *he* is the one we care to condemn or save (from lack of literary merit or death), while the woman in the picture (garrulous Wife or silent maiden) fades into the background.

WORKS CITED

Cannon, Christopher. "*Raptus* in the Chaumpaigne Release and a Newly Discovered Document Concerning the Life of Geoffrey Chaucer." *Speculum* 68 (1993): 74–94.

Fuss, Diana. *Essentially Speaking: Feminism, Nature and Difference.* New York: Routledge, 1989.

Galloway, Andrew. "Marriage Sermons, Polemical Sermons, and *The Wife of Bath's Prologue*: A Generic Excursus." *Studies in the Age of Chaucer* 14 (1992): 3–30.

Gilbert, Sandra, and Susan Gubar. *The Madwoman in the Attic.* New Haven: Yale UP, 1979.

Green, Richard Firth. *Poets and Princepleasers.* Toronto: U of Toronto P, 1980.

Guillaume de Lorris and Jean de Meun. *Le Roman de la Rose.* Ed. Ernest Langlois. 5 vols. Paris: Didots (vols. 1–2), Champion (vols. 3–4), 1914–24. Trans. Charles Dahlberg, *The Romance of the Rose.* Hanover, NH: UP of New England, 1971, 1983. Alternate trans. Frances Horgan. Oxford: Oxford UP, 1994.

Hanna, Ralph, III. "*Compilatio* and the Wife of Bath: Latin Backgrounds, Ricardian Texts." *Latin and Vernacular: Studies in Late-Medieval Texts and Manuscripts*. Ed. A. J. Minnis. Woodbridge: Boydell and Brewer, 1989. 1–11.

Hansen, Elaine Tuttle. *Chaucer and the Fictions of Gender*. Berkeley: U of California P, 1992.

Lipking, Lawrence. "Aristotle's Sister: A Poetics of Abandonment." *Critical Inquiry* 10 (1983): 61–81.

Middle English Dictionary. Ed. Sherman Kuhn. Ann Arbor: U of Michigan P, 1983.

Patterson, Lee. "'For the Wyves Love of Bath': Feminine Rhetoric and Poetic Resolution in the *Roman de la Rose* and the *Canterbury Tales*." *Speculum* 58 (1983): 656–95.

Root, Jerry. "'Space to Speke': The Wife of Bath and the Discourse of Confession." *Chaucer Review* 28 (1994): 252–74.

Sanders, Barry. "Chaucer's Dependence on Sermon Structure in the *Wife of Bath's Prologue and Tale*." *Studies in Medieval Culture* 4 (1974): 437–45.

Storm, Melvin. "Uxor and Alisoun: Noah's Wife in the Flood Plays and Chaucer's Wife of Bath." *Modern Language Quarterly* 48 (1987): 303–19.

Woolf, Virginia. *A Room of One's Own*. New York: Harcourt, 1957.

Glossary of Critical
and Theoretical Terms

Most terms have been glossed parenthetically where they first appear in the text. Mainly, the glossary lists terms that are too complex to define in a phrase or a sentence or two. A few of the terms listed are discussed at greater length elsewhere (feminist criticism, for instance); these terms are defined succinctly and a page reference to the longer discussion is provided.

AFFECTIVE FALLACY First used by William K. Wimsatt and Monroe C. Beardsley to refer to what they regarded as the erroneous practice of interpreting texts according to the psychological responses of readers. "The Affective Fallacy," they wrote in a 1946 essay later republished in *The Verbal Icon* (1954), "is a confusion between the poem and its *results* (what it *is* and what it *does*). . . . It begins by trying to derive the standards of criticism from the psychological effects of a poem and ends in impressionism and relativism." The affective fallacy, like the intentional fallacy (confusing the meaning of a work with the author's expressly intended meaning), was one of the main tenets of the New Criticism, or formalism. The affective fallacy has recently been contested by reader-response critics, who have deliberately dedicated their efforts to describing the way individual readers and "interpretive communities" go about "making sense" of texts.

See also: Authorial Intention, Formalism, Reader-Response Criticism.

AUTHORIAL INTENTION Defined narrowly, an author's intention in writing a work, as expressed in letters, diaries, interviews, and conversations. Defined more broadly, "intentionality" involves unexpressed motivations, designs, and purposes, some of which may have remained unconscious.

The debate over whether critics should try to discern an author's intentions (conscious or otherwise) is an old one. William K. Wimsatt and Monroe C. Beardsley, in an essay first published in the 1940s, coined the term "intentional fallacy" to refer to the practice of basing interpretations on the expressed or implied intentions of authors, a practice they judged to be erroneous. As proponents of the New Criticism, or formalism, they argued that a work of literature is an object in itself and should be studied as such. They believed that it is sometimes helpful to learn what an author intended, but the critic's real purpose is to show what is actually in the text, not what an author intended to put there.

See also: Affective Fallacy, Formalism.

BASE   *See* Marxist Criticism.

BINARY OPPOSITIONS   *See* Oppositions.

BLANKS   *See* Gaps.

CANON   Since the fourth century, used to refer to those books of the Bible that the Christian church accepts as being Holy Scripture. The term has come to be applied more generally to those literary works given special status, or "privileged," by a culture. Works we tend to think of as "classics" or the "Great Books" produced by Western culture — texts that are found in every anthology of American, British, and world literature — would be among those that constitute the canon.

Recently, Marxist, feminist, minority, and postcolonial critics have argued that, for political reasons, many excellent works never enter the canon. Canonized works, they claim, are those that reflect — and respect — the culture's dominant ideology and/or perform some socially acceptable or even necessary form of "cultural work." Attempts have been made to broaden or redefine the canon by discovering valuable texts, or versions of texts, that were repressed or ignored for political reasons. These have been published both in traditional and in nontraditional anthologies. The most outspoken critics of the canon, especially radical critics practicing cultural criticism, have called into question the whole concept of canon or "canonicity." Privileging no form of artistic expression that reflects and revises the culture, these critics treat cartoons, comics, and soap operas with the same cogency and respect they accord novels, poems, and plays.

See also: Cultural Criticism, Feminist Criticism, Ideology, Marxist Criticism.

CONFLICTS, CONTRADICTIONS   *See* Gaps.

CULTURAL CRITICISM   A critical approach that is sometimes referred to as "cultural studies" or "cultural critique." Practitioners of cultural criticism oppose "high" definitions of culture and take seriously popular cultural forms. Grounded in a variety of continental European influences, cultural criticism nonetheless gained institutional force in England, in 1964, with the founding of the Centre for Contemporary Cultural Studies at Birmingham University. Broadly interdisciplinary in its scope and approach, cultural criticism views the text as the locus and catalyst of a complex network of political and economic discourses. Cultural critics share with Marxist critics an interest in the ideological contexts of cultural forms.

DECONSTRUCTION   A poststructuralist approach to literature that is strongly influenced by the writings of the French philosopher Jacques Derrida. Deconstruction, partly in response to structuralism and formalism, posits the undecidability of meaning for all texts. In fact, as the deconstructionist critic J. Hillis Miller points out, "deconstruction is not a dismantling of the structure of a text but a demonstration that it has already dismantled itself." See "What Is Deconstruction?" pp. 221–29.

DIALECTIC   Originally developed by Greek philosophers, mainly Socrates and Plato, as a form and method of logical argumentation; the term later came to denote a philosophical notion of evolution. The German philosopher G. W. F. Hegel described dialectic as a process whereby a thesis, when countered by an antithesis, leads to the synthesis of a new idea. Karl Marx and Friedrich Engels, adapting Hegel's idealist theory, used the phrase "dialectical materialism" to discuss the way in which a revolutionary class war might lead to the synthesis of a new social economic order. The American Marxist critic Fredric Jameson has coined the phrase "dialectical criticism" to refer to a Marxist critical approach that synthesizes structuralist and poststructuralist methodologies.

See also: Marxist Criticism, Poststructuralism, Structuralism.

DIALOGIC   *See* Discourse.

DISCOURSE   Used specifically, can refer to (1) spoken or written discussion of a subject or area of knowledge; (2) the words in, or text of, a narrative as opposed to its story line; or (3) a "strand" within a given narrative that argues a certain point or defends a given value system.

More generally, "discourse" refers to the language in which a subject or area of knowledge is discussed or a certain kind of business is transacted. Human knowledge is collected and structured in discourses. Theology and medicine are defined by their discourses, as are politics, sexuality, and literary criticism.

A society is generally made up of a number of different discourses or "discourse communities," one or more of which may be dominant or serve the dominant ideology. Each discourse has its own vocabulary, concepts, and rules, knowledge of which constitutes power. The psychoanalyst and psychoanalytic critic Jacques Lacan has treated the unconscious as a form of discourse, the patterns of which are repeated in literature. Cultural critics, following Mikhail Bakhtin, use the word "dialogic" to discuss the dialogue *between* discourses that takes place within language or, more specifically, a literary text.

See also: Cultural Criticism, Ideology, Narrative, Psychoanalytic Criticism.

FEMINIST CRITICISM   An aspect of the feminist movement whose primary goals include critiquing masculine-dominated language and literature by showing how they reflect a masculine ideology; writing the history of unknown or undervalued women writers, thereby earning them their rightful place in the literary canon; and helping create a climate in which women's creativity may be fully realized and appreciated. See "What Is Feminist Criticism?" pp. 255–62.

FIGURE   *See* Metaphor, Metonymy, Symbol.

FORMALISM   Also referred to as the New Criticism, formalism reached its height during the 1940s and 1950s, but it is still practiced today. Formalists treat a work of literary art as if it were a self-contained, self-referential object. Rather than basing their interpretations of a text on the reader's response, the author's stated intentions, or parallels between the text and historical contexts (such as the author's life), formalists concentrate on the relationships *within* the text that give it its own distinctive character or form. Special attention is paid to repetition, particularly of images or symbols, but also of sound effects and rhythms in poetry.

Because of the importance placed on close analysis and the stress on the text as a carefully crafted, orderly object containing observable formal patterns, formalism has often been seen as an attack on Romanticism and impressionism, particularly impressionistic criticism. It has sometimes even been called an "objective" approach to literature. Formalists are more likely than certain other critics to believe and say that the meaning of a text can be known objectively. For instance, reader-response critics see meaning as a function either of each reader's experience or of the norms that govern a particular "interpretive community," and deconstructors argue that texts mean opposite things at the same time.

Formalism was originally based on essays written during the 1920s and 1930s by T. S. Eliot, I. A. Richards, and William Empson. It was significantly developed later by a group of American poets and critics, including R. P. Blackmur, Cleanth Brooks, John Crowe Ransom, Allen Tate, Robert Penn Warren, and William K. Wimsatt. Although we associate formalism with certain principles and terms (such as the "Affective Fallacy" and the "Intentional Fallacy" as defined by Wimsatt and Monroe C. Beardsley), formalists were trying to make a cultural statement rather than establish a critical dogma. Generally southern, religious, and culturally conservative, they advocated the inherent value of literary works (particularly of literary works regarded as beautiful art objects) because they were sick of the growing ugliness of modern life and contemporary events. Some recent theorists even suggest that the rising popularity of formalism after World War II was a feature of American isolationism, the formalist tendency to isolate literature from biography and history being a manifestation of the American fatigue with wider involvements.

See also: Affective Fallacy, Authorial Intention, Deconstruction, Reader-Response Criticism, Symbol.

GAPS When used by reader-response critics familiar with the theories of Wolfgang Iser, refers to "blanks" in texts that must be filled in by readers. A gap may be said to exist whenever and wherever a reader perceives something to be missing between words, sentences, paragraphs, stanzas, or chapters. Readers respond to gaps actively and creatively, explaining apparent inconsistencies in point of view, accounting for jumps in chronology, speculatively supplying information missing from plots, and resolving problems or issues left ambiguous or "indeterminate" in the text.

Reader-response critics sometimes speak as if a gap actually exists in a text; a gap is, of course, to some extent a product of readers' perceptions. Different readers may find gaps in different texts, and different gaps in the same text. Furthermore, they may fill these gaps in different ways, which is why, a reader-response critic might argue, works are interpreted in different ways.

Although the concept of the gap has been used mainly by reader-response critics, it has also been used by critics taking other theoretical approaches. Practitioners of deconstruction might use "gap" when speaking of the radical contradictoriness of a text. Marxists have used the term to speak of everything from the gap that opens up between economic base and cultural superstructure to the two kinds of conflicts or contradictions to be found in literary texts. The first of these, they would argue, results from the fact that texts reflect ideology, within which certain subjects cannot be covered, things that cannot be said, contradictory views that cannot be recognized as contradictory. The second kind of conflict, contradiction, or gap within a text results from the fact that works don't just reflect ideology: they are also fictions that, consciously or unconsciously, distance themselves from the same ideology.

See also: Deconstruction, Ideology, Marxist Criticism, Reader-Response Criticism.

GENDER CRITICISM Developing out of feminist criticism in the mid-1980s, this fluid and inclusive movement by its nature defies neat definition. Its practitioners include, but are not limited to, self-identified feminists, gay and lesbian critics, queer and performance theorists, and poststructuralists interested in deconstructing oppositions such as masculine/feminine, heterosexual/homosexual. This diverse group of critics shares an interest in interrogating categories of gender and sexuality and exploring the relationships between them, although it does not necessarily share any central assumptions about the nature of these categories. For example, some gender critics insist that all gender identities are cultural constructions, but others have maintained a belief in essential gender identity. Often gender critics are more interested in examining gender issues through a literary text than a literary text through gender issues.

GENRE A French word referring to a kind or type of literature. Individual works within a genre may exhibit a distinctive form, be governed by certain conventions, and/or represent characteristic subjects. Tragedy, epic, and romance are all genres.

Perhaps inevitably, the term "genre" is used loosely. Lyric poetry is a genre, but so are characteristic *types* of the lyric, such as the sonnet, the ode, and the elegy. Fiction is a genre, as are detective fiction and science fiction. The list of genres grows constantly as critics establish new lines of connection between individual works and discern new categories of works with common characteristics. Moreover, some writers form hybrid genres by combining the characteristics of several in a single work.

Knowledge of genres helps critics to understand and explain what is conventional and unconventional, borrowed and original, in a work.

HEGEMONY Given intellectual currency by the Italian communist Antonio Gramsci, the word (a translation of *egemonia*) refers to the pervasive system of assumptions, meanings, and values — the web of ideologies, in other words — that shapes the way things look, what they mean, and therefore what reality *is* for the majority of people within a given culture.

See also: Ideology, Marxist Criticism.

IDEOLOGY A set of beliefs underlying the customs, habits, and/or practices common to a given social group. To members of that group, the beliefs seem obviously true, natural, and even universally applicable. They may seem just as obviously arbitrary, idiosyncratic, and even false to outsiders or members of another group who adhere to another ideology. Within a society, several ideologies may coexist, or one or more may be dominant.

Ideologies may be forcefully imposed or willingly subscribed to. Their component beliefs may be held consciously or unconsciously. In either case, they come to form what Johanna M. Smith has called "the unexamined ground of our experience." Ideology governs our perceptions, judgments, and prejudices — our sense of what is acceptable, normal, and deviant. Ideology may cause a revolution; it may also allow discrimination and even exploitation.

Ideologies are of special interest to sociologically oriented critics of literature because of the way in which authors reflect or resist prevailing views in their texts. Some Marxist critics have argued that literary texts reflect and reproduce the ideologies that produced them; most, however, have shown how ideologies are riven with contradictions that works of literature manage to expose and widen. Still other Marxists have focused on the way in which texts themselves are characterized by gaps, conflicts, and contradictions between their ideological and anti-ideological functions.

Feminist critics have addressed the question of ideology by seeking to expose (and thereby call into question) the patriarchal ideology mirrored or inscribed in works written by men — even men who have sought to counter sexism and break down sexual stereotypes. New historicists have been interested in demonstrating the ideological underpinnings not only of literary representations but also of our interpretations of them. Fredric Jameson, an American Marxist critic, argues that all thought is ideological, but that ideological thought that knows itself as such stands the chance of seeing through and transcending ideology.

See also: Cultural Criticism, Feminist Criticism, Marxist Criticism, New Historicism.

IMAGINARY ORDER   One of the three essential orders of the psychoanalytic field (see Real and Symbolic Order), it is most closely associated with the senses (sight, sound, touch, taste, and smell). The infant, who by comparison to other animals is born premature and thus is wholly dependent on others for a prolonged period, enters the Imaginary order when it begins to experience a unity of body parts and motor control that is empowering. This usually occurs between six and eighteen months, and is called by Lacan the "mirror stage" or "mirror phase," in which the child anticipates mastery of its body. It does so by identifying with the *image* of wholeness (that is, seeing its own image in the mirror, experiencing its mother as a whole body, and so on). This sense of oneness, and also difference from others (especially the mother or primary caretaker), is established through an image or a vision of harmony that is both a mirroring and a "mirage of maturation" or false sense of individuality and independence. The Imaginary is a metaphor for unity, is related to the visual order, and is always part of human subjectivity. Because the subject is fundamentally separate from others and also internally divided (conscious/unconscious), the apparent coherence of the Imaginary, its fullness and grandiosity, is always false, a *mis*recognition that the ego (or "me") tries to deny by imagining itself as coherent and empowered. The Imaginary operates in conjunction with the Real and Symbolic and is not a "stage" of development equivalent to Freud's "pre-oedipal stage," nor is it prelinguistic.

See also: Psychoanalytic Criticism, Real, Symbolic Order.

IMPLIED READER A phrase used by some reader-response critics in place of the phrase "the reader." Whereas "the reader" could refer to any idiosyncratic individual who happens to have read or to be reading the text, "the implied reader" is *the* reader intended, even created, by the text. Other reader-response critics seeking to describe this more generally conceived reader have spoken of the "informed reader" or the "narratee," who is "the necessary counterpart of a given narrator."

See also: Reader-Response Criticism.

INTENTIONAL FALLACY *See* Authorial Intention.

INTENTIONALITY *See* Authorial Intention.

INTERTEXTUALITY The condition of interconnectedness among texts. Every author has been influenced by others, and every work contains explicit and implicit references to other works. Writers may consciously or unconsciously echo a predecessor or precursor; they may also consciously or unconsciously disguise their indebtedness, making intertextual relationships difficult for the critic to trace.

Reacting against the formalist tendency to view each work as a freestanding object, some poststructuralist critics suggested that the meaning of a work emerges only intertextually, that is, within the context provided by other works. But there has been a reaction, too, against this type of intertextual criticism. Some new historicist critics suggest that literary history is itself too narrow a context and that works should be interpreted in light of a larger set of cultural contexts.

There is, however, a broader definition of intertextuality, one that refers to the relationship between works of literature and a wide range of narratives and discourses that we don't usually consider literary. Thus defined, intertextuality could be used by a new historicist to refer to the significant interconnectedness between a literary text and nonliterary discussions of or discourses about contemporary culture. Or it could be used by a poststructuralist to suggest that a work can be recognized and read only within a vast field of signs and tropes that is *like* a text and that makes any single text self-contradictory and "undecidable."

See also: Discourse, Formalism, Narrative, New Historicism, Poststructuralism, Trope.

MARXIST CRITICISM An approach that treats literary texts as material products, describing them in broadly historical terms. In Marxist criticism, the text is viewed in terms of its production and consumption, as a product *of* work that does identifiable cultural work of its own. Following Karl Marx, the founder of communism, Marxist critics have used the terms "base" to refer to economic reality and "superstructure" to refer to the corresponding or "homologous" infrastructure consisting of politics, law, philosophy, religion, and the arts. Also following Marx, they have used the word "ideology" to refer to that set of cultural beliefs that literary works at once reproduce, resist, and revise. See "What Is Marxist Criticism?" pp. 155–66.

METAPHOR The representation of one thing by another related or similar thing. The image (or activity or concept) used to represent or "figure" something else is known as the "vehicle" of the metaphor; the thing represented is called the "tenor." In other words, the vehicle is what we substitute for the tenor. The relationship between vehicle and tenor can provide much additional meaning. Thus, instead of saying, "Last night I read a book," we might say, "Last night I plowed through a book." "Plowed through" (or the activity of plowing) is the vehicle of our metaphor; "read" (or the act of reading) is the tenor, the thing being figured. The increment in meaning through metaphor is fairly obvious. Our audience knows not only *that* we read but also *how* we read, because to read a book in the way that a plow rips through earth is surely to read in a relentless, unreflective way. Note that in the sentence above, a new metaphor — "rips through" — has been used to explain an old one. This serves (which is a metaphor) as an example of just how thick (another metaphor) language is with metaphors!

Metaphor is a kind of "trope" (literally, a "turning," that is, a figure of speech that alters or "turns" the meaning of a word or phrase). Other tropes include allegory, conceit, metonymy, personification, simile, symbol, and synecdoche. Traditionally, metaphor and symbol have been viewed as the principal tropes; minor tropes have been categorized as *types* of these two major ones. Similes, for instance, are usually defined as simple metaphors that usually employ "like" or "as" and state the tenor outright, as in "My love is like a red, red rose." Synecdoche involves a vehicle that is a *part* of the tenor, as in "I see a sail" meaning "I see a boat." Metonymy is viewed as a metaphor involving two terms commonly if arbitrarily associated with (but not fundamentally or intrinsically related to) each other. Recently, however, deconstructors such as Paul de Man and J. Hillis Miller have questioned the "privilege" granted to metaphor and the metaphor/metonymy distinction or "opposition." They have suggested that all metaphors are really metonyms and that all figuration is arbitrary.

See also: Deconstruction, Metonymy, Oppositions, Symbol.

METONYMY The representation of one thing by another that is commonly and often physically associated with it. To refer to a writer's handwriting as his or her "hand" is to use a metonymic "figure" or "trope." The image or thing used to represent something else is known as the "vehicle" of the metonym; the thing represented is called the "tenor."

Like other tropes (such as metaphor), metonymy involves the replacement of one word or phrase by another. Liquor may be referred to as "the bottle," a monarch as "the crown." Narrowly defined, the vehicle of a metonym is arbitrarily, not intrinsically, associated with the tenor. In other words, the bottle just happens to be what liquor is stored in and poured from in our culture. The hand may be involved in the production of handwriting, but so are the brain and the pen. There is no special, intrinsic likeness between a crown and a monarch; it's just that crowns traditionally sit on monarchs' heads and not on the heads of university professors. More broadly, "metonym" and "metonymy" have been used by recent critics to refer to a wide range of figures and tropes. Deconstructors have questioned the distinction between metaphor and metonymy.

See also: Deconstruction, Metaphor, Trope.

NARRATIVE   A story or a telling of a story, or an account of a situation or of events. A novel and a biography of a novelist are both narratives, as are Freud's case histories.

Some critics use the word "narrative" even more generally; Brook Thomas, a new historicist, has critiqued "narratives of human history that neglect the role human labor has played."

NEW CRITICISM   *See* Formalism.

NEW HISTORICISM   First practiced and articulated in the late 1970s and early 1980s in the work of critics such as Stephen Greenblatt — who named this movement in contemporary critical theory — and Louis Montrose, its practitioners share certain convictions, primarily that literary critics need to develop a high degree of historical consciousness and that literature should not be viewed apart from other human creations, artistic or otherwise. They share a belief in referentiality — a belief that literature refers to and is referred to by things outside itself — that is fainter in the works of formalist, poststructuralist, and even reader-response critics. Discarding old distinctions between literature, history, and the social sciences, new historicists agree with Greenblatt that the "central concerns" of criticism "should prevent it from permanently sealing off one type of discourse from another, or decisively separating works of art from the minds and lives of their creators and their audiences." See "What Is the New Historicism?" pp. 115–26.

See also: Authorial Intention, Deconstruction, Formalism, Ideology, Poststructuralism, Psychoanalytic Criticism.

OPPOSITIONS   A concept highly relevant to linguistics, since linguists maintain that words (such as "black" and "death") have meaning not in themselves but in relation to other words ("white" and "life"). Jacques Derrida, a poststructuralist philosopher of language, has suggested that in the West we think in terms of these "binary oppositions" or dichotomies, which on examination turn out to be evaluative hierarchies. In other words, each opposition — beginning/end, presence/absence, or consciousness/unconsciousness — contains one term that our culture views as superior and one term that we view as negative or inferior.

Derrida has "deconstructed" a number of these binary oppositions, including two — speech/writing and signifier/signified — that he believes to be central to linguistics in particular and Western culture in general. He has concurrently critiqued the "law" of noncontradiction, which is fundamental to Western logic. He and other deconstructors have argued that a text can contain opposed strands of discourse and, therefore, mean opposite things: reason *and* passion, life *and* death, hope *and* despair, black *and* white. Traditionally, criticism has involved choosing between opposed or contradictory meanings and arguing that one is present in the text and the other absent.

French feminists have adopted the ideas of Derrida and other deconstructors, showing not only that we think in terms of such binary oppositions as male/female, reason/emotion, and active/passive, but that we also associate reason and activity with masculinity and emotion and passivity with femininity. Because of this, they have concluded that language is "phallocentric," or masculine-dominated.

See also: Deconstruction, Discourse, Feminist Criticism, Poststructuralism.

PHALLUS The symbolic value of the penis that organizes libidinal development and which Freud saw as a stage in the process of human subjectivity. Lacan viewed the Phallus as the representative of a fraudulent power (male over female) whose "law" is a principle of psychic division (conscious/unconscious) and sexual difference (masculine/feminine). The Symbolic order (*see* Symbolic Order) is ruled by the Phallus, which of itself has no inherent meaning *apart from* the power and meaning given to it by individual cultures and societies, and represented by the name of the father as lawgiver and namer.

POSTSTRUCTURALISM The general attempt to contest and subvert structuralism initiated by deconstructors and certain other critics associated with psychoanalytic, Marxist, and feminist theory. Structuralists, using linguistics as a model and employing semiotic (sign) theory, posit the possibility of knowing a text systematically and revealing the "grammar" behind its form and meaning. Poststructuralists argue against the possibility of such knowledge and description. They counter that texts can be shown to contradict not only structuralist accounts of them but also themselves. In making their adversarial claims, they rely on close readings of texts and on the work of theorists such as Jacques Derrida and Jacques Lacan.

Poststructuralists have suggested that structuralism rests on distinctions between "signifier" and "signified" (signs and the things they point toward), "self" and "language" (or "text"), texts and other texts, and text and world that are overly simplistic, if not patently inaccurate. Poststructuralists have shown how all signifieds are also signifiers, and they have treated texts as "intertexts." They have viewed the world as if it *were* a text (we desire a certain car because it *symbolizes* achievement) and the self as the subject, as well as the user, of language; for example, we may shape and speak through language, but it also shapes and speaks through us.

See also: Deconstruction, Feminist Criticism, Intertextuality, Psychoanalytic Criticism, Semiotics, Structuralism.

PSYCHOANALYTIC CRITICISM Grounded in the psychoanalytic theories of Sigmund Freud, it is one of the oldest critical methodologies still in use. Freud's view that works of literature, like dreams, express secret, unconscious desires led to criticism and interpreted literary works as manifestations of the authors' neuroses. More recently, psychoanalytic critics have come to see literary works as skillfully crafted artifacts that may appeal to *our* neuroses by tapping into our repressed wishes and fantasies. Other forms of psychological criticism that diverge from Freud, although they ultimately derive from his insights, include those based on the theories of Carl Jung and Jacques Lacan. See "What Is Psychoanalytic Criticism?" pp. 189–98.

READER-RESPONSE CRITICISM An approach to literature that, as its name implies, considers the way readers respond to texts, as they read. Stanley Fish describes the method by saying that it substitutes for one question, "What does this sentence mean?" a more operational question, "What does this sentence do?" Reader-response criticism shares with deconstruction a strong textual orientation and a reluctance to define a single meaning for a work. Along with psychoanalytic criticism, it shares an interest in the dynamics of mental response to textual cues.

REAL One of the three orders of subjectivity (*see* Imaginary Order and Symbolic Order), the Real is the intractable and substantial world that resists and exceeds interpretation. The Real cannot be imagined, symbolized, or known directly. It constantly eludes our efforts to name it (death, gravity, the physicality of objects are examples of the Real), and thus challenges both the Imaginary and the Symbolic Orders. The Real is fundamentally "Other," the mark of the divide between conscious and unconscious, and is signaled in language by gaps, slips, speechlessness, and the sense of the uncanny. The Real is not what we call "reality." It is the stumbling block of the Imaginary (which thinks it can "imagine" anything, including the Real) and of the Symbolic, which tries to bring the Real under its laws (the Real exposes the "phallacy" of the Law of the Phallus). The Real is frightening; we try to tame it with laws and language and call it "reality."

See also: Imaginary Order, Psychoanalytic Criticism, Symbolic Order.

SEMIOLOGY, SEMIOTIC *See* Semiotics.

SEMIOTICS The study of signs and sign systems and the way meaning is derived from them. Structuralist anthropologists, psychoanalysts, and literary critics developed semiotics during the decades following 1950, but much of the pioneering work had been done at the turn of the century by the founder of modern linguistics, Ferdinand de Saussure, and the American philosopher Charles Sanders Peirce.

Semiotics is based on several important distinctions, including the distinction between "signifier" and "signified" (the sign and what it points toward) and the distinction between "langue" and "parole." *Langue* (French for "tongue," as in "native tongue," meaning language) refers to the entire system within which individual utterances or usages of language have meaning; *parole* (French for "word") refers to the particular utterances or usages. A principal tenet of semiotics is that signs, like words, are not significant in themselves, but instead have meaning only in relation to other signs and the entire system of signs, or langue.

The affinity between semiotics and structuralist literary criticism derives from this emphasis placed on langue, or system. Structuralist critics, after all, were reacting against formalists and their procedure of focusing on individual words as if meanings didn't depend on anything external to the text.

Poststructuralists have used semiotics but questioned some of its underlying assumptions, including the opposition between signifier and signified. The feminist poststructuralist Julia Kristeva, for instance, has used the word "semiotic" to describe feminine language, a highly figurative, fluid form of discourse that she sets in opposition to rigid, symbolic masculine language.

See also: Deconstruction, Feminist Criticism, Formalism, Oppositions, Poststructuralism, Structuralism, Symbol.

SIMILE *See* Metaphor.

SOCIOHISTORICAL CRITICISM *See* New Historicism.

STRUCTURALISM A science of humankind whose proponents attempted to show that all elements of human culture, including literature, may be understood as parts of a system of signs. Structuralism, according to Robert Scholes, was a reaction to "'modernist' alienation and despair."

Using Ferdinand de Saussure's linguistic theory, European structuralists such as Roman Jakobson, Claude Lévi-Strauss, and Roland Barthes (before his shift toward poststructuralism) attempted to develop a "semiology" or "semiotics" (science of signs). Barthes, among others, sought to recover literature and even language from the isolation in which they had been studied and to show that the laws that govern them govern all signs, from road signs to articles of clothing.

Particularly useful to structuralists were two of Saussure's concepts: the idea of "phoneme" in language and the idea that phonemes exist in two kinds of relationships: "synchronic" and "diachronic." A phoneme is the smallest consistently significant unit in language; thus, both "a" and "an" are phonemes, but "n" is not. A diachronic relationship is that which a phoneme has with those that have preceded it in time and those that will follow it. These "horizontal" relationships produce what we might call discourse or narrative and what Saussure called "parole." The synchronic relationship is the "vertical" one that a word has in a given instant with the entire system of language ("langue") in which it may generate meaning. "An" means what it means in English because those of us who speak the language are using it in the same way at a given time.

Following Saussure, Lévi-Strauss studied hundreds of myths, breaking them into their smallest meaningful units, which he called "mythemes." Removing each from its diachronic relations with other mythemes in a single myth (such as the myth of Oedipus and his mother), he vertically aligned those mythemes that he found to be homologous (structurally correspondent). He then studied the relationships within as well as between vertically aligned columns, in an attempt to understand scientifically, through ratios and proportions, those thoughts and processes that humankind has shared, both at one particular time and across time. One could say, then, that structuralists followed Saussure in preferring to think about the overriding langue or language of myth, in which each mytheme and mytheme-constituted myth fits meaningfully, rather than about isolated individual paroles or narratives. Structuralists followed Saussure's lead in believing what the poststructuralist Jacques Derrida later decided he could not subscribe to — that sign systems must be understood in terms of binary oppositions. In analyzing myths and texts to find basic structures, structuralists tended to find that opposite terms modulate until they are finally resolved or reconciled by some intermediary third term. Thus, a structuralist reading of *Paradise Lost* would show that the war between God and the bad angels becomes a rift between God and sinful, fallen man, the rift then being healed by the Son of God, the mediating third term.

See also: Deconstruction, Discourse, Narrative, Poststructuralism, Semiotics.

SUPERSTRUCTURE   *See* Marxist Criticism.

SYMBOL   A thing, image, or action that, although it is of interest in its own right, stands for or suggests something larger and more complex — often an idea or a range of interrelated ideas, attitudes, and practices.

Within a given culture, some things are understood to be symbols: the flag of the United States is an obvious example. More subtle cultural symbols might be the river as a symbol of time and the journey as a symbol of life and its manifold experiences.

Instead of appropriating symbols generally used and understood within their culture, writers often create symbols by setting up, in their works, a complex but identifiable web of associations. As a result, one object, image, or action suggests others, and often, ultimately, a range of ideas.

A symbol may thus be defined as a metaphor in which the "vehicle," the thing, image, or action used to represent something else, represents many related things (or "tenors") or is broadly suggestive. The urn in Keats's "Ode on a Grecian Urn" suggests many interrelated concepts, including art, truth, beauty, and timelessness.

Symbols have been of particular interest to formalists, who study how meanings emerge from the complex, patterned relationships between images in a work, and psychoanalytic critics, who are interested in how individual authors and the larger culture both disguise and reveal unconscious fears and desires through symbols. Recently, French feminists have also focused on the symbolic. They have suggested that, as wide-ranging as it seems, symbolic language is ultimately rigid and restrictive. They favor semiotic language and writing, which, they contend, is at once more rhythmic, unifying, and feminine.

See also: Feminist Criticism, Metaphor, Psychoanalytic Criticism, Trope.

SYMBOLIC ORDER One of the three orders of subjectivity (see Imaginary Order and Real), it is the realm of law, language, and society; it is the repository of generally held cultural beliefs. Its symbolic system is language, whose agent is the father or lawgiver, the one who has the power of naming. The human subject is commanded into this preestablished order by language (a process that begins long before a child can speak) and must submit to its orders of communication (grammar, syntax, and so on). Entrance into the Symbolic order determines subjectivity according to a primary law of referentiality that takes the male sign (phallus, see Phallus) as its ordering principle. Lacan states that both sexes submit to the Law of the Phallus (the law of order, language, and differentiation) but their individual relation to the law determines whether they see themselves as — and are seen by others to be — either "masculine" or "feminine." The Symbolic institutes repression (of the Imaginary), thus creating the unconscious, which itself is structured like the language of the symbolic. The unconscious, a timeless realm, cannot be known directly, but it can be understood by a kind of translation that takes place in language — psychoanalysis is the "talking cure." The Symbolic is not a "stage" of development (as is Freud's "oedipal stage") nor is it set in place once and for all in human life. We constantly negotiate its threshold (in sleep, in drunkenness) and can "fall out" of it altogether in psychosis.

See also: Imaginary Order, Psychoanalytic Criticism, Real.

SYNECDOCHE *See* Metaphor, Metonymy.

TENOR *See* Metaphor, Metonymy, Symbol.

TROPE A figure, as in "figure of speech." Literally a "turning," that is, a turning or twisting of a word or phrase to make it mean something else. Principal tropes include metaphor, metonymy, personification, simile, and synecdoche.

See also: Metaphor, Metonymy.

VEHICLE *See* Metaphor, Metonymy, Symbol.

About the Contributors

THE VOLUME EDITOR

Peter G. Beidler is the Lucy G. Moses Distinguished Professor of English at Lehigh University. He has published on Chaucer, Native American literature, and American literature. This is his second volume in the Bedford Case Studies in Contemporary Criticism series; the first was on Henry James's *The Turn of the Screw* (1995). In 1983 he was named National Professor of the Year by the Council for Advancement and Support of Education. He spent the 1995–96 academic year at Baylor University as the Robert Foster Cherry Distinguished Teaching Professor.

THE CRITICS

Laurie Finke is associate professor of women's and gender studies at Kenyon College. She is the author of *Feminist Theory, Women's Writing* (1993) and coeditor of *Medieval Texts and Contemporary Readers* (1987) and *Literary Criticism and Theory* (1989).

Louise O. Fradenburg is associate professor of English at the University of California, Santa Barbara. She has published articles on Chaucer, on late-medieval Scottish culture, and on medieval studies.

She is the author of *City, Marriage, Tournament: Arts of Rule in Late Medieval Scotland* (1991). She has edited a collection of essays on *Women and Sovereignty* (1992) and is currently coediting a collection of essays on sexuality in premodern Europe.

Elaine Tuttle Hansen is professor of English at Haverford College. She is author of *The Solomon Complex: Reading Wisdom in Old English Poetry* (1988) and *Chaucer and the Fictions of Gender* (1992). She has recently completed a book tentatively titled *Mother Without Child: Contemporary Fiction and the Crisis of Motherhood.*

H. Marshall Leicester, Jr., is professor of English literature at Cowell College at the University of California, Santa Cruz. He is the author of *The Disenchanted Self: Representing the Subject in the Canterbury Tales* (1990) and articles on Chaucer, medieval literature, culture, opera, and film.

Lee Patterson is professor of English at Yale University. He writes on medieval literature and on theories of historical understanding, especially in relation to the Middle Ages. Among his publications are *Negotiating the Past: The Historical Understanding of Medieval Literature* (1987) and *Chaucer and the Subject of History* (1991).

THE SERIES EDITOR

Ross C Murfin, general editor of Case Studies in Contemporary Criticism, is dean of the College of Arts and Sciences and professor of English at the University of Miami. He has taught at Yale University and the University of Virginia and has published scholarly studies of Joseph Conrad, Thomas Hardy, Nathaniel Hawthorne, and D. H. Lawrence.